Building Microservices
with Spring

Master design patterns of the Spring framework to build smart, efficient microservices

Dinesh Rajput
Rajesh R V

BIRMINGHAM - MUMBAI

Building Microservices with Spring

First published: December 2018

Production reference: 1181218

Published by Packt Publishing Ltd.
Livery Place
35 Livery Street
Birmingham
B3 2PB, UK.

ISBN 978-1-78995-564-4

www.packtpub.com

`mapt.io`

Mapt is an online digital library that gives you full access to over 5,000 books and videos, as well as industry leading tools to help you plan your personal development and advance your career. For more information, please visit our website.

Why subscribe?

- Spend less time learning and more time coding with practical eBooks and Videos from over 4,000 industry professionals

- Improve your learning with Skill Plans built especially for you

- Get a free eBook or video every month

- Mapt is fully searchable

- Copy and paste, print, and bookmark content

Packt.com

Did you know that Packt offers eBook versions of every book published, with PDF and ePub files available? You can upgrade to the eBook version at `www.packt.com` and as a print book customer, you are entitled to a discount on the eBook copy. Get in touch with us at `customercare@packtpub.com` for more details.

At `www.packt.com`, you can also read a collection of free technical articles, sign up for a range of free newsletters, and receive exclusive discounts and offers on Packt books and eBooks.

Contributors

About the authors

Dinesh Rajput is a founder of Dineshonjava (dot) com, a blog for Spring and Java techies. He is a Spring enthusiast and a Pivotal Certified Spring Professional. He has written two bestselling books, Spring 5 Design Patterns and Mastering Spring Boot 2.0. Mastering Spring Boot 2.0 is the Amazon #1 best-selling book on Java. He has more than 10 years of experience with various aspects of Spring and cloud-native development, such as REST APIs and microservice architecture. He is currently working as an architect at a leading company. He has worked as a tech lead at Bennett, Coleman & Co. Ltd, and Paytm. He has a master's degree in computer engineering from JSS Academy of Technical Education, Noida, and lives in Noida with his family.

Rajesh R V is a seasoned IT architect with extensive experience in diversified technologies and more than 18 years of airline IT experience.

He received a degree in computer engineering from the University of Cochin, India, and he joined the JEE community during the early days of EJB. During his course as an architect, he worked on many large-scale, mission-critical projects, including the new generation Passenger Reservation System (iFly Res) and next generation Cargo Reservation System (Skychain, CROAMIS) in the Airline domain.

At present, as a chief architect at Emirates, Rajesh handles the solution architecture portfolio spread across various capabilities, such as JEE, SOA, NoSQL, IoT, cognitive computing, mobile, UI, and integration. At Emirates, the Open Travel Platform (OTP) architected by him earned the group the prestigious 2011 Red Hat Innovation Award in the Carved Out Costs category. In 2011, he introduced the innovative concept of the Honeycomb architecture based on the hexagonal architecture pattern for transforming the legacy mainframe system.

Rajesh has a deep passion for technology and architecture. He also holds several certifications, such as BEA Certified Weblogic Administrator, Sun Certified Java Enterprise Architect, Open Group Certified TOGAF practitioner, Licensed ZapThink Architect in SOA, and IASA global CITA-A Certified Architecture Specialist.

He has written Spring Microservices and reviewed Service-Oriented Java Business Integration by Packt Publishing.

Packt is searching for authors like you

If you're interested in becoming an author for Packt, please visit authors.packtpub.com and apply today. We have worked with thousands of developers and tech professionals, just like you, to help them share their insight with the global tech community. You can make a general application, apply for a specific hot topic that we are recruiting an author for, or submit your own idea.

Table of Contents

Preface

Getting Started with Spring Microservices begins with an overview of the Spring Framework 5.0, its design patterns, and its guidelines that enable you to implement responsive microservices at scale. You will learn how to use GoF patterns in application design. You will understand the dependency injection pattern, which is the main principle behind the decoupling process of the Spring Framework and makes it easier to manage your code. Then, you will learn how to use proxy patterns in aspect-oriented programming and remoting. Moving on, you will understand the JDBC template patterns and their use in abstracting database access.

After understanding the basics, you will move on to more advanced topics, such as reactive streams and concurrency. Written to the latest specifications of Spring that focuses on Reactive Programming, the Learning Path teaches you how to build modern, internet-scale Java applications in no time.

Next, you will understand how Spring Boot is used to deploying serverless autonomous services by removing the need to have a heavyweight application server. You'll also explore ways to deploy your microservices to Docker and managing them with Mesos.

By the end of this Learning Path, you will have the clarity and confidence for implementing microservices using Spring Framework.

This Learning Path includes content from the following Packt products:

• Spring 5 Microservices by Rajesh R V
• Spring 5 Design Patterns by Dinesh Rajput

Who this book is for

Getting Started with Spring Microservices is ideal for Spring developers who want to use design patterns to solve common design problems and build cloud-ready, Internet-scale applications, and simple RESTful services.

What this book covers

Chapter 1, *Getting Started with the Spring Framework 5.0 and Design Patterns*, gives an overview of the Spring 5 Framework and all new features of the Spring 5 Framework, including some basic examples of DI and AOP. You'll also get an overview of the great Spring portfolio.

Chapter 2, *Overview of GOF Design Patterns - Core Design Patterns*, gives an overview of the Core Design Pattern of the GoF Design Patterns family, including some best practices for an application design. You'll also get an overview of the common problems solving with design patterns.

Chapter 3, *Wiring Beans using Dependency Injection Pattern*, explores dependency injection pattern and detail about the configuration of Spring in an application, showing you various ways of configurations in your application. This includes a configuration with XML, Annotation, Java, and Mix.

Chapter 4, *Spring Aspect Oriented Programming with Proxy and Decorator Pattern*, explores how to use Spring AOP to decouple cross-cutting concerns from the objects that they service. This chapter also sets the stage for later chapters where you'll use AOP to provide declarative services such as transactions, security, and caching.

Chapter 5, *Accessing Database with Spring and JDBC Template Patterns*, explores how to access the data with Spring and JDBC; here, you'll see how to use Spring's JDBC abstraction and JDBC Template to query relational databases in a way that is far simpler than native JDBC.

Chapter 6, *Improving Application Performance Using Caching Patterns*, shows how to improve application performance by avoiding the database altogether if the data needed is readily available. So, I will show you how Spring provides support for caching data.

Chapter 7, *Implementing Reactive Design Patterns*, explores the Reactive Programming Model, which is programming with asynchronous data streams. You'll see how the Reactive System is implemented in the Spring Web Module.

Chapter 8, *Implementing Concurrency Patterns*, takes a closer look at concurrency when handling multiple connections inside a web server. As outlined in our architectural model, request handling is decoupled from application logic.

Chapter 9, *Demystifying Microservices*, gives you an introduction to microservices. This chapter covers the background, evaluation, and fundamental concepts of microservices.

Chapter 10, *Related Architecture Styles and Use Cases*, covers the relationship with Service-Oriented Architecture, the concepts of cloud native and Twelve Factor applications, and explains some of the common use cases.

Chapter 11, *Building Microservices with Spring Boot*, introduces building REST and message-based microservices using the Spring Framework and how to wrap them with Spring Boot. In addition, we will also explore some core capabilities of Spring Boot.

Chapter 12, *Scale Microservices with Spring Cloud Components*, shows you how to scale previous examples using Spring Cloud stack capabilities. It details the architecture and different components of Spring Cloud and how they integrate together.

Chapter 13, *Logging and Monitoring Microservices*, covers the importance of logging and monitoring aspects when developing microservices. Here, we look at the details of some of the best practices when using microservices, such as centralized logging and monitoring capabilities using open source tools and how to integrate them with Spring projects.

Chapter 14, *Containerizing Microservices with Docker*, explains containerization concepts in the context of microservices. Using Mesos and Marathon, it demonstrates next-level implementation to replace the custom life cycle manager for large deployments.

Chapter 15, *Scaling Dockerized Microservices with Mesos and Marathon*, explains auto-provisioning and deployment of microservices. Here, we will also learn how to use Docker containers in the preceding example for large-scale deployments.

To get the most out of this book

This book can be read without a computer or laptop at hand, in which case you need nothing more than the book itself. Although to follow the examples in the book, you need Java 8, which you can download from http://www.oracle.com/technetwork/java/javase/downloads/jdk8-downloads-2133151.html. You will also need your favorite IDE for the examples, but I have used the Software Spring Tool Suite; download the latest version of Spring Tool Suite (STS) from https://spring.io/tools/sts/all according to your system OS. The Java 8 and STS work on a variety of platforms--Windows, macOS, and Linux.

Other software components required are as follows:

- Spring Cloud Dalston RELEASE
- elasticsearch-1.5.2
- kibana-4.0.2-darwin-x64
- logstash-2.1.2
- Docker version (17.03.1-ce)
- Docker Hub
- Mesos version 1.2.0
- Docker version 17.03.1-ce
- Marathon version 3.4.9

Download the example code files

You can download the example code files for this book from your account at
`www.packt.com`. If you purchased this book elsewhere, you can visit
`www.packt.com/support` and register to have the files emailed directly to you.

You can download the code files by following these steps:

1. Log in or register at `www.packt.com`.
2. Select the **SUPPORT** tab.
3. Click on **Code Downloads & Errata**.
4. Enter the name of the book in the **Search** box and follow the onscreen instructions.

Once the file is downloaded, please make sure that you unzip or extract the folder using the latest version of:

- WinRAR/7-Zip for Windows
- Zipeg/iZip/UnRarX for Mac
- 7-Zip/PeaZip for Linux

The code bundle for the book is also hosted on GitHub
at `https://github.com/PacktPublishing/Building-Microservices-with-Spring`. In case
there's an update to the code, it will be updated on the existing GitHub repository.

We also have other code bundles from our rich catalog of books and videos available at https://github.com/PacktPublishing/. Check them out!

Conventions used

There are a number of text conventions used throughout this book.

`CodeInText`: Indicates code words in text, database table names, folder names, filenames, file extensions, pathnames, dummy URLs, user input, and Twitter handles. Here is an example: "The `EventEmitter` object is defined in the events module of Node.js."

A block of code is set as follows:

```
if (anotherNote instanceof Note) {
  ... it's a Note, so act on it as a Note
}
```

Any command-line input or output is written as follows:

```
$ npm update express
$ npm update
```

Bold: Indicates a new term, an important word, or words that you see onscreen. For example, words in menus or dialog boxes appear in the text like this. Here is an example: "If you need something different, click on the **DOWNLOADS** link in the header for all possible downloads: "

Warnings or important notes appear like this.

Tips and tricks appear like this.

Get in touch

Feedback from our readers is always welcome.

General feedback: If you have questions about any aspect of this book, mention the book title in the subject of your message and email us at customercare@packtpub.com.

Errata: Although we have taken every care to ensure the accuracy of our content, mistakes do happen. If you have found a mistake in this book, we would be grateful if you would report this to us. Please visit www.packt.com/submit-errata, selecting your book, clicking on the Errata Submission Form link, and entering the details.

Piracy: If you come across any illegal copies of our works in any form on the Internet, we would be grateful if you would provide us with the location address or website name. Please contact us at copyright@packt.com with a link to the material.

If you are interested in becoming an author: If there is a topic that you have expertise in and you are interested in either writing or contributing to a book, please visit authors.packtpub.com.

Reviews

Please leave a review. Once you have read and used this book, why not leave a review on the site that you purchased it from? Potential readers can then see and use your unbiased opinion to make purchase decisions, we at Packt can understand what you think about our products, and our authors can see your feedback on their book. Thank you!

For more information about Packt, please visit packt.com.

1
Getting Started with Spring Framework 5.0 and Design Patterns

This chapter will help you gain a better understanding of the Spring Framework with modules, and use the design patterns that are responsible for the success of Spring. This chapter will cover every major module of the Spring Framework. We begin with an introduction to the Spring Framework. We will have a look at the new features and enhancement introduced in Spring 5. We will also understand the design patterns used in the major modules of the Spring Framework.

At the end of this chapter, you will understand how Spring works, and how Spring solves the common problems of the design level of the enterprise application by using design patterns. You will know how to improve loose coupling between the components of applications and how to simplify application development by using Spring with design patterns.

This chapter will cover the following topics:

- Introduction of the Spring Framework
- Simplifying application development using Spring and its pattern
    - Using the power of the POJO pattern
    - Injecting dependencies
    - Applying aspects to address cross-cutting concerns
    - Applying a template pattern to eliminate boilerplate code

- Creating a Spring container for containing beans using the Factory pattern
  - Creating a container with an application context
  - The life of a bean in the container
- Spring modules
- New features in Spring Framework 5.0

Introducing Spring Framework

In the early days of Java, there were lots of heavier enterprise Java technologies for enterprise applications that provided enterprise solutions to programmers. However, it was not easy to maintain the applications because it was tightly coupled with the framework. A couple of years ago, apart from Spring, all Java technologies were heavier, like EJB. At the time, Spring was introduced as an alternative technology especially made for EJB because Spring provided a very simple, leaner, and lighter programming model compared with other existing Java technologies. Spring makes this possible by using many available design patterns, but it focused on the **Plain Old Java Object** (**POJO**) programming model. This model provided the simplicity to the Spring Framework. It also empowered ideas such as the **dependency injection** (**DI**) pattern and **Aspect-Oriented Programming** (**AOP**) by using the Proxy pattern and Decorator pattern.

The Spring Framework is an open source application framework and a Java-based platform that provides comprehensive infrastructure support for developing enterprise Java applications. So developers don't need to care about the infrastructure of the application; they should be focused on the business logic of the application rather than handling the configuration of the application. All infrastructure, configuration, and meta-configuration files, either Java-based configuration or XML-based configuration, both are handled by the Spring Framework. So this framework makes you more flexible in building an application with a POJOs programming model rather than a non-invasive programming model.

The Spring **Inversion of Control** (**IoC**) container is the heart of the entire framework. It helps glue together the different parts of the application, thus forming a coherent architecture. Spring MVC components can be used to build a very flexible web tier. The IOC container simplifies the development of the business layer with POJOs.

Spring simplifies the application development and removes a lot of the dependency on the other APIs. Let's see some examples of how you, as an application developer, can benefit from the Spring platform:

- All application classes are simple POJO classes--Spring is not invasive. It does not require you to extend framework classes or implement framework interfaces for most use cases.
- Spring applications do not require a Java EE application server, but they can be deployed on one.
- You can execute a method in a database transaction by using transaction management in Spring Framework without having any third-party transactional API.
- Using Spring, you can use a Java method as a request handler method or remote method, like a `service()` method of a servlet API, but without dealing with the servlet API of the servlet container.
- Spring enables you to use a local `java` method as a message handler method without using a **Java Message Service (JMS)** API in the application.
- Spring also enables you to use the local `java` method as a management operation without using a **Java Management Extensions (JMX)** API in the application.
- Spring serves as a container for your application objects. Your objects do not have to worry about finding and *establishing* connections with each other.
- Spring instantiates the beans and injects the dependencies of your objects into the application--it serves as a life cycle manager of the beans.

Simplifying application development using Spring and its pattern

Developing an enterprise application using the traditional Java platform has a lot of limitations when it comes to organizing the basic building blocks as individual components for reusability in your application. Creating reusable components for basic and common functionality is best design practice, so you cannot ignore it. To address the reusability problem in your application, you can use various design patterns, such as the Factory pattern, Abstract Factory pattern, Builder pattern, Decorator pattern, and Service Locator pattern, to compose the basic building blocks into a coherent whole, such as class and object instances, to promote the reusability of components. These patterns address the common and recursive application problems. Spring Framework simply implements these patterns internally, providing you with an infrastructure to use in a formalized way.

There are lots of complexities in enterprise application development, but Spring was created to address these, and makes it possible to simplify the process for developers. Spring isn't only limited to server-side development--it also helps simplifies things regarding building projects, testability, and loose coupling. Spring follows the POJO pattern, that is, a Spring component can be any type of POJO. A component is a self-contained piece of code that ideally could be reused in multiple applications.

Since this book is focused on all **design patterns** that are adopted by the Spring Framework to simplify Java development, we need to discuss or at least provide some basic implementation and consideration of design patterns and the best practices to design the infrastructure for enterprise application development. Spring uses the following strategies to make java development easy and testable:

- Spring uses the power of the *POJO pattern* for lightweight and minimally invasive development of enterprise applications
- It uses the power of the **dependency injection pattern** (**DI pattern**) for loose coupling and makes a system interface oriented
- It uses the power of the *Decorator and Proxy design pattern* for declarative programming through aspects and common conventions
- It uses the power of the *Template Design pattern* for eliminating boilerplate code with aspects and templates

In this chapter, I'll explain each of these ideas, and also show concrete examples of how Spring simplifies Java development. Let's start with exploring how Spring remains minimally invasive by encouraging POJO-oriented development by using the POJO pattern.

Using the power of the POJO pattern

There are many other frameworks for Java development that lock you in by forcing you to extend or implement one of their existing classes or interfaces; Struts, Tapestry, and earlier versions of EJB had this approach. The programming model of these frameworks is based on the invasive model. This makes it harder for your code to find bugs in the system, and sometimes it will render your code unintelligible. However, if you are working with Spring Framework, you don't need to implement or extend its existing classes and interfaces, so this is simply POJO-based implementation, following a non-invasive programming model. It makes it easier for your code to find bugs in the system, and keeps the code understandable.

Spring allows you to do programming with very simple non Spring classes, which means there is no need to implement Spring-specific classes or interfaces, so all classes in the Spring-based application are simply POJOs. That means you can compile and run these files without dependency on Spring libraries; you cannot even recognize that these classes are being used by the Spring Framework. In Java-based configuration, you will use Spring annotations, which is the worst case of the Spring-based application.

Let's look at this with the help of the following example:

```
package com.packt.chapter1.spring;
public class HelloWorld {
  public String hello() {
    return "Hello World";
  }
}
```

The preceding class is a simple POJO class with no special indication or implementation related to the framework to make it a Spring component. So this class could function equally well in a Spring application as it could in a non-Spring application. This is the beauty of Spring's non-invasive programming model. Another way that Spring empowers POJO is by collaborating with other POJOs using the DI pattern. Let's see how DI works to help decouple components.

Injecting dependencies between POJOs

The term *dependency injection* is not new-it is used by PicoContainer. Dependency injection is a design pattern that promotes loose coupling between the Spring components--that is, between the different collaborating POJOs. So by applying DI to your complex programming, your code will become simpler, easier to understand, and easier to test.

In your application, many objects are working together for a particular functionality as per your requirement. This collaboration between the objects is actually known as dependency injection. Injecting dependency between the working components helps you to unit test every component in your application without tight coupling.

In a working application, what the end user wants is to see the output. To create the output, a few objects in the application work together and are sometimes coupled. So when you are writing these complex application classes, consider the reusability of these classes and make these classes as independent as possible. This is a best practice of coding that will help you in unit testing these classes independently.

How DI works and makes things easy for development and testing

Let's look at DI pattern implementation in your application. It makes things easy to understand, loosely coupled, and testable across the application. Suppose we have a simple application (something more complex than a *Hello World* example that you might make in your college classes). Every class is working together to perform some business task and help build business needs and expectations. That means that each class in the application has its measure of responsibility for a business task, together with other collaborating objects (its dependencies). Let's look at the following image. This dependency between the objects can create complexity and tight coupling between the dependent objects:

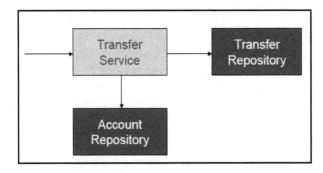

The TransferService component is traditionally dependent on two other components: TransferRepository and AccountRepository

A typical application system consists of several parts working together to carry out a use case. For example, consider the `TransferService` class, shown next.

`TransferService` using direct instantiation:

```
package com.packt.chapter1.bankapp.transfer;
public class TransferService {
  private AccountRepository accountRepository;
  public TransferService () {
    this.accountRepository = new AccountRepository();
  }
  public void transferMoney(Account a, Account b) {
    accountRepository.transfer(a, b);
  }
}
```

The `TransferService` object needs an `AccountRepository` object to make money transfer from account a to account b. Hence, it creates an instance of the `AccountRepository` object directly and uses it. But direct instantiation increases coupling and scatters the object creation code across the application, making it hard to maintain and difficult to write a unit test for `TransferService`, because, in this case, whenever you want to test the `transferMoney()` method of the `TransferService` class by using the `assert` to unit test, then the `transfer()` method of the `AccountRepository` class is also called unlikely by this test. But the developer is not aware about the dependency of `AccountRepository` on the `TransferService` class; at least, the developer is not able to test the `transferMoney()` method of the `TransferService` class using unit testing.

In enterprise applications, coupling is very dangerous, and it pushes you to a situation where you will not be able to do any enhancement in the application in the future, where any further changes in such an application can create a lot of bugs, and where fixing these bugs can create new bugs. Tightly coupled components are one of the reasons for major problems in these applications. Unnecessary tightly coupled code makes your application non-maintainable, and as time goes by, its code will not be reused, as it cannot be understood by other developers. But sometimes a certain amount of coupling is required for an enterprise application because completely uncoupled components are not possible in real-world cases. Each component in the application has some responsibility for a role and business requirement, to the extent that all components in the application have to be aware of the responsibility of the other components. That means coupling is necessary sometimes, but we have to manage the coupling between required components very carefully.

Using factory helper pattern for dependent components

Let's try another method for dependent objects using the Factory pattern. This design pattern is based on the GOF factory design pattern to create object instances by using a factory method. So this method actually centralizes the use of the new operator. It creates the object instances based on the information provided by the client code. This pattern is widely used in the dependency injection strategy.

`TransferService` using factory helper:

```
package com.packt.chapter1.bankapp.transfer;
public class TransferService {
  private AccountRepository accountRepository;
  public TransferService() {
    this.accountRepository =
      AccountRepositoryFactory.getInstance("jdbc");
  }
  public void transferMoney(Account a, Account b) {
    accountRepository.transfer(a, b);
  }
}
```

In the preceding code, we use the Factory pattern to create an object of
`AccountRepository`. In software engineering, one of the best practices of application
design and development is **program-to-interface** (**P2I**). According to this practice, concrete
classes must implement an interface that is used in the client code for the caller rather than
using a concrete class. By using P2I, you can improve the preceding code. Therefore, we can
easily replace it with a different implementation of the interface with little impact on the
client code. So programming-to-interface provides us with a method involving low
coupling. In other words, there is no direct dependency on a concrete implementation
leading to low coupling. Let's look at the following code. Here, `AccountRepository` is an
interface rather than a class:

```
public interface AccountRepository{
  void transfer();
  //other methods
}
```

So we can implement it as per our requirement, and it is dependent upon the client's
infrastructure. Suppose we want an `AccountRepository` during the development phase
with JDBC API. We can provide a `JdbcAccountRepositry` concrete implementation of the
`AccountRepositry` interface, as shown here:

```
public class JdbcAccountRepositry implements AccountRepositry{
  //...implementation of methods defined in AccountRepositry
  // ...implementation of other methods
}
```

In this pattern, objects are created by factory classes to make it easy to maintain, and this avoids scattering the code of object creation across other business components. With a factory helper, it is also possible to make object creation configurable. This technique provides a solution for tight coupling, but we are still adding factory classes to the business component for fetching collaborating components. So let's see the DI pattern in the next section and look at how to solve this problem.

Using DI pattern for dependent components

According to the DI pattern, dependent objects are given their dependencies at the time of the creation of the objects by some factory or third party. This factory coordinates each object in the system in such a way that each dependent object is not expected to create their dependencies. This means that we have to focus on defining the dependencies instead of resolving the dependencies of collaborating objects in the enterprise application. Let's look at the following image. You will learn that dependencies are injected into the objects that need them:

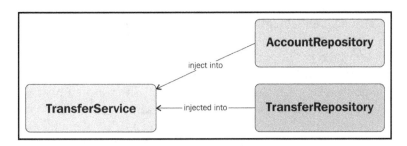

Dependency injection between the different collaborating components in the application

To illustrate this point, let's look at `TransferService` in the next section--a `TransferService` has dependency with `AccountRepository` and `TransferRepository`. Here, `TransferService` is capable of transferring money by any kind implementation of `TransferRepository`, that is, we can either use `JdbcTransferRepository` or `JpaTransferRepository`, depending on whichever comes along according to the deployment environment.

`TransferServiceImpl` is flexible enough to take on any `TransferRepository` it's given:

```
package com.packt.chapter1.bankapp;
public class TransferServiceImpl implements TransferService {
   private TransferRepository transferRepository;
   private AccountRepository  accountRepository;
   public TransferServiceImpl(TransferRepository transferRepository,
     AccountRepository  accountRepository) {
      this.transferRepository =
       transferRepository;//TransferRepository is injected
      this.accountRepository  = accountRepository;
      //AccountRepository is injected
   }
   public void transferMoney(Long a, Long b, Amount amount) {
      Account accountA = accountRepository.findByAccountId(a);
      Account accountB = accountRepository.findByAccountId(b);
      transferRepository.transfer(accountA, accountB, amount);
   }
}
```

Here you can see that `TransferServiceImpl` doesn't create its own repositories implementation. Instead, we have given the implementation of repositories at the time of construction as a constructor argument. This is a type of DI known as *constructor injection*. Here we have passed the repository interface type as an argument of the constructor. Now `TransferServiceImpl` could use any implementation of repositories, either JDBC, JPA, or mock objects. The point is that `TransferServiceImpl` isn't coupled to any specific implementation of repositories. It doesn't matter what kind of repository is used to transfer an amount from one account to another account, as long as it implements the repositories interfaces. If you are using the DI pattern of the Spring Framework, loose coupling is one of the key benefits. The DI pattern always promotes P2I, so each object knows about its dependencies by their associated interface rather than associated implementation, so the dependency can easily be swapped out with another implementation of that interface instead of changing to its dependent class implementation.

Spring provides support for assembling such an application system from its parts:

- Parts do not worry about finding each other
- Any part can easily be swapped out

The method for assembling an application system by creating associations between application parts or components is known as **wiring**. In Spring, there are many ways to wire collaborating components together to make an application system. For instance, we could use either an XML configuration file or a Java configuration file.

Now let's look at how to inject the dependencies of `TransferRepository` and `AccountRepository` into a `TransferService` with Spring:

```xml
<?xml version="1.0" encoding="UTF-8"?>
<beans xmlns="http://www.springframework.org/schema/beans"
xmlns:xsi="http://www.w3.org/2001/XMLSchema-instance"
xsi:schemaLocation="http://www.springframework.org/schema/beans
http://www.springframework.org/schema/beans/spring-beans.xsd">
<bean id="transferService"
 class="com.packt.chapter1.bankapp.service.TransferServiceImpl">
    <constructor-arg ref="accountRepository"/>
    <constructor-arg ref="transferRepository"/>
</bean>
<bean id="accountRepository" class="com.
 packt.chapter1.bankapp.repository.JdbcAccountRepository"/>
<bean id="transferRepository" class="com.
 packt.chapter1.bankapp.repository.JdbcTransferRepository"/>
</beans>
```

Here, `TransferServiceImpl`, `JdbcAccountRepository`, and `JdbcTransferRepository` are declared as beans in Spring. In the case of the `TransferServiceImpl` bean, it's constructed, passing a reference to the `AccountRepository` and `TransferRepository` beans as constructor arguments. You might like to know that Spring also allows you to express the same configuration using Java.

Spring offers Java-based configuration as an alternative to XML:

```java
package com.packt.chapter1.bankapp.config;

import org.springframework.context.annotation.Bean;
import org.springframework.context.annotation.Configuration;

import com.packt.chapter1.bankapp.repository.AccountRepository;
import com.packt.chapter1.bankapp.repository.TransferRepository;
import
 com.packt.chapter1.bankapp.repository.jdbc.JdbcAccountRepository;
import
 com.packt.chapter1.bankapp.repository.jdbc.JdbcTransferRepository;
import com.packt.chapter1.bankapp.service.TransferService;
import com.packt.chapter1.bankapp.service.TransferServiceImpl;

@Configuration
public class AppConfig {
 @Bean
 public TransferService transferService(){
    return new TransferServiceImpl(accountRepository(),
```

```
      transferRepository());
  }
  @Bean
  public AccountRepository accountRepository() {
    return new JdbcAccountRepository();
  }
  @Bean
  public TransferRepository transferRepository() {
    return new JdbcTransferRepository();
  }
}
```

The benefits of the dependency injection pattern are the same whether you are using an XML-based or a Java-based configuration:

- Dependency injection promotes loose coupling. You can remove hard-coded dependencies with best practice P2I, and you could provide dependencies from outside the application by using the Factory pattern and its built-in swappable and pluggable implementation
- The DI pattern promotes the composition design of object-oriented programming rather than inheritance programming

Although `TransferService` depends on an `AccountRepository` and `TransferRepository`, it doesn't care about what type (JDBC or JPA) of implementations of `AccountRepository` and `TransferRepository` are used in the application. Only Spring, through its configuration (XML- or Java-based), knows how all the components come together and are instantiated with their required dependencies using the DI pattern. DI makes it possible to change those dependencies with no changes to the dependent classes--that is, we could use either a JDBC implementation or a JPA implementation without changing the implementation of `AccountService`.

In a Spring application, an implementation of the application context (Spring offers `AnnotationConfigApplicationContext` for Java-based and `ClassPathXmlApplicationContext` for XML-based implementations) loads bean definitions and wires them together into a Spring container. The application context in Spring creates and wires the Spring beans for the application at startup. Look into the implementation of the Spring application context with Java-based configuration--It loads the Spring configuration files (`AppConfig.java` for Java and `Sprig.xml` for XML) located in the application's classpath. In the following code, the `main()` method of the `TransferMain` class uses a `AnnotationConfigApplicationContext` class to load the configuration class `AppConfig.java` and get an object of the `AccountService` class.

Spring offers Java-based configuration as an alternative to XML:

```
package com.packt.chapter1.bankapp;

import org.springframework.context.ConfigurableApplicationContext;
import
 org.springframework.context.annotation
 .AnnotationConfigApplicationContext;

import com.packt.chapter1.bankapp.config.AppConfig;
import com.packt.chapter1.bankapp.model.Amount;
import com.packt.chapter1.bankapp.service.TransferService;

public class TransferMain {

  public static void main(String[] args) {
    //Load Spring context
    ConfigurableApplicationContext applicationContext =
      new AnnotationConfigApplicationContext(AppConfig.class);
    //Get TransferService bean
    TransferService transferService =
     applicationContext.getBean(TransferService.class);
      //Use transfer method
    transferService.transferAmmount(1001, 2001,
     new Amount(2000.0));
    applicationContext.close();
  }

}
```

Here we have a quick introduction to the dependency injection pattern. You'll learn a lot more about the DI pattern in the coming chapters of this book. Now let's look at another way of simplifying Java development using Spring's declarative programming model through aspects and proxy patterns.

Applying aspects for cross cutting concerns

In a Spring application, the DI pattern provides us with loose coupling between collaborating software components, but **Aspect-Oriented Programming** in Spring (Spring **AOP**) enables you to capture common functionalities that are repetitive throughout your application. So we can say that Spring AOP promotes loose coupling and allows cross-cutting concerns, listed as follows, to be separated in a most elegant fashion. It allows these services to be applied transparently through declaration. With Spring AOP, it is possible to write custom aspects and configure them declaratively.

The generic functionalities that are needed in many places in your application are:

- Logging and tracing
- Transaction management
- Security
- Caching
- Error handling
- Performance monitoring
- Custom business rules

The components listed here are not part of your core application, but these components have some additional responsibilities, commonly referred to as cross-cutting concerns because they tend to cut across multiple components in a system beyond their core responsibilities. If you put these components with your core functionalities, thereby implementing cross-cutting concerns without modularization, it will have two major problems:

- **Code tangling**: A coupling of concerns means that a cross-cutting concern code, such as a security concern, a transaction concern, and a logging concern, is coupled with the code for business objects in your application.
- **Code scattering**: Code scattering refers to the same concern being spread across modules. This means that your concern code of security, transaction, and logging is spread across all modules of the system. In other words, you can say there is a duplicity of the same concern code across the system.

The following diagram illustrates this complexity. The business objects are too intimately involved with the cross-cutting concerns. Not only does each object know that it's being logged, secured, and involved in a transactional context, but each object is also responsible for performing those services assigned only to it:

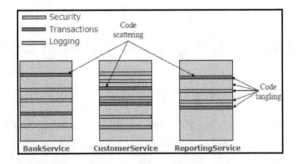

Cross-cutting concerns, such as logging, security and transaction, are often scattered about in modules where those tasks are not their primary concern

Spring AOP enables the modularization of cross-cutting concerns to avoid tangling and scattering. You can apply these modularized concerns to the core business components of the application declaratively without affecting the aforementioned the above components. The aspects ensure that the POJOs remain plain. Spring AOP makes this magic possible by using the Proxy Design Pattern. We will discuss the Proxy Design pattern more in the coming chapters of this book.

How Spring AOP works

The following points describe the work of Spring AOP:

- **Implement your mainline application logic**: Focusing on the core problem means that, when you are writing the application business logic, you don't need to worry about adding additional functionalities, such as logging, security, and transaction, between the business codes-Spring AOP takes care of it.
- **Write aspects to implement your cross-cutting concerns**: Spring provides many aspects out of the box, which means you can write additional functionalities in the form of the aspect as independent units in Spring AOP. These aspects have additional responsibilities as cross-cutting concerns beyond the application logic codes.
- **Weave the aspects into your application**: Adding the cross-cutting behaviors to the right places, that is, after writing the aspects for additional responsibilities, you could declaratively inject them into the right places in the application logic codes.

Let's look at an illustration of AOP in Spring:

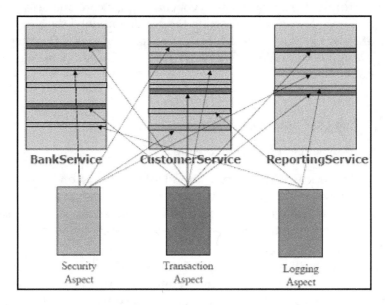

BankService CustomerService ReportingService

Security Aspect   Transaction Aspect   Logging Aspect

AOP-based system evolution--this leaves the application components to focus on their specific business functionalities

In the preceding diagram, Spring AOP separates the cross-cutting concerns, for example, security, transaction, and logging, from the business modules, that is, `BankService`, `CustomerService`, and `ReportingService`. These cross-cutting concerns are applied to predefined points (stripes in the preceding diagram) of the business modules at the running time of the application.

Suppose that you want to log the messages before and after calling the `transferAmmount()` method of `TransferService` using the services of a `LoggingAspect`. The following listing shows the `LoggingAspect` class you might use.

`LoggingAspect` call is used for logging the system for `TransferService`:

```
package com.packt.chapter1.bankapp.aspect;

import org.aspectj.lang.annotation.After;
import org.aspectj.lang.annotation.Aspect;
import org.aspectj.lang.annotation.Before;

@Aspect
public class LoggingAspect {
  @Before("execution(* *.transferAmount(..))")
  public void logBeforeTransfer(){
```

```
    System.out.println("####LoggingAspect.logBeforeTransfer()
    method called before transfer amount####");
  }
  @After("execution(* *.transferAmount(..))")
  public void logAfterTransfer(){
    System.out.println("####LoggingAspect.logAfterTransfer() method
    called after transfer amount####");
  }
}
```

To turn LoggingAspect into an aspect bean, all you need to do is declare it as one in the Spring configuration file. Also, to make it an aspect, you have to add the @Aspect annotation to this class. Here's the updated AppConfig.java file, revised to declare LoggingAspect as an aspect.

Declaring LoggingAspect as an aspect and enabling the Apsect proxy feature of Spring AOP:

```
package com.packt.chapter1.bankapp.config;

import org.springframework.context.annotation.Bean;
import org.springframework.context.annotation.Configuration;
import
 org.springframework.context.annotation.EnableAspectJAutoProxy;

import com.packt.chapter1.bankapp.aspect.LoggingAspect;
import com.packt.chapter1.bankapp.repository.AccountRepository;
import com.packt.chapter1.bankapp.repository.TransferRepository;
import
 com.packt.chapter1.bankapp.repository.jdbc.JdbcAccountRepository;
import
 com.packt.chapter1.bankapp.repository.jdbc.JdbcTransferRepository;
import com.packt.chapter1.bankapp.service.TransferService;
import com.packt.chapter1.bankapp.service.TransferServiceImpl;

@Configuration
@EnableAspectJAutoProxy
public class AppConfig {
  @Bean
  public TransferService transferService(){
    return new TransferServiceImpl(accountRepository(),
    transferRepository());
  }
  @Bean
  public AccountRepository accountRepository() {
    return new JdbcAccountRepository();
  }
```

```
@Bean
public TransferRepository transferRepository() {
  return new JdbcTransferRepository();
}
@Bean
public LoggingAspect loggingAspect() {
  return new LoggingAspect();
}
}
```

Here, we're using Spring's AOP configuration based on Java to declare the `LoggingAspect` bean as an aspect. First, we declare `LoggingAspect` as a bean. Then we annotate that bean with the `@Aspect` annotation.

We annotate `logBeforeTransfer()` of `LoggingAspect` with the `@Before` annotation so that this method is called before the `transferAmount()` is executed. This is called **before advice**. Then, we annotate another method of `LoggingAspect` with the `@After` annotation to declare that the `logAfterTransfer()` method should be called after `transferAmount()` has executed. This is known as **after advice**.

`@EnableAspectJAutoProxy` is used to enable Spring AOP features in the application. This annotation actually forces you to apply proxy to some of the components that are defined in the spring configuration file. We'll talk more about Spring AOP later, in Chapter 4, *Spring Aspect Oriented Programming with Proxy and Decorator Pattern*. For now, it's enough to know that you've asked Spring to call `logBeforeTransfer()` and `logAferTransfer()` of `LoggingAspect` before and after the `transferAmount()` method of the `TransferService` class. For now, there are two important points to take away from this example:

- `LoggingAspect` is still a POJO (if you ignore the `@Aspect` annotation or are using XML-based configuration)--nothing about it indicates that it's to be used as an aspect.
- It is important to remember that `LoggingAspect` can be applied to `TransferService` without `TransferService` needing to explicitly call it. In fact, `TransferService` remains completely unaware of the existence of `LoggingAspect`.

Let's move to another way that Spring simplifies Java development.

Applying the template pattern to eliminate boilerplate code

At one point in the enterprise application, we saw some code that looked like code we had already written before in the same application. That is actually boilerplate code. It is code that we often have to write again and again in the same application to accomplish common requirements in different parts of the application. Unfortunately, there are a lot of places where Java APIs involve a bunch of boilerplate code. A common example of boilerplate code can be seen when working with JDBC to query data from a database. If you've ever worked with JDBC, you've probably written something in code that deals with the following:

- Retrieving a connection from the connection pool
- Creating a `PreparedStatement` object
- Binding SQL parameters
- Executing the `PreparedStatement` object
- Retrieving data from the `ResultSet` object and populating data container objects
- Releasing all database resources

Let's look at the following code, it contains boilerplate code with the JDBC API of the Java:

```java
public Account getAccountById(long id) {
  Connection conn = null;
  PreparedStatement stmt = null;
  ResultSet rs = null;
  try {
    conn = dataSource.getConnection();
    stmt = conn.prepareStatement(
      "select id, name, amount from " +
      "account where id=?");
    stmt.setLong(1, id);
    rs = stmt.executeQuery();
    Account account = null;
    if (rs.next()) {
      account = new Account();
      account.setId(rs.getLong("id"));
      account.setName(rs.getString("name"));
      account.setAmount(rs.getString("amount"));
    }
    return account;
  } catch (SQLException e) {
  } finally {
      if(rs != null) {
        try {
```

```
          rs.close();
        } catch(SQLException e) {}
      }
      if(stmt != null) {
        try {
          stmt.close();
        } catch(SQLException e) {}
      }
      if(conn != null) {
        try {
          conn.close();
        } catch(SQLException e) {}
      }
    }
    return null;
  }
```

In the preceding code, we can see that the JDBC code queries the database for an account name and amount. For this simple task, we have to create a connection, then create a statement, and finally query for the results. We also have to catch `SQLException`, a checked exception, even though there's not a lot you can do if it's thrown. Lastly, we have to clean up the mess, closing down the connection statement and result set. This could also force it to handle JDBC's exception, so you must catch `SQLException` here as well. This kind of boilerplate code seriously hurts reusability.

Spring JDBC solves the problem of boilerplate code by using the Template Design pattern, and it makes life very easy by removing the common code in templates. This makes the data access code very clean and prevents nagging problems, such as connection leaks, because the Spring Framework ensures that all database resources are released properly.

The Template Design pattern in Spring

Let's see how to go about using the Template Design pattern in spring:

- Define the outline or skeleton of an algorithm

1. Leave the details for specific implementations until later.
2. Hide away large amounts of boilerplate code.

- Spring provides many template classes:
- `JdbcTemplate`
- `JmsTemplate`
- `RestTemplate`

- `WebServiceTemplate`
- Most hide low-level resource management

Let's look at the same code that we used earlier with Spring's `JdbcTemplate` and how it removes the boilerplate code.

Use `JdbcTemplates` to let your code the focus on the task:

```
public Account getAccountById(long id) {
   return jdbcTemplate.queryForObject(
      "select id, name, amoount" +
      "from account where id=?",
       new RowMapper<Account>() {
          public Account mapRow(ResultSet rs,
           int rowNum) throws SQLException {
             account = new Account();
             account.setId(rs.getLong("id"));
             account.setName(rs.getString("name"));
             account.setAmount(rs.getString("amount"));
             return account;
          }
      },
   id);
}
```

As you can see in the preceding code, this new version of `getAccountById()` is much simpler as compared to the boiler plate code, and here the method is focused on selecting an account from the database rather than creating a database connection, creating a statement, executing the query, handling the SQL exception, and finally closing the connection as well. With the template, you have to provide the SQL query and a `RowMapper` used for mapping the resulting set data to the domain object in the template's `queryForObject()` method. The template is responsible for doing everything for this operation, such as database connection and so on. It also hides a lot of boilerplate code behind the framework.

We have seen in this section how Spring attacks the complexities of Java development with the power of POJO-oriented development and patterns such as the DI pattern, the Aspect-using Proxy pattern, and the Template method design pattern.

In the next section, we will look at how to use a Spring container to create and manage the Spring beans in the application.

Using a Spring container to manage beans with the Factory pattern

Spring provides us with a container, and our application objects live in this Spring container. As shown in the following diagram, this container is responsible for creating and managing the objects:

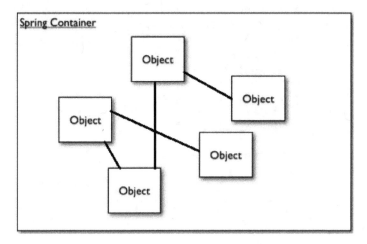

In a Spring application, our application objects live in this Spring container

The **Spring Container** also wires the many **Object** together according to its configuration. It is configured with some initialized parameters, and manages their complete life cycle from start to finish.

Basically, there are two distinct types of Spring container:

- Bean factory
- Application contexts

Bean factory

In the Spring Framework, the `org.springframework.beans.factory.BeanFactory` interface provides the bean factory, which is a Spring IoC container. `XmlBeanFactory` is an implementation class for this interface. This container reads the configuration metadata from an XML file. It is based on the GOF factory method design pattern--it creates, manages, caches, and wires the application objects in a sophisticated manner. The bean factory is merely an object pool where objects are created and managed by configuration. For small applications, this is sufficient, but enterprise applications demand more, so spring provides another version of the spring container with more features.

In the next section, we will learn about the application context and how Spring creates it in the application.

Application contexts

In the Spring Framework, the `org.springframework.context.ApplicationContext` interface also provides Spring's IoC container. It is simply a wrapper of the bean factory, providing some extra application context services, such as support for AOP and, hence, declarative transaction, security, and instrumentation support such as support for message resources required for internationalization, and the ability to publish application events to interested event listeners.

Creating a container with an application context

Spring provides several flavors of application context as a bean container. There are multiple core implementations of the `ApplicationContext` interface, as shown here:

- `FileSystemXmlApplicationContext`: This class is an implementation of `ApplicationContext` that loads application context bean definitions from the configuration files (XML) located in the file system.
- `ClassPathXmlApplicationContext`: This class is an implementation of `ApplicationContext` that loads application context bean definitions from the configuration files (XML) located in the classpath of the application.
- `AnnotationConfigApplicationContext`: This class is an implementation of `ApplicationContext` that loads application context bean definitions from the configuration classes (Java based) from the class path of the application.

Spring provides you with a web-aware implementation of the `ApplicationContext` interface, as shown here:

- `XmlWebApplicationContext`: This class is a web-aware implementation of `ApplicationContext` that loads application context bean definitions from the configuration files (XML) contained in a web application.
- `AnnotationConfigWebApplicationContext`: This class is a web-aware implementation of `ApplicationContext` that loads Spring web application context bean definitions from one or more Java-based configuration classes.

We can use either one of these implementations to load beans into a bean factory. It depends upon our application configuration file locations. For example, if you want to load your configuration file `spring.xml` from the file system in a specific location, Spring provides you with a `FileSystemXmlApplicationContext`, class that looks for the configuration file `spring.xml` in a specific location within the file system:

```
ApplicationContext context = new
 FileSystemXmlApplicationContext("d:/spring.xml");
```

In the same way, you can also load your application configuration file `spring.xml` from the classpath of your application by using a `ClassPathXmlApplicationContext` class provided by Spring. It looks for the configuration file `spring.xml` anywhere in the classpath (including JAR files):

```
ApplicationContext context = new
 ClassPathXmlApplicationContext("spring.xml");
```

If you are using a Java configuration instead of an XML configuration, you can use `AnnotationConfigApplicationContext`:

```
ApplicationContext context = new
 AnnotationConfigApplicationContext(AppConfig.class);
```

After loading the configuration files and getting an application context, we can fetch beans from the Spring container by calling the `getBean()` method of the application context:

```
TransferService transferService =
 context.getBean(TransferService.class);
```

In the following section, we will learn about the Spring bean life cycle, and how a Spring container reacts to the Spring bean to create and manage it.

Life of a bean in the container

The Spring application context uses the Factory method design pattern to create Spring beans in the container in the correct order according to the given configuration. So the Spring container has the responsibility of managing the life cycle of the bean from creation to destruction. In the normal java application, Java's `new` keyword is used to instantiate the bean, and it's ready to use. Once the bean is no longer in use, it's eligible for garbage collection. But in the Spring container, the life cycle of the bean is more elaborate. The following image shows the life cycle of a typical Spring bean:

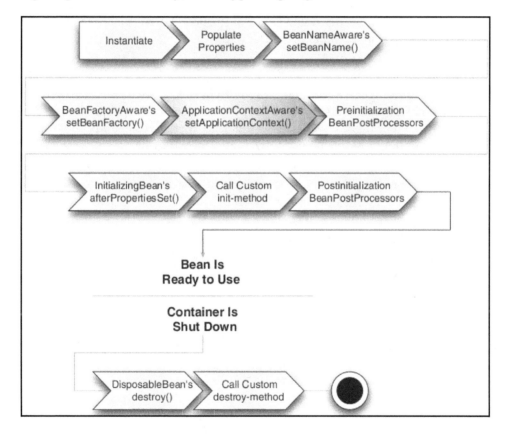

The life cycle of a Spring bean in the Spring container is as follows:

1. Load all bean definitions, creating an ordered graph.
2. Instantiate and run `BeanFactoryPostProcessors` (you can update bean definitions here).
3. Instantiate each bean.

4. Spring injects the values and bean references into the beans' properties.

5. Spring passes the ID of the bean to the `setBeanName()` method of the `BeanNameAware` interface if any bean implements it.

6. Spring passes the reference of the bean factory itself to the `setBeanFactory()` method of `BeanFactoryAware` if any bean implements it.

7. Spring passes the reference of the application context itself to the `setApplicationContext()` method of `ApplicationContextAware` if any bean implements it.

8. `BeanPostProcessor` is an interface, and Spring allows you to implement it with your bean, and modifies the instance of the bean before the initializer is invoked in the Spring bean container by calling its `postProcessBeforeInitialization()`.

9. If your bean implements the `InitializingBean` interface, Spring calls its `afterPropertiesSet()` method to initialize any process or loading resource for your application. It's dependent on your specified initialization method. There are other methods to achieve this step, for example, you can use the `init-method` of the `<bean>` tag, the `initMethod` attribute of the `@Bean` annotation, and JSR 250's `@PostConstruct` annotation.

10. `BeanPostProcessor` is an interface, and spring allows you to implement it with your bean. It modifies the instance of the bean after the initializer is invoked in the spring bean container by calling its `postProcessAfterInitialization()`.

11. Now your bean is ready to use in the step, and your application can access this bean by using the `getBean()` method of the application context. Your beans remain live in the application context until it is closed by calling the `close()` method of the application context.

12. If your bean implements the `DisposibleBean` interface, Spring calls its `destroy()` method to destroy any process or clean up the resources of your application. There are other methods to achieve this step-for example, you can use the `destroy-method` of the `<bean>` tag, the `destroyMethod` attribute of the `@Bean` annotation, and JSR 250's `@PreDestroy` annotation.

13. These steps show the life cycle of Spring beans in the container.

14. The next section describes the modules that are provided by the Spring Framework.

Spring modules

Spring Framework has several distinct modules for a specific set of functionalities, and they work more or less independently of the others. This system is very flexible, so the developer can choose only those required for the enterprise application. For example, a developer can just use the Spring DI module and build the rest of the application with non-Spring components. So, Spring provides integration points to work with other frameworks and APIs--for example, you can use the Spring Core DI pattern only with the Struts application. In case the development team is more proficient in using Struts, it can be used instead of Spring MVC while the rest of the application uses Spring components and features, such as JDBC and transactions. So while the developers need to deploy the required dependencies with the Struts application, there is no need to add a whole Spring Framework.

Here is an overview of the entire module structure:

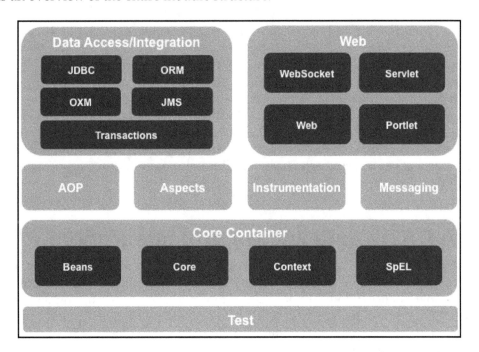

The various modules of the Spring Framework

Let's look at each of Spring's modules and see how each fits in to the bigger picture.

Core Spring container

This module of the Spring Framework uses lot of the design pattern such as the Factory method design pattern, DI pattern, Abstract Factory Design pattern, Singleton Design pattern, Prototype Design pattern, and so on. All other Spring modules are dependent on this module. You'll implicitly use these classes when you configure your application. It is also called the IoC container and is central to Spring's support for dependency injection, which manages how the beans in a Spring application are created, configured, and managed. You can create Spring container either by using the implementations of `BeanFactory` or the implementations of the `ApplicationContext`. This module contains the Spring bean factory, which is the portion of Spring that provides the DI.

Spring's AOP module

Spring AOP is a Java-based AOP Framework with AspectJ integration. It uses dynamic proxies for aspect weaving and focuses on using AOP to solve enterprise problems. This module is based on Proxy and Decorator Design patterns. This module enables the modularization of cross-cutting concerns to avoid tangling and eliminate scattering. Like DI, it supports loose coupling between the core business service and cross-cutting concerns. You can implement your custom aspects and configure them declaratively in your application without impacting on the code of business objects. It provides much flexibility in the code; you could remove or change the aspect logic without touching the code of the business objects. This is a very important module of the spring framework, so I will discuss it in detail in `Chapter 4`, *Spring Aspect Oriented Programming with Proxy and Decorator Pattern* of this book.

Spring DAO - data access and integration

Spring DAO and Spring JDBC make life very easy by using templates to remove the common code. The templates implement the GOF template method design pattern and provide suitable extension points to plug in custom code. If you are working with a traditional JDBC application, you have to write lots of boilerplate code to, for example, create a database connection, create a statement, find a result set, handle SQLException, and finally close the connection. If you are working with a Spring JDBC Framework with a DAO layer, then you do not have to write boilerplate code, unlike a traditional JDBC application. That means that Spring allows you to keep your application code clean and simple.

Spring's ORM

Spring also provides support to ORM solutions, and it provides integration with ORM tools for easy persistence of POJO objects in relational databases. This module actually provides an extension to the Spring DAO module. Like JDBC-based templates, Spring provides ORM templates to work with leading ORM products, such as Hibernate, JPA, OpenJPA, TopLink, iBATIS, and so on.

Spring web MVC

Spring provides a web and remote module for the enterprise web application. This module helps build highly flexible web applications, leveraging the complete benefits of the Spring IOC container. This module of Spring uses the patterns such as the MVC architectural pattern, Front Controller pattern, and the DispatcherServlet Pattern, and it seamlessly integrates with the servlet API. The Spring web module is very pluggable and flexible. We can add any of the view technologies, such as JSP, FreeMarker, Velocity, and so on. We can also integrate it with other frameworks, such as Struts, Webwork, and JSF, using spring IOC and DI.

New features in Spring Framework 5.0

Spring 5.0 is the freshest release of Spring available. There are a lot of exciting new features in Spring 5.0, including the following:

- Support for JDK 8 + 9 and Java EE 7 Baseline:

  Spring 5 supports Java 8 as a minimum requirement, as the entire framework codebase is based on Java 8.

  Spring Framework required at least Java EE 7 to run Spring Framework 5.0 applications. That means it requires Servlet 3.1, JMS 2.0, JPA 2.1.

- Deprecated and removed packages, classes, and methods:

  In Spring 5.0, some packages have been either removed or deprecated. It has had a package called `mock.static` removed from the spring-aspects module, and hence there is no support for `AnnotationDrivenStaticEntityMockingControl`.

Packages such as `web.view.tiles2` and `orm.hibernate3/hibernate4` have also been removed as of Spring 5.0. Now, in the latest spring framework, Tiles 3 and Hibernate 5 are being used.

The Spring 5.0 framework doesn't support Portlet, Velocity, JasperReports, XMLBeans, JDO, Guava (and so on) anymore.

Some deprecated classes and methods of earlier versions of Spring have been removed as of Spring 5.0.

- Adding the new reactive programming model:

    This model of programming has been introduced in the Spring 5.0 Framework. Let's look at the following listed point about the reactive programming model.

    Spring 5 introduced the Spring-core module `DataBuffer` and encoder/decoder abstractions with non-blocking semantics into the reactive programming model.

    Using the reactive model, Spring 5.0 provides the Spring-web module for HTTP message codec implementations with **JSON (Jackson)** and **XML (JAXB)** support.

    The Spring reactive programming model added a new `spring-web-reactive` module with reactive support for the `@Controller` programming model, adapting reactive streams to Servlet 3.1 containers, as well as non-Servlet runtimes, such as Netty and Undertow.

    Spring 5.0 also introduced a new `WebClient` with reactive support on the client side to access services.

As listed here, you can see that there are a lot of exciting new features and enhancements in the Spring Framework 5. So in this book, we will look at many of these new features with examples and their adopted design patterns.

Summary

After reading this chapter, you should now have a good overview of the Spring Framework and its most-used design patterns. I highlighted the problem with the J2EE traditional application, and how Spring solves these problems and simplifies Java development by using lots of design patterns and good practices to create an application. Spring aims to make enterprise Java development easier and to promote loosely coupled code. We have also discussed Spring AOP for cross-cutting concerns and the DI pattern for use with loose coupling and pluggable Spring components so that the objects don't need to know where their dependencies come from or how they're implemented. Spring Framework is an enabler for best practices and effective object design. Spring Framework has two important features--First it has a Spring container to create and manage the life of beans and second it provides support to several modules and integration to help simplify Java development.

2

Overview of GOF Design Patterns - Core Design Patterns

In this chapter, you'll be given an overview of GOF Design Patterns, including some best practices for making an application design. You'll also get an overview of common problem--solving with design patterns.

I will explain the design patterns that are commonly used by the Spring Framework for better design and architecture. We are all in a global world, which means that if we have services in the market, they can be accessed across the Globe. Simply put, now is the age of the distributed computing system. So first, what is a distributed system? It's an application that is divided into smaller parts that run simultaneously on different computers and the smaller parts communicate over the network, generally using protocols. These smaller parts are called **tiers**. So if we want to create a distributed application, n-tier architecture is a better choice for that type of application. But developing an n-tier distributed application is a complex and challenging job. Distributing the processing into separate tiers leads to better resource utilization. It also support the allocation of tasks to experts who are best suited to work and develop a particular tier. Many challenges exist in developing distributed applications, some of which are detailed here:

- Integration between the tiers
- Transaction management
- Concurrency handling of enterprise data
- Security of the application and so on

So my focus in this book is on simplifying Java EE application design and development by applying patterns and best practices with the Spring Framework. In this book, I will cover some common GOF Design Patterns, and how Spring adopted these for providing the best solutions to the aforementioned listed problems of enterprise application because the design of distributed objects is an immensely complicated task, even for experienced professionals. You need to consider critical issues, such as scalability, performance, transactions, and so on, before drafting a final solution. That solution is described as a pattern.

At the end of this chapter, you will understand how design patterns provide the best solution to address any design-related and development-related issues, and how to start development with the best practices. Here, you will get more ideas about GOF Design Patterns, with real-life examples. You will get information about how the Spring Framework implements these design patterns internally to provide the best enterprise solution.

This chapter will cover the following points:

- Introducing the power of design patterns
- Common GOF Design Patterns overview
    - Core design patterns
        - Creational design patterns
        - Structural design patterns
        - Behavioral design patterns
    - J2EE design patterns
        - Design patterns at presentation layer
        - Design patterns at business layer
        - Design patterns at integration layer
- Some best practices for Spring application development

Introducing the power of design patterns

So what is a design pattern? Actually, the phrase design pattern is not associated with any programming language, and also it doesn't provide language-specific solutions to problems. A design pattern is associated with the solution to repetitive problems. For example, if any problem occurs frequently, a solution to that problem has been used effectively. Any non-reusable solution to a problem can't be considered a pattern, but the problem must occur frequently in order to have a reusable solution, and to be considered as a pattern. So a design pattern is a software engineering concept describing recurring solutions to common problems in software design. Design patterns also represent the best practices used by experienced object-oriented software developers.

When you make a design for an application, you should consider all the solutions to common problems, and these solutions are called **design patterns**. The understanding of design patterns must be good across the developer team so that the staff can communicate with each other effectively. In fact, you may be familiar with some design patterns; however, you may not have used well-known names to describe them. This book will take you through a step-by-step approach and show you examples that use Java while you learn design pattern concepts.

A design pattern has three main characteristics:

- A Design pattern is *specific to a particular scenario* rather than a specific platform. So its context is the surrounding condition under which the problem exists. The context must be documented within the pattern.
- Design patterns have been *evolved to provide the best solutions* to certain problems faced during software development. So this should be limited by the context in which it is being considered.
- Design patterns are *the remedy for the problems under consideration*.

For example, if a developer is referring to the GOF Singleton design pattern and signifies the use of a single object, then all developers involved should understand that you need to design an object that will only have a single instance in the application. So the Singleton design pattern will be composed of a single object and the developers can tell each other that the program is following a Singleton pattern.

Common GoF Design Pattern overview

The authors Erich Gamma, Richard Helm, Ralph Johnson, and John Vlissides are often referred to as the GoF, or Gang of Four. They published a book titled *Design Patterns: Elements of Reusable Object-Oriented Software,* which initiated the concept of design patterns in software development.

In this chapter, you will learn what GOF patterns are and how they help solve common problems encountered in object-oriented design.

The **Gang of Four (GoF)** patterns are 23 classic software design patterns providing recurring solutions to common problems in software design. The patterns are defined in the book *Design Patterns: Elements of Reusable Object-Oriented Software*. These patterns are categorized into two main categories:

- Core Design Patterns
- J2EE Design Patterns

Furthermore, **Core Design Patterns** are also subdivided into three main categories of design pattern, as follows:

- **Creational Design Pattern**: Patterns under this category provide a way to construct objects when constructors will not serve your purpose. The creation logic of objects is hidden. The programs based on these patterns are more flexible in deciding object creation according to your demands and your use cases for the application.
- **Structural Design Pattern**: Patterns under this category deal with the composition of classes or objects. In the enterprise application, there are two commonly used techniques for reusing functionality in object-oriented systems: one is class Inheritance and the other is the Object Composition Concept of inheritance. The Object Composition Concept of inheritance is used to compose interfaces and define ways to compose objects to obtain new functionalities.
- **Behavioral Design Pattern**: Patterns under this category, characterize the ways in which classes or objects interact and distribute responsibility. These design patterns are specifically concerned with communication between objects. The behavioral design pattern is used to control and reduce complicated application flow in the enterprise application.

Now, let's look at the other category, the **JEE Design patterns**. This is the other main category of design patterns. Application design can be immensely simplified by applying Java EE design patterns. Java EE design patterns have been documented in Sun's Java Blueprints. These Java EE Design patterns provide time-tested solution guidelines and best practices for object interaction in the different layers of a Java EE application. These design patterns are specifically concerned with the following listed layers:

- Design pattern at the presentation layer
- Design pattern at the business layer
- Design pattern at the integration layer

Let's explore creational design patterns in the upcoming section.

Creational design patterns

Let's look at the underlying design patterns of this category and how Spring Framework adopts them to provide loose coupling between components and create and manage the lifecycle of Spring components. Creational design patterns are associated with the method of object creation. The creation logic of the object is hidden to the caller of this object.

We are all aware of how to create an object using the `new` keyword in Java, as follows:

```
Account account = new Account();
```

But this way is not suitable for some cases, because it is a hardcoded way of creating an object. It is also not a best practice to create an object because the object might be changed according to the nature of the program. Here, the creational design pattern provides the flexibility to create an object according to the nature of the program.

Now let's look at the different design patterns under this category.

Factory design pattern

Define an interface for creating an object, but let subclasses decide which class to instantiate. Factory Method lets a class defer instantiation to subclasses.
- GOF Design Pattern

The Factory design pattern is a creational design pattern. The Factory design pattern is also known as the Factory method design pattern. According to this design pattern, you get an object of a class without exposing the underlying logic to the client. It assigns a new object to the caller by using a common interface or abstract class. This means that the design pattern hides the actual logic of the implementation of an object, how to create it, and which class to instantiate it in. So the client shouldn't worry about creating, managing, and destroying an object-the Factory pattern takes responsibility for these tasks. The Factory pattern is one of the most-used design patterns in Java.

Let's look at the benefits of the Factory pattern:

- The Factory pattern promotes loose coupling between collaborating components or classes by using interfaces rather than binding application-specific classes into the application code
- Using this pattern, you can get an implementation of an object of classes that implement an interface, at runtime
- The object life cycle is managed by the factory implemented by this pattern

Now let's discuss some common problems where you should apply the Factory design pattern:

- This pattern removes the burden on the developer to create and manage the objects
- This pattern removes the tight coupling between collaboration components because a component doesn't know what subclasses it will be required to create
- Avoid hard code to create an object of the class

Implementing the Factory design pattern in Spring Framework

Spring Framework transparently uses this Factory design pattern to implement Spring containers using `BeanFactory` and `ApplicationContext` interfaces. Spring's container works based on the Factory pattern to create spring beans for the Spring application and also manages the life cycle of every Spring bean. `BeanFactory` and `ApplicationContext` are factory interfaces, and Spring has lots of implementing classes. The `getBean()` method is the factory method that gives you Spring beans accordingly.

Let's see a sample implementation of the Factory design pattern.

Sample implementation of the Factory design pattern

There are two classes `SavingAccount` and `CurrentAccount` implementing an interface `Account`. So, you can create a `Factory` class with a method that takes one or more arguments and its return type is `Account`. This method is known as the Factory method because it creates the instances of either `CurrentAccount` or `SavingAccount`. The `Account` interface is used for loose coupling. So, according to the passed arguments in the factory method, it chooses which subclass to instantiate. This factory method will have the superclass as its return type:

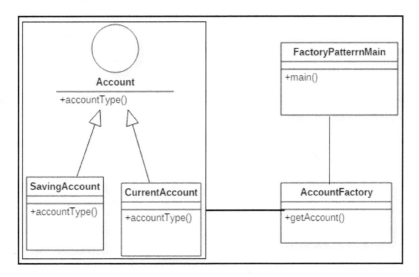

UML Diagram for the Factory design pattern

Let's look at this design pattern in the following example. Here, I am going to create an `Account` interface and some concrete classes that implement the `Account` interface:

```
package com.packt.patterninspring.chapter2.factory;
public interface Account {
   void accountType();
}
```

Now let's create `SavingAccount.java`, which will implement the `Account` interface:

```
package com.packt.patterninspring.chapter2.factory;
public class SavingAccount implements Account{
  @Override
  public void accountType() {
     System.out.println("SAVING ACCOUNT");
  }
}
```

Same with `CurrentAccount.java`, it will also implement the `Account` interface:

```
package com.packt.patterninspring.chapter2.factory;
public class CurrentAccount implements Account {
  @Override
  public void accountType() {
     System.out.println("CURRENT ACCOUNT");
  }
}
```

A Factory class `AccountFactory` is now going to be defined. `AccountFactory` generates an object of the concrete class, either `SavingAccount` or `CurrentAccount`, based on the account type given as an argument to the Factory method:

`AccountFactory.java` is a Factory to produce the `Account` type object:

```
package com.packt.patterninspring.chapter2.factory.pattern;
import com.packt.patterninspring.chapter2.factory.Account;
import com.packt.patterninspring.chapter2.factory.CurrentAccount;
import com.packt.patterninspring.chapter2.factory.SavingAccount;
public class AccountFactory {
  final String CURRENT_ACCOUNT = "CURRENT";
  final String SAVING_ACCOUNT  = "SAVING";
  //use getAccount method to get object of type Account
  //It is factory method for object of type Account
  public Account getAccount(String accountType){
     if(CURRENT_ACCOUNT.equals(accountType)) {
            return new CurrentAccount();
     }
     else if(SAVING_ACCOUNT.equals(accountType)){
            return new SavingAccount();
     }
     return null;
  }
}
```

`FactoryPatternMain` is the main calling class of `AccountFactory` to get an `Account` object. It will pass an argument to the factory method that contains information of the account type, such as `SAVING` and `CURRENT`. `AccountFactory` returns the object of the type that you passed to the factory method.

Let's create a demo class `FactoryPatterMain.java` to test the factory method design pattern:

```
package com.packt.patterninspring.chapter2.factory.pattern;
import com.packt.patterninspring.chapter2.factory.Account;
public class FactoryPatterMain {
  public static void main(String[] args) {
    AccountFactory accountFactory = new AccountFactory();
    //get an object of SavingAccount and call its accountType()
    method.
    Account savingAccount = accountFactory.getAccount("SAVING");
    //call accountType method of SavingAccount
    savingAccount.accountType();
    //get an object of CurrentAccount and call its accountType()
    method.
    Account currentAccount = accountFactory.getAccount("CURRENT");
    //call accountType method of CurrentAccount
    currentAccount.accountType();
  }
}
```

You can test this file and see the output on the console, which should look like this:

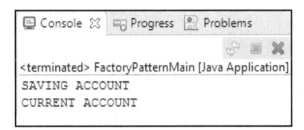

Now that we've seen the Factory design pattern, let's turn to a different variant of it-the Abstract factory design pattern.

Abstract factory design pattern

Provide an interface for creating families of related or dependent objects without specifying their concrete classes. - GOF Design Patterns

The Abstract Factory pattern comes under the creational design pattern. It is a high-level design pattern compared to the factory method design pattern. According to this design pattern, you just define an interface or abstract class to create a related dependent object without specifying its concrete subclass. So here, the abstract factory returns a factory of classes. Let me simplify it for you. You have a set of factory method design patterns, and you just put these factories under a factory using the factory design pattern, which means that it is simply a factory of factories. And there is no need to take the knowledge about all of the factories into the factory--you can make your program using a top-level factory.

In the Abstract Factory pattern, an interface is responsible for creating a factory of related objects without explicitly specifying their classes. Each generated factory can give the objects as per the Factory pattern.

The benefits of the Abstract Factory pattern are as follows:

- The Abstract Factory Design provides loose coupling between the component families. It also isolates the client code from concrete classes.
- This design pattern is a higher-level design than the Factory pattern.
- This pattern provides better consistency at construction time of objects across the application.
- This pattern easily swaps component families.

Common problems where you should apply the Abstract factory design pattern

When you design a Factory pattern for object creation in your application, there are times when you want a particular set of related objects to be created with certain constraints and apply the desired logic across the related objects in your application. You can achieve this design by creating another factory inside the factory for a set of related objects and apply the required constraints. You can also program the logic to a set of related objects.

When you want to customize the instantiation logic of related objects, then you could use this design pattern.

Implementing the Abstract factory design pattern in the Spring Framework

In the Spring Framework, the `FactoryBean` interface is based on the Abstract Factory design pattern. Spring provides a lot of implementation of this interface, such as `ProxyFactoryBean`, `JndiFactoryBean`, `LocalSessionFactoryBean`, `LocalContainerEntityManagerFactoryBean`, and so on. A `FactoryBean` is also useful to help Spring construct objects that it couldn't easily construct itself. Often this is used to construct complex objects that have many dependencies. It might also be used when the construction logic itself is highly volatile and depends on the configuration.

For example, in Spring Framework, one of the `FactoryBean` implementations is `LocalSessionFactoryBean`, which is used to get a reference of a bean that was associated with the hibernate configuration. It is a specific configuration concerning the data source. It should be applied before you get an object of `SessionFactory`. You can use the `LocalSessionFactoryBean` to apply the specific data source configuration in a consistent way. You may inject the result of a FactoryBean's `getObject()` method into any other property.

Let's create a sample implementation of the Abstract Factory design pattern.

Sample implementation of the Abstract Factory design pattern

I am going to create a `Bank` and `Account` interface and some concrete classes implementing these interfaces. Here, I also create an abstract factory class, `AbstractFactory`. I have some factory classes, `BankFactory` and `AccountFactory`; these classes extend the `AbstractFactory` class. I will also create a `FactoryProducer` class to create the factories.

Let's see this design pattern in the following image:

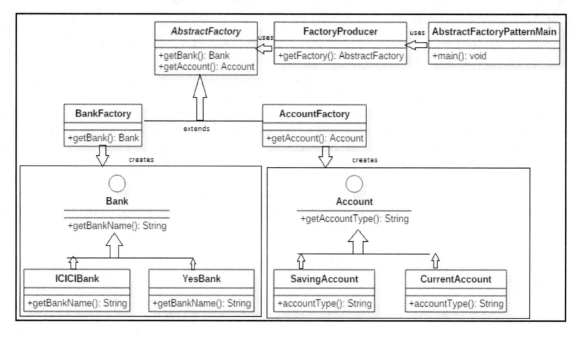

UML diagram for the Abstract Factory design pattern

Create a demo class, `AbstractFactoryPatternMain`; it uses `FactoryProducer` to get an `AbstractFactory` object. Here, I pass information such as `ICICI`, `YES` to `AbstractFactory` to get an object of `Bank`, and I also pass information such as `SAVING`, `CURRENT` to `AbstractFactory` to get an `Account` type.

Here is the code for `Bank.java`, which is an interface:

```
package com.packt.patterninspring.chapter2.model;
public interface Bank {
   void bankName();
}
```

Now let's create `ICICIBank.java`, which implements the `Bank` interface:

```
package com.packt.patterninspring.chapter2.model;
public class ICICIBank implements Bank {
  @Override
  public void bankName() {
    System.out.println("ICICI Bank Ltd.");
  }
}
```

Let's create another `YesBank.java`, an implementing `Bank` interface:

```
package com.packt.patterninspring.chapter2.model;
public class YesBank implements Bank{
  @Override
  public void bankName() {
      System.out.println("Yes Bank Pvt. Ltd.");
  }
}
```

In this example, I am using the same interface and implementing classes of `Account` as I used in the Factory pattern example in this book.

`AbstractFactory.java` is an abstract class that is used to get factories for `Bank` and `Account` objects:

```
package com.packt.patterninspring.chapter2.abstractfactory.pattern;
import com.packt.patterninspring.chapter2.model.Account;
import com.packt.patterninspring.chapter2.model.Bank;
public abstract class AbstractFactory {
  abstract Bank getBank(String bankName);
  abstract Account getAccount(String accountType);
}
```

`BankFactory.java` is a factory class extending `AbstractFactory` to generate an object of the concrete class based on the given information:

```
package com.packt.patterninspring.chapter2.abstractfactory.pattern;
import com.packt.patterninspring.chapter2.model.Account;
import com.packt.patterninspring.chapter2.model.Bank;
import com.packt.patterninspring.chapter2.model.CurrentAccount;
import com.packt.patterninspring.chapter2.model.SavingAccount;
public class AccountFactory extends AbstractFactory
{
    final String CURRENT_ACCOUNT = "CURRENT";
final String SAVING_ACCOUNT = "SAVING";
@Override
Bank getBank(String bankName)
```

```
        {
            return null;
        }
    //use getAccount method to get object of type Account
    //It is factory method for object of type Account
        @Override
        public Account getAccount(String accountType){
            if(CURRENT_ACCOUNT.equals(accountType))
            {
                return new CurrentAccount();
            }
            else if(SAVING_ACCOUNT.equals(accountType))
            {
                return new SavingAccount();
            }
            return null;
        }
    }
```

AccountFactory.java is a factory class that extends AbstractFactory.java to generate an object of the concrete class based on the given information:

```
package com.packt.patterninspring.chapter2.abstractfactory.pattern;
import com.packt.patterninspring.chapter2.model.Account;
import com.packt.patterninspring.chapter2.model.Bank;
import com.packt.patterninspring.chapter2.model.CurrentAccount;
import com.packt.patterninspring.chapter2.model.SavingAccount;
public class AccountFactory extends AbstractFactory {
  final String CURRENT_ACCOUNT = "CURRENT";
  final String SAVING_ACCOUNT  = "SAVING";
  @Override
  Bank getBank(String bankName) {
      return null;
  }
  //use getAccount method to get object of type Account
  //It is factory method for object of type Account
  @Override
  public Account getAccount(String accountType){
    if(CURRENT_ACCOUNT.equals(accountType)) {
            return new CurrentAccount();
    }
    else if(SAVING_ACCOUNT.equals(accountType)){
            return new SavingAccount();
    }
    return null;
  }
}
```

`FactoryProducer.java` is a class that creates a Factory generator class to get factories by passing a piece of information, such as `Bank` or `Account`:

```java
package com.packt.patterninspring.chapter2.abstractfactory.pattern;
public class FactoryProducer {
   final static String BANK    = "BANK";
   final static String ACCOUNT = "ACCOUNT";
   public static AbstractFactory getFactory(String factory){
      if(BANK.equalsIgnoreCase(factory)){
            return new BankFactory();
      }
      else if(ACCOUNT.equalsIgnoreCase(factory)){
            return new AccountFactory();
      }
      return null;
   }
}
```

`FactoryPatterMain.java` is a demo class for the Abstract Factory design pattern. `FactoryProducer` is a class to get `AbstractFactory` in order to get the factories of concrete classes by passing a piece of information, such as the type:

```java
package com.packt.patterninspring.chapter2.factory.pattern;
import com.packt.patterninspring.chapter2.model.Account;
public class FactoryPatterMain {
   public static void main(String[] args) {
      AccountFactory accountFactory = new AccountFactory();
      //get an object of SavingAccount and call its accountType()
      method.
      Account savingAccount = accountFactory.getAccount("SAVING");
      //call accountType method of SavingAccount
      savingAccount.accountType();
      //get an object of CurrentAccount and call its accountType()
      method.
      Account currentAccount = accountFactory.getAccount("CURRENT");
      //call accountType method of CurrentAccount
      currentAccount.accountType();
   }
}
```

You can test this file and see the output on the console:

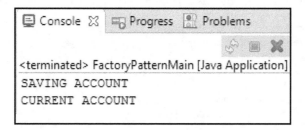

Now that we've seen the abstract Factory design pattern, let's turn to a different variant of it-the singleton design pattern.

Singleton design pattern

Ensure a class has only one instance and provide a global point of access to it - GOF Design Patterns

The Singleton pattern is a creational design pattern, it is one of the simplest design patterns in Java. According to the singleton design pattern, the class provides the same single object for each call--that is, it is restricting the instantiation of a class to one object and provides a global point of access to that class. So the class is responsible for creating an object and also ensures that only a single object should be created for each client call for this object. This class doesn't allow a direct instantiation of an object of this class. It allows you to get an object instance only by an exposed static method.

This is useful when exactly one object is needed to coordinate actions across the system. You can create a single pattern using two forms, as listed here:

- **Early instantiation**: Creation of instance at load time
- **Lazy instantiation**: Creation of instance when required

Benefits of the Singleton pattern:

- It provides controller access to crucial (usually heavy object) classes, such as the connection class for DB and the `SessionFactory` class in hibernate
- It saves heaps of memory
- It is a very efficient design for multithreaded environments
- It is more flexible because the class controls the instantiation process, and the class has the flexibility to change the instantiation process
- It has low latency

Common problems where you should apply Singleton pattern

The Singleton pattern solves only one problem--if you have a resource that can only have a single instance, and you need to manage that single instance, then you need a singleton. Normally, if you want to create a database connection with the given configuration in the distributed and multithread environment, it might be the case that every thread can create a new database connection with a different configuration object, if you don't follow the singleton design. With the Singleton pattern, each thread gets the same database connection object with the same configuration object across the system. It is mostly used in multithreaded and database applications. It is used in logging, caching, thread pools, configuration settings, and so on.

Singleton design pattern implementation in the Spring Framework

The Spring Framework provides a Singleton scoped bean as a singleton pattern. It is similar to the singleton pattern, but it's not exactly the same as the Singleton pattern in Java. According to the Singleton pattern, a scoped bean in the Spring Framework means a single bean instance per container and per bean. If you define one bean for a particular class in a single Spring container, then the Spring container creates one and only one instance of the class defined by that bean definition.

Let's create a sample application of the singleton design pattern.

Sample implementation of the Singleton design pattern

In the following code example, I will be creating a class with a method to create an instance of this class if one does not exist. If the instance is already present, then it will simply return the reference of that object. I have also taken thread safety into consideration, and so I have used a synchronized block here before creating the object of that class.

Let's check out the UML diagram for the Singleton design pattern:

```
package com.packt.patterninspring.chapter2.singleton.pattern;
public class SingletonClass {
   private static SingletonClass instance = null;
   private SingletonClass() {
   }
   public static SingletonClass getInstance() {
     if (instance == null) {
       synchronized(SingletonClass.class){
           if (instance == null) {
               instance = new SingletonClass();
           }
       }
     }
     return instance;
   }
 }
}
```

One thing to be noted in the preceding code is that I have written a private constructor of the `SingletonClass` class to make sure that there is no way to create the object of that class. This example is based on lazy initialization, which means that the program creates an instance on demand the first time. So you could also eagerly instantiate the object to improve the runtime performance of your application. Let's see the same `SingletonClass` with eager initialization:

```
package com.packt.patterninspring.chapter2.singleton.pattern;
public class SingletonClass {
   private static final SingletonClass INSTANCE =
       new SingletonClass();
   private SingletonClass() {}
   public static SingletonClass getInstance() {
     return INSTANCE;
   }
 }
}
```

Now that we've seen the singleton design pattern, let's turn to a different variant of it--the Prototype design pattern.

Prototype design pattern

Specify the kind of objects to create using a prototypical instance, and create new objects by copying this prototype. - GOF Design Patterns

The Prototype pattern comes under the creational design pattern family of GOF patterns in software development. This pattern is used to create the objects by using a clone method of objects. It is determined by a prototypical instance. In the enterprise application, object creation is costly in terms of creating and initializing the initial properties of objects. If such a type of object is already in your hand, then you go for the prototype pattern; you just copy an existing similar object instead of creating it, which is time-consuming.

This pattern involves implementing a prototype interface, it creates a clone of the current object. This pattern is used when the direct creation of the object is costly. For example, say that an object is to be created after a costly database operation. We can cache the object, returns its clone on the next request, and update the database as and when it is needed, thus reducing database calls.

Benefits of the Prototype design pattern

The following list shows the benefits of using the Prototype pattern:

- Reduces the time to create the time-consuming objects by using the prototype pattern
- This pattern reduces subclassing
- This pattern adds and removes objects at runtime
- This pattern configures the application with classes dynamically

Let's see the UML class structure of the Prototype design pattern.

UML class structure

The following UML diagram shows all the components of the Prototype design pattern:

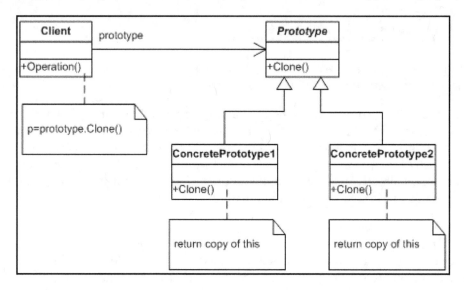

UML diagram for Prototype design pattern

Let's see these components as listed in following points:

- **Prototype**: The Prototype is an interface. It is uses the clone method to create instances of this interface type.

- **ConcretePrototype**: This is a concrete class of the Prototype interface to implement an operation to clone itself.

- **Client**: This is a `caller` class to create a new object of a Prototype interface by calling a `clone` method of the prototype interface.

Let's see a sample implementation of the prototype design pattern.

Sample implementation of the Prototype design pattern

I am going to create an abstract `Account` class and concrete classes extending the `Account` class. An `AccountCache` class is defined as a next step, which stores account objects in a `HashMap` and returns their clone when requested. Create an abstract class implementing the `Clonable` interface.

```
package com.packt.patterninspring.chapter2.prototype.pattern;
public abstract class Account implements Cloneable{
  abstract public void accountType();
  public Object clone() {
    Object clone = null;
    try {
      clone = super.clone();
    }
    catch (CloneNotSupportedException e) {
      e.printStackTrace();
    }
    return clone;
  }
}
```

Now let's create concrete classes extending the preceding class:

Here's the `CurrentAccount.java` file:

```
package com.packt.patterninspring.chapter2.prototype.pattern;
public class CurrentAccount extends Account {
  @Override
  public void accountType() {
    System.out.println("CURRENT ACCOUNT");
  }
}
```

Here's how `SavingAccount.java` should look:

```
package com.packt.patterninspring.chapter2.prototype.pattern;
public class SavingAccount extends Account{
  @Override
  public void accountType() {
    System.out.println("SAVING ACCOUNT");
  }
}
```

Let's create a class to get concrete classes in the `AccountCache.java` file:

```
package com.packt.patterninspring.chapter2.prototype.pattern;
import java.util.HashMap;
import java.util.Map;
public class AccountCache {
    public static Map<String, Account> accountCacheMap =
        new HashMap<>();
    static{
      Account currentAccount = new CurrentAccount();
      Account savingAccount = new SavingAccount();
      accountCacheMap.put("SAVING", savingAccount);
      accountCacheMap.put("CURRENT", currentAccount);
    }
 }
```

`PrototypePatternMain.java` is a demo class that we will use to test the design pattern `AccountCache` to get the `Account` object by passing a piece of information, such as the type, and then call the `clone()` method:

```
package com.packt.patterninspring.chapter2.prototype
    .pattern;
public class PrototypePatternMain {
  public static void main(String[] args) {
    Account currentAccount = (Account)
      AccountCache.accountCacheMap.get("CURRENT").clone();
    currentAccount.accountType();
    Account savingAccount = (Account)
      AccountCache.accountCacheMap.get("SAVING") .clone();
    savingAccount.accountType();
  }
}
```

We've covered this so far and it's good. Now let's look at the next design pattern.

Builder design pattern

Separate the construction of a complex object from its representation so that the same construction process can create different representations. - GOF Design Patterns

The Builder design pattern is used to construct a complex object step by step, and finally it will return the complete object. The logic and process of object creation should be generic so that you can use it to create different concrete implementations of the same object type. This pattern simplifies the construction of complex objects and it hides the details of the object's construction from the client caller code. When you are using this pattern, remember you have to build it one step at a time, which means you have to break the object construction login into multiple phases, unlike other patterns, such as the abstract factory and the factory method pattern, which the object in a single step.

Benefits of the Builder pattern:

- This pattern provides you with complete isolation between the construction and representation of an object
- This pattern allows you to construct the object in multiple phases, so you have greater control over the construction process
- This pattern provides the flexibility to vary an object's internal representation

UML class structure

The following UML diagram shows all the components of the Builder design pattern:

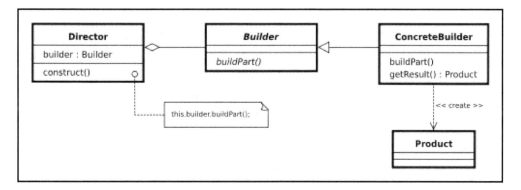

UML diagram for the Builder design pattern:

- **Builder** (AccountBuilder): This is an abstract class or interface for creating the details of an Account object.

- **ConcreteBuilder**: This is an implementation to construct and assemble details of the account by implementing the Builder interface.

- **Director**: This constructs an object using the Builder interface.

- **Product** (Account): This represents the complex object under construction. `AccountBuilder` builds the account's internal representation and defines the process by which it's assembled.

Implementing the Builder pattern in the Spring Framework

The Spring Framework implements the Builder design pattern transparently in some functionalities. The following classes are based on the Builder design pattern in the Spring Framework:

- `EmbeddedDatabaseBuilder`
- `AuthenticationManagerBuilder`
- `UriComponentsBuilder`
- `BeanDefinitionBuilder`
- `MockMvcWebClientBuilder`

Common problems where you should apply Builder pattern

In an enterprise application, you can apply the Builder pattern where the object creation has been done by using multiple steps. In each step, you do a portion of the process. In this process, you set some required parameters and some optional parameters, and after the final step, you will get a complex object.

The Builder pattern is an object creation software design pattern. The intention is to abstract the steps of construction so that different implementations of these steps can construct different representations of objects. Often, the Builder pattern is used to build products in accordance with the composite pattern.

Sample implementation of the Builder design pattern

In the following code example, I am going to create an `Account` class that has
`AccountBuilder` as an inner class. The `AccountBuilder` class has a method to create an
instance of this class:

```
package com.packt.patterninspring.chapter2.builder.pattern;
public class Account {
  private String accountName;
  private Long accountNumber;
  private String accountHolder;
  private double balance;
  private String type;
  private double interest;
  private Account(AccountBuilder accountBuilder) {
    super();
    this.accountName = accountBuilder.accountName;
    this.accountNumber = accountBuilder.accountNumber;
    this.accountHolder = accountBuilder.accountHolder;
    this.balance = accountBuilder.balance;
    this.type = accountBuilder.type;
    this.interest = accountBuilder.interest;
  }
  //setters and getters
   public static class AccountBuilder {
    private final String accountName;
    private final Long accountNumber;
    private final String accountHolder;
    private double balance;
    private String type;
    private double interest;
    public AccountBuilder(String accountName,
        String accountHolder, Long accountNumber) {
      this.accountName = accountName;
      this.accountHolder = accountHolder;
      this.accountNumber = accountNumber;
    }
    public AccountBuilder balance(double balance) {
      this.balance = balance;
      return this;
    }
    public AccountBuilder type(String type) {
      this.type = type;
      return this;
    }
    public AccountBuilder interest(double interest) {
      this.interest = interest;
      return this;
```

```
        }
        public Account build() {
            Account user =  new Account(this);
            return user;
        }
    }
    public String toString() {
    return "Account [accountName=" + accountName + ",
        accountNumber=" + accountNumber + ", accountHolder="
        + accountHolder + ", balance=" + balance + ", type="
        + type + ", interest=" + interest + "]";
    }
}
```

`AccountBuilderTest.java` is a demo class that we will use to test the design pattern.
Let's look at how to build an `Account` object by passing the initial information to the object:

```
package com.packt.patterninspring.chapter2.builder.pattern;
public class AccountBuilderTest {
  public static void main(String[] args) {
    Account account = new Account.AccountBuilder("Saving
        Account", "Dinesh Rajput", 11111)
            .balance(38458.32)
            .interest(4.5)
            .type("SAVING")
            .build();
    System.out.println(account);
  }
}
```

You can test this file and see the output on the console:

```
<terminated> AccountBuilderTest [Java Application] C:\Program Files\Java\jre1.8.0_131\bin\javaw.exe (27-Jun-2017, 2:10:21 AM)
Account [accountName=Saving Account, accountNumber=1111, accountHolder=Dinesh Rajput, balance=38458.32, type=SAVING, interest=4.5]
```

Summary

After reading this chapter, the reader should now have a good idea about the overview of GOF creational design patterns and its best practices. I highlighted the problems that come from not using design patterns in enterprise application development, and how Spring solves these problems by using the creational design patterns and good practices in the application. In this chapter, I have mentioned only one of the Creational Design pattern categories out of the three main categories of the GOF Design Patterns. The Creational design pattern is used for the creation of object instances, and also applies constraints at the creation time in the enterprise application in a specific manner using the Factory, Abstract Factory, Builder, Prototype, and Singleton patterns.

3
Wiring Beans using the Dependency Injection Pattern

In the previous chapter, you learned about the **Gang of Four** (**GOF**) design patterns with examples and use cases of each. Now, we will go into more detail about injecting beans and the configuration of dependencies in a Spring application, where you will see the various ways of configuring in a Spring application. This includes configuration with XML, Annotation, Java, and Mix.

Everyone loves movies, right? Well, if not movies, how about plays, or dramas, or theatre? Ever wondered what would happen if the different team members didn't speak to each other? By team I don't just mean the actors, but the sets team, make-up personnel, audio-visual guys, sound system guys, and so on. It is needless to say that every member has an important contribution towards the end product, and an immense amount of coordination is required between these teams.

A blockbuster movie is a product of hundreds of people working together toward a common goal. Similarly, great software is an application where several objects work together to meet some business target. As a team, every object must be aware of the other, and communicate with each other to get their jobs done.

In a banking system, the money transfer service must be aware of the account service, and the account service must be aware of the accounts repository, and so on. All these components work together to make the banking system workable. In Chapter 1, *Getting Started with Framework 5.0 and Design Patterns*, you saw the same banking example created with the traditional approach, that is, creating objects using construction and direct object initiation. This traditional approach leads to complicated code, is difficult to reuse and unit test, and is also highly coupled to one another.

But in Spring, objects have a responsibility to do their jobs without the need to find and create the other dependent objects that are required in their jobs. The Spring container takes the responsibility to find or create the other dependent objects, and to collaborate with their dependencies. In the previous example of the banking system, the transfer service depends on the account service, but it doesn't have to create the account service, so the dependency is created by the container, and is handed over to the dependent objects in the application.

In this chapter, we will discuss the behind-the-scenes story of the Spring-based application with reference to the **dependency injection (DI)** pattern, and how it works. By the end of this chapter, you will understand how the objects of your Spring-based application create associations between them, and how Spring wires these objects for a job done. You will also learn many ways to wire beans in Spring.

This chapter will cover the following topics:

- The dependency injection pattern
- Types of dependency injection patterns
- Resolving dependency using the Abstract Factory pattern
- Lookup-method injection pattern
- Configuring beans using the Factory pattern
- Configuring dependencies
- Common best practices for configuring dependencies in an application

The dependency injection pattern

In any enterprise application, coordination between the working objects is very important for a business goal. The relationship between objects in an application represents the dependency of an object, so each object would get the job done with coordination of the dependent objects in the application. Such required dependencies between the objects tend to be complicated and with tight-coupled programming in the application. Spring provides a solution to the tight-coupling code of an application by using the dependency injection pattern. Dependency injection is a design pattern, which promotes the loosely coupled classes in the application. This means that the classes in the system depend on the behavior of others, and do not depend on instantiation of object of the classes. The dependency injection pattern also promotes programming to interface instead of programming to implementation. Object dependencies should be on an interface, and not on concrete classes, because a loosely coupled structure offers you greater reusability, maintainability, and testability.

Solving problems using the dependencies injection pattern

In any enterprise application, a common problem to handle is how to configure and wire together the different elements to achieve a business goal--for example, how to bind together the controllers at the web layer with the services and repository interfaces written by different members of the team without knowing about the controllers of the web layers. So, there are a number frameworks that provide a solution for this problem by using lightweight containers to assemble the components from different layers. Examples of such types of frameworks are PicoContainer and Spring Framework.

The containers of PicoContainer and Spring use a number of design patterns to solve the problem of assembling the different components of different layers. Here, I am going to discuss one of these design patterns--the dependency injection pattern. Dependency injection provides us with a decoupled and loosely coupled system. It ensures construction of the dependent object. In the following example, we'll demonstrate how the dependency injection pattern solves the common problems related to collaboration between the various layered components.

Without dependency injection

In the following Java example, first of all, let's see what is a dependency between two classes? Take a look at the following class diagram:

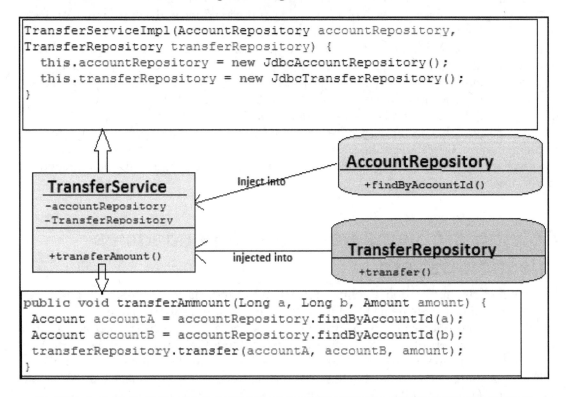

TransferService has dependencies with AccountRepository and TransferRepository for transferAmount() method with Direct Instantiation of repositories classes.

As seen in the preceding diagram, the **TransferService** class contains two member variables, **AccountRepository** and **TransferRepository.** These are initialized by the **TransferService** constructor. **TransferService** controls which implementation of the repositories is used. It also controls their construction. In this situation, **TransferService** is said to have a hard-coded dependency on the following example:

Following is the `TransferServiceImpl.java` file:

```java
public class TransferServiceImpl implements TransferService {
    AccountRepository accountRepository;
    TransferRepository transferRepository;
    public TransferServiceImpl(AccountRepository accountRepository,
    TransferRepository transferRepository) {
        super();
        // Specify a specific implementation in the constructor
        instead of using dependency injection
        this.accountRepository = new JdbcAccountRepository();
        this.transferRepository = new JdbcTransferRepository();
    }
    // Method within this service that uses the accountRepository and
    transferRepository
    @Override
    public void transferAmmount(Long a, Long b, Amount amount) {
        Account accountA = accountRepository.findByAccountId(a);
        Account accountB = accountRepository.findByAccountId(b);
        transferRepository.transfer(accountA, accountB, amount);
    }
}
```

In the preceding example, the `TransferServiceImpl` class has dependencies of two classes, that is `AccountRepository` and `TransferRepository`. The `TransferServiceImpl` class has two member variables of the dependent classes, and initializes them through its constructor by using the JDBC implementation of repositories such as `JdbcAccountRepository` and `JdbcTransferRepository`. The `TransferServiceImpl` class is tightly coupled with the JDBC implementation of repositories; in case the JDBC implementation is changed to a JPA implementation, you have to change your `TransferServiceImpl` class as well.

According to the SOLID (Single Responsibility Principle, Open Closed Principle, Liskov's Substitution Principle, Interface Segregation Principle, Dependency Inversion Principle) principles, a class should have a single responsibility in the application, but in the preceding example, the `TransferServiceImpl` class is also responsible for constructing the objects of `JdbcAccountRepository` and `JdbcTransferRepository` classes. We can't use direction instantiation of objects in the class.

In our first attempt to avoid the direct instantiation logic in the `TransferServiceImpl`
class, we can use a `Factory` class that creates instances of `TransferServiceImpl`.
According to this idea, `TransferServiceImpl` minimizes the dependency from
`AccountRepository` and `TransferRepository`--earlier we had a tightly coupled
implementation of the repositories, but now it refers only to the interface, as shown in the
following diagram:

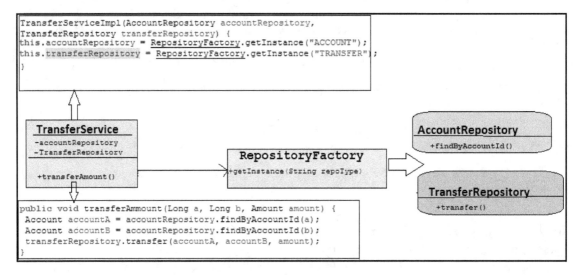

TransferService has dependencies with AccountRepository and TransferRepository for transferAmount() method with Factory of repositories classes.

But the `TransferServiceImpl` class is, again, tightly coupled with the implementation of
the `RepositoryFactory` class. Moreover, this process is not suitable for cases where we
have more number of dependencies, which increases either the `Factory` classes or the
complexity of the `Factory` class. The repository classes can also have other dependencies.

The following code uses the `Factory` class to get the `AccountRepository` and
`TransferRepository` classes:

Following is the `TransferServiceImpl.java` file:

```
package com.packt.patterninspring.chapter4.bankapp.service;
public class TransferServiceImpl implements TransferService {
   AccountRepository accountRepository;
   TransferRepository transferRepository;
   public TransferServiceImpl(AccountRepository accountRepository,
   TransferRepository transferRepository) {
      this.accountRepository = RepositoryFactory.getInstance();
      this.transferRepository = RepositoryFactory.getInstance();
```

```
    }
    @Override
    public void transferAmount(Long a, Long b, Amount amount) {
        Account accountA = accountRepository.findByAccountId(a);
        Account accountB = accountRepository.findByAccountId(b);
        transferRepository.transfer(accountA, accountB, amount);
    }
}
```

In the preceding code example, we have minimized tight coupling, and removed direction object instantiation from the TransferServiceImpl class, but this is not the optimal solution.

With dependency injection pattern

The Factory idea avoids direct instantiation of an object of a class, and we also have to create another module that is responsible for wiring the dependencies between classes. This module is known as a **dependency injector**, and is based on the **Inversion of Control (IoC)** pattern. According to the IoC Framework, the Container it is responsible for object instantiation, and to resolve the dependencies among classes in the application. This module has its own life cycle of construction and destruction for the object defined under its scope.

In the following diagram, we have used the dependency injection pattern to resolve the dependencies of the TransferServiceImpl class:

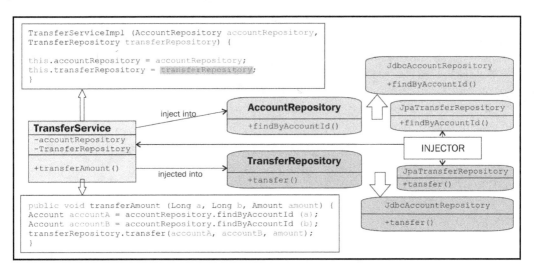

Using dependency injection design pattern to resolve dependencies for TransferService.

In the following example, we have used an interface to resolve the dependencies:

Following is the `TransferServiceImpl.java` file:

```
package com.packt.patterninspring.chapter4.bankapp.service;
public class TransferServiceImpl implements TransferService {
  AccountRepository accountRepository;
  TransferRepository transferRepository;
  public TransferServiceImpl(AccountRepository accountRepository,
  TransferRepository transferRepository) {
    this.accountRepository = accountRepository;
    this.transferRepository = transferRepository;
  }
  @Override
  public void transferAmmount(Long a, Long b, Amount amount) {
    Account accountA = accountRepository.findByAccountId(a);
    Account accountB = accountRepository.findByAccountId(b);
    transferRepository.transfer(accountA, accountB, amount);
  }
}
```

In the `TransferServiceImpl` class, we passed references of the `AccountRepository` and `TransferRepository` interfaces to the constructor. Now the `TransferServiceImpl` class is loosely coupled with the implementation repository class (use any flavor, either JDBC or JPA implementation of repository interfaces), and the framework is responsible for wiring the dependencies with the involved dependent class. Loose coupling offers us greater reusability, maintainability, and testability.

The Spring Framework implements the dependency injection pattern to resolve dependencies among the classes in a Spring application. Spring DI is based on the IoC concept, that is, the Spring Framework has a container where it creates, manages, and destructs the objects; it is known as a Spring IoC container. The objects lying within the Spring container are known as **Spring beans**. There are many ways to wire beans in a Spring application. Let's take a look at the three most common approaches for configuring the Spring container.

In the following section, we'll look at the types of the dependency injection pattern; you can configure the dependencies by using either one of them.

Types of dependency injection patterns

The following are the types of dependency injections that could be injected into your application:

- Constructor-based dependency injection
- Setter-based dependency injection

Constructor-based dependency injection pattern

Dependency injection is a design pattern to resolve the dependencies of dependent classes, and dependencies are nothing but object attributes. The injector has to be constructed for the dependent objects by using one of the ways constructor injection or setter injection. A constructor injection is one of the ways of fulfilling these object attributes at the time of creation to instantiate the object. An object has a public constructor that takes dependent classes as constructor arguments to inject the dependencies. You can declare more than one constructor into the dependent class. Earlier, only the PicoContainer Framework is used a constructor-based dependency injection to resolve dependencies. Currently, the Spring Framework also supports constructor injections to resolve dependencies.

Advantages of the constructor injection pattern

The following are the advantages if you use a constructor injection in your Spring application:

- Constructor-based dependency injection is more suitable for mandatory dependencies, and it makes a strong dependency contract
- Constructor-based dependency injection provides a more compact code structure than others
- It supports testing by using the dependencies passed as constructor arguments to the dependent class
- It favors the use of immutable objects, and does not break the information hiding principle

Disadvantages of constructor injection pattern

The following is the only drawback of this constructor-based injection pattern:

- It may cause circular dependency. (Circular dependency means that the dependent and the dependency class are also dependents on each other, for example, class A depends on Class B and Class B depends on Class A)

Example of constructor-based dependency injection pattern

Let's see the following example for constructor-based dependency injection. In the following code, we have a `TransferServiceImpl` class, and its constructor takes two arguments:

```
public class TransferServiceImpl implements TransferService {
  AccountRepository accountRepository;
  TransferRepository transferRepository;
  public TransferServiceImpl(AccountRepository accountRepository,
  TransferRepository transferRepository) {
    this.accountRepository = accountRepository;
    this.transferRepository = transferRepository;
  }
  // ...
}
```

The repositories will also be managed by the Spring container, and, as such, will have the `datasource` object for database configuration injected into them by the container, as follows:

Following is the `JdbcAccountRepository.java` file:

```
public class JdbcAccountRepository implements AccountRepository{
  JdbcTemplate jdbcTemplate;
  public JdbcAccountRepository(DataSource dataSource) {
    this.jdbcTemplate = new JdbcTemplate(dataSource);
  }
  // ...
}
```

Following is the `JdbcTransferRepository.java` file:

```
public class JdbcTransferRepository implements TransferRepository{
  JdbcTemplate jdbcTemplate;
  public JdbcTransferRepository(DataSource dataSource) {
    this.jdbcTemplate = new JdbcTemplate(dataSource);
  }
   // ...
}
```

You can see in the preceding code the JDBC implementation of the repositories as `AccountRepository` and `TransferRepository`. These classes also have one argument constructor to inject the dependency with the `DataSource` class.

Let's see another way of implementing a dependency injection in the enterprise application, which is setter injection.

Setter-based dependency injection

The injector of the container has another way to wire the dependency of the dependent object. In setter injection, one of the ways to fulfil these dependencies is by providing a setter method in the dependent class. Object has a public setter methods that takes dependent classes as method arguments to inject dependencies. For setter-based dependency injection, the constructor of the dependent class is not required. There are no changes required if you change the dependencies of the dependent class. Spring Framework and PicoContainer Framework support setter injection to resolve the dependencies.

Advantages of setter injection

The following are the advantages if you use the setter injection pattern in your Spring application:

- Setter injection is more readable than the constructor injection
- Setter injection solves the circular dependency problem in the application
- Setter injection allows costly resources or services to be created as late as possible, and only when required
- Setter injection does not require the constructor to be changed, but dependencies are passed through public properties that are exposed

Disadvantage of the setter injection

The following are the drawbacks of the setter injection pattern:

- Security is lesser in the setter injection pattern, because it can be overridden
- A setter-based dependency injection does not provide a code structure as compact as the constructor injection
- Be careful whenever you use setter injection, because it is not a required dependency

Example of a setter-based dependency injection

Let's see the following example for setter-based dependency injection. The following `TransferServiceImpl` class, has setter methods with one argument of the repository type:

Following is the `TransferServiceImpl.java` file:

```
public class TransferServiceImpl implements TransferService {
    AccountRepository accountRepository;
    TransferRepository transferRepository;
    public void setAccountRepository(AccountRepository
    accountRepository) {
        this.accountRepository = accountRepository;
    }
    public void setTransferRepository(TransferRepository
    transferRepository) {
        this.transferRepository = transferRepository;
    }
    // ...
}
```

Similarly, let's define a setter for the repositories' implementations as follows:

Following is the `JdbcAccountRepository.java` file:

```
public class JdbcAccountRepository implements AccountRepository{
    JdbcTemplate jdbcTemplate;
    public setDataSource(DataSource dataSource) {
        this.jdbcTemplate = new JdbcTemplate(dataSource);
    }
    // ...
}
```

Following is the `JdbcTransferRepository.java` file:

```
public class JdbcTransferRepository implements TransferRepository{
   JdbcTemplate jdbcTemplate;
   public setDataSource(DataSource dataSource) {
     this.jdbcTemplate = new JdbcTemplate(dataSource);
 }
  // ...
}
```

You can see in the preceding code the JDBC implementation of the repositories as `AccountRepository` and `TransferRepository`. These classes have a setter method with one argument to inject the dependency with the `DataSource` class.

Constructor versus setter injection and best practices

The Spring Framework provides support for both types of dependency injection patterns. Both, the constructor and setter injection pattern, assemble the elements in the system. The choice between the setter and constructor injections depends on your application requirement, and the problem at hand. Let's see the following table, which lists some differences between the constructor and setter injections, and some best practices to select which one is suitable in your application.

Constructors injection	Setter injection
A class with constructor takes arguments; it is very compact sometimes, and clear to understand what it creates.	Here, the object is constructed, but it is not clear whether its attributes are initialized or not.
This is a better choice when the dependency is mandatory.	This is suitable when the dependency is not mandatory.
It allows you to hide the object attributes that are immutable, because it does not have setters for these object attributes. To ensure the immutable nature of the object, use the constructor injection pattern instead of the setter injection.	It doesn't ensure the immutable nature of the object.
It creates circular dependency in your application.	It solves the problem of circular dependency in your application. In this case, the setter injection is a better choice than constructor.

It is not suitable for scalar value dependencies in the application.	If you have simple parameters such as strings and integers as dependencies, the setter injection is better to use, because each setter name indicates what the value is supposed to do.

In the next section, you'll learn how to configure the injector to find the beans and wire them together, and how the injector manages the beans. Here, I will use the Spring configuration for the dependency injection pattern.

Configuring the dependency injection pattern with Spring

In this section, I will explain the process required to configure dependencies in an application. The mainstream injectors are Google Guice, Spring, and Weld. In this chapter, I am using the Spring Framework, so, we will see the Spring configuration here. The following diagram is a high-level view of how Spring works:

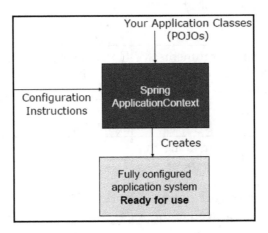

How Spring works using dependency injection pattern

In the preceding diagram, the **Configuration Instruction** is the meta configuration of your application. Here, we define the dependencies in **Your Application Classes (POJOs)**, and initialize the Spring container to resolve the dependency by combining the POJOs and **Configuration Instructions**, and finally, you have a fully configured and executable system or application.

As you have seen in the preceding diagram, the Spring container creates the beans in your application, and assembles them for relationships between those objects via the DI pattern. The Spring container creates the beans based on the configuration that we give to the framework, so, it's your responsibility to tell Spring which beans to create, and how to wire them together.

Spring is very flexible in configuring the dependency of Spring beans. The following are three ways to configure the metadata of your application:

1. **Dependency injection pattern with Java-based configuration**—it is an explicit configuration in Java.
2. **Dependency injection pattern with Annotation-based configuration**—it is an implicit bean discovery, and automatic wiring.
3. **Dependency injection pattern with XML-based configuration**—it is an explicit configuration in XML.

Spring provides three choices to wire beans in Spring. You must select one of the choices, but no single choice is the best match for any application. It depends on your application, and you can also mix and match these choices into a single application. Let's now discuss the dependency injection pattern with Java-based configuration in detail.

Dependency injection pattern with Java-based configuration

As of Spring 3.0, it provides a Java-based Spring configuration to wire the Spring beans. Take a look at the following Java configuration class (`AppConfig.java`) to define the Spring bean and their dependencies. The Java-based configuration for dependency injection is a better choice, because it is more powerful and type-safe.

Creating a Java configuration class - AppConfig.java

Let's create an `AppConfig.java` configuration class for our example:

```
package com.packt.patterninspring.chapter4.bankapp.config;
import org.springframework.context.annotation.Configuration;
@Configuration
public class AppConfig {
    //..
}
```

The preceding `AppConfig` class is annotated with the `@Configuration` annotation, which indicates that it is a configuration class of the application that contains the details on bean definitions. This file will be loaded by the Spring application context to create beans for your application.

Let's now see how you can declare the `TransferService`, `AccountRepository` and `TransferRepository` beans in `AppConfig`.

Declaring Spring beans into configuration class

To declare a bean in a Java-based configuration, you have to write a method for the desired type object creation in the configuration class, and annotate that method with `@Bean`. Let's see the following changes made in the `AppConfig` class to declare the beans:

```
package com.packt.patterninspring.chapter4.bankapp.config;
import org.springframework.context.annotation.Bean;
import org.springframework.context.annotation.Configuration;
@Configuration
public class AppConfig {
  @Bean
  public TransferService transferService(){
    return new TransferServiceImpl();
  }
  @Bean
  public AccountRepository accountRepository() {
    return new JdbcAccountRepository();
  }
  @Bean
  public TransferRepository transferRepository() {
    return new JdbcTransferRepository();
  }
}
```

In the preceding configuration file, I declared three methods to create instances for `TransferService`, `AccountRepository`, and `TransferRepository`. These methods are annotated with the `@Bean` annotation to indicate that they are responsible for instantiating, configuring, and initializing a new object to be managed by the Spring IoC container. Each bean in the container has a unique bean ID; by default, a bean has an ID same as the `@Bean` annotated method name. In the preceding case, the beans will be named as `transferService`, `accountRepository`, and `transferRepository`. You can also override that default behavior by using the name attribute of the `@Bean` annotation as follows:

```
@Bean(name="service")
public TransferService transferService(){
  return new TransferServiceImpl();
}
```

Now `"service"` is the bean name of that bean `TransferService`.

Let's see how you can inject dependencies for the `TransferService`, `AccountRepository`, and `TransferRepository` beans in `AppConfig`.

Injecting Spring beans

In the preceding code, I declared the beans `TransferService`, `AccountRepository`, and `TransferRepository`; these beans had no dependencies. But, actually, the `TransferService` bean depends on `AccountRepository` and `TransferRepository`. Let's see the following changes made in the `AppConfig` class to declare the beans:

```
package com.packt.patterninspring.chapter4.bankapp.config;
import org.springframework.context.annotation.Bean;
import org.springframework.context.annotation.Configuration;
@Configuration
public class AppConfig {
  @Bean
  public TransferService transferService(){
    return new TransferServiceImpl(accountRepository(),
    transferRepository());
  }
  @Bean
  public AccountRepository accountRepository() {
    return new JdbcAccountRepository();
  }
  @Bean
  public TransferRepository transferRepository() {
    return new JdbcTransferRepository();
```

```
      }
   }
```

In the preceding example, the simplest way to wire up beans in a Java-based configuration is to refer to the referenced bean's method. The `transferService()` method constructs the instance of the `TransferServiceImpl` class by calling the arguments constructor that takes `AccountRepository` and `TransferRepository`. Here, it seems that the constructor of the `TransferServiceImpl` class is calling the `accountRepository()` and `transferRepository()` methods to create instances of `AccountRepository` and `TransferRepository` respectively, but it is not an actual call to create instances. The Spring container creates instances of `AccountRepository` and `TransferRepository`, because the `accountRepository()` and `transferRepository()` methods are annotated with the `@Bean` annotation. Any call to the bean method by another bean method will be intercepted by Spring to ensure the default singleton scope of the Spring beans by that method is returned rather than allowing it to be invoked again.

Best approach to configure the dependency injection pattern with Java

In the previous configuration example, I declared the `transferService()` bean method to construct an instance of the `TransferServiceImpl` class by using its arguments constructor. The bean methods, `accountRepository()` and `transferRepository()`, are passed as arguments of the constructor. But in an enterprise application, a lot of configuration files depend on the layers of the application architecture. Suppose the service layer and the infrastructure layer have their own configuration files. That means that the `accountRepository()` and `transferRepository()` methods may be in different configuration files, and the `transferService()` bean method may be in another configuration file. Passing bean methods into the constructor is not a good practice for configuration of the dependency injection pattern with Java. Let's see a different and the best approach to configuring the dependency injection:

```
package com.packt.patterninspring.chapter4.bankapp.config;
import org.springframework.context.annotation.Bean;
import org.springframework.context.annotation.Configuration;
@Configuration
public class AppConfig {
  @Bean
  public TransferService transferService(AccountRepository
  accountRepository, TransferRepository transferRepository){
    return new TransferServiceImpl(accountRepository,
    transferRepository);
  }
```

```
@Bean
public AccountRepository accountRepository() {
  return new JdbcAccountRepository();
}
@Bean
public TransferRepository transferRepository() {
  return new JdbcTransferRepository();
}
}
```

In the preceding code, the transferService() method asks for AccountRepository and TransferRepository as parameters. When Spring calls transferService() to create the TransferService bean, it autowires AccountRepository and TransferRepository into the configuration method. With this approach, the transferService() method can still inject AccountRepository and TransferRepository into the constructor of TransferServiceImpl without explicitly referring to the accountRepository() and transferRepository() @Bean methods.

Let's now take a look at dependency injection pattern with XML-based configuration.

Dependency injection pattern with XML-based configuration

Spring provides dependency injection with XML-based configuration from the very beginning. It is the primary way of configuring a Spring application. According to me, every developer should have an understanding of how to use XML with a Spring application. In this section, I am going to explain the same example as discussed in the previous section of Java-based configuration with reference to XML-based configuration.

Creating an XML configuration file

In the section on Java-based configuration, we had created an `AppConfig` class annotated with the `@Configuration` annotation. Similarly, for XML-based configuration, we will now create an `applicationContext.xml` file rooted with a `<beans>` element. The following simplest possible example shows the basic structure of XML-based configuration metadata:

Following is the `applicationContext.xml` file:

```
<?xml version="1.0" encoding="UTF-8"?>
<beans xmlns="http://www.springframework.org/schema/beans"
 xmlns:xsi="http://www.w3.org/2001/XMLSchema-instance"
 xsi:schemaLocation="http://www.springframework.org/schema/beans
 http://www.springframework.org/schema/beans/spring-beans.xsd">
 <!-- Configuration for bean definitions go here -->
</beans>
```

The preceding XML file is a configuration file of the application which contains the details on bean definitions. This file is also loaded by the XML-flavored implementation of `ApplicationContext` to create beans for your application. Let's see how you can declare the `TransferService`, `AccountRepository` and `TransferRepository` beans in the preceding XML file.

Declaring Spring beans in an XML file

As with Java, we have to declare a class as a Spring bean into Spring's XML-based configuration by using an element of the Spring-beans schema as a `<bean>` element. The `<bean>` element is the XML analogue to JavaConfig's `@Bean` annotation. We add the following configuration to the XML-based configuration file:

```
<bean id="transferService"
 class="com.packt.patterninspring.chapter4.
 bankapp.service.TransferServiceImpl"/>
<bean id="accountRepository"
 class="com.packt.patterninspring.chapter4.
 bankapp.repository.jdbc.JdbcAccountRepository"/>
<bean id="transferService"
 class="com.packt.patterninspring.chapter4.
 bankapp.repository.jdbc.JdbcTransferRepository"/>
```

In the preceding code, I have created a very simple bean definition. In this configuration, the `<bean>` element has an `id` attribute to identify the individual bean definition. The `class` attribute is expressed as the fully qualified class name to create this bean. The value of the `id` attribute refers to collaborating objects. So let's see how to configure the collaborating beans to resolve the dependencies in the application.

Injecting Spring beans

Spring provides these two ways to define the DI pattern to inject the dependency with the dependent bean in an application:

- Using constructor injection
- Using setter injection

Using constructor injection

For the DI pattern with the construction injection, Spring provides you two basic options as the `<constructor-arg>` element and c-namespace introduced in Spring 3.0. c-namespace has less verbosity in the application, which is the only difference between them--you can choose any one. Let's inject the collaborating beans with the construction injection as follows:

```
<bean id="transferService"
 class="com.packt.patterninspring.chapter4.
 bankapp.service.TransferServiceImpl">
 <constructor-arg ref="accountRepository"/>
 <constructor-arg ref="transferRepository"/>
</bean>
<bean id="accountRepository"
 class="com.packt.patterninspring.chapter4.
 bankapp.repository.jdbc.JdbcAccountRepository"/>
<bean id="transferRepository"
 class="com.packt.patterninspring.chapter4.
 bankapp.repository.jdbc.JdbcTransferRepository"/>
```

In the preceding configuration, the `<bean>` element of `TransferService` has two `<constructor-arg>`. This tells it to pass a reference to the beans whose IDs are `accountRepository` and `transferRepository` to the constructor of `TransferServiceImpl`.

As of Spring 3.0, the c-namespace, similarly, has a more succinct way of expressing constructor args in XML. For using this namespace, we have to add its schema in the XML file, as follows:

```xml
<?xml version="1.0" encoding="UTF-8"?>
<beans xmlns="http://www.springframework.org/schema/beans"
 xmlns:xsi="http://www.w3.org/2001/XMLSchema-instance"
 xmlns:c="http://www.springframework.org/schema/c"
 xsi:schemaLocation="http://www.springframework.org/schema/beans
 http://www.springframework.org/schema/beans/spring-beans.xsd">
<bean id="transferService"
 class="com.packt.patterninspring.chapter4.
 bankapp.service.TransferServiceImpl"
 c:accountRepository-ref="accountRepository" c:transferRepository-
 ref="transferRepository"/>
<bean id="accountRepository"
 class="com.packt.patterninspring.chapter4.
 bankapp.repository.jdbc.JdbcAccountRepository"/>
<bean id="transferRepository"
 class="com.packt.patterninspring.chapter4.
 bankapp.repository.jdbc.JdbcTransferRepository"/>
 <!-- more bean definitions go here -->
</beans>
```

Let's see how to set up these dependencies with the setter injection.

Using setter injection

Using the injection, Spring also provides you with two basic options as the <property> element and p-namespace introduced in Spring 3.0. The p-namespace also reduced verbosity of code in the application, which is the only difference between them, you can choose any one. Let's inject the collaborating beans with the setter injection as follows:

```xml
<bean id="transferService"
 class="com.packt.patterninspring.chapter4.
 bankapp.service.TransferServiceImpl">
 <property name="accountRepository"  ref="accountRepository"/>
 <property name="transferRepository" ref="transferRepository"/>
</bean>
<bean id="accountRepository"
 class="com.packt.patterninspring.chapter4.
 bankapp.repository.jdbc.JdbcAccountRepository"/>
<bean id="transferRepository"
 class="com.packt.patterninspring.chapter4.
 bankapp.repository.jdbc.JdbcTransferRepository"/>
```

In the preceding configuration, the <bean> element of TransferService has two <property> elements which tell it to pass a reference to the beans whose IDs are accountRepository and transferRepository to the setter methods of TransferServiceImpl, as follows:

```
package com.packt.patterninspring.chapter4.bankapp.service;

import com.packt.patterninspring.chapter4.bankapp.model.Account;
import com.packt.patterninspring.chapter4.bankapp.model.Amount;
import com.packt.patterninspring.chapter4.bankapp.
 repository.AccountRepository;
import com.packt.patterninspring.chapter4.bankapp.
 repository.TransferRepository;

public class TransferServiceImpl implements TransferService {
  AccountRepository accountRepository;
  TransferRepository transferRepository;
  public void setAccountRepository(AccountRepository
  accountRepository) {
    this.accountRepository = accountRepository;
  }
  public void setTransferRepository(TransferRepository
  transferRepository) {
    this.transferRepository = transferRepository;
  }
  @Override
  public void transferAmmount(Long a, Long b, Amount amount) {
    Account accountA = accountRepository.findByAccountId(a);
    Account accountB = accountRepository.findByAccountId(b);
    transferRepository.transfer(accountA, accountB, amount);
  }
}
```

In the preceding file, if you use this Spring bean without setter methods, the properties accountRepository and transferRepository will be initialized as null without injecting the dependency.

As of Spring 3.0, the p-namespace, similarly, has a more succinct way of expressing property in XML. For using this namespace, we have to add its schema in the XML file as follows:

```xml
<?xml version="1.0" encoding="UTF-8"?>
<beans xmlns="http://www.springframework.org/schema/beans"
  xmlns:xsi="http://www.w3.org/2001/XMLSchema-instance"
  xmlns:p="http://www.springframework.org/schema/p"
  xsi:schemaLocation="http://www.springframework.org/schema/beans
  http://www.springframework.org/schema/beans/spring-beans.xsd">
<bean id="transferService"
 class="com.packt.patterninspring.chapter4.bankapp.
 service.TransferServiceImpl"
 p:accountRepository-ref="accountRepository" p:transferRepository-
 ref="transferRepository"/>
<bean id="accountRepository"
 class="com.packt.patterninspring.chapter4.
 bankapp.repository.jdbc.JdbcAccountRepository"/>
<bean id="transferRepository"
 class="com.packt.patterninspring.chapter4.
 bankapp.repository.jdbc.JdbcTransferRepository"/>
<!-- more bean definitions go here -->
</beans>
```

Let's now take a look at the dependency injection pattern with Annotation-based configuration.

Dependency injection pattern with Annotation-based configuration

As discussed in the previous two sections, we defined the DI pattern with Java-and XML-based configurations, and these two options define dependencies explicitly. It creates the Spring beans by using either the @Bean annotated method in the AppConfig Java file, or the <bean> element tag in the XML configuration file. By these methods, you can also create the bean for those classes which lie outside the application, that is, classes that exist in third-party libraries. Now let's discuss another way to create Spring beans, and define the dependencies between them by using implicit configuration through the Stereotype annotations.

What are Stereotype annotations?

The Spring Framework provides you with some special annotations. These annotations are used to create Spring beans automatically in the application context. The main stereotype annotation is @Component. By using this annotation, Spring provides more Stereotype meta annotations such as @Service, used to create Spring beans at the Service layer, @Repository, which is used to create Spring beans for the repositories at the DAO layer, and @Controller, which is used to create Spring beans at the controller layer. This is depicted in the following diagram:

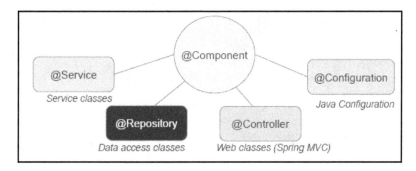

By using these annotations, Spring creates automatic wiring in these two ways:

- **Component scanning:** In this, Spring automatically searches the beans to be created in the Spring IoC container
- **Autowiring:** In this, Spring automatically searches the bean dependencies in the Spring IoC container

Implicitly, the DI pattern configuration reduces the verbosity of an application, and minimizes explicit configuration. Let's demonstrate component scanning and autowiring in the same example as discussed previously. Here, Spring will create the beans for TransferService, TransferRepository, and AccountRepository by discovering them, and automatically inject them to each other as per the defined dependencies.

Creating auto searchable beans using Stereotype annotations

Let's see the following `TransferService` interface. Its implementation is annotated with `@Component`. Please refer to the following code:

```
package com.packt.patterninspring.chapter4.bankapp.service;
public interface TransferService {
  void transferAmmount(Long a, Long b, Amount amount);
}
```

The preceding interface is not important for this approach of configuration--I have taken it just for loose coupling in the application. Let's see its implementation, which is as follows:

```
package com.packt.patterninspring.chapter1.bankapp.service;
import org.springframework.stereotype.Component;
@Component
public class TransferServiceImpl implements TransferService {
  @Override
  public void transferAmmount(Long a, Long b, Amount amount) {
    //business code here
  }
}
```

You can see in the preceding code that `TransferServiceImpl` is annotated with the `@Component` annotation. This annotation is used to identify this class as a component class, which means, it is eligible to scan and create a bean of this class. Now there is no need to configure this class explicitly as a bean either by using XML or Java configuration--Spring is now responsible for creating the bean of the `TransferServiceImpl` class, because it is annotated with `@Component`.

As mentioned earlier, Spring provides us meta annotations for the `@Component` annotation as `@Service`, `@Repository`, and `@Controller`. These annotations are based on a specific responsibility at different layers of the application. Here, `TransferService` is the service layer class; *as a best practice of Spring configuration*, we have to annotate this class with the specific annotation, `@Service`, rather than with the generic annotation, `@Component`, to create the bean of this class. The following is the code for the same class annotated with the `@Service` annotation:

```
package com.packt.patterninspring.chapter1.bankapp.service;
import org.springframework.stereotype.Service;
@Service
public class TransferServiceImpl implements TransferService {
  @Override
  public void transferAmmount(Long a, Long b, Amount amount) {
```

```
      //business code here
    }
  }
```

Let's see other classes in the application--these are the `implementation` classes of `AccountRepository`--and the `TransferRepository` interfaces are the repositories working at the DAO layer of the application. *As a best practice,* these classes should be annotated with the `@Repository` annotation rather than using the `@Component` annotation as shown next.

`JdbcAccountRepository.java` implements the `AccountRepository` interface:

```java
package com.packt.patterninspring.chapter4.bankapp.repository.jdbc;
import org.springframework.stereotype.Repository;
import com.packt.patterninspring.chapter4.bankapp.model.Account;
import com.packt.patterninspring.chapter4.bankapp.model.Amount;
import com.packt.patterninspring.chapter4.bankapp.repository.
  AccountRepository;
@Repository
public class JdbcAccountRepository implements AccountRepository {
  @Override
  public Account findByAccountId(Long accountId) {
    return new Account(accountId, "Arnav Rajput", new
    Amount(3000.0));
  }
}
```

And `JdbcTransferRepository.java` implements the `TransferRepository` interface:

```java
package com.packt.patterninspring.chapter4.bankapp.repository.jdbc;
import org.springframework.stereotype.Repository;
import com.packt.patterninspring.chapter4.bankapp.model.Account;
import com.packt.patterninspring.chapter4.bankapp.model.Amount;
import com.packt.patterninspring.chapter4.bankapp.
  repository.TransferRepository;
@Repository
public class JdbcTransferRepository implements TransferRepository {
  @Override
  public void transfer(Account accountA, Account accountB, Amount
  amount) {
    System.out.println("Transfering amount from account A to B via
    JDBC implementation");
  }
}
```

In Spring, you have to enable component scanning in your application, because it is not enabled by default. You have to create a configuration Java file, and annotate it with `@Configuration` and `@ComponentScan`. This class is used to search out classes annotated with `@Component`, and to create beans from them.

Let's see how Spring scans the classes which are annotated with any stereotype annotations.

Searching beans using component scanning

The following minimum configuration is required to search beans using component scanning in a Spring application:

```
package com.packt.patterninspring.chapter4.bankapp.config;

import org.springframework.context.annotation.ComponentScan;
import org.springframework.context.annotation.Configuration;

@Configuration
@ComponentScan
public class AppConfig {
}
```

The `AppConfig` class defines a Spring wiring configuration class same as the Java-based Spring configuration in the previous section. There is one thing to be observed here--the `AppConfig` file has one more `@ComponentScan`, as earlier it had only the `@Configuration` annotation. The configuration file `AppConfig` is annotated with `@ComponentScan` to enable component scanning in Spring. The `@ComponentScan` annotation scans those classes that are annotated with `@Component` by default in the same package as the configuration class. Since the `AppConfig` class is in the `com.packt.patterninspring.chapter4.bankapp.config` package, Spring will scan only this package and its sub packages. But our component application classes are in the `com.packt.patterninspring.chapter1.bankapp.service` and `com.packt.patterninspring.chapter4.bankapp.repository.jdbc` packages, and these are not subpackages of `com.packt.patterninspring.chapter4.bankapp.config`. In this case, Spring allows to override the default package scanning of the `@ComponentScan` annotation by setting a base package for component scanning. Let's specify a different base package. You only need to specify the package in the `value` attribute of `@ComponentScan`, as shown here:

```
@Configuration
@ComponentScan("com.packt.patterninspring.chapter4.bankapp")
public class AppConfig {
```

```
    }
```

Or you can define the base packages with the `basePackages` attribute, as follows:

```
@Configuration
@ComponentScan(basePackages="com.packt.patterninspring.
chapter4.bankapp")
public class AppConfig {
    }
```

In the `@ComponentScan` annotation, the `basePackages` attribute can accept an array of Strings, which means that we can define multiple base packages to scan component classes in the application. In the previous configuration file, Spring will scan all classes of `com.packt.patterninspring.chapter4.bankapp package`, and all the subpackages underneath this package. *As a best practice*, always define the specific base packages where the components classes exist. For example, in the following code, I define the base packages for the service and repository components:

```
package com.packt.patterninspring.chapter4.bankapp.config;
import org.springframework.context.annotation.ComponentScan;
import org.springframework.context.annotation.Configuration;
@Configuration
@ComponentScan(basePackages=
{"com.packt.patterninspring.chapter4.
bankapp.repository.jdbc","com.packt.patterninspring.
chapter4.bankapp.service"})
public class AppConfig {
    }
```

Now Spring scans only `com.packt.patterninspring.chapter4.bankapp.repository.jdbc` and `com.packt.patterninspring.chapter4.bankapp.service packages`, and its subpackages if they exist. instead of doing a wide range scanning like in the earlier examples.

Rather than specify the packages as simple String values of the `basePackages` attribute of `@ComponentScan`, Spring allows you to specify them via classes or interfaces as follows:

```
package com.packt.patterninspring.chapter4.bankapp.config;
import org.springframework.context.annotation.ComponentScan;
import org.springframework.context.annotation.Configuration;
import com.packt.patterninspring.chapter4.bankapp.
  repository.AccountRepository;
import com.packt.patterninspring.chapter4.
  bankapp.service.TransferService;
@Configuration
```

```
@ComponentScan(basePackageClasses=
{TransferService.class,AccountRepository.class})
public class AppConfig {

}
```

As you can see in the preceding code, the `basePackages` attribute has been replaced with `basePackageClasses`. Now Spring will identify the component classes in those packages where `basePackageClasses` will be used as the base package for component scanning.

It should find the `TransferServiceImpl`, `JdbcAccountRepository`, and `JdbcTransferRepository` classes, and automatically create the beans for these classes in the Spring container. Explicitly, there is no need to define the bean methods for these classes to create Spring beans. Let's turn on component scanning via XML configuration, then you can use the `<context:component-scan>` element from Spring's context namespace. Here is a minimal XML configuration to enable component scanning:

```
<?xml version="1.0" encoding="UTF-8"?>
<beans xmlns="http://www.springframework.org/schema/beans"
xmlns:xsi="http://www.w3.org/2001/XMLSchema-instance"
xmlns:context="http://www.springframework.org/schema/context"
xsi:schemaLocation="http://www.springframework.org/schema/beans
http://www.springframework.org/schema/beans/spring-beans.xsd
http://www.springframework.org/schema/context
http://www.springframework.org/schema/context/spring-context.xsd">
<context:component-scan base-
package="com.packt.patterninspring.chapter4.bankapp" />
</beans>
```

In the preceding XML file, the `<context:component-scan>` element is same the `@ComponentScan` annotation in the Java-based configuration for component scanning.

Annotating beans for autowiring

Spring provides support for automatic bean wiring. This means that Spring automatically resolves the dependencies that are required by the dependent bean by finding other collaborating beans in the application context. Bean Autowiring is another way of DI pattern configuration. It reduces verbosity in the application, but the configuration is spread throughout the application. Spring's `@Autowired` annotation is used for auto bean wiring. This `@Autowired` annotation indicates that autowiring should be performed for this bean.

In our example, we have `TransferService` which has dependencies of `AccountRepository` and `TransferRepository`. Its constructor is annotated with `@Autowired` indicating that when Spring creates the `TransferService` bean, it should instantiate that bean by using its annotated constructor, and pass in two other beans, `AccountRepository` and `TransferRepository`, which are dependencies of the `TransferService` bean. Let's see the following code:

```
package com.packt.patterninspring.chapter4.bankapp.service;
import org.springframework.beans.factory.annotation.Autowired;
import org.springframework.stereotype.Service;
import com.packt.patterninspring.chapter4.bankapp.model.Account;
import com.packt.patterninspring.chapter4.bankapp.model.Amount;
import com.packt.patterninspring.chapter4.bankapp.
  repository.AccountRepository;
importcom.packt.patterninspring.chapter4.
  bankapp.repository.TransferRepository;
@Service
public class TransferServiceImpl implements TransferService {
  AccountRepository accountRepository;
  TransferRepository transferRepository;
@Autowired
public TransferServiceImpl(AccountRepository accountRepository,
TransferRepository transferRepository) {
  super();
  this.accountRepository = accountRepository;
  this.transferRepository = transferRepository;
}
@Override
public void transferAmmount(Long a, Long b, Amount amount) {
  Account accountA = accountRepository.findByAccountId(a);
  Account accountB = accountRepository.findByAccountId(b);
  transferRepository.transfer(accountA, accountB, amount);
}
}
```

 Note--As of Spring 4.3, the `@Autowired` annotation is no more required if you define only one construct with arguments in that class. If class has multiple argument constructors, then you have to use the `@Autowired` annotation on any one of them.

The @Autowired annotation is not limited to the construction; it can be used with the setter method, and can also be used directly in the field, that is, an autowired class property directly. Let's see the following line of code for setter and field injection.

Using @Autowired with setter method

Here you can annotate the setter method's setAccountRepository and setTransferRepository with the @Autowired annotation. This annotation can be used with any method. There is no specific reason to use it with the setter method only. Please refer to the following code:

```
public class TransferServiceImpl implements TransferService {
  //...
  @Autowired
  public void setAccountRepository(AccountRepository
  accountRepository) {
    this.accountRepository = accountRepository;
  }
  @Autowired
  public void setTransferRepository(TransferRepository
  transferRepository) {
    this.transferRepository = transferRepository;
  }
  //...
}
```

Using @Autowired with the fields

Here you can annotate those class properties which are required for this class to achieve a business goal. Let's see the following code:

```
public class TransferServiceImpl implements TransferService {
  @Autowired
  AccountRepository accountRepository;
  @Autowired
  TransferRepository transferRepository;
  //...
}
```

In the preceding code, the `@Autowired` annotation resolves the dependency by `type` and then by `name` if the property name is the same as the bean name in the Spring container. By default, the `@Autowired` dependency is a required dependency--it raises an exception if the dependency is not resolved, it doesn't matter whether we have used it with a constructor or with the setter method. You can override the required behavior of the `@Autowired` annotation by using the `required` attribute of this annotation. You can set this attribute with the Boolean value `false` as follows:

```
@Autowired(required = false)
public void setAccountRepository(AccountRepository
accountRepository) {
   this.accountRepository = accountRepository;
}
```

In the preceding code, we have set the required attribute with the Boolean value `false`. In this case, Spring will attempt to perform autowiring, but if there are no matching beans, it will leave the bean unwired. But as a best practice of code, you should avoid setting its value as false until it is absolutely necessary.

The Autowiring DI pattern and disambiguation

The `@Autowiring` annotation reduces verbosity in the code, but it may create some problems when two of the same type of beans exist in the container. Let's see what happens in that situation, with the following example:

```
@Service
public class TransferServiceImpl implements TransferService {
@Autowired
public TransferServiceImpl(AccountRepository accountRepository) {
... }
}
```

The preceding snippet of code shows that the `TransferServiceImpl` class has a dependency with a bean of type `AccountRepository`, but the Spring container contains two beans of the same type, that is, the following:

```
@Repository
public class JdbcAccountRepository implements AccountRepository
{..}
@Repository
public class JpaAccountRepository implements AccountRepository {..}
```

As seen from the preceding code, there are two implementations of the AccountRepository interface--one is JdbcAccountRepository and another is JpaAccountRepository. In this case, the Spring container will throw the following exception at startup time of the application:

```
At startup: NoSuchBeanDefinitionException, no unique bean of type
[AccountRepository] is defined: expected single bean but found 2...
```

Resolving disambiguation in Autowiring DI pattern

Spring provides one more annotation, @Qualifier, to overcome the problem of disambiguation in autowiring DI. Let's see the following snippet of code with the @Qualifier annotation:

```
@Service
public class TransferServiceImpl implements TransferService {
@Autowired
public TransferServiceImpl( @Qualifier("jdbcAccountRepository")
AccountRepository accountRepository) { ... }
```

Now I have wired the dependency by name rather than by type by using the @Qualifier annotation. So, Spring will search the bean dependency with the name "jdbcAccountRepository" for the TransferServiceImpl class. I have given the names of the beans as follows:

```
@Repository("jdbcAccountRepository")
public class JdbcAccountRepository implements AccountRepository
{..}
@Repository("jpaAccountRepository")
public class JpaAccountRepository implements AccountRepository {..}
```

@Qualifier, also available with the method injection and field injection component names, should not show implementation details unless there are two implementations of the same interface.

Let's now discuss some best practices to choose the DI pattern configuration for your Spring application.

Resolving dependency with Abstract Factory pattern

If you want to add the if...else conditional configuration for a bean, you can do so, and also add some custom logic if you are using Java configuration. But in the case of an XML configuration, it is not possible to add the if...then...else conditions. Spring provides the solution for conditions in an XML configuration by using the Abstract Factory Pattern. Use a factory to create the bean(s) you want, and use any complex Java code that you need in the factory's internal logic.

Implementing the Abstract Factory Pattern in Spring (FactoryBean interface)

The Spring Framework provides the FactoryBean interface as an implementation of the Abstract Factory Pattern. A FactoryBean is a pattern to encapsulate interesting object construction logic in a class. The FactoryBean interface provides a way to customize the Spring IoC container's instantiation logic. You can implement this interface for objects that are themselves factories. Beans implementing FactoryBean are auto-detected.

The definition of this interface is as follows:

```
public interface FactoryBean<T> {
  T getObject() throws Exception;
  Class<T> getObjectType();
  boolean isSingleton();
}
```

As per the preceding definition of this interface, the dependency injection using the FactoryBean and it causes getObject() to be invoked transparently. The isSingleton() method returns true for singleton, else it returns false. The getObjectType() method returns the object type of the object returned by the getObject() method.

Implementation of FactoryBean interface in Spring

`FactoryBean` is widely used within Spring as the following:

- `EmbeddedDatabaseFactoryBean`
- `JndiObjectFactoryBean`
- `LocalContainerEntityManagerFactoryBean`
- `DateTimeFormatterFactoryBean`
- `ProxyFactoryBean`
- `TransactionProxyFactoryBean`
- `MethodInvokingFactoryBean`

Sample implementation of FactoryBean interface

Suppose you have a `TransferService` class whose definition is thus:

```
package com.packt.patterninspring.chapter4.bankapp.service;
import com.packt.patterninspring.chapter4.
 bankapp.repository.IAccountRepository;
public class TransferService {
  IAccountRepository accountRepository;
  public TransferService(IAccountRepository accountRepository){
    this.accountRepository = accountRepository;
  }
  public void transfer(String accountA, String accountB, Double
  amount){
    System.out.println("Amount has been tranferred");
  }
}
```

And you have a `FactoryBean` whose definition is thus:

```
package com.packt.patterninspring.chapter4.bankapp.repository;
import org.springframework.beans.factory.FactoryBean;
public class AccountRepositoryFactoryBean implements
FactoryBean<IAccountRepository> {
  @Override
  public IAccountRepository getObject() throws Exception {
    return new AccountRepository();
  }
  @Override
  public Class<?> getObjectType() {
    return IAccountRepository.class;
  }
  @Override
```

```
    public boolean isSingleton() {
      return false;
    }
  }
```

You could wire up an `AccountRepository` instance using a hypothetical `AccountRepositoryFactoryBean` like this:

```xml
<?xml version="1.0" encoding="UTF-8"?>
<beans xmlns="http://www.springframework.org/schema/beans"
xmlns:xsi="http://www.w3.org/2001/XMLSchema-instance"
xmlns:c="http://www.springframework.org/schema/c"
xsi:schemaLocation="http://www.springframework.org/schema/beans
http://www.springframework.org/schema/beans/spring-beans.xsd">
<bean id="transferService" class="com.packt.patterninspring.
 chapter4.bankapp.service.TransferService">
 <constructor-arg ref="accountRepository"/>
</bean>
<bean id="accountRepository"
 class="com.packt.patterninspring.chapter4.
  bankapp.repository.AccountRepositoryFactoryBean"/>
</beans>
```

In the preceding example, the `TransferService` class depends on the `AccountRepository` bean, but in the XML file, we have defined `AccountRepositoryFactoryBean` as an `accountRepository` bean. The `AccountRepositoryFactoryBean` class implements the `FactoryBean` interface of Spring. The result of the `getObject` method of `FactoryBean` will be passed, and not the actual `FactoryBean` itself. Spring injects that object returned by `FactoryBean`'s `getObjectType()` method, and the object type returned by `FactoryBean`'s `getObjectType()`; the scope of this bean is decided by the `FactoryBean`'s `isSingleton()` method.

The following is the same configuration for the `FactoryBean` interface in a Java Configuration:

```java
package com.packt.patterninspring.chapter4.bankapp.config;
import org.springframework.context.annotation.Bean;
import org.springframework.context.annotation.Configuration;
import com.packt.patterninspring.chapter4.bankapp.
 repository.AccountRepositoryFactoryBean;
import com.packt.patterninspring.chapter4.
 bankapp.service.TransferService;
@Configuration
public class AppConfig {
  public TransferService transferService() throws Exception{
```

```
      return new TransferService(accountRepository().getObject());
  }
@Bean
public AccountRepositoryFactoryBean accountRepository(){
  return new AccountRepositoryFactoryBean();
}
}
```

As other normal beans in the Spring container, the Spring `FactoryBean` also has all the other characteristics of any other Spring bean, including the life cycle hooks and services that all beans in the Spring container enjoy.

Best practices for configuring the DI pattern

The following are the best practices for configuring the DI pattern:

- Configuration files should be separated categorically. Application beans should be separate from infrastructure beans. Currently, it's a bit difficult to follow.

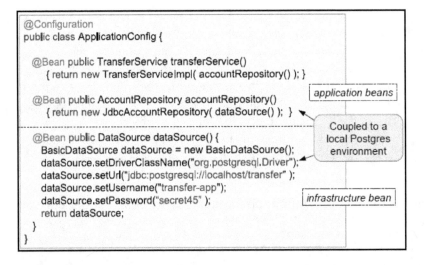

- Always specify the component name; never rely on generated names by the container.
- It is a best practice to give a name along with a description of what the pattern does, where to apply it, and the problems it addresses.

- The best practices for component scanning are as follows:
  - The components are scanned at startup, and it scans the JAR dependencies as well.
  - **Bad practice:** It scans all the packages of com and org. It increases the startup time of the application. Avoid such type of component scanning:

```
@ComponenttScan (( {{ "org", "com" }} ))
```

  - **Optimized:** It scans only the specific packages as defined by us.

```
@ComponentScan ( {
 "com.packt.patterninspring.chapter4.
 bankapp.repository",
 "com.packt.patterninspring.chapter4.bankapp.service"}
 )
```

- Best practices in choosing implicit configuration:
  - Choose annotation-based configurations for frequently changing beans
  - It allows for very rapid development
  - It is a single place to edit the configuration
- Best practices in choosing explicit via Java configuration:
  - It is centralized in one place
  - Strong type checking enforced by the compiler
  - Can be used for all classes
- Spring XML Best Practices: XML has been around for a long time, there are many shortcuts and useful techniques available in XML configuration as well, they are listed follow:
  - factory-method and factory-bean attributes
  - Bean Definition Inheritance
  - Inner Beans
  - p and c namespaces
  - Using collections as Spring beans

Summary

After reading this chapter, you should now have a good idea about DI design patterns, and the best practices for applying those patterns. Spring deals with the plumbing part, so, you can focus on solving the domain problem by using the dependency injection pattern. The DI pattern frees the object of the burden of resolving its dependencies. Your object is handed everything that it needs to work. The DI pattern simplifies your code, improves code reusability, and testability. It promotes programming to interfaces, and conceals the implementation details of dependencies. The DI pattern allows for centralized control over the object's life cycle. You can configure DI via two ways--explicit configuration and implicit configuration. Explicit configuration can be configured through XML-or Java-based configuration; it provides centralized configuration. But implicit configuration is based on annotations. Spring provides stereotype annotations for Annotation-based configuration. This configuration reduces the verbosity of code in the application, but it spreads out across the application files.

4

Spring Aspect Oriented Programming with Proxy and Decorator pattern

Before you start reading this chapter, I want to share something with you; as I was writing this chapter, my wife Anamika, was taking a selfie and uploading it to several social media sites such as Facebook and WhatsApp. She keeps a track of the *likes*, However, uploading more photos uses more mobile data, and mobile data costs money. I rarely use social media as I prefer to avoid paying more to the internet company. Every month, the internet company knows how much to bill us. Now consider what would happen if the internet usage, total call duration and bill calculation was meticulously planned and managed by us? It's possible that some obsessive internet users would manage it and I'm really clueless as to how.

Calculating billing for internet usage and calls is an important function, but it is still not predominant for most internet users. For those like my wife, taking selfies, uploading photos to social media, and watching videos on YouTube are the kinds of things that most internet users are actively involved in. Managing and calculating their internet bill is a passive action for internet users.

Similarly some modules of the enterprise applications are like the internet billing calculator for our internet usage. There are some modules in the application that have important functionalities that need to be placed at multiple points in the application. But it is unexpected to explicitly call these functionalities at every points. Functionalities such as logging, security, and transaction management are important for your application but your business objects are not actively participating in it because your business objects need to focus on the business domain problems they're designed for, and leave certain aspects to be handled by someone else.

In software development, there are specific tasks to be performed at certain points in an application. These tasks or functions are known as **cross-cutting concerns**. In an application, all cross-cutting concerns are separate from the business logic of this application. Spring provides a module **Aspect-Oriented Programming (AOP)** to separate these cross-cutting concerns from the business logic.

As in Chapter 3, *Wiring Beans using Dependency Injection Pattern*, you learned about the dependency injection to configure and resolve dependencies of collaborating objects in the application. Whereas DI promotes programming to interface and decoupling application objects from each other, Spring AOP promotes decoupling between the application's business logic and the cross-cutting concerns in the application.

In our bankapp example, transferring money from one account to another account is a business logic but logging this activity and securing the transaction are cross-cutting concerns in our bankapp application. That means logging, security, and transaction are common examples of the application of aspects.

In this chapter, you will explore Spring's support for aspects. It will cover the following points:

- Proxy pattern in Spring
- Adapter design pattern to handle load time weaving
- Decorator design pattern
- Aspect-oriented programming
- Problems resolved by AOP
- Core AOP concepts
- Defining point cuts
- Implementing Advices
- Creating aspects
- Understanding AOP proxies

Before we go further into our Spring AOP discussion, let's first understand the implemented patterns under the Spring AOP Framework, and see how these patterns are applied.

Proxy pattern in Spring

Proxy design pattern provides an object of class that has the functionality of another class. This pattern comes under the structural design pattern of GOF design patterns. According to GOF pattern, *Provide a surrogate or placeholder for another object to control access to it*. The intent of this design pattern is to provide a different class for another class with its functionality to the outer world.

Proxying classes using Decorator pattern in Spring

AAccording to GOF book, *Attach additional responsibilities to an object dynamically. Decorators provide a flexible alternative to subclassing for extending functionality.* This pattern allows you to add and remove behaviors to an individual object at the runtime dynamically or statically without changing the existing behavior of other associated objects from the same class.

In Spring AOP, CGLIB is used to create the proxy in the application. CGLIB proxying works by generating a subclass of the target class at runtime. Spring configures this generated subclass to delegate method calls to the original target--the subclass is used to implement the Decorator pattern, weaving in the advice.

Spring provides two ways to create the proxy in the application.

- CGLIB proxy
- JDK proxy or dynamic proxy

Let's see the following table:

JDK proxy	CGLIB proxy
Also called **dynamic proxies**	NOT built into JDK
API is built into the JDK	Included in Spring JARs
Requirements: Java interface(s)	Used when interface not available
All interfaces proxied	Cannot be applied to final classes or methods

Let's see the following figure:

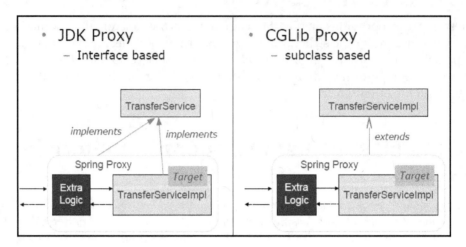

Note--CGLIB proxying has one issue to be considered, that is, final methods can't be advised, as they can't be overridden.

In the following section let's learn more about the cross-cutting concerns.

What are cross-cutting concerns?

In any application, there is some generic functionality that is needed in many places. But this functionality is not related to the application's business logic. Suppose you perform a role-based security check before every business method in your application. Here security is a cross-cutting concern. It is required for any application but it is not necessary from the business point of view, it is a simple generic functionality we have to implement in many places in the application. The following are examples of the cross-cutting concerns for the enterprise application.

- Logging and tracing
- Transaction management
- Security
- Caching

- Error handling
- Performance monitoring
- Custom business rules

Let's see how we will implement these cross-cutting concerns in our application by using aspects of Spring AOP.

What is Aspect-Oriented Programming?

As mentioned earlier, **Aspect-Oriented Programming** (**AOP**) enables modularization of cross-cutting concerns. It complements **Object-oriented programming** (**OOP**) which is another programing paradigm. OOP has class and object as key elements but AOP has aspect as key element. Aspects allow you to modularize some functionality across the application at multiple points. This type of functionality is known as **cross-cutting concerns**. For example, security is one of the cross-cutting concerns in the application, because we have to apply it at multiple methods where we want security. Similarly, transaction and logging are also cross-cutting concerns for the application and many more. Let's see in the following figure how these concerns are applied to the business modules:

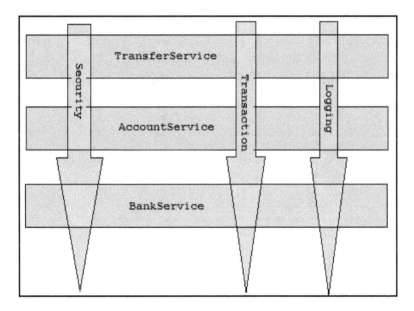

As you can see in the preceding figure, there are three main business modules as **TransferService**, **AccountService**, and **BankService**. All business modules require some common functionality such as **Security**, **Transaction** management and **Logging**.

Let's check out what problems we have to face in the application if we do not use the Spring AOP.

Problems resolved by AOP

As stated earlier, aspects enable modularization of cross-cutting concerns. So if you are not using aspects, then modularization of some cross-cutting functionality is not possible. It tends to mix the cross-cutting functionality with the business modules. If you use a common object-oriented principle to reuse the common functionalities such as security, logging and transaction management, *you need to use* inheritance or composition. But here using inheritance can violate the single responsibility of SOLID principles and also increase object hierarchy. Also, the composition can be complicated to handle across the application. That means, failing to modularize cross-cutting concerns leads to two main problems as follows:

- Code tangling
- Code scattering

Code tangling

It is a coupling of concerns in the application. Code tangling occurs when there is a mixing of cross-cutting concerns with the application's business logic. It promotes tight coupling between the cross-cutting and business modules. Let's see the following code to understand more about code tangling:

```
public class TransferServiceImpl implements TransferService {
   public void transfer(Account a, Account b, Double amount) {
      //Security concern start here
      if (!hasPermission(SecurityContext.getPrincipal())) {
        throw new AccessDeniedException();
      }
      //Security concern end here
      //Business logic start here
      Account aAct = accountRepository.findByAccountId(a);
      Account bAct = accountRepository.findByAccountId(b);
      accountRepository.transferAmount(aAct, bAct, amount);
      ...
   }
}
```

As you can see in the preceding code, security concern code (highlighted) is mixing with application's business logic code. This situation is an example of code tangling. Here we have only included security concern, but in the enterprise application you have to implement multiple cross-cutting concerns such as logging, transaction management and so on. In such cases, it will be even more complicated to manage the code and make any change to the code, which may cause critical bugs in the code as follows in the figure:

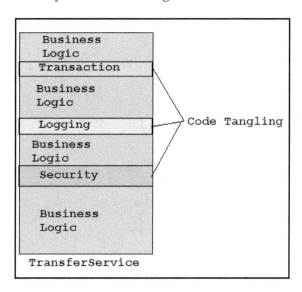

In the preceding figure, you can see there are three cross-cutting concerns which are distributed across the `TransferService` business class and cross-cutting concerns logic mixing with `AccountService`'s business logic. This coupling between the concerns and application's logic is called **code tangling**. Let's see another main problem if we are using aspects for cross-cutting concern.

Code scattering

This means that the same concern is spread across modules in the application. Code scattering promotes the duplicity of the concern's code across the application modules. Let's see the following code to understand more about code scattering:

```
public class TransferServiceImpl implements TransferService {
    public void transfer(Account a, Account b, Double amount) {
        //Security concern start here
        if (!hasPermission(SecurityContext.getPrincipal()) {
            throw new AccessDeniedException();
        }
```

```
        //Security concern end here
        //Business logic start here
        ...
    }
}

public class AccountServiceImpl implements AccountService {
    public void withdrawl(Account a, Double amount) {
        //Security concern start here
        if (!hasPermission(SecurityContext.getPrincipal()) {
            throw new AccessDeniedException();
        }
        //Security concern end here
        //Business logic start here
        ...
    }
}
```

As you can see in the preceding code, there are two modules for the application,
`TransferService` and `AccountService`. Both modules have the same cross-cutting
concern code for the security. The bold highlighted code in both business modules are the
same, it means there is code duplication here. The following figure illustrates code
scattering:

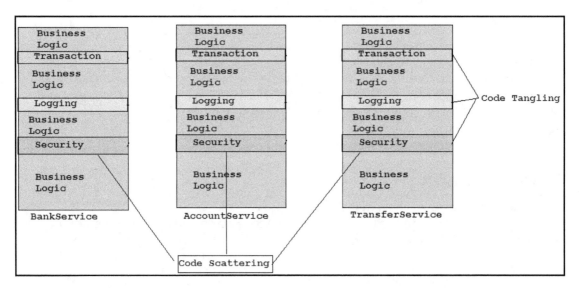

In the preceding figure, there are three business modules **TransferService**, **AccountService**, and **BankService**. Each business module contains cross-cutting concerns such as **Security**, **Logging** and **Transaction** management. All modules have the same code of concerns in the application. It is actually duplication of concerns code across the application.

Spring AOP provides solution for these two problems that is, code tangling and code scattering in the Spring application. Aspects enable modularization of cross-cutting concerns to avoid tangling and to eliminate scattering. Let's see in further section how AOP solves these problems.

How AOP Works to solve problems

Spring AOP allows you to keep cross-cutting concern logic separate from the mainline application logic. That means, you can implement your mainline application logic and only focus on the core problem of the application. And you can write aspects to implement your cross-cutting concerns. Spring provides many aspects out-of-the-box. After creating the aspects, you can add these aspects that is, cross-cutting behaviors to the right places into your application. Let's see the following figure that illustrates the functionality of AOP:

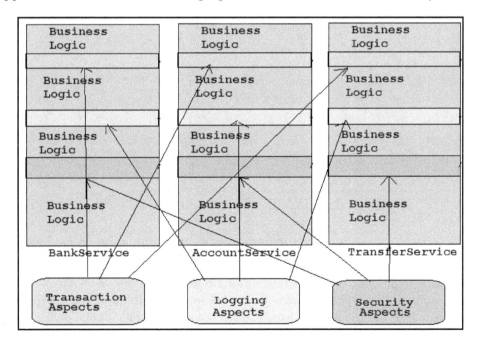

As you can see in the preceding figure, all aspects such as Security, Logging, and Transaction aspect are implemented separately in the application. We have added these aspects at the right places in the applications. Now our application logic is separate from the concerns. Let's see the following section defining the core AOP concepts and use AOP's terminology in your application.

Core AOP terminology and concepts

As with other technologies, AOP has its own vocabularies. Let's start to learn some core AOP concepts and terminology. Spring used the AOP paradigm for the Spring AOP module. But unfortunately, terms used in the Spring AOP Framework are Spring-specific. These terms are used to describe AOP modules and features, but these aren't intuitive. In spite of this, these terms are used in order to understand AOP. Without an understanding of the AOP idiom you will not be able to understand AOP functionality. Basically, AOP is defined in terms of advice, pointcuts, and join points. Let's see the following figure that illustrates about the core AOP concepts and how they are tied together in the framework:

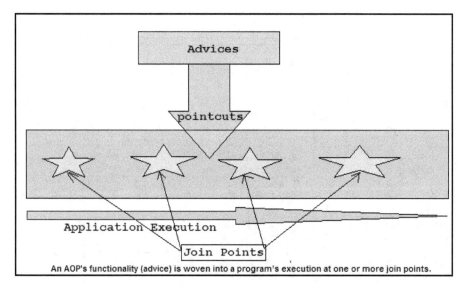

An AOP's functionality (advice) is woven into a program's execution at one or more join points.

In the preceding figure, you can see an AOP functionality, it is known as **Advices** and it is implemented into multiple points. These points are known as **Joint Points**, these are defined by using an expression. These expression are known as **pointcuts**. Let's understand these terms in detail using an example (remember my wife's internet bill story?).

Advice

An internet plan is used for calculating the bill according to data usage in MB or GB by the internet company. The internet company has a list of customers, also and they also company calculates the internet bill for them. So calculating bills and sending it to the customers is a core job for the internet company but not for customers. Likewise, each aspect has its own main job and also has a purpose for doing this job. The job of an aspect is known as advice in the AOP.

As you know now, advice is a job, aspect will perform this job, so there are some questions that come to in mind, when to perform this job and what will be in this job. Will this job be performed before a business method is invoked? Or will it be performed after the business method is invoked? Or will it be performed both before and after method invocation? Or it will be performed when business method throws an exception. Sometime this business method is also called the **advised method**. Let's see the following five kinds of advises used by Spring aspects:

- **Before:** Advice's job executes before the `advised` method is invoked.

 If the advice throws an exception, target will not be called - this is a valid use of a Before Advice.

- **After:** Advice's job executes after the advised method completes regardless of whether an exception has been thrown by the target or not.
- **After-returning:** Advice's job executes after the advised method successfully completes. For example, if a business method returns without throwing an exception.
- **After-throwing:** Advice's job executes if the advised method exits by throwing an exception.
- **Around:** This is one of the most powerful advice of Spring AOP, this advice surrounds the advised method, providing some advice's job before and after the advised method is invoked.

In short, advice's job code to be executed at each selected point that is, Join Point, let's look into another term of AOP.

Join Point

The internet company provides internet to many customers. Each customer has an internet plan and that plan needs to be used for their bill calculation. With the help of each internet plan, the company could potentially calculates the internet bill for all customers. Similarly, your application may have multiple number of places to apply advice. These places in the application are called **join points**. A join point is a point in the execution of a program such as a method call or exception thrown. In these points, Spring aspect inserts concern functionality in your application. Let's see how AOP knows about the join points and discuss another term of AOP concepts.

Pointcut

Internet company makes a number of internet plans according to usage of internet data (customers like my wife need more data) because it is not possible for any internet company to provide same plan for all customers or a unique plan for each customer. Instead, each plan is assigned to the subset of the customers. In the same way, an advice is not necessary to apply to all join points in an application. You can define an expression that selects one or more Join Points in the application. This expression is known as **pointcut**. It helps to narrow down the join points advised by an aspect. Let's see another term of AOP that is Aspect.

Aspect

An internet company knows which customer has what internet plan. On the basis of this information the internet company calculates an internet bill and sends it to the customer. In this example internet company is an aspect, internet plans are pointcuts and customers are join points, and calculating internet bills by the company is an advice. Likewise, in your application, an aspect is a module that encapsulates pointcuts and advice. Aspects know what it does; where and when it does it in the application. Let's see how AOP applies the aspect to the business methods.

Weaving

Weaving is a technique by which aspects are combined with the business code. This is a process of applying aspects to a target object by creating a new proxy object. Weaving can be done at the compile time or at class load time, or at runtime. Spring AOP uses the runtime weaving by using proxy pattern.

You have seen lot of terms used in the AOP. You must know about this terminology whenever your learn about any AOP Framework either AspectJ or Spring AOP. Spring has used AspectJ Framework to implement Spring AOP Framework. Spring AOP supports limited features of AspectJ. Spring AOP provides proxy-based AOP solution. Spring only supports the method joint points. Now you have some basic idea about Spring AOP and how it works, let's move on the next topics how to define pointcuts in the Spring's declarative AOP model.

Defining pointcuts

As mentioned before, pointcuts are used to define a point where advice would be applied. So pointcut is one of the most important elements of an aspect in the application. Let's understand how to define pointcuts. In Spring AOP, we can use expression language to define the pointcuts. Spring AOP uses AspectJ's pointcut expression language for selecting where to apply advice. Spring AOP supports a subset of the pointcut designators available in AspectJ because as you know, Spring AOP is proxy-based and some designators do not support proxy-based AOP. Let's see following table has Spring AOP supported designators.

Spring supported AspectJ designators	Description
execution	It matches the join points by method executions, it is primary pointcut designator supported by Spring AOP.
within	It matches the join points by limit within certain types.
this	It limits matching to join points where the bean reference is an instance of the given type.
target	It limits matching to join points where the target object is of a given type.
args	It limits matching to join points where the arguments are instances of the given types.
@target	It limits matching to join points where the target object has an annotation of the given type.
@args	It limits matching to join points where the runtime, type of the actual arguments passed have annotations of the given type.
@within	It limits matching to join points where the declared type of the target object has the given type annotation.
@annotation	It limits matching to join points where the subject of the join point has the given annotation.

As listed earlier, Spring supported pointcut designators, execution is primary pointcut designator. So here I will only show you how to define pointcuts using execution designators. Let's see how to write the pointcut expression in the application.

Writing pointcuts

We can write pointcuts by using execution designator as follows:

- **execution(<method pattern>)**: The method must match the pattern as defined follows
- **Can chain together to create composite pointcuts by using following operators**: `&& (and), || (or), ! (not)`
- **Method pattern**: Following is method pattern:
    - `[Modifiers] ReturnType [ClassType]`
    - `MethodName ([Arguments]) [throws ExceptionType]`

In the preceding method pattern, values within bracket `[ ]` that is, modifiers, `ClassType`, arguments and exceptions are all optional values. There is no need to define it for every pointcut using execution designator. Value without brackets such as `ReturnType`, and `MethodName` are mandatory to define.

Let's define a `TransferService` interface:

```
package com.packt.patterninspring.chapter6.bankapp.service;
public interface TransferService {
   void transfer(String accountA, String accountB, Long amount);
}
```

`TransferService` is a service for transferring amounts from one to another account. Let's say that you want to write a logging aspect that triggers off `TransferService`'s `transfer()` method. The following figure illustrates a pointcut expression that can be used to apply advice whenever the `transfer()` method is executed:

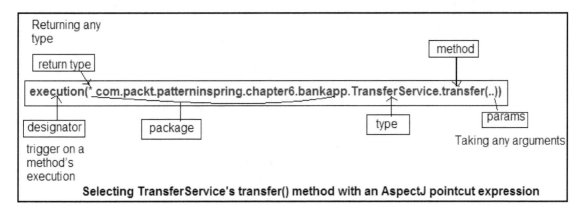

Selecting TransferService's transfer() method with an AspectJ pointcut expression

As in the preceding figure, you can see, I used the `execution()` designator to select join point `TransferService`'s `transfer()` method. In preceding expression in figure, I have used an asterisk at the beginning of the expression. This means that method can return any type. And after asterisk, I have specified a fully qualified class name and name of method as `transfer()`. As method arguments, I have used double dot (..), it means that the pointcut can select a method whose name is `transfer()` with no parameter or any number of parameters.

Let's see following some more pointcut expressions to select join points:

- Any class or package:
    - **execution(void transfer*(String))**: Any method starting with transfer that takes a single String parameter and has a void return type
    - **execution(* transfer(*))**: Any method named `transfer()` that takes a single parameter
    - **execution(* transfer(int, ..))**: Any method named transfer whose first parameter is an int (the "`..`" signifies zero or more parameters may follow)
- Restrict by class:
    - `execution(void com.packt.patterninspring.chapter6.bankapp.service.TransferServiceImpl.*(..))`: Any void method in the `TransferServiceImpl` class, it is including any sub-class, but will be ignored if a different implementation is used.

- Restrict by interface:
    - `execution(void com.packt.patterninspring.chapter6.bankapp.service.TransferService.transfer(*))`: Any void `transfer()` method taking one argument, in any object implementing `TransferService`, it is more flexible choice--works if implementation changes.
- Using Annotations
    - `execution(@javax.annotation.security.RolesAllowed void transfer*(..))`: Any void method whose name starts with `transfer` that is annotated with the `@RolesAllowed` annotation.
- Working with packages
    - `execution(* com..bankapp.*.*(..))`: There is one directory between `com` and `bankapp`
    - `execution(* com.*.bankapp.*.*(..))`: There may be several directories between `bankapp` and `com`
    - `execution(* *..bankapp.*.*(..))`: Any sub-package called `bankapp`

Now that you have seen that the basics of writing pointcuts, let's see how to write the advice and declare the aspects that use those pointcuts

Creating aspects

As I said earlier, *aspects* is one of the most important terms in the AOP. Aspect merges the pointcuts and advices in the application. Let's see how to define aspect in the application.

You've already defined the `TransferService` interface as the subject of your aspect's pointcuts. Now let's use AspectJ annotations to create an aspect.

Define aspects using Annotation

Suppose in your bank application, you want to generate log for a money transfer service for auditing and tracking to understand customers' behaviors. A business never succeeds without understanding its customers. Whenever you will think about it from the perspective of a business, an auditing is required but isn't central to the function of the business itself; it's a separate concern. Therefore, it makes sense to define the auditing as an aspect that's applied to a transfer service. Let's see the following code which shows the Auditing class that defines the aspects for this concern:

```
package com.packt.patterninspring.chapter6.bankapp.aspect;

import org.aspectj.lang.annotation.AfterReturning;
import org.aspectj.lang.annotation.AfterThrowing;
import org.aspectj.lang.annotation.Aspect;
import org.aspectj.lang.annotation.Before;

@Aspect
public class Auditing {

  //Before transfer service
  @Before("execution(* com.packt.patterninspring.chapter6.bankapp.
  service.TransferService.transfer(..))")
  public void validate(){
    System.out.println("bank validate your credentials before
    amount transferring");
  }

  //Before transfer service
  @Before("execution(* com.packt.patterninspring.chapter6.bankapp.
  service.TransferService.transfer(..))")
  public void transferInstantiate(){
    System.out.println("bank instantiate your amount
    transferring");
  }

  //After transfer service
  @AfterReturning("execution(* com.packt.patterninspring.chapter6.
  bankapp.service.TransferService.transfer(..))")
  public void success(){
    System.out.println("bank successfully transferred amount");
  }

  //After failed transfer service
  @AfterThrowing("execution(* com.packt.patterninspring.chapter6.
  bankapp.service.TransferService.transfer(..))")
  public void rollback() {
```

```
            System.out.println("bank rolled back your transferred amount");
    }
  }
```

As you can see how the `Auditing` class is annotated with `@Aspect` annotation. It means this class is not just Spring bean, it is an aspect of the application. And `Auditing` class has some methods, these are advices and define some logic within these methods. As we know that before beginning to transfer amount from an account to another, bank will validate (`validate ()`) the use credentials and after that instantiate (`transferInstantiate()`) this service. After successful validation (`success ()`) amount is transferred and the bank audits it. But if the amount transferring fails in any case, then the bank should roll back (`rollback ()`) that amount.

As you can see, all methods of `Auditing` aspects are annotated with advice annotations to indicate when those methods should be called. Spring AOP provides five type advice annotations for defining advice. Let's see in the following table:

Annotation	Advice
`@Before`	It is used for before advice, `advice`'s method executes before the advised method is invoked.
`@After`	It is used for after advice, advice's method execute after the advised method executes normally or abnormally doesn't matter.
`@AfterReturning`	It used for after returning advice, advice's method execute after the advised method complete successfully.
`@AfterThrowing`	It used for after throwing advice, advice's method execute after the method terminate abnormally by throwing an exception.
`@Around`	It is used for around advice, advice's method executes before and after the advised method invoked.

Let's see the implementation of advices and how these work in the application.

Implementing Advice

As you know that, Spring provides five types of advices, let's see work flow of one by one.

Advice type - Before

Let's see the following figure for before advice. This advice executes the before the target method:

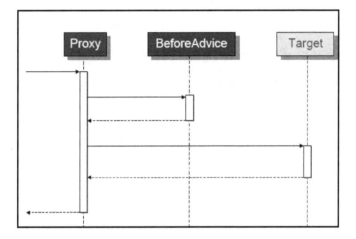

As you can see in figure, before advice is executed first and then it calls the **Target** method. As we know that Spring AOP is proxy-based. So a **Proxy** object is created of target class. It is based on Proxy design pattern and Decorator Design Pattern.

Before Advice example

Let's see the use of @Before annotation:

```
//Before transfer service
@Before("execution(* com.packt.patterninspring.chapter6.
bankapp.service.TransferService.transfer(..))")
public void validate(){
   System.out.println("bank validate your credentials before amount
   transferring");
}

//Before transfer service
@Before("execution(* com.packt.patterninspring.chapter6.
```

```
bankapp.service.TransferService.transfer(..))")
public void transferInstantiate(){
   System.out.println("bank instantiate your amount transferring");
}
```

 Note--if the advice throws an exception, target will not be called--this is a valid use of a Before Advice.

Now you have seen the before advice, let's have a look into another type advice.

Advice Types: After Returning

Let's see the following figure for after returning advice. This advice executes the after the **Target** method executed successfully:

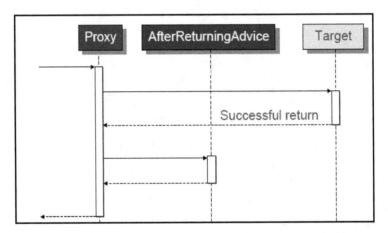

As you can see in figure, the after returning advice is executed after the target returns successfully. This advice will never execute if target throws any exception in the application.

After Returning Advice example

Let's see the use of the @AfterReturning annotation:

```
//After transfer service
@AfterReturning("execution(* com.packt.patterninspring.chapter6.
bankapp.service.TransferService.transfer(..))")
public void success(){
   System.out.println("bank successfully transferred amount");
}
```

Now you have seen the after returning advice, let's move to another type advice in the Spring AOP.

Advice Types: After Throwing

Let's see the following figure for after throwing advice. This advice executes the after the target method terminated abnormally. It mean the target method throws any exception, then this advice will be executed. Please refer to the following diagram:

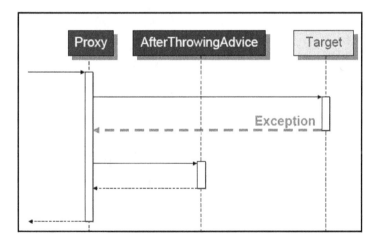

As you can see in figure, the after throwing advice is executed after the target throws an exception. This advice will never execute if the target doesn't throw any exception in the application.

After Throwing Advice example

Let's see the use of the @AfterThrowing annotation:

```
//After failed transfer service
@AfterThrowing("execution(* com.packt.patterninspring.chapter6.
bankapp.service.TransferService.transfer(..))")
public void rollback() {
   System.out.println("bank rolled back your transferred amount");
}
```

You can also use the @AfterThrowing annotation with the throwing attribute, it only invokes advice if the right exception type is thrown:

```
//After failed transfer service
@AfterThrowing(value = "execution(*
com.packt.patterninspring.chapter6.
bankapp.service.TransferService.transfer(..))", throwing="e"))
public void rollback(DataAccessException e) {
   System.out.println("bank rolled back your transferred amount");
}
```

Execute every time a TransferService class throws an exception of type DataAccessException.

The @AfterThrowing advice will not stop the exception from propagating. However, it can throw a different type of exception.

Advice Types: After

Let's see the following figure for **AfterAdvice**. This advice executes after the **Target** method is terminated normally or abnormally. It doesn't matter that **Target** method throws any exception or executes without any exception:

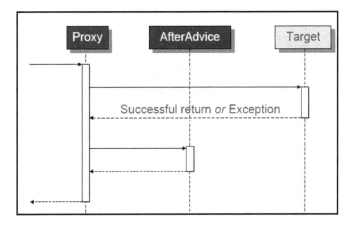

As you can see in figure, the after advice is executed after the target method terminates by throwing any exception or normally.

After Advice example

Let's see the use of @After annotation:

```
//After transfer service
@After ("execution(* com.packt.patterninspring.chapter6.
bankapp.service.TransferService.transfer(..))")
public void trackTransactionAttempt(){
   System.out.println("bank has attempted a transaction");
}
```

Use @After annotation called regardless of whether an exception has been thrown by the target or not.

Advice Types - Around

Let's see the following figure for **AroundAdvice**. This advice executes both times before and after the **Target** method is invoked. This advice is very powerful advice of Spring AOP. Many features of the Spring Framework are implemented by using this advice. This is the only advice in Spring which has capability to stop or proceed the target method execution. Please refer to the following diagram:

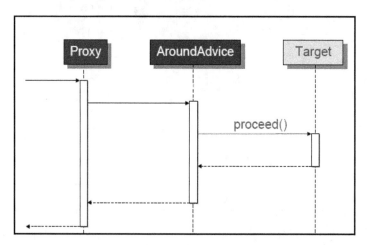

As you can see in the preceding figure, **AroundAdvice** executed two times, first time it is executed before the advised method and second time it is executed after advised method is invoked. And also this advice calls the `proceed()` method to execute the advised method in the application. Let's see the following example:

Around Advice example

Let's see the use of the `@Around` annotation:

```
@Around(execution(*    com.packt.patterninspring.chapter6.
bankapp.service.TransferService.createCache(..)))
public Object cache(ProceedingJoinPoint point){
Object value = cacheStore.get(CacheUtils.toKey(point));
if (value == null) {
  value = point.proceed();
  cacheStore.put(CacheUtils.toKey(point), value);
}
return value;
}
```

Here I used `@Around` annotation and a `ProceedingJoinPoint`, it inherits from Join Point and adds the `proceed()` method. As you can see in this example, this advice proceeds to target only if value is not already in the cache.

You have seen how to implement the advice in the application using annotations and how to create aspect and how to define pointcuts by annotations. In this example, we are using Auditing as an aspect class and it is annotated with `@Aspect` annotation, but this annotation will not work if you don't enable AOP proxy behavior of the Spring.

Let's see the following Java configuration file, `AppConfig.java`, you can turn on auto-proxying by applying the `@EnableAspectJAutoProxy` annotation at the class level:

```
package com.packt.patterninspring.chapter6.bankapp.config;

import org.springframework.context.annotation.Bean;
import org.springframework.context.annotation.ComponentScan;
import org.springframework.context.annotation.Configuration;
import org.springframework.context.annotation.
   EnableAspectJAutoProxy;

import com.packt.patterninspring.chapter6.bankapp.aspect.Auditing;

@Configuration
@EnableAspectJAutoProxy
@ComponentScan
public class AppConfig {
  @Bean
  public Auditing auditing() {
     return new Auditing();
  }
}
```

If you're using XML configuration, let's see how to wire your beans in Spring and how to enable Spring AOP feature by using the `<aop:aspectj-autoproxy>` element from Spring's AOP namespace:

```
<?xml version="1.0" encoding="UTF-8"?>
<beans xmlns="http://www.springframework.org/schema/beans"
  xmlns:xsi="http://www.w3.org/2001/XMLSchema-instance"
  xmlns:context="http://www.springframework.org/schema/context"
  xmlns:aop="http://www.springframework.org/schema/aop"
  xsi:schemaLocation="http://www.springframework.org/schema/aop
  http://www.springframework.org/schema/aop/spring-aop.xsd
  http://www.springframework.org/schema/beans
  http://www.springframework.org/schema/beans/spring-beans.xsd
  http://www.springframework.org/schema/context
```

```
          http://www.springframework.org/schema/context/spring-
          context.xsd">
          <context:component-scan base-
          package="com.packt.patterninspring.chapter6.bankapp" />
          <aop:aspectj-autoproxy />
          <bean class="com.packt.patterninspring.chapter6.
          bankapp.aspect.Auditing" />
      </beans>
```

Let's see how you can declare aspects in a Spring XML configuration file.

Define aspects using XML configuration

As we know that, we can configure beans in the XML based configuration, similarly you can declare aspects in the XML configuration. Spring provides another AOP namespace and it offers many elements that are used to declare aspects in XML, let's see in the following tables:

Annotation	Parallel XML element	Purpose of XML element
@Before	<aop:before>	It defines before advice.
@After	<aop:after>	It defines after advice.
@AfterReturning	<aop:after-returning>	It defines after returning advice.
@AfterThrowing	<aop:after-throwing>	It defines after throwing advice.
@Around	<aop:around>	It defines around advice.
@Aspect	<aop:aspect>	It defines an aspect.
@EnableAspectJAutoProxy	<aop:aspectj-autoproxy>	It enables annotation-driven aspects using @AspectJ.
@Pointcut	<aop:pointcut>	It defines a pointcut.
--	<aop:advisor>	It define AOP adviser
--	<aop:config>	It is top level AOP element

As you can see in the preceding table, a number of AOP namespace elements are parallel to the corresponding annotation available in the Java based configuration. Let's see the following same example in the XML based configuration, first have a look into the aspect class Auditing. Let's remove all of those AspectJ annotations as shown in following code:

```
package com.packt.patterninspring.chapter6.bankapp.aspect;

public class Auditing {
  public void validate(){
    System.out.println("bank validate your credentials before
    amount transferring");
  }
  public void transferInstantiate(){
    System.out.println("bank instantiate your amount
    transferring");
  }
  public void success(){
    System.out.println("bank successfully transferred amount");
  }
  public void rollback() {
    System.out.println("bank rolled back your transferred amount");
  }
}
```

As you can see the preceding code, now our aspect class doesn't indicate that it is an aspect class. It is a basic Java POJO class with some methods. Let's see in next section how to declare advices in XML configuration:

```
<aop:config>
  <aop:aspect ref="auditing">
    <aop:before pointcut="execution(*
    com.packt.patterninspring.chapter6.bankapp.
    service.TransferService.transfer(..))"
    method="validate"/>
    <aop:before pointcut="execution(*
    com.packt.patterninspring.chapter6.bankapp.
    service.TransferService.transfer(..))"
    method="transferInstantiate"/>
    <aop:after-returning pointcut="execution(*
    com.packt.patterninspring.chapter6.
    bankapp.service.TransferService.transfer(..))"
    method="success"/>
    <aop:after-throwing pointcut="execution(*
    com.packt.patterninspring.chapter6.bankapp.
    service.TransferService.transfer(..))"
    method="rollback"/>
  </aop:aspect>
```

```
</aop:config>
```

As you can see, <aop-config> is using a top level element. In <aop:config>, you declare other elements like <aop:aspect>, this element has ref attribute and it references to the POJO bean Auditing. It indicates that Auditing is an aspect class in the application. Now <aop-aspect> element has advices and pointcuts elements. All logics are same as we have defined in Java configuration.

Let's see in the next section how spring create AOP proxy.

Understanding AOP proxies

As you know that, Spring AOP is proxy-based. It mean Spring creates the proxy to weave the aspect between the business logic that is, in target object. It is based on the Proxy and Decorator design pattern. Let's see TransferServiceImpl class as an implementation of TransferService interface:

```java
package com.packt.patterninspring.chapter6.bankapp.service;
import org.springframework.stereotype.Service;
public class TransferServiceImpl implements TransferService {
    @Override
    public void transfer(String accountA, String accountB, Long
    amount) {
        System.out.println(amount+" Amount has been tranfered from
        "+accountA+" to "+accountB);
    }
}
```

Caller invokes this service (transfer() method) directly by the object reference, let's see the following figure to illustrate more:

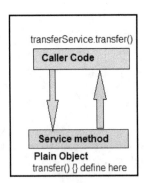

As you can see that caller could directly call the service and do the task assigned to it.

But you declare this `TransferService` as a target for the aspect. Since this is done, things change slightly. Now this class wrapped by proxy and client code actually doesn't call this service directly, it calls routed by this proxy. Let's see the following diagram.

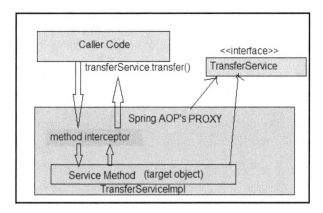

As you can see in the preceding diagram, Spring apply the AOP-proxy to the object in the following sequence:

1. Spring creates a proxy weaving aspect and target.
2. Proxy also implements target interface, that is, `TransferServive` interface.
3. All calls for transfer service method `transfer()` routed through proxy interceptor.
4. Matching advice is executed.
5. Then `target` method is executed.

As preceding list, is the flow when you call the method that has the proxy created by Spring.

You have seen in this chapter the Spring AOP Framework, it has actually implemented some part of the AspectJ Framework using proxy-based aspect weaving. I think, this gave good knowledge about Spring AOP.

Summary

In this chapter, we have seen the Spring AOP Framework and used design patterns behind this module. AOP is a very powerful paradigm and it complements the Object oriented programming. **Aspect-Oriented Programming (AOP)** modularizes cross-cutting concerns such as Logging, Security and Transaction. An aspect is a Java class annotated with `@Aspect` annotation. It defines a module containing the crosscutting behavior. This module separates from the application's business logic. We can reuse it in our application with other business modules without making any changes.

In Spring AOP, behavior is implemented as an advice method. You have learned in Spring, there are five types as Before, AfterThrowing, AfterReturning, After and Around. Around advice is a very powerful advice, there are interesting features implemented by using Around advice. You've learned how to weave these advices using load time weaving.

You have seen how to declare Pointcuts in the Spring application and pointcuts select joinpoints where advice applies.

Now we'll move to the essential part and look at how spring works in the backend to connect with database and read data for the application. Starting in the next chapter, you'll see how to build applications using JDBC template in Spring.

5
Accessing a Database with Spring and JDBC Template Patterns

In earlier chapters, you learned about Spring core modules like the Spring IoC container, the DI pattern, container life cycle, and the used design patterns. Also you have seen how Spring makes magic using AOP. Now is the right time to move into the battlefield of real Spring applications with persisting data. Do you remember your first application during college days where you dealt with database access? That time, you probably, had to write boring boilerplate code to load database drivers, initialize your data-access framework, open connections, handle various exceptions, and to close connections. You also had to be very careful about that code. If anything went wrong, you would not have been able to make a database connection in your application, even though you would've invested a lot of time in such boring code, apart from writing the actual SQL and business code.

Because we always try to make things better and simpler, we have to focus on the solution to that tedious work for data-access. Spring comes with a solution for the tedious and boring work for data-access--it removes the code of data access. Spring provides data-access frameworks to integrate with a variety of data-access technologies. It allows you to use either JDBC directly or any **object-relational mapping (ORM)** framework, like Hibernate, to persist your data. Spring handles all the low-level code for data access work in your application; you can just write your SQL, application logic, and manage your application's data rather than investing time in writing code for making and closing database connections, and so on.

Now, you can choose any technology, such as JDBC, Hibernate, the **Java Persistence API** (**JPA**), or others. to persist your application's data. Irrespective of what you choose, Spring provides support for all these technologies for your application. In this chapter, we will explore Spring's support for JDBC. It will cover the following points:

- The best approach to designing your data access
- Implementing the template design pattern
- Problems with the traditional JDBC
- Solving problems with the Spring `JdbcTemplate`
- Configuring the data source
- Using the object pool design pattern to maintain database connections
- Abstracting database access by the DAO pattern
- Working with `JdbcTemplate`
- The Jdbc callback interfaces
- Best practices for configuring `JdbcTemplate` in the application

Before we go on to discuss more about JDBC and the template design pattern, let's first see the best approach to define the data-access tier in the layered architecture.

The best approach to designing your data-access

In previous chapters, you have seen that one of Spring's goals is to allow you to develop applications by following one of the OOPs principles of coding to interfaces. Any enterprise application needs to read data and write data to any kind of database, and to meet this requirement, we have to write the persistence logic. Spring allows you to avoid the scattering of persistence logic across all the modules in your application. For this, we can create a different component for data access and persistence logic, and this component is known as a **data access object** (**DAO**). Let's see, in the following diagram, the best approach to create modules in layered applications:

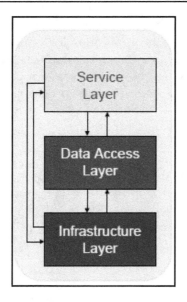

As you can see in the preceding diagram, for a better approach, many enterprise applications consist of the following three logical layers:

- **The service layer** (or application layer): This layer of the application exposes high-level application functions like use-cases and business logic. All application services are defined here.
- **The data access layer**: This layer of the application defines an interface to the application's data repository (such as a Relational or NoSQL database). This layer has the classes and interfaces which have the data-access logic's data persisting in the application.
- **The infrastructure layer**: This layer of the application exposes low-level services to the other layers, such as configuring DataSource by using the database URL, user credentials, and so on. Such configuration comes under this layer.

In the previous figure, you can see that the **Service Layer** collaborates with the **Data Access Layer**. To avoid coupling between the application logic and data-access logic, we should expose their functionality through interfaces, as interfaces promote decoupling between the collaborating components. If we use the data-access logic by implementing interfaces, we can configure any particular data-access strategy to the application without making any changes in the application logic in the **Service Layer**. The following diagram shows the proper approach to designing our data-access layer:

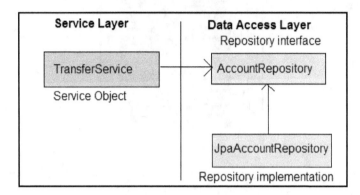

As shown in the preceding figure, your application service objects, that is, **TransferService**, don't handle their own data access. Instead, they delegate data access to the repositories. The repository's interface, that is, **AccountRepository** in your application, keeps it loosely coupled to the service object. You could configure any variant of the implementations-either the Jpa implementation of **AccountRepository** (**JpaAccountRepository**), or the Jdbc implementation of **AccountRepository** (**JdbcAccountRepository**).

Spring not only provides loose coupling between the application components working at the different layers in the layered architecture, but also helps to manage the resources in the enterprise layered architecture application. Let's see how Spring manages the resources, and what design pattern is using by Spring to solve the resource management problem.

The resource management problem

Let's understand the resource management problem with the help of a real example. You must've ordered pizza online sometime. If so, what are the steps involved in the process, from the time of ordering the pizza till its delivery? There are many steps to this process-- We first go to the online portal of the pizza company, select the size of the pizza and the toppings. After that, we place our order and check out. The order is accepted by the nearest pizza shop; they prepare our pizza accordingly, put the toppings on accordingly, wrap this pizza in the bag, the delivery boy comes to your place and hands over the pizza to you, and, finally, you enjoy your pizza with your friend. Even though there are many steps to this process, you're actively involved in only a couple of them. The pizza company is responsible for cooking the pizza and delivering it smoothly. You are involved only when you need to be, and other steps are taken care of by the pizza company. As you saw in this example, there are many steps involved in managing this process, and we also have to assign the resources to each step accordingly such that it is treated as a complete task without any break in the flow. This is a perfect scenario for a powerful design pattern, the template method pattern. The Spring framework implements this template design pattern to handle such type scenarios in the DAO layer of an application. Let's see what problems we face if we don't use Spring, and work with the traditional application instead.

In a traditional application, we work with the JDBC API to access the data from the database. It is a simple application where we access and persist the data using the JDBC API, and for this application, the following steps are required:

1. Define the connection parameters.
2. Access a data source, and establish a connection.
3. Begin a transaction.
4. Specify the SQL statement.
5. Declare the parameters, and provide parameter values.
6. Prepare and execute the statement.
7. Set up the loop to iterate through the results.
8. Do the work for each iteration--execute the business logic.
9. Process any exception.
10. Commit or roll back the transaction.
11. Close the connection, statement, and resultset.

If you use the Spring Framework for the same application, then you have to write the code for some steps of the preceding list of steps, while spring takes care of all the steps involving the low-level processes such as establishing a connection, beginning a transaction, processing any exception in the data layer, and closing the connection. Spring manages these steps by using the Template method design pattern, which we'll study in the next section.

Implementing the template design pattern

Define the skeleton of an algorithm in an operation, deferring some steps to subclasses. Template Method lets subclasses redefine certain steps of an algorithm without changing the algorithm's structure.

-GOF Design Pattern

Template method design pattern is widely used, and comes under the structural design pattern of the GOF design pattern family. This pattern defines the outline or skeleton of an algorithm, and leaves the details to specific implementations later. This pattern hides away large amounts of boilerplate code. Spring provides many template classes, such as `JdbcTemplate`, `JmsTemplate`, `RestTemplate`, and `WebServiceTemplate`. Mostly, this pattern hides the low-level resource management as discussed earlier in the pizza example.

In the example, the process is ordering a pizza for home delivery from an online portal. The process followed by the pizza company has some fixed steps for each customer, like taking the order, preparing the pizza, adding the toppings according to the customer's specifications, and delivering it to the customer's address. We can add these steps, or define these steps to a specific algorithm. The system can then implement this algorithm accordingly.

Spring implements this pattern to access data from a database. In a database, or any other technology, there are some steps that are always common, such as establishing a connection to the database, handling transactions, handling exceptions, and some clean up actions which are required for each data access process. But there are also some steps which are not fixed, but depend on the application's requirement. It is the responsibility of the developer to define these steps. But spring allows us to separate the fixed and dynamic parts of the data-access process into different parts as templates and callbacks. All fixed steps come under the template, and dynamic custom steps come under callbacks. The following figure describes the two in detail:

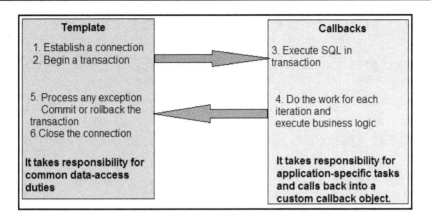

As you can see in the preceding figure, all the fixed parts of the process for data access wraps to the template classes of the Spring Framework as open and close connection, open and close statements, handling exceptions, and managing resources. But the other steps like writing SQLs, declaring connection parameters, and so on are parts of the callbacks, and callbacks are handled by the developer.

Spring provides several implementations of the Template method design pattern such as `JdbcTemplate`, `JmsTemplate`, `RestTemplate`, and `WebServiceTemplate`, but in this chapter, I will explain only its implementation for the JDBC API as `JdbcTemplate`. There is another variant of `JdbcTemplate-NamedParameterJdbcTemplate`, which wraps a `JdbcTemplate` to provide named parameters instead of the traditional JDBC "?" placeholders.

Problems with the traditional JDBC

The following are the problems we have to face whenever we work with the traditional JDBC API:

- **Redundant results due to error-prone code**: The traditional JDBC API required a lot of tedious code to work with the data access layer. Let's see the following code to connect the Database and execute the desired query:

```
public List<Account> findByAccountNumber(Long accountNumber) {
  List<Account> accountList = new ArrayList<Account>();
  Connection conn = null;
  String sql = "select account_name,
  account_balance from ACCOUNT where account_number=?";
  try {
    DataSource dataSource = DataSourceUtils.getDataSource();
    conn = dataSource.getConnection();
```

```
      PreparedStatement ps = conn.prepareStatement(sql);
      ps.setLong(1, accountNumber);
      ResultSet rs = ps.executeQuery();
      while (rs.next()) {
        accountList.add(new Account(rs.getString(
          "account_name"), ...));
      }
    } catch (SQLException e) { /* what to be handle here? */ }
    finally {
      try {
        conn.close();
      } catch (SQLException e) { /* what to be handle here ?*/ }
    }
    return accountList;
  }
```

As you can see in the preceding code, there are some lines which are highlighted; only this bold code matters-the rest is boilerplate. Also, this code handles the SQLException in the application inefficiently, because the developer doesn't know what should be handled there. Let's now look at another problem in the traditional JDBC code.

- **Leads to poor exception handling**: In the preceding code, the exceptions in the application are handled very poorly. The developers are not aware of what exceptions are to be handled here. SQLException is a checked Exception, which means it forces the developers to handle errors, but if you can't handle it, you must declare it. It is a very bad way of handling exceptions, and the intermediate methods must declare exception(s) from all methods in the code. It is a form of tight coupling.

Solving problems with Spring's JdbcTemplate

Spring's JdbcTemplate solves both the problems listed in the last section. JdbcTemplate greatly simplifies the use of the JDBC API, and it eliminates repetitive boilerplate code. It alleviates the common causes of bugs, and handles SQLExceptions properly without sacrificing power. It provides full access to the standard JDBC constructs. Let's see the same code using Spring's JdbcTemplate class to solve these two problems:

- **Removing redundant code from the application using JdbcTemplate**: Suppose you want a count of the accounts in a bank. The following code is required if you use the JdbcTemplate class:

```
int count = jdbcTemplate.queryForObject("SELECT COUNT(*)
  FROM ACCOUNT", Integer.class);
```

If you want to access the list of accounts for a particular user ID:

```
List<Account> results = jdbcTemplate.query(someSql,
  new RowMapper<Account>() {
    public Account mapRow(ResultSet rs, int row) throws
     SQLException {
       // map the current row to an Account object
    }
});
```

As you can see in the preceding code, you don't need to write the code for Open and Close database connection, for preparing a statement to execute query, and so on.

- **Data Access Exceptions**: Spring provides a consistent exception hierarchy to handle technology-specific exceptions like SQLException to its own exception class hierarchy with DataAccessException as the root exception. Spring wraps these original exceptions into different unchecked exceptions. Now Spring does not force the developers to handle these exceptions at development time. Spring provides the DataAccessException hierarchy to hide whether you are using JPA, Hibernate, JDBC, or similar. Actually, it is a hierarchy of sub-exceptions, and not just one exception for everything. It is consistent across all the supported data access technologies. The following diagram depicts the Spring Data Access Exception hierarchy:

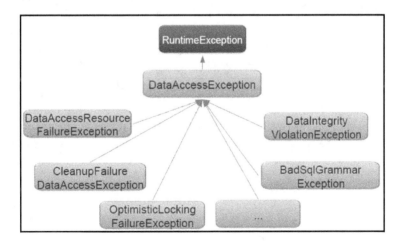

- As you can see in the preceding figure, Spring's `DataAccessException` extends the `RuntimeException`, that is, it is an unchecked exception. In an enterprise application, unchecked exceptions can be thrown up the call hierarchy to the best place to handle it. The good thing is that the methods in between don't know about it in the application.

Let's first discuss how to configure Spring with a data source to be able to connect the database, before declaring the templates and repositories in a Spring application.

Configuring the data source and object pool pattern

In the Spring Framework, DataSource is part of the JDBC API, and it provides a connection to the database. It hides many boilerplate codes for connection pooling, exception handling, and transaction management issues from the application code. As a developer, you let it focus on your business logic only. Don't worry about connection pooling, exception handling, and managing transactions; it is the responsibility of the application administrators how they set up the container managed data source in production. You just write the code, and test that code.

In an enterprise application, we can retrieve DataSource in several ways. We can use the JDBC driver to retrieve DataSource, but it is not the best approach to create DataSource in the production environment. As performance is one of the key issues during application development, Spring implements the object pool pattern to provide DataSource to the application in a very efficient way. The object pool pattern says that *creation of objects is expensive rather than reuse.*

Spring allows us to implement the object pool pattern for reusing the DataSource object in the application. You can use either the application server and container-managed pool (JNDI), or you can create a container by using third-party libraries such as DBCP, c3p0, and so on. These pools help to manage the available data sources in a better way.

In your Spring application, there are several options to configure the data-source beans, and they are as follows:

- Configuring data source using a JDBC driver
- Implementing the object pool design pattern to provide data source objects
    - Configuring the data source using JNDI
    - Configuring the data source using pool connections
        - Implementing the Builder pattern to create an embedded data source
- Let's see how to configure a data-source bean in a Spring application.

Configuring a data source using a JDBC driver

Using a JDBC driver to configure a data-source bean is the simplest data source in Spring. The three data source classes provided by Spring are as follows:

- `DriverManagerDataSource`: It always creates a new connection for every connection request
- `SimpleDriverDataSource`: It is similar to the `DriverManagerDataSource` except that it works with the JDBC driver directly
- `SingleConnectionDataSource`: It returns the same connection for every connection request, but it is not a pooled data source

Let's see the following code for configuring a data source bean using the `DriverManagerDataSource` class of Spring in your application:

In Java-based configuration, the code is as follows:

```
DriverManagerDataSource dataSource = new DriverManagerDataSource();
dataSource.setDriverClassName("org.h2.Driver");
dataSource.setUrl("jdbc:h2:tcp://localhost/bankDB");
dataSource.setUsername("root");
dataSource.setPassword("root");
```

In XML-based configuration, the code will be like this:

```
<bean id="dataSource"
 class="org.springframework.jdbc.datasource
 .DriverManagerDataSource">
 <property name="driverClassName" value="org.h2.Driver"/>
 <property name="url" value="jdbc:h2:tcp://localhost/bankDB"/>
 <property name="username" value="root"/>
 <property name="password" value="root"/>
</bean>
```

The data source defined in the preceding code is a very simple data source, and we can use it in the development environment. It is not a suitable data source for production. I, personally, prefer to use JNDI to configure the data source for the production environment. Let's see how.

Let's implement the object pool design pattern to provide data source objects *by* configuring the data source *using* JNDI.

In a Spring application, you can configure a data source by using the JNDI lookup. Spring provides the `<jee:jndi-lookup>` element from Spring's JEE namespace. Let's see the code for this configuration.

In XML configuration, the code is given as follows:

```
<jee:jndi-lookup id="dataSource"
 jndi-name="java:comp/env/jdbc/datasource" />
```

In Java configuration, the code is as follows:

```
@Bean
public JndiObjectFactoryBean dataSource() {
    JndiObjectFactoryBean jndiObject = new JndiObjectFactoryBean();
    jndiObject.setJndiName("jdbc/datasource");
    jndiObject.setResourceRef(true);
    jndiObject.setProxyInterface(javax.sql.DataSource.class);
    return jndiObject;
}
```

Application servers like WebSphere or JBoss allow you to configure data sources to be prepared via JNDI. Even a web container like Tomcat allows you to configure data sources to be prepared via JNDI. These servers manage the data sources in your application. It is beneficial, because the performance of the data source will be greater, as the application servers are often pooled. And they can be managed completely external to the application. This is one of the best ways to configure a data source to be retrieved via JNDI. If you are not able to retrieve through the JNDI lookup in production, you can choose another, better option, which we'll discuss next.

Configuring the data source using pool connections

The following open-sources technologies provide pooled data sources:

- Apache commons DBCP
- c3p0
- BoneCP

The following code configures DBCP's `BasicDataSource`.

The XML-based DBCP configuration is given as follows:

```
<bean id="dataSource"
  class="org.apache.commons.dbcp.BasicDataSource"
  destroy-method="close">
  <property name="driverClassName" value="org.h2.Driver"/>
  <property name="url" value="jdbc:h2:tcp://localhost/bankDB"/>
  <property name="username" value="root"/>
  <property name="password" value="root"/>
  <property name="initialSize" value="5"/>
  <property name="maxActive" value="10"/>
</bean>
```

The Java-based DBCP configuration is as follows:

```
@Bean
public BasicDataSource dataSource() {
   BasicDataSource dataSource = new BasicDataSource();
   dataSource.setDriverClassName("org.h2.Driver");
   dataSource.setUrl("jdbc:h2:tcp://localhost/bankDB");
   dataSource.setUsername("root");
   dataSource.setPassword("root");
   dataSource.setInitialSize(5);
   dataSource.setMaxActive(10);
   return dataSource;
}
```

As you can see in the preceding code, there are many other properties which are introduced for a pooled data sources provider. The properties of the `BasicDataSource` class in Spring are listed next:

- `initialSize`: This is the number of connections created at the time of initialization of the pool.
- `maxActive`: This is the maximum number of connections that can be allocated from the pool at the time of initialization of the pool. If you set this value to 0, that means there's no limit.
- `maxIdle`: This is the maximum number of connections that can be idle in the pool without extras being released. If you set this value to 0, that means there's no limit.
- `maxOpenPreparedStatements`: This is the maximum number of prepared statements that can be allocated from the statement pool at the time of initialization of the pool. If you set this value to 0, that means there's no limit.
- `maxWait`: This is the maximum waiting time for a connection to be returned to the pool before an exception is thrown. If you set it to 1, it means wait indefinitely.
- `minEvictableIdleTimeMillis`: This is the maximum time duration a connection can remain idle in the pool before it's eligible for eviction.
- `minIdle`: This is the minimum number of connections that can remain idle in the pool without new connections being created.

Implementing the Builder pattern to create an embedded data source

In application development, the embedded database is very useful, because it doesn't require a separate database server that your application connects. Spring provides one more data source for embedded databases. It is not powerful enough for the production environment. We can use the embedded data source for the development and testing environment. In Spring, the jdbc namespace configures an embedded database, H2, as follows:

In XML configuration, H2 is configured as follows:

```
<jdbc:embedded-database id="dataSource" type="H2">
 <jdbc:script location="schema.sql"/>
 <jdbc:script location="data.sql"/>
</jdbc:embedded-database>
```

In Java configuration, H2 is configured as follows:

```
@Bean
public DataSource dataSource(){
  EmbeddedDatabaseBuilder builder =
    new EmbeddedDatabaseBuilder().setType(EmbeddedDatabaseType.H2);
  builder.addScript("schema.sql");
  builder.addScript("data.sql");
  return builder.build();
}
```

As you can see in the preceding code, Spring provides the EmbeddedDatabaseBuilder class. It actually implements the Builder design pattern to create the object of the EmbeddedDatabaseBuilder class.

Let's see one more design pattern in the next section.

Abstracting database access using the DAO pattern

The data access layer works as an aspect between the business layer and the database. Data accessing depends on the business call, and it varies depending on the source of the data for example database, flat files, XML, and so on. So, we can abstract all access by providing an interface. This is known as the data access object pattern. From the application's point of view, it makes no difference when it accesses a relational database or parses XML files using a DAO.

In an earlier version, EJB provided entity beans managed by the container; they were distributed, secure, and transactional components. These beans were very transparent to the client, that is, for the service layer in the application, they had automatic persistence without the care of underlying database. But mostly, the features offered by these entity beans were not required for your application, as you needed to persist data to the database. Due to *this*, some non-required features of the entity beans, like network traffic, increased, and your application's performance was impacted. And that time, the entity beans needed to run inside the EJB containers, which is why it was very difficult to test.

In a nutshell, if you are working with the traditional JDBC API or earlier EJB versions, you will face the following problems in your application:

- In a traditional JDBC application, you merge the business tier logic with persistence logic.
- The Persistence tier or DAO layer is not consistent for the service layer or business tier. But DAO should be consistent for the service layer in an enterprise application.
- In a traditional JDBC application, you have to handle a lot of boilerplate code like making and closing connection, preparing statement, handling exceptions, and so on. It degrades reusability and increases development time.
- With EJB, the entity bean was created *as* an overhead to the application, and was difficult to test.

Let's see how spring solves these problems.

The DAO pattern with the Spring Framework

Spring provides a comprehensive JDBC module to design and develop JDBC-based DAOs. These DAOs in the application take care of all the boilerplate code of the JDBC API, and help to provide a consistent API for data access. In the Spring JDBC, DAO is a generic object to access data for the business tier, and it provides a consistent interface to the services at the business tier. The main goal behind the DAO's classes is to abstract the underlying data access logic from the services at the business tier.

In our previous example, we saw how the pizza company helped us to understand the resource management problem, and now, we will continue with our bank application. Let's see the following example on how to implement DAOs in an application. Suppose, in our bank application, we want the total number accounts in a branch in the city. For this, we will first create an interface for the DAO. It promotes programming to interface, as discussed earlier. It is one of the best practices of the design principles. This DAO interface will be injected with the services at the business tier, and we can create a number of concrete classes of the DAO interface according to the underlying databases in the application. That means our DAO layer will be consistent for the business layer. Let's create a DAO interface as following:

```
package com.packt.patterninspring.chapter7.bankapp.dao;
public interface AccountDao {
  Integer totalAccountsByBranch(String branchName);
}
```

Let's see a concrete implementation of the DAO interface using Spring's `JdbcDaoSupport` class:

```
package com.packt.patterninspring.chapter7.bankapp.dao;

import org.springframework.jdbc.core.support.JdbcDaoSupport;
public class AccountDaoImpl extends JdbcDaoSupport implements
 AccountDao {
  @Override
  public Integer totalAccountsByBranch(String branchName) {
    String sql = "SELECT count(*) FROM Account WHERE branchName =
    "+branchName;
    return this.getJdbcTemplate().queryForObject(sql,
    Integer.class);
  }
}
```

In the preceding code, you can see that the `AccountDaoImpl` class implements the `AccountDao` DAO interface, and it extends Spring's `JdbcDaoSupport` class to ease development with JDBC-based. This class provides a `JdbcTemplate` to its subclasses by using `getJdbcTemplate()`. The `JdbcDaoSupport` class is associated with a data source, and supplies the `JdbcTemplate` object for use in the DAO.

Working with JdbcTemplate

As you learned earlier, Spring's `JdbcTemplate` solves two main problems in the application. It solves the redundant code problem as well as poor exception handling of the data access code in the application. Without `JdbcTemplate` in your application, only 20% of the code is required for querying a row, but 80% is boilerplate which handles exceptions and manages resources. If you use `JdbcTemplate`, then there is no need to worry about the 80% boilerplate code. Spring's `JdbcTemplate`, in a nutshell, is responsible for the following:

- Acquisition of the connection
- Participation in the transaction
- Execution of the statement
- Processing of the result set
- Handling any exceptions
- Release of the connection

Let's see when to use `JdbcTemplate` in the application, and how to create it.

When to use JdbcTemplate

`JdbcTemplate` is useful in standalone applications, and anytime when JDBC is needed. It is suitable in utility or test code to clean up messy legacy code. Also, in any layered application, you can implement a repository or data access object. Let's see how to create it in an application.

Creating a JdbcTemplate in an application

If you want to create an object of the JdbcTemplate class to access data in your Spring application, you need to remember that it requires a DataSource to create the database connection. Let's create a template once, and reuse it. Do not create one for each thread, it is thread-safe after construction:

```
JdbcTemplate template = new JdbcTemplate(dataSource);
```

Let's configure a JdbcTemplate bean in Spring with the following @Bean method:

```
@Bean
public JdbcTemplate jdbcTemplate(DataSource dataSource) {
  return new JdbcTemplate(dataSource);
}
```

In the preceding code, we use the constructor injection to inject the DataSource with the JdbcTemplate bean in the Spring application. The dataSource bean being referenced can be any implementation of javax.sql.DataSource. Let's see how to use the JdbcTemplate bean in your JDBC-based repository to access the database in your application.

Implementing a JDBC-based repository

We can use the Spring's JdbcTemplate class to implement the repositories in a Spring application. Let's see how to implement the repository class based on the JDBC template:

```
package com.packt.patterninspring.chapter7.bankapp.repository;

import java.sql.ResultSet;
import java.sql.SQLException;

import javax.sql.DataSource;

import org.springframework.jdbc.core.JdbcTemplate;
import org.springframework.jdbc.core.RowMapper;
import org.springframework.stereotype.Repository;
import com.packt.patterninspring.chapter7.bankapp.model.Account;
@Repository
public class JdbcAccountRepository implements AccountRepository{
  JdbcTemplate jdbcTemplate;
  public JdbcAccountRepository(DataSource dataSource) {
    super();
    this.jdbcTemplate = new JdbcTemplate(dataSource);
  }
```

```
@Override
public Account findAccountById(Long id){
   String sql = "SELECT * FROM Account WHERE id = "+id;
   return jdbcTemplate.queryForObject(sql,
    new RowMapper<Account>(){
      @Override
      public Account mapRow(ResultSet rs, int arg1) throws
      SQLException {
        Account account = new Account(id);
        account.setName(rs.getString("name"));
        account.setBalance(new Long(rs.getInt("balance")));
        return account;
      }
   });
  }
}
```

In the preceding code, the `DataSource` bean is injected with the `JdbcAccountRepository` class by using the constructor injection. By using this DataSource, we created a `JdbcTemplate` object for accessing the data. The following methods are provided by `JdbcTemplate` to access data from the database:

- `queryForObject(..)`: This is a query for simple java types (`int`, `long`, `String`, `Date` ...) and for custom domain objects.
- `queryForMap(..)`: This is used when expecting a single row. `JdbcTemplate` returns each row of a `ResultSet` as a Map.
- `queryForList(..)`: This is used when expecting multiple rows.

 Note that `queryForInt` and `queryForLong` have been deprecated since Spring 3.2; you can just use `queryForObject` instead (API improved in Spring 3).

Often, it is useful to map relational data into domain objects, for example, a `ResultSet` to an Account in the last code. Spring's `JdbcTemplate` supports this by using a callback approach. Let's discuss Jdbc callback interfaces in the next section.

Jdbc callback interfaces

Spring provides three callback interfaces for JDBC as follows:

- **Implementing RowMapper**: Spring provides a `RowMapper` interface for mapping a single row of a `ResultSet` to an object. It can be used for both single and multiple row queries. It is parameterized as of Spring 3.0:

```
public interface RowMapper<T> {
  T mapRow(ResultSet rs, int rowNum)
  throws SQLException;
}
```

- Let's understand this with the help of an example.

Creating a RowMapper class

In the following example, a class, `AccountRowMapper`, implements the `RowMapper` interface of the Spring Jdbc module:

```
package com.packt.patterninspring.chapter7.bankapp.rowmapper;

import java.sql.ResultSet;
import java.sql.SQLException;
import org.springframework.jdbc.core.RowMapper;
import com.packt.patterninspring.chapter7.bankapp.model.Account;
public class AccountRowMapper implements RowMapper<Account>{
  @Override
  public Account mapRow(ResultSet rs, int id) throws SQLException {
    Account account = new Account();
    account.setId(new Long(rs.getInt("id")));
    account.setName(rs.getString("name"));
    account.setBalance(new Long(rs.getInt("balance")));
    return account;
  }
}
```

In the preceding code, a class, `AccountRowMapper`, maps a row of the result set to the domain object. This row-mapper class implements the `RowMapper` callback interface of the Spring Jdbc module.

Query for single row with JdbcTemplate

Let's now see how the row-mapper maps a single row to the domain object in the application in the following code:

```
public Account findAccountById(Long id){
    String sql = "SELECT * FROM Account WHERE id = "+id;
    return jdbcTemplate.queryForObject(sql, new AccountRowMapper());
}
```

Here, there is no need to add typecasting for the Account object. The `AccountRowMapper` class maps the rows to the Account objects.

Query for multiple rows

The following code shows how the row mapper maps multiple rows to the list of domain objects:

```
public List<Account> findAccountById(Long id){
    String sql = "SELECT * FROM Account ";
    return jdbcTemplate.queryForList(sql, new AccountRowMapper());
}
```

RowMapper is the best choice when each row of a `ResultSet` maps to a domain object.

Implementing RowCallbackHandler

Spring provides a simpler `RowCallbackHandler` interface when there is no return object. It is used to stream rows to a file, converting the rows to XML, and filtering them before adding to a collection. But filtering in SQL is much more efficient, and is faster than the JPA equivalent for big queries. Let's look at the following example:

```
public interface RowCallbackHandler {
    void processRow(ResultSet rs) throws SQLException;
}
```

Example for using a RowCallbackHandler

The following code is an example of a `RowCallbackHandler` in the application:

```
package com.packt.patterninspring.chapter7.bankapp.callbacks;
import java.sql.ResultSet;
import java.sql.SQLException;
import org.springframework.jdbc.core.RowCallbackHandler;
public class AccountReportWriter implements RowCallbackHandler {
    public void processRow(ResultSet resultSet) throws SQLException {
```

```
      // parse current row from ResultSet and stream to output
      //write flat file, XML
   }
}
```

In preceding code, we have created a `RowCallbackHandler` implementation; the `AccountReportWriter` class implements this interface to process the result set returned from the database. Let's see the following code how to use AccountReportWriter call back class:

```
@Override
public void generateReport(Writer out, String branchName) {
   String sql = "SELECT * FROM Account WHERE branchName = "+
    branchName;
   jdbcTemplate.query(sql, new AccountReportWriter());
}
```

`RowCallbackHandler` is the best choice when no value should be returned from the callback method for each row, especially for large queries.

Implementing ResultSetExtractor

Spring provides a `ResultSetExtractor` interface for processing an entire `ResultSet` at once. Here, you are responsible for iterating the `ResultSet`, for example, for mapping the entire `ResultSet` to a single object. Let's see the following example:

```
public interface ResultSetExtractor<T> {
   T extractData(ResultSet rs) throws SQLException,
   DataAccessException;
}
```

Example for using a ResultSetExtractor

The following line of code implements the `ResultSetExtractor` interface in the application:

```
package com.packt.patterninspring.chapter7.bankapp.callbacks;

import java.sql.ResultSet;
import java.sql.SQLException;
import java.util.ArrayList;
import java.util.List;

import org.springframework.dao.DataAccessException;
import org.springframework.jdbc.core.ResultSetExtractor;
```

```
import com.packt.patterninspring.chapter7.bankapp.model.Account;

public class AccountExtractor implements
 ResultSetExtractor<List<Account>> {
   @Override
   public List<Account> extractData(ResultSet resultSet) throws
    SQLException, DataAccessException {
      List<Account> extractedAccounts = null;
      Account account = null;
      while (resultSet.next()) {
        if (extractedAccounts == null) {
          extractedAccounts = new ArrayList<>();
          account = new Account(resultSet.getLong("ID"),
           resultSet.getString("NAME"), ...);
        }
        extractedAccounts.add(account);
      }
      return extractedAccounts;
   }
}
```

This preceding class, `AccountExtractor`, implements `ResultSetExtractor`, and it is used to create an object for the entire data of the result set returned from the database. Let's see how to use this class in your application:

```
public List<Account> extractAccounts() {
   String sql = "SELECT * FROM Account";
   return jdbcTemplate.query(sql, new AccountExtractor());
}
```

The previous code is responsible for accessing all the accounts of a bank, and for preparing a list of accounts by using the `AccountExtractor` class. This class implements the `ResultSetExtractor` callback interface of the Spring Jdbc module.

`ResultSetExtractor` is the best choice when multiple rows of a `ResultSet` map to a single object.

Best practices for Jdbc and configuring JdbcTemplate

Instances of the JdbcTemplate class are thread-safe once configured. As a best practice of configuring the JdbcTemplate in a Spring application, it should be constructed in the constructor injection or setter injection of the data source bean in your DAO classes by passing that data source bean as a constructor argument of the JdbcTemplate class. This leads to DAOs that look, in part, like the following:

```
@Repository
public class JdbcAccountRepository implements AccountRepository{
  JdbcTemplate jdbcTemplate;
  public JdbcAccountRepository(DataSource dataSource) {
    super();
    this.jdbcTemplate = new JdbcTemplate(dataSource);
  }
  //...
}
```

Let's see some best practices to configure a database and write the code for the DAO layer:

- If you want to configure the embedded database at the time of development of the application, as the best practice, the embedded database will always be assigned a uniquely generated name. This is because in the Spring container, the embedded database is made available by configuring a bean of type javax.sql.DataSource, and that data source bean is injected to the data access objects.
- Always use object pooling; this can be achieved in two ways:
  - **Connection pooling**: It allows the pool manager to keep the connections in a *pool* after they are closed
  - **Statement pooling**: It allows the driver to reuse the prepared Statement objects.
    - Choose the commit mode carefully
    - Consider removing the auto-commit mode for your application, and use manual commit instead to better control the commit logic, as follows:

```
Connection.setAutoCommit(false);
```

Summary

An application without data is like a car without fuel. Data is the heart of an application. Some applications may exist in the world without data, but these applications are simply showcase applications such as static blogs. Data is an important part of an application, and you need to develop data-access code for your application. This code should very simple, robust, and customizable.

In a traditional Java application, you could use JDBC to access the data. It is a very basic way, but sometimes, it is very messy to define specifications, handle JDBC exceptions, make database connections, load drivers, and so on. Spring simplifies these things by removing the boilerplate code and simplifying JDBC exception handling. You just write your SQL that should be executed in the application, and the rest is managed by the Spring framework.

In this chapter, you have seen how Spring provides support at the backend for data access and data persistence. JDBC is useful, but using the JDBC API directly is a tedious and error-prone task. `JdbcTemplate` simplifies data access, and enforces consistency. Data access with Spring uses the layered architecture principles-the higher layers should not know about data management. It isolates SQLException via Data Access Exceptions, and creates a hierarchy to make them easier to handle.

6
Improving Application Performance Using Caching Patterns

In previous chapters, we have seen how Spring works in the backend to access data for the application. We also saw how the Spring JDBC Module provides the `JdbcTemplate` helper class for database access. Spring provides support for integration with ORM solutions such as Hibernate, JPA, JDO, and so on, and manages transactions across application. Now, in this chapter, we will see how Spring provides caching support to improve application performance.

Do you ever face a volley of questions from your wife when you return home very late in the night from your office? Yes, I know it is very irritating to answer so many questions when you are tired and exhausted. It is even more irritating when you're asked the same questions over and over again..

Some questions can be answered with a *Yes* or *No*, but for some questions, you have to explain in detail. Consider what will happen if you are asked another lengthy question again after some time! Similarly, there are some stateless components in an application, where the components have been designed in such a way that they ask the same questions over and over again to complete each task individually. Similar to some questions asked by your wife, some questions in the system take a while to fetch the appropriate data--it may have some major complex logic behind it, or maybe, it has to fetch data from the database, or call a remote service.

If we know that the answer of a question is not likely to change frequently, we can remember the answer to that question for later when it is asked again by the same system. It doesn't make sense to go through the same channel to fetch it again, as it will impact your application's performance, and will be a wasteful use of your resources. In an enterprise application, caching is a way to store those frequently needed answers so that we fetch from the cache instead of going through the proper channel to get the answer for the same question over and over again. In this chapter, we will discuss Spring's Cache Abstraction feature, and how Spring declaratively supports caching implementation. It will cover the following points:

- What is a cache?
- Where do we do this caching?
- Understanding the cache abstraction
- Enabling caching via the Proxy pattern
- Declarative Annotation-based caching
- Declarative XML-based caching
- Configuring the cache storage
- Implementing custom cache annotations
- Caching best practices

Let's begin.

What is cache?

In very simple terms, **cache** is a memory block where we store preprocessed information for the application. In this context, a key-value storage, such as a map, may be a cache in the application. In Spring, cache is an interface to abstract and represent caching. A cache interface provides some methods for placing objects into a cache storage, it can retrieve from the cache storage for given key, it can update the object in the cache storage for a given key, it remove the object from the cache storage for a given key. This cache interface provides many functions to operate with cache.

Where do we use caching?

We use caching in cases where a method always returns the same result for the same argument(s). This method could do anything such as calculate data on the fly, execute a database query, and request data via RMI, JMS, and a web-service, and so on. A unique key must be generated from the arguments. That's the cache key.

Understanding cache abstraction

Basically, caching in Java applications is applied to the Java methods to reduce the number of executions for the same information available in the cache. That means, whenever these Java methods are invoked, the cache abstraction applies the cache behavior to these methods based on the given arguments. If the information for the given argument is already available in the cache, then it is returned without having to execute the target method. If the required information is not available in the cache, then the `target` method is executed, and the result is cached and returned to the caller. Cache abstraction also provides other cache-related operations such as updating and/or removing the contents in the cache. These operations are useful when the data changes in the application sometimes.

Spring Framework provides cache abstraction for Spring applications by using the `org.springframework.cache.Cache` and `org.springframework.cache.CacheManager` interfaces. Caching requires the use of an actual storage to store the cache data. But cache abstraction only provides caching logic. It doesn't provide any physical storage to store the cached data. So, developers need to implement the actual storage for caching in the application. If you have a distributed application, then you will need to configure your cache provider accordingly. It depends on the use cases of your application. You can either make a copy of the same data across nodes for a distributed application, or you can make a centralized cache.

There are several cache providers in the market, which you could use as per as your application requirement. Some of them are as follows:

- Redis
- `OrmLiteCacheClient`
- `Memcached`
- In Memory Cache
- Aws DynamoDB Cache Client
- Azure Cache Client

To implement cache abstraction in your application, you have to take care of the following tasks:

- **Caching declaration**: This means that you have to recognize those methods in the application that need to be cached, and annotate these methods either with caching annotations, or you can use XML configuration by using Spring AOP
- **Cache configuration**: This means that you have to configure the actual storage for the cached data--the storage where the data is stored and read from

Let's now see how we can enable Spring's cache abstraction in a Spring application.

Enabling caching via the Proxy pattern

You can enable Spring's cache abstraction in the following two ways:

- Using Annotation
- Using the XML namespace

Spring transparently applies caching to the methods of Spring beans by using AOP. Spring applies proxy around the Spring beans where you declare the methods that need to be cached. This proxy adds the dynamic behavior of caching to the Spring beans. The following diagram illustrates the caching behavior:

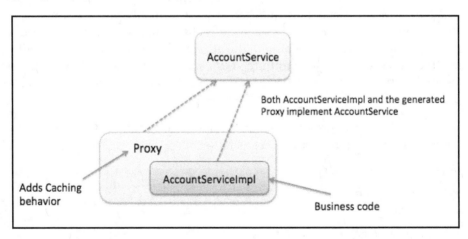

In the preceding diagram, you can see that Spring applies **Proxy** to the **AccountServiceImpl** class to add the caching behavior. Spring uses the GoF proxy pattern to implement caching in the application.

Let's look at how to enable this feature in a Spring application.

Enabling the caching proxy using Annotation

As you already know, Spring provides lots of features, but they are, mostly, disabled. You must enable these feature before using it. If you want to use Spring's cache abstraction in your application, you have to enable this feature. If you are using Java configuration, you can enable cache abstraction of Spring by adding the @EnableCaching annotation to one of your configuration classes. The following configuration class shows the @EnableCaching annotation:

```
package com.packt.patterninspring.chapter9.bankapp.config;

import org.springframework.cache.CacheManager;
import org.springframework.cache.annotation.EnableCaching;
import org.springframework.cache.concurrent.
  ConcurrentMapCacheManager;
import org.springframework.context.annotation.Bean;
import org.springframework.context.annotation.ComponentScan;
import org.springframework.context.annotation.Configuration;

@Configuration
@ComponentScan(basePackages=
{"com.packt.patterninspring.chapter9.bankapp"})
@EnableCaching //Enable caching
public class AppConfig {
  @Bean
  public AccountService accountService() { ... }

  //Declare a cache manager
  @Bean
  public CacheManager cacheManager() {
      CacheManager cacheManager = new ConcurrentMapCacheManager();
      return cacheManager;
  }
}
```

In the preceding Java configuration file, we added the @EnableCaching annotation to the configuration class AppConfig.java; this annotation indicates to the Spring Framework to enable Spring cache behavior for the application.

Let's now look at how to enable Spring's cache abstraction by using XML configuration.

Enabling the Caching Proxy using the XML namespace

If you're configuring your application with XML, you can enable annotation-driven caching with the `<cache:annotation-driven>` element from Spring's cache namespace, as follows:

```xml
<?xml version="1.0" encoding="UTF-8"?>
<beans xmlns="http://www.springframework.org/schema/beans"
  xmlns:xsi="http://www.w3.org/2001/XMLSchema-instance"
  xmlns:context="http://www.springframework.org/schema/context"
  xmlns:jdbc="http://www.springframework.org/schema/jdbc"
  xmlns:tx="http://www.springframework.org/schema/tx"
  xmlns:aop="http://www.springframework.org/schema/aop"
  xmlns:cache="http://www.springframework.org/schema/cache"
  xsi:schemaLocation="http://www.springframework.org/schema/jdbc
  http://www.springframework.org/schema/jdbc/spring-jdbc-4.3.xsd
  http://www.springframework.org/schema/cache
  http://www.springframework.org/schema/cache/spring-cache-4.3.xsd
  http://www.springframework.org/schema/beans
  http://www.springframework.org/schema/beans/spring-beans.xsd
  http://www.springframework.org/schema/context
  http://www.springframework.org/schema/context/spring-context.xsd
  http://www.springframework.org/schema/aop
  http://www.springframework.org/schema/aop/spring-aop-4.3.xsd
  http://www.springframework.org/schema/tx
  http://www.springframework.org/schema/tx/spring-tx-4.3.xsd">
  <!-- Enable caching -->
  <cache:annotation-driven />
  <context:component-scan base-
  package="com.packt.patterninspring.chapter9.bankapp"/>
  <!-- Declare a cache manager -->
  <bean id="cacheManager"
  class="org.springframework.cache.concurrent.
  ConcurrentMapCacheManager" />
</beans>
```

As seen in the preceding configuration files, whether you use Java configuration or XML configuration, the annotation @EnableCaching and namespace `<cache:annotation-driven>` enables Spring's cache abstraction by creating an aspect with pointcuts that trigger off of Spring's caching annotations.

Let's see how to use Spring's caching annotations to define cache boundaries.

Declarative Annotation-based caching

In Spring applications, Spring's abstraction provides the following Annotations for caching declaration:

- @Cacheable: This indicates that before execution of the actual method, look at the return value of that method in the cache. If the value is available, return this cached value, if the value is not available, then invoke the actual method, and put the returned value into the cache.
- @CachePut: This updates the cache without checking if the value is available or not. It always invokes the actual method.
- @CacheEvict: This is responsible for triggering cache eviction.
- @Caching: This is used for grouping multiple annotations to be applied on a method at once.
- @CacheConfig: This indicates to Spring to share some common cache-related settings at the class level.

Let us now take a closer look at each annotation.

The @Cacheable annotation

@Cacheable marks a method for caching. Its result is stored in a cache. For all subsequent invocations of that method with the same arguments, it will fetch data from the cache using a key. The method will not be executed. The following are the @Cacheable attributes:

- **value**: This is the name of cache to use
- **key**: This is the key for each cached data item
- **condition**: This is a SpEL expression to evaluate true or false; if it is false, then the result of caching is not applied to the method call
- **unless**: This too is a SpEL expression; if it is true, it prevents the return value from being put in the cache

You can use SpEL and argument(s) of method. Let's look at the following code for the simplest declaration of the @Cacheable annotation. It requires the name of the cache associated with that method. Please refer to the following code:

```
@Cacheable("accountCache ")
public Account findAccount(Long accountId) {...}
```

In the preceding code, the `findAccount` method is annotated with the `@Cacheable` annotation. This means that this method is associated with a cache. The name of the cache is **accountCache**. Whenever this method is called for a particular `accountId`, the cache is checked for the return value of this method for the given `accountId`. You can also give multiple names to the cache as shown next:

```
@Cacheable({"accountCache ", "saving-accounts"})
public Account findAccount(Long accountId) {...}
```

The @CachePut annotation

As mentioned earlier, the `@Cacheable` and `@CachePut` annotations both have the same goal, that is, to populate a cache. But their working is slightly different from each other. `@CachePut` marks a method for caching, and its result is stored in a cache. For each invocation of that method with the same arguments, it always invokes the actual method without checking whether the return value of that method is available in the cache or not. The following are `@CachePut` attributes:

- **value**: This is the name of the cache to use
- **key**: This is the key for each cached data item
- **condition**: This is a SpEL expression to evaluate true or false; if false, then the result of caching is not applied to the method call
- **unless**: This is also a SpEL expression; if it is true, it prevents the return value from being put in the cache

You can also use SpEL and argument(s) of method for the `@CachePut` annotation. The following code is the simplest declaration of the `@CachePut` annotation:

```
@CachePut("accountCache ")
public Account save(Account account) {...}
```

In the preceding code, when `save()` is invoked, it saves the `Account`. Then the returned Account is placed in the `accountCache` cache.

As mentioned earlier, the cache is populated by the method based on the argument of the method. It is actually a default cache key. In case of the `@Cachable` annotation, the `findAccount(Long accountId)` method has `accountId` as an argument, the `accountId` is used as the cache key for this method. But in case of the `@CachePut` annotation, the only parameter of `save()` is an Account. It is used as the cache key. It doesn't seem fine to use `Account` as a cache key. In this case, you need the cache key to be the ID of the newly saved Account and not the Account itself. So, you need to customize the key generation behavior. Let's see how you can customize the cache key.

Customizing the cache key

You can customize the cache key by using a key attribute of `@Cacheable` and the `@CachePut` annotation. The cache key is derived by a SpEL expression using properties of the object as highlighted key attribute in the following snippet of code. Let's look at the following examples:

```
@Cacheable(cacheNames=" accountCache ", key="#accountId")
public Account findAccount(Long accountId)

@Cacheable(cacheNames=" accountCache ", key="#account.accountId")
public Account findAccount(Account account)

@CachePut(value=" accountCache ", key="#account.accountId")
Account save(Account account);
```

You can see in the preceding code snippets how we have created the cache key by using the key attribute of the `@Cacheable` annotation.

Let's see another attribute of these annotations in a Spring application.

Conditional caching

Spring's caching annotations allow you to turn off caching for some cases by using the condition attribute of `@Cacheable` and `@CachePut` annotations. These are given a SpEL expression to evaluate the conditional value. If the value of the conditional expression is true, the method is cached. If the value of the conditional expression is false, the method is not cached, but is executed every time without performing any caching operations no matter what values in the cache or what arguments are used. Let's see an example. The following method will be cached only if the passed argument has a value greater than or equal to `2000`:

```
@Cacheable(cacheNames="accountCache", condition="#accountId >=
2000")
public Account findAccount(Long accountId);
```

There is a one more attribute of the `@Cacheable` and `@CachePut` annotations-- `unless`. This is also given a SpEL expression. This attribute may seem the same as the condition attribute but there is some difference between them. Unlike condition, the `unless` expressions are evaluated after the method has been called. It prevents the value from being placed in the cache. Let's see the following example--We only want to cache when the bank name does not contain HDFC:

```
@Cacheable(cacheNames="accountCache", condition="#accountId >=
2000", unless="#result.bankName.contains('HDFC')")
public Account findAccount(Long accountId);
```

As you can see in the preceding code snippet, we have used both attributes--`condition` and `unless`. But the `unless` attribute has a SpEL expression as `#result.bankName.contains('HDFC')`. In this expression, the result is a SpEL extension or cache SpEL metadata. The following is a list of the caching metadata that is available in SpEL:

Expression	Description
`#root.methodName`	The name of the cached method
`#root.method`	The cached method, that is, the method being invoked
`#root.target`	It evaluates the target object being invoked
`#root.targetClass`	It evaluates the class of the target object being invoked
`#root.caches`	An array of caches against which the current method is executed
`#root.args`	An array of the arguments passed into the cached method
`#result`	The return value from the cached method; only available in unless expressions for `@CachePut`

Spring's @CachePut and @Cacheable annotations should never be used on the same method, because they have different behaviors. The @CachePut annotation forces the execution of the cache method in order to update the caches. But the @Cacheable annotation executes the cached method only if the return value of the method is not available on the cache.

You have seen how to add information to the cache by using Spring's @CachePut and @Cacheable annotations in a Spring application. But how can we remove that information from the cache? Spring's cache abstraction provides another annotation for removing cached data from the cache--the @CacheEvict annotation. Let's see how to remove the cached data from the cache by using the @CacheEvict annotation.

The @CacheEvict annotation

Spring's cache abstraction not only allows populating caches, but also allows removing the cached data from the cache. There is a stage in the application where you have to remove stale or unused data from the cache. In that case, you can use the @CacheEvict annotation, because it doesn't add anything to the cache unlike the @Cacheable annotation. The @CacheEvict annotation is used only to perform cache eviction. Let's see how this annotation makes the remove() method of AccountRepository as a cache eviction:

```
@CacheEvict("accountCache ")
void remove(Long accountId);
```

As you can see in the preceding code snippet, the value associated with the argument, accountId, is removed from the accountCache cache when the remove() method is invoked. The following are @Cacheable attributes:

- **value**: This is an array of names of the cache to use
- **key**: This is a SpEL expression to evaluate the cache key to be used
- **condition**: This is a SpEL expression to evaluate true or false; if it is false, then the result of caching is not being applied to the method call
- **allEntries**: This implies that if the value of this attribute is true, all entries will be removed from the caches

- **beforeInvocation**: This means that if the value of this attribute is true, the entries are removed from the cache before the method is invoked, and if the value of this attribute is false (the default), the entries are removed after a successful method invocation

> We can use the `@CacheEvict` annotation on any method, even a `void` one, because it only removes the value from the cache. But in case of the `@Cacheable` and `@CachePut` annotations, we have to use a non-void return value method, because these annotations require a result to be cached.

The @Caching annotation

Spring's cache abstraction allows you to use multiple annotations of the same type for caching a method by using the `@Caching` annotation in a Spring application. The `@Caching` annotation groups other annotations such as `@Cacheable`, `@CachePut`, and `@CacheEvict` for the same method. For example:

```
@Caching(evict = {
  @CacheEvict("accountCache "),
  @CacheEvict(value="account-list", key="#account.accountId") })
  public List<Account> findAllAccount(){
  return (List<Account>) accountRepository.findAll();
}
```

The @CacheConfig annotation

Spring's cache abstraction allows you to annotate `@CacheConfig` at the class level to avoid repeated mentioning in each method. In some cases, applying customizations of the caches to all methods can be quite tedious. Here, you can use the `@CacheConfig` annotation to all operations of the class. For example:

```
@CacheConfig("accountCache ")
public class AccountServiceImpl implements AccountService {

  @Cacheable
  public Account findAccount(Long accountId) {
    return (Account) accountRepository.findOne(accountId);
  }
}
```

You can see in the preceding code snippet that the `@CacheConfig` annotation is used at the class level, and it allows you to share the `accountCache` cache with all the `cacheable` methods.

 Since Spring's cache abstraction module uses proxies, you should use the cache annotations only with public visibility methods. In all non-public methods, these annotations do not raise any error, but non-public methods annotated with these annotations do not show any caching behaviors.

We have already seen that Spring also offers XML namespace to configure and implement cache in a Spring application. Let's see how in the next section.

Declarative XML-based caching

To keep your configuration codes of caching separate from business codes, and to maintain loose coupling between the Spring-specific annotations and your source code, XML-based caching configuration is much more elegant than the annotation-based one. So, to configure Spring cache with XML, let's use the cache namespace along with the AOP namespace, because caching is an AOP activity, and it uses the Proxy pattern behind the declarative caching behavior.

```xml
<?xml version="1.0" encoding="UTF-8"?>
<beans xmlns="http://www.springframework.org/schema/beans"
 xmlns:xsi="http://www.w3.org/2001/XMLSchema-instance"
 xmlns:context="http://www.springframework.org/schema/context"
 xmlns:aop="http://www.springframework.org/schema/aop"
 xmlns:cache="http://www.springframework.org/schema/cache"
 xsi:schemaLocation="http://www.springframework.org/schema/cache
 http://www.springframework.org/schema/cache/spring-cache-4.3.xsd
 http://www.springframework.org/schema/beans
 http://www.springframework.org/schema/beans/spring-beans.xsd
 http://www.springframework.org/schema/context
 http://www.springframework.org/schema/context/spring-context.xsd
 http://www.springframework.org/schema/aop
 http://www.springframework.org/schema/aop/spring-aop-4.3.xsd">
 <!-- Enable caching -->
 <cache:annotation-driven />
 <!-- Declare a cache manager -->
 <bean id="cacheManager"class="org.springframework.cache.
 concurrent.ConcurrentMapCacheManager" />
</beans>
```

You can see in the preceding XML file that we have included the `cache` and `aop` namespaces. The cache namespace defines the caching configurations by using the following elements:

XML element	Caching Description
`<cache:annotation-driven>`	It is equivalent to `@EnableCaching` in Java configuration, and is used to enable the caching behavior of Spring.
`<cache:advice>`	It defines caching advice
`<cache:caching>`	It is equivalent to the `@Caching` annotation, and is used to group a set of caching rules within the caching advice
`<cache:cacheable>`	It is equivalent to the `@Cacheable` annotation; it makes any method cacheable
`<cache:cache-put>`	It is equivalent to the `@CachePut` annotation, and is used to populate a cache
`<cache:cache-evict>`	It is equivalent to the `@CacheEvict` annotation, and is used for cache eviction.

Let's see the following example based on XML-based configuration.

Create a configuration file, `spring.xml` as follows:

```xml
<?xml version="1.0" encoding="UTF-8"?>
<beans xmlns="http://www.springframework.org/schema/beans"
xmlns:xsi="http://www.w3.org/2001/XMLSchema-instance"
xmlns:context="http://www.springframework.org/schema/context"
xmlns:aop="http://www.springframework.org/schema/aop"
xmlns:cache="http://www.springframework.org/schema/cache"
xsi:schemaLocation="http://www.springframework.org/schema/cache
http://www.springframework.org/schema/cache/spring-cache-4.3.xsd
http://www.springframework.org/schema/beans
http://www.springframework.org/schema/beans/spring-beans.xsd
http://www.springframework.org/schema/context
http://www.springframework.org/schema/context/spring-context.xsd
http://www.springframework.org/schema/aop
http://www.springframework.org/schema/aop/spring-aop-4.3.xsd">
<context:component-scan base-
package="com.packt.patterninspring.chapter9.bankapp.service,
com.packt.patterninspring.chapter9.bankapp.repository"/>

<aop:config>
<aop:advisor advice-ref="cacheAccount" pointcut="execution(*
com.packt.patterninspring.chapter9.bankapp.service.*.*(..))"/>
</aop:config>
<cache:advice id="cacheAccount">
```

```
<cache:caching>
  <cache:cacheable cache="accountCache" method="findOne" />
    <cache:cache-put cache="accountCache" method="save"
    key="#result.id" />
    <cache:cache-evict cache="accountCache" method="remove" />
    </cache:caching>
  </cache:advice>

<!-- Declare a cache manager -->
<bean id="cacheManager" class="org.springframework.cache.concurrent.
ConcurrentMapCacheManager" />
</beans>
```

In the preceding XML configuration file, the highlighted code is the Spring cache configuration. In the cache configuration, the first thing that you see is the declared `<aop:config>` then `<aop:advisor>`, which have references to the advice whose ID is cacheAccount, and also has a pointcut expression to match the advice. The advice is declared with the `<cache:advice>` element. This element can have many `<cache:caching>` elements. But, in our example, we have only one `<cache:caching>` element, which has a `<cache:cacheable>` element, a `<cache:cache-put>`, and one `<cache:cache-evict>` element; each declare a method from the pointcut as being cacheable.

Let's see the Service class of the application with cache annotations:

```
package com.packt.patterninspring.chapter9.bankapp.service;

import org.springframework.beans.factory.annotation.Autowired;
import org.springframework.cache.annotation.CacheEvict;
import org.springframework.cache.annotation.CachePut;
import org.springframework.cache.annotation.Cacheable;
import org.springframework.stereotype.Service;

import com.packt.patterninspring.chapter9.bankapp.model.Account;
import com.packt.patterninspring.chapter9.
bankapp.repository.AccountRepository;

@Service
public class AccountServiceImpl implements AccountService{
@Autowired
AccountRepository accountRepository;

@Override
@Cacheable("accountCache")
public Account findOne(Long id) {
  System.out.println("findOne called");
```

```
        return accountRepository.findAccountById(id);
    }

    @Override
    @CachePut("accountCache")
    public Long save(Account account) {
        return accountRepository.save(account);
    }

    @Override
    @CacheEvict("accountCache")
    public void remove(Long id) {
        accountRepository.findAccountById(id);
    }
}
```

In the preceding file definition, we have used Spring's cache annotations to create the cache in the application. Now let's see how to configure the cache storage in an application.

Configuring the cache storage

Spring's cache abstraction provides a lot of storage integration. Spring provides CacheManager for each memory storage. You can just configure CacheManager with the application. Then the CacheManager is responsible for controlling and managing the Caches. Let's explore how to set up the CacheManager in an application.

Setting up the CacheManager

You must specify a cache manager in the application for storage, and some cache provider given to the CacheManager, or you can write your own CacheManager. Spring provides several cache managers in the org.springframework.cache package, for example, ConcurrentMapCacheManager, which creates a ConcurrentHashMap for each cache storage unit.

```
    @Bean
    public CacheManager cacheManager() {
        CacheManager cacheManager = new ConcurrentMapCacheManager();
        return cacheManager;
    }
```

`SimpleCacheManager`, `ConcurrentMapCacheManager`, and others are cache managers of the Spring Framework's cache abstraction. But Spring provides support for integration with third-party cache managers, as we will see in the following section.

Third-party cache implementations

Spring's `SimpleCacheManager` is ok for testing, but has no cache control options (overflow, eviction). So we have to use third-party alternatives like the following:

- Terracotta's EhCache
- Google's Guava and Caffeine
- Pivotal's Gemfire

Let's see one of the configurations of third-party cache managers.

Ehcache-based cache

Ehcache is one of the most popular cache providers. Spring allows you to integrate with Ehcache by configuring `EhCacheCacheManager` in the application. Take for example, the following Java configuration:

```
@Bean
public CacheManager cacheManager(CacheManager ehCache) {
  EhCacheCacheManager cmgr = new EhCacheCacheManager();
  cmgr.setCacheManager(ehCache);
  return cmgr;
}
@Bean
public EhCacheManagerFactoryBean ehCacheManagerFactoryBean() {
  EhCacheManagerFactoryBean eh = new EhCacheManagerFactoryBean();
  eh.setConfigLocation(new
  ClassPathResource("resources/ehcache.xml"));
  return eh;
}
```

In the preceding code, the bean method, `cacheManager()`, creates an object of `EhCacheCacheManager`, and set it with the `CacheManager` of Ehcache. Here, Ehcache's `CacheManager` is injected into Spring's `EhCacheCacheManager`. The second bean method, `ehCacheManagerFactoryBean()`, creates and returns an instance of `EhCacheManagerFactoryBean`. Because it's a Factory bean, it will return an instance of `CacheManager`. An XML file, `ehcache.xml`, has the Ehcache configuration. Let's refer to the following code for `ehcache.xml`:

```xml
<ehcache>
    <cache name="accountCache" maxBytesLocalHeap="50m"
     timeToLiveSeconds="100">
    </cache>
</ehcache>
```

The contents of the `ehcache.xml` file vary from application to application, but you need to declare, at least, a minimal cache. For example, the following Ehcache configuration declares a cache named **accountCache** with 50 MB of maximum heap storage and a time-to-live of 100 seconds:

XML-based configuration

Let's create XML based configuration for the Eache, and it is configuring here `EhCacheCacheManager`. Please refer to the following code:

```xml
<bean id="cacheManager"
 class="org.springframework.cache.ehcache.EhCacheCacheManager"
 p:cache-manager-ref="ehcache"/>

<!-- EhCache library setup -->
<bean id="ehcache"
  class="org.springframework.cache.ehcache.
  EhCacheManagerFactoryBean" p:config-
  location="resources/ehcache.xml"/>
```

Similarly, in case of the XML configuration, you have to configure the cache manager for ehcache, configure the `EhCacheManagerFactoryBean` class, and set the config-location value with `ehcache.xml`, which has the Ehcache configuration as defined in the previous section.

There are many more third-party caching storages which have integration support with the Spring Framework. In this chapter, I have discussed only the ECache manager.

In the following section, we'll discuss how Spring allows you to create your own custom annotation for caching.

Creating custom caching annotations

Spring's cache abstraction allows you to create custom caching annotations for your application to recognize the cache method for the cache population or cache eviction. Spring's @Cacheable and @CacheEvict annotations are used as Meta annotations to create custom cache annotation. Let's see the following code for custom annotations in an application:

```
@Retention(RetentionPolicy.RUNTIME)
@Target({ElementType.METHOD})
@Cacheable(value="accountCache", key="#account.id")
public @interface SlowService {
}
```

In the preceding code snippet, we have defined a custom annotation named as SlowService, which is annotated with Spring's @Cacheable annotation. If we use @Cacheable in the application, then we have to configure it as the following code:

```
@Cacheable(value="accountCache", key="#account.id")
public Account findAccount(Long accountId)
```

Let's replace the preceding configuration with our defined custom annotation, with the following code:

```
@SlowService
public Account findAccount(Long accountId)
```

As you can see, we use only the @SlowService annotation to make a method cacheable in the application.

Now let's move on to the next section, where we'll see which are the best practices we should consider at the time of cache implementation in anapplication.

Top caching best practices to be used in a web application

In your enterprise web application, proper use of caching enables the web page to be rendered very fast, minimizes the database hits, and reduces the consumption of the server's resources such as memory, network, and so on. Caching is a very powerful technique to boost your application's performance by storing stale data in the cache memory. The following are the best practices which should be considered at the time of design and development of a web application:

- In your Spring web application, Spring's cache annotations such as `@Cacheable`, `@CachePut`, and `@CacheEvict` should be used on concrete classes instead of application interfaces. However, you can annotate the interface method as well, using interface-based proxies. Remember that Java annotations are not inherited from interfaces, which means that if you are using class-based proxies by setting the attribute `proxy-target-class="true"`, then Spring cache annotations are not recognized by the proxying.
- If you have annotated any method with the `@Cacheable`, @CachePut, or `@CacheEvict` annotations, then never call it directly by another method of the same class if you want to benefit from the cache in the application. This is because in direct calling of a cached method, the Spring AOP proxy is never applied.
- In an enterprise application, Java Maps or any key/value collections should never be used as a Cache. Any key/value collection cannot be a Cache. Sometimes, developers use java map as a custom caching solution, but it is not a caching solution, because Cache provides more than a key/value storage, like the following:
  - Cache provides eviction policies
  - You can set the max size limit of Cache
  - Cache provides a persistent store
  - Cache provides weak reference keys
  - Cache provides statistics
    - The Spring Framework provides the best declarative approach to implement and configure the Cache solution in an application. So, always use the cache abstraction layer--it provides flexibility in the application. We know that the `@Cacheable` annotation allows you to separate business logic code from the caching cross-cutting concern.

- Be careful whenever you use cache in the application. Always use cache in a place where it is actually required such as a web service or an expensive database call, because every caching API has an overhead.

- At the time of cache implementation in an application, you have to ensure that the data in the cache is in sync with the data storage. You can use distributed cache managers like Memcached for proper cache strategy implementation to provide considerable performance.

- You should use cache only as second option if data fetching is very difficult from the database because of slow database queries. It is because, whenever we use caching behavior in the application, first the value is checked in the cache if not available then it execute actual method, so it would be unnecessary.

- In this chapter, we saw how caching helps to improve the performance of anapplication. Caching mostly works on the service layer of the application. In your application, there is a data returned by a method; we can cache that data if the application code calls it over and over again from the same requirement. Caching is a great way to avoid execution of the application method for the same requirements. The return value of the method for a specific parameter is stored in a cache whenever this method is invoked for the first time. For further calls of the same method for same parameter, the value is retrieved from that cache. Caching improves application performance by avoiding some resource and time consuming operations for same answers like performing a database query.

Summary

Spring provides Cache Manager to manage caching in a Spring application. In this chapter, you have seen how to define the caching manager for a particular caching technology. Spring provides some annotations for caching such as `@Cacheable`, `@CachePut`, and `@CacheEvict`, which we can use in our Spring application. We can also configure caching in the Spring application by using the XML configuration. Spring framework provides cache namespace to achieve this. The `<cache:cacheable>`, `<cache:cache-put>`, and `<cache:cache-evict>` elements are used instead of the corresponding annotations.

Spring makes it possible to manage caching in anapplication by using Aspect-Oriented Programming. Caching is a cross-cutting concern for the Spring Framework. That means, caching is as an aspect in the Spring application. Spring implements caching by using around advice of the Spring AOP module.

Implementing Reactive Design Patterns

7

In this chapter, we will explore one of the most important features of the Spring 5 Framework, which is reactive pattern programming. The Spring 5 Framework introduced this new feature with the Spring web reactive module. We will discuss this module in this chapter. Before that, let's have a look at reactive patterns. What is the reactive pattern, and why is it growing more popular nowadays? I will start my discussion on reactive pattern with the following statement made by **Satya Nadella**, CEO, Microsoft Corporation:

> *Every business out there now is a software company, is a digital company.*

The topics we will cover here are as follows:

- Why reactive pattern?
- The reactive pattern principles
- Blocking calls
- Non-blocking calls
- Back-pressure
- Implementing the reactive pattern using the Spring Framework
- The Spring web reactive module

Understanding application requirement over the years

If you go back 10 to 15 years, there were very few internet users, and far less online portals for end users compared to what we have today. Nowadays, we cannot think of a life without a computer or without any online system. In short, we have become extremely dependent on computers and online computing for personal as well as business use. Every business model is moving towards digitalization. The Prime Minister of India, Mr. Narendra Damodardas Modi has launched a Digital India campaign to ensure that the Government's services are made available to citizens electronically by improved online infrastructure, increasing internet connectivity, and by making the country digitally empowered in the field of technology.

All this implies that the number of internet users is increasing dramatically. According to the Ericsson Mobility Report,

> *The Internet of Things (IoT) is expected to surpass mobile phones as the largest category of connected devices in 2018.*

There has been a tremendous growth of mobile internet users, and there is no sign of that slowing down anytime soon. In these sectors, by definition, the server side has to handle millions of connected devices concurrently. The following table compares the infrastructure and application requirements today with the requirement from 10 years back:

RequirementsNowTen years ago

Server nodes	More than 1000 nodes required.	Ten nodes were enough.
Response times	Takes milliseconds to serve requests, and send back responses.	Took seconds to response.
Maintenance downtimes	Currently, there is no or zero maintenance downtime required.	Took hours of maintenance downtime.
Data volume	Data for the current application that increased to TBs from PBs.	Data was in GBs.

You can see the differences in the requirement of resources in the preceding table. These requirements have increased, because we now expect responses immediately, within the second. At the same time, the complexity of tasks given to computers have also increased. These tasks are not just pure computation in a mathematical sense, but also in requesting the responses to be distilled from enormous amounts of data. So, now we have to focus the performance of such systems by designing a single computer in the form of multi-core CPUs, possibly, combined in multi-socket servers. The first thing on our minds is to make the system responsive. It is the first of the reactive traits-responsiveness. We will explore more of this in this chapter, along with the following topics:

- Why reactive pattern
- Reactive pattern principles
- Blocking calls
- Non-blocking calls
- Back-pressure
- Implementing reactive pattern using the Spring Framework
- Spring Web reactive module
- Implementing reactive at server side
- Implementing reactive at client side
- Request and response body type conversion

This chapter will teach you how to make a system responsive in the face of any variable load, partial outages, program failure, and more. Nowadays, systems are distributed across different nodes to efficiently serve requests.

Let's look at the aforementioned topics in detail.

Understanding the reactive pattern

Today, the modern applications must be more robust, more resilient, more flexible, and better positioned to meet the requirements of the organizations, because, in the recent couple of years, the requirements for applications have changed dramatically. As we have seen in the last table, 10 to 15 years ago, a large application had 10 server nodes, the response time taken to serve a request was in seconds, we required a couple of hours of downtime for maintenance and deployment, and the data was in gigabytes. But today, an application requires thousands of server nodes, because it is accessed by multiple channels such as mobile devices. The server responses are expected within milliseconds, and the downtime for deployment and maintenance is near to 0%. Data has been increased from terabytes to petabytes.

Ten-year old systems cannot fulfill the requirements of today's applications; we need a system that can fulfill all user's requirements either at the application level or the system level, which means we need a responsive system. Responsiveness is one of the properties of the reactive pattern. We want a system that must be responsive, resilient, elastic, and message-driven. We know these systems as reactive systems. These systems are more flexible, loosely-coupled, and scalable.

A system must react to failure and stay available, that is, it should be resilient, and the system must react to variable load conditions, and not be overloaded. The system should react to events--event-driven or message-driven. If all these properties are associated with a system, then it will be responsive, that is, if a system reacts to its users, it is responsive. To create a reactive system, we must focus on the system level and application level. Let's see first the all reactive traits.

The reactive pattern traits

The following are the principles of the Reactive pattern:

- **Responsive**: This is the goal of each application today.
- **Resilient**: This is required to make an application responsive.
- **Scalable**: This is also required to make an application responsive; without resilience and scalability, it is impossible to achieve responsiveness.
- **Message-driven**: A message-driven architecture is the base of a scalable and resilient application, and ultimately, it makes a system responsive. Message-driven either based on the event-driven or actor-based programming model.

The preceding points mentioned are core principles of the reactive pattern. Let's explore each principle of the reactive pattern in detail, and understand why all of them must be applied together in order to make a reactive system with quality software for a modern context application, which is able to handle millions of parallel requests in milliseconds without any failure. Let's first understand these principles with the following diagram:

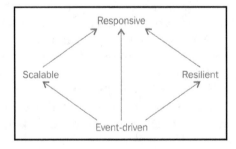

As you can see in the preceding diagram, to make a system reactive, we need scalability and resilience. To make a system scalable and resilient, we need an event-driven or message-driven architecture of the application. Ultimately, these principles, scalability, resilience, and event-driven architecture make a system responsive to the client. Let's see these properties in detail.

Responsiveness

When we say that a system or an application is responsive, it means that the application or system responds quickly to all users in a given time in all conditions, and that is in good condition as well as bad. It ensures a consistent positive user experience.

Responsiveness is required for a system for usability and utility. A responsive system means that up on system failure, either because of an external system or a spike in traffic, the failures are detected quickly, and dealt with effectively in a short time without the users knowing of the failure. An end user must be able to interact with the system by providing rapid and consistent response times. A user must not face any failure during interaction with the system, and it must deliver a consistent quality of service to the user. That consistent behavior solves the failures and builds end-user confidence in the system. Quickness and a positive user experience under various conditions make a system responsive. It depends on the two other traits of a reactive application or system, that is, resilience and scalability. Another trait, that is, event-driven or message-driven architecture, provides the overall foundation for a responsive system. The following diagram illustrates a responsive system:

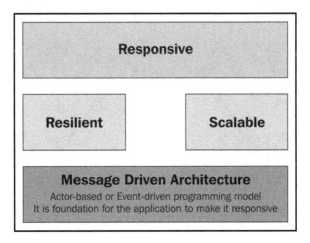

As you can see in the preceding diagram, a responsive system depends on resilient and scalability of the system, and these depend on its event-driven architecture. Let's look at the other traits of a reactive application.

Resilience

When we design and develop a system, we have consider all conditions--good and bad. If we consider only the good conditions, then we tend to implement a system that may fail after just a few days. A major application failure results in downtime and data loss and damages your application's reputation in the market.

So, we have to focus on every condition to ensure the responsiveness of the application under all conditions. Such a system or application is known as a resilient system.

Every system must be resilient to ensure responsiveness. If a system is not resilient, it will be unresponsive after a failure. So, a system must be responsive in the face of failure as well. In the whole system, failure can exist in any component of the application or system. So, each component in the system must be isolated from each other so that at the time of failure of a component, we can recover it without compromising the system as a whole. Recovery of an individual component is achieved by replication. If a system is resilient, then it must have replication, containment, isolation, and delegation. Take a look at the following diagram, which illustrates the resilient traits of a reactive application or system:

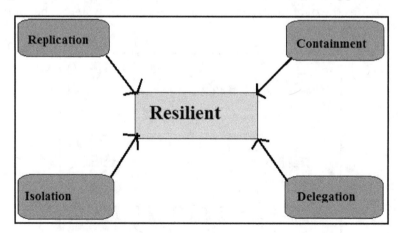

As you can see in the preceding diagram, resilience is achieved by replication, containment, isolation, and delegation. Let's discuss these points in detail:

- **Replication**: This ensures high-availability, where necessary, at the time of component failure.
- **Isolation**: This means that the failure of each component must be isolated, which is achieved by decoupling the components as much as possible. Isolation is needed for a system to self-heal. If your system has isolation in place, then you can easily measure the performance of each component, and check the memory and CPU usage. Moreover, the failure of one component won't impact the responsiveness of the overall system or application.
- **Containment**: The result of decoupling is containment of the failure. It helps avoid failure in the system as a whole.
- **Delegation**: After failure, the recovery of each component is delegated to another component. It is possible only when our system is composable.

Modern applications not only depend on the internal infrastructure but are also integrated with other web services via network protocols. So, our applications must be resilient at their core in order to stay responsive under a variety of real-world in the opposite conditions. Our applications must not only be resilient at the application level but also at the system level.

Let's see another principle of the reactive pattern.

Scalable

Resiliency and scalability together make a system consistently responsive. A scalable system or an elastic system can easily be upgraded under a varying workload. A reactive system can be made scalable on demand by increasing and decreasing the resources allocated to service these inputs. It supports multiple scaling algorithms by providing relevant live performance for the scalability of the application. We can achieve scalability by using cost-effective software and cheap commodity hardware (for example, the Cloud).

An application is scalable if it can be extended according to its usage, in the following ways:

- **scale-up**: It makes use of parallelism in multi-core systems.
- **scale-out**: It makes use of multi-server nodes. Location transparency and resilience are important for this.

Minimizing the shared mutable state is very important for scalability.

 Elasticity and Scalability are both the same! Scalability is all about the efficient use of resources already available, while elasticity is all about adding new resources to your application on demand when the needs of the system changed. So, eventually, the system can be made responsive anyway--by either using the existing resources of the system or by adding new resources to the system.

Let's see the final foundation of the resilient and scalability of the reactive pattern, that is, message-driven architecture.

Message-driven architecture

A message-driven architecture is the base of a responsive application. A message-driven application can be an event-driven and actor-based application. It can also be a combination of both architectures--event-driven and actor-based architecture.

In event-driven architecture, events and event observers play the main role. Events happen, but are not directed to a specific address; event listeners listen to these events, and take actions. But in message-driven architecture, the messages have a proper direction to the destination. Let's look at the following diagram that illustrates message-driven and event-driven architectures:

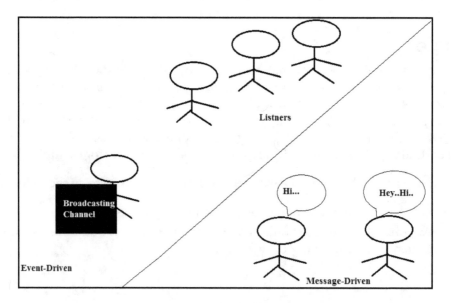

As you can see in the preceding diagram, in event-driven architecture, if an event happens, then listeners listen to it. But in the message-driven one, one generated message communication has an addressable recipient and a single purpose.

Asynchronous message-driven architecture acts as the foundation for a reactive system by establishing limitations between the components. It ensures loose coupling, isolation, and location transparency. Isolation between components fully depends on the loose coupling between them. And isolations and loose coupling develop the base of resilience and elasticity.

A large system has multiple components. These components either have smaller applications, or they may have reactive properties. This means that the reactive design principles have to apply at all levels of the scale to make a large system composable.

Traditionally, large systems are composed of multiple threads which communicate with a shared synchronized state. It tends to have strong coupling and is hard to compose, and it also tends to block stage. But, for now, all large systems are composed of loosely coupled event handlers. And events can be handled asynchronously without blocking.

Let's look at the blocking and non-blocking programming models.

In very simple terms, reactive programming is all about non-blocking applications that are asynchronous and event-driven, and require a small number of threads to scale vertically rather than horizontally.

Blocking calls

In a system, a call may be holding the resources while other calls wait for the same resources. These resources are released when the other one finishes using them.

Let's come to the technical words--actually, blocking a call means some operations in the application or system that take a longer time to complete, such as file I/O operations and database access using blocking drives. The following is a diagram of blocking calls for the JDBC operation in a system:

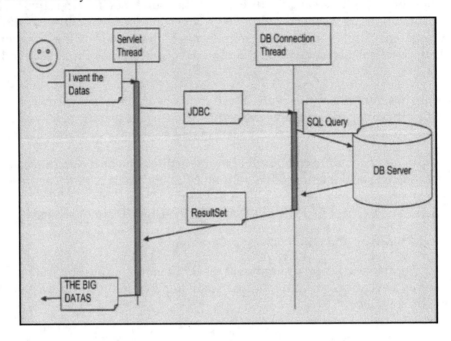

As you can see in the preceding diagram, the blocking operations, shown here in red, are the ones where the user calls the servlet to fetch data, then that moves to the JDBC and DB connection with the DB server. Until that time, the current thread waits for the result set from the DB server. If the DB server has latency, then this wait time can increase. That means that thread execution depends on the DB server latency.

Let's look at how to make this a non-blocking execution.

Non-blocking calls

Non-blocking execution of a program means that a thread competes for a resource without waiting for it. A non-blocking API for the resources allows calling the resources without waiting for the blocked call such as database access and network calls. If the resources are not available at the time of calling, then it moves to other work rather than waiting for the blocked resources. The system is notified when the blocked resources are available.

Take a look at the following diagram that shows the JDBC connection to access data without the blocking thread execution:

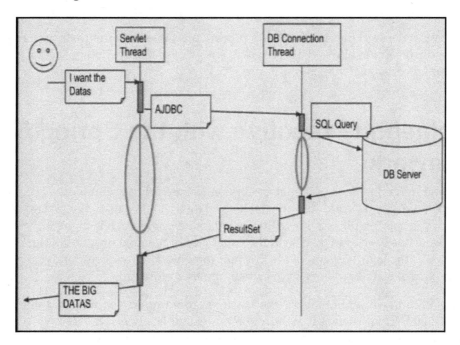

As you can see in the preceding diagram, thread execution does not wait for the result set from the DB server. The thread makes the DB connection and SQL statement for the DB server. If the DB server has latency in the response, then the thread moves on to do other work rather than be blocked waiting for the resource to become available.

Back-pressure

A reactive application is never given up in overload conditions. Back-pressure is a key aspect of a reactive application. It is a mechanism to ensure that the reactive application doesn't overwhelm the consumers. It tests aspects for the reactive application. It tests the system response gracefully under any load.

The back-pressure mechanism ensures that the system is resilient under load. In a back-pressure condition, the system makes itself scalable by applying other resources to help distribute the load.

Until now, we have seen the reactive pattern principles; these are mandatory to make a system responsive in the blue sky or grey sky. Let's see, in the upcoming section how Spring 5 implements reactive programming.

Implementing reactive with the Spring 5 Framework

The most highlighted feature of the latest version of the Spring Framework is the new reactive stack web framework. Reactive is the update that takes us to the future. This area of technology is gaining popularity with every passing day, which is the reason why Spring Framework 5.0 has been launched with the capability of reactive programming. This addition makes the latest version of the Spring Framework convenient for event-loop style processing, which enables scaling with a small number of threads.

The Spring 5 Framework implements the reactive programming pattern by using the reactor internally for its own reactive support. A reactor is a Reactive Stream implementation that extends the basic Reactive Streams. Twitter has been implemented as a reactive passed by using Reactive Streams.

Reactive Streams

Reactive Streams provide a protocol or rule for asynchronous stream processing with non-blocking back-pressure. This standard is also adopted by Java 9 in the form of `java.util.concurrent.Flow`. Reactive Streams is composed of four simple Java interfaces. These interfaces are `Publisher`, `Subscriber`, `Subscription`, and `Processor`. But the main goal of the Reactive Streams is handling the backpressure. As discussed earlier, backpressure is a process that allows a receiver to ask about a data quantity from the emitter.

You can use the following Maven dependency for adding Reactive Streams in your application development:

```
<dependency>
    <groupId>org.reactivestreams</groupId>
    <artifactId>reactive-streams</artifactId>
    <version>1.0.1</version>
```

```
    </dependency>
    <dependency>
        <groupId>org.reactivestreams</groupId>
        <artifactId>reactive-streams-tck</artifactId>
        <version>1.0.1</version>
    </dependency>
```

The preceding Maven dependency code adds the required libraries for the Reactive Streams in your application. In the upcoming section, we'll see how Spring implements Reactive Streams in the web module of Spring and the Spring MVC Framework.

Spring Web reactive module

As of Spring 5.0 Framework, Spring has introduced a new module for reactive programming--the spring-web-reactive module. It is based on Reactive Streams. Basically, this module uses the Spring MVC module with reactive programming, so, you can still use the Spring MVC module for your web application either separately or with the spring-web-reactive module.

This new module in the Spring 5.0 Framework contains support for the Reactive-web-functional- based programming model. It also supports the Annotation-based programming model. The Spring-web-reactive module contains support for reactive HTTP and WebSocket clients to call the reactive server application. It also enables the reactive web client to make a connection with a reactive HTTP connection with a reactive web application.

The following diagram shows a Spring-web-reactive module with its components that give reactive behavior to the Spring web application:

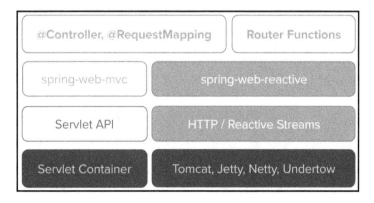

As you can see in the preceding diagram, there are two parallel modules--one for the traditional Spring MVC framework, and the other for the Spring-reactive web modules. On the left side in the diagram are the Spring-MVC-related components such as the @MVC controllers, **spring-web-mvc module**, **Servlet API module**, and **Servlet Container.** On the right side in the diagram are the spring-web-reactive related components such as the Router Functions, spring-web-reactive module, HTTP/Reactive Streams, Reactive version of Tomcat, and so on. **Spring-web-reactive** related components such as the **Router Functions**, **spring-web-reactive module**, **HTTP/Reactive Streams**, Reactive version of Tomcat, and so on.

In the preceding diagram, you must focus on the placement of the modules. Each module on the same level has comparisons between the traditional Spring MVC and Spring-web-reactive modules. These comparisons are given as follows:

- In the Spring web reactive modules, the Router functions are similar to the @MVC controllers in the Spring MVC modules such as the `@Controller`, `@RestController`, and `@RequestMapping` annotations.
- The Spring-web-reactive module is parallel to the Spring-web-MVC modules.
- In the traditional Spring MVC Framework, we use the Servlet API for the `HttpServletRequest` and `HttpServletResponse` in the servlet container. But in the Spring-web-reactive framework, we use HTTP/Reactive Streams, which creates `HttpServerRequest` and `HttpServerResponse` under the reactive support of the tomcat server.
- We can user Servlet Container for the traditional Spring MVC Framework, but a reactive-supported server is required for the Spring-web-reactive application. Spring provides support for Tomcat, Jetty, Netty, and Undertow.

Let's now see how to implement a reactive web application by using the Spring web reactive module.

Implementing a reactive web application at the server side

Spring reactive web modules support both programming models--Annotation-based or the Functional-based programming model. Let's see how these models work on the server side:

- **Annotations-based programming model**: It is based on MVC annotations such as `@Controller`, `@RestController`, `@RequestMapping`, and many more. Annotations are supported by the Spring MVC framework for server-side programming for a web application.
- **Functional programming model:** It is a new paradigm of programming supported by the Spring 5 Framework. It is based on the Java 8 Lambda style routing and handling. Scala also provides the functional programming paradigm.

The following are the Maven dependencies that we have to add for a reactive web application based on Spring Boot:

```xml
<parent>
    <groupId>org.springframework.boot</groupId>
    <artifactId>spring-boot-starter-parent</artifactId>
    <version>2.0.0.M3</version>
    <relativePath/> <!-- lookup parent from repository -->
</parent>

<properties>
    <project.build.sourceEncoding>UTF-
    8</project.build.sourceEncoding>
    <project.reporting.outputEncoding>UTF
    -8</project.reporting.outputEncoding>
    <java.version>1.8</java.version>
</properties>

<dependencies>
    <dependency>
        <groupId>org.springframework.boot</groupId>
        <artifactId>spring-boot-starter-webflux</artifactId>
    </dependency>

    <dependency>
        <groupId>org.springframework.boot</groupId>
        <artifactId>spring-boot-starter-test</artifactId>
        <scope>test</scope>
    </dependency>
    <dependency>
```

```
                    <groupId>io.projectreactor</groupId>
                    <artifactId>reactor-test</artifactId>
                    <scope>test</scope>
            </dependency>
        </dependencies>
```

As you can see in the preceding Maven configuration file for dependencies, we have added the `spring-boot-starter-webflux` and `reactor-test` dependencies to the application.

Let's create a reactive web application based on the Annotation-based programming model.

The Annotation-based programming model

Annotations such as `@Controller` and `@RestController` of Spring MVC are supported on the reactive side. There is no difference till now between the traditional Spring MVC and Spring web with reactive module. The actual difference starts after the `@Controller` annotation configuration declaration, that is, when we go to the internal working of the Spring MVC, starting with `HandlerMapping` and `HandlerAdapter`.

The main difference between the traditional Spring MVC and Spring web reactive comes into play in the request-handling mechanism. Spring MVC without reactive handles the requests using the blocking `HttpServletRequest` and the `HttpServletResponse` interfaces of the Servlet API, but the Spring web reactive framework is non-blocking, and operates on the reactive `ServerHttpRequest` and `ServerHttpResponse` rather than on `HttpServletRequest` and `HttpServletResponse`.

Let's see the following example with a reactive controller:

```
package com.packt.patterninspring.chapter11.
    reactivewebapp.controller;

import org.reactivestreams.Publisher;
import org.springframework.beans.factory.annotation.Autowired;
import org.springframework.web.bind.annotation.GetMapping;
import org.springframework.web.bind.annotation.PathVariable;
import org.springframework.web.bind.annotation.PostMapping;
import org.springframework.web.bind.annotation.RequestBody;
import org.springframework.web.bind.annotation.RestController;

import com.packt.patterninspring.chapter11.
    reactivewebapp.model.Account;
import  com.packt.patterninspring.chapter11.
    reactivewebapp.repository.AccountRepository;
```

```
import reactor.core.publisher.Flux;
import reactor.core.publisher.Mono;

@RestController
public class AccountController {
  @Autowired
  private AccountRepository repository;
  @GetMapping(value = "/account")
  public Flux<Account> findAll() {
    return repository.findAll().map(a -> new
      Account(a.getId(), a.getName(),
        a.getBalance(), a.getBranch())));
  }
  @GetMapping(value = "/account/{id}")
  public Mono<Account> findById(@PathVariable("id") Long id) {
    return repository.findById(id)
      .map(a -> new Account(a.getId(), a.getName(), a.getBalance(),
        a.getBranch())));
  }
  @PostMapping("/account")
  public Mono<Account> create(@RequestBody
    Publisher<Account> accountStream) {
    return repository
      .save(Mono.from(accountStream)
      .map(a -> new Account(a.getId(), a.getName(), a.getBalance(),
        a.getBranch()))))
      .map(a -> new Account(a.getId(), a.getName(), a.getBalance(),
        a.getBranch())));
  }
}
```

As you can see in the preceding Controller code of `AccountController.java`, I have used the same Spring MVC annotations such as `@RestController` to declare a controller class, and `@GetMapping` and `@PostMapping` are used to create the request handler methods for the GET and POST request methods respectively.

Let's focus on the return types of the handler methods. These methods return values as **Mono** and **Flux** types. These are types of the reactive steams provided by the reactor framework. Also, the handler method takes the request body using the Publisher type.

Reactor is a Java Framework from the Pivotal open-source team. It builds directly on Reactive Streams, so there is no need for a bridge. The Reactor IO project provides wrappers around low-level network runtimes like Netty and Aeron. Reactor is a "4th Generation" library according to David Karnok's Generations of Reactive classification.

Let's look at the same controller class using the functional programming model to handle requests.

The functional programming model

The functional programming model uses the API that has functional interfaces such as `RouterFunction` and `HandlerFunction`. It uses Java 8 Lambda style programming with routing and request handling instead of the Spring MVC annotations. They are simple, but powerful, building blocks for creating web applications.

The following is an example of functional request handling:

```
package com.packt.patterninspring.chapter11.web.reactive.function;

import static org.springframework.http.MediaType.APPLICATION_JSON;
import static org.springframework.web.reactive.
  function.BodyInserters.fromObject;

import org.springframework.web.reactive.
  function.server.ServerRequest;
import org.springframework.web.reactive.
  function.server.ServerResponse;

import com.packt.patterninspring.chapter11.
  web.reactive.model.Account;
import com.packt.patterninspring.chapter11.
  web.reactive.repository.AccountRepository;

import reactor.core.publisher.Flux;
import reactor.core.publisher.Mono;

public class AccountHandler {

  private final AccountRepository repository;

  public AccountHandler(AccountRepository repository) {
     this.repository = repository;
  }

  public Mono<ServerResponse> findById(ServerRequest request) {
    Long accountId = Long.valueOf(request.pathVariable("id"));
    Mono<ServerResponse> notFound =
      ServerResponse.notFound().build();
    Mono<Account> accountMono =
     this.repository.findById(accountId);
    return accountMono
```

```
        .flatMap(account ->      ServerResponse.ok().contentType
        (APPLICATION_JSON).body(
           fromObject(account)))
        .switchIfEmpty(notFound);
    }
    public Mono<ServerResponse> findAll(ServerRequest request) {
      Flux<Account> accounts = this.repository.findAll();
      return ServerResponse.ok().contentType
      (APPLICATION_JSON).body(accounts,
         Account.class);
    }
    public Mono<ServerResponse> create(ServerRequest request) {
      Mono<Account> account = request.bodyToMono(Account.class);
      return   ServerResponse.ok().build(this.
      repository.save(account));
    }
  }
```

In the preceding code, the class file, `AccountHandler.java`, is based on the functional
reactive programming model. Here, I have used the reactor framework to handle the
request. Two functional interfaces, `ServerRequest` and `ServerResponse`, are used to
handle requests and to generate responses.

Let's see the Repositories classes of this application. The following `AccountRepository`
and `AccountRepositoryImpl` classes are the same for both type of applications-
Annotation-based and the functional-based programming model.

Let's create an interface `AccountRepository.java` class as follows:

```
package com.packt.patterninspring.chapter11.
  reactivewebapp.repository;
import com.packt.patterninspring.chapter11.
  reactivewebapp.model.Account;

import reactor.core.publisher.Flux;
import reactor.core.publisher.Mono;

public interface AccountRepository {
  Mono<Account> findById(Long id);
  Flux<Account> findAll();
  Mono<Void> save(Mono<Account> account);
}
```

The preceding code is an interface, let's implements this interface with the `AccountRepositoryImpl.java` class as following:

```java
package com.packt.patterninspring.chapter11.
  web.reactive.repository;

import java.util.Map;
import java.util.concurrent.ConcurrentHashMap;

import org.springframework.stereotype.Repository;

import com.packt.patterninspring.chapter11.web.
  reactive.model.Account;

import reactor.core.publisher.Flux;
import reactor.core.publisher.Mono;

@Repository
public class AccountRepositoryImpl implements AccountRepository {
  private final Map<Long, Account> accountMap = new
  ConcurrentHashMap<>();
  public AccountRepositoryImpl() {
    this.accountMap.put(10001, new Account(10001,
    "Dinesh Rajput", 500001,
      "Sector-1"));
    this.accountMap.put(20001, new Account(20001,
    "Anamika Rajput", 600001,
      "Sector-2"));
    this.accountMap.put(30001, new Account(30001,
    "Arnav Rajput", 700001,
      "Sector-3"));
    this.accountMap.put(40001, new Account(40001,
   "Adesh Rajput", 800001,
      "Sector-4"));
  }
  @Override
  public Mono<Account> findById(Long id) {
    return Mono.justOrEmpty(this.accountMap.get(id));
  }

  @Override
  public Flux<Account> findAll() {
    return Flux.fromIterable(this.accountMap.values());
  }

  @Override
  public Mono<Void> save(Mono<Account> account) {
    return account.doOnNext(a -> {
```

```
        accountMap.put(a.getId(), a);
        System.out.format("Saved %s with id %d%n", a, a.getId());
    }).thenEmpty(Mono.empty());
    // return accountMono;
    }
}
```

As you can see in the preceding code, we created the `AccountRepository` class. This class has only three methods: `findById()`, `findAll()`, and `save()`. We implemented these methods according to the business requirements. In this repository class, I have, especially, used the Flux and Mono react types to make it a reactive-based application.

Let's create the server for the functional-based programming model. In Annotation-based programming, we use the simple tomcat container to deploy the web application. But for this functional-based programming, we have to create a Server class to start the Tomcat server or Reactor server, as follows:

```
package com.packt.patterninspring.chapter11.web.reactive.function;

//Imports here

public class Server {

    public static final String HOST = "localhost";
    public static final int TOMCAT_PORT = 8080;
    public static final int REACTOR_PORT = 8181;
    //main method here, download code for GITHUB
    public RouterFunction<ServerResponse> routingFunction() {
        AccountRepository repository = new AccountRepositoryImpl();
        AccountHandler handler = new AccountHandler(repository);

        return nest(path("/account"), nest(accept(APPLICATION_JSON),
            route(GET("/{id}"), handler::findById)
            .andRoute(method(HttpMethod.GET), handler::findAll)
            ).andRoute(POST("/").and(contentType
            (APPLICATION_JSON)), handler::create));
    }

    public void startReactorServer() throws InterruptedException {
        RouterFunction<ServerResponse> route = routingFunction();
        HttpHandler httpHandler = toHttpHandler(route);

        ReactorHttpHandlerAdapter adapter = new
            ReactorHttpHandlerAdapter(httpHandler);
        HttpServer server = HttpServer.create(HOST, REACTOR_PORT);
        server.newHandler(adapter).block();
    }
```

```
    public void startTomcatServer() throws LifecycleException {
        RouterFunction<?> route = routingFunction();
        HttpHandler httpHandler = toHttpHandler(route);

        Tomcat tomcatServer = new Tomcat();
        tomcatServer.setHostname(HOST);
        tomcatServer.setPort(TOMCAT_PORT);
        Context rootContext = tomcatServer.addContext("",
            System.getProperty("java.io.tmpdir"));
        ServletHttpHandlerAdapter servlet = new
            ServletHttpHandlerAdapter(httpHandler);
        Tomcat.addServlet(rootContext, "httpHandlerServlet", servlet);
        rootContext.addServletMapping("/", "httpHandlerServlet");
        tomcatServer.start();
    }
}
```

As you can see in the preceding `Server.java` class file, I have added both, the Tomcat and Reactor servers. The Tomcat server uses port 8080, but the Reactor server uses the port `8181`.

This `Server.java` class has three methods. The first method, `routingFunction()`, is responsible for handling client requests by using the `AccountHandler` class. It depends on the `AccountRepository` class. The second method, `startReactorServer()`, is responsible for starting the Reactor server by using the `ReactorHttpHandlerAdapter` class of the reactor server. This class takes an object of the `HttpHandler` class as a constructor argument to create the request handler mapping. Similarly, the third method, `startTomcatServer()`, is responsible for starting the Tomcat server. And it is bound to the `HttpHandler` object through a reactor adapter class, `ServletHttpHandlerAdapter`.

You can run this server class file as a Java application, and see the output on the browser by typing the URL, `http://localhost:8080/account/`:

```
[
  - {
        id: 2000,
        name: "Anamika Rajput",
        branch: "Sector-2",
        balance: 60000
    },
  - {
        id: 4000,
        name: "Adesh Rajput",
        branch: "Sector-4",
        balance: 80000
    },
  - {
        id: 1000,
        name: "Dinesh Rajput",
        branch: "Sector-1",
        balance: 50000
    },
  - {
        id: 3000,
        name: "Arnav Rajput",
        branch: "Sector-3",
        balance: 70000
    }
]
```

You can also type the same URL with port `8181` for the Reactor server, as follows, and you will get the same output:

```
http://localhost:8181/account/
```

In this section, you learned how to create a reactive web application using the Spring-web-reactive module. We created the web application by using both the programming paradigms: Annotation-based and Functional-based.

In the next section, we'll discuss client-side code, and how a client accesses the reactive web application.

Implementing a Reactive Client-Side application

The Spring 5 Framework introduces a functional and reactive WebClient. It is a fully non-blocking and reactive web client, and an alternative to RestTemplate. It creates the network input and output in the form of reactive ClientHttpRequest and ClientHttpRespones. It creates the body of the request and response in the form of Flux<DataBuffer> instead of InputStream and OutputStream.

Let's see the code for the web client, which creates a Client.java class:

```java
package com.packt.patterninspring.chapter11.web.reactive.function;

//Imports here

public class Client {

  private ExchangeFunction exchange = ExchangeFunctions.create(new
    ReactorClientHttpConnector());

  public void findAllAccounts() {
    URI uri = URI.create(String.format("http://%s:%d/account",
    Server.HOST,
      Server.TOMCAT_PORT));
    ClientRequest request = ClientRequest.method(HttpMethod.GET,
    uri).build();

    Flux<Account> account = exchange.exchange(request)
    .flatMapMany(response -> response.bodyToFlux(Account.class));

      Mono<List<Account>> accountList = account.collectList();
      System.out.println(accountList.block());
  }

  public void createAccount() {
    URI uri = URI.create(String.format("http://%s:%d/account",
    Server.HOST,
      Server.TOMCAT_PORT));
    Account jack = new Account(50001, "Arnav Rajput", 5000001,
    "Sector-5");

    ClientRequest request = ClientRequest.method(HttpMethod.POST,
    uri)
```

```
            .body(BodyInserters.fromObject(jack)).build();

        Mono<ClientResponse> response = exchange.exchange(request);

        System.out.println(response.block().statusCode());
    }
}
```

The preceding class, `Client.java`, is a web client class for `Server.java`. It has two methods. The first method is `findAllAccounts()`. It fetches all accounts from the account repository. It uses the `org.springframework.web.reactive.function.client.` The `ClientRequest` interface to create a request to the `http://localhost:8080/account/` URI with the `GET` http method. By using the `org.springframework.web.reactive.function.client.` The `ExchangeFunction` interface, it calls the server, and fetches the result as the JSON format. Similarly, the other method, `createAccount()`, creates a new account in the server by using the URI with the `POST` method `http://localhost:8080/account/`.

Let's run the Client class as a Java application and see the output on the console, which is as follows:

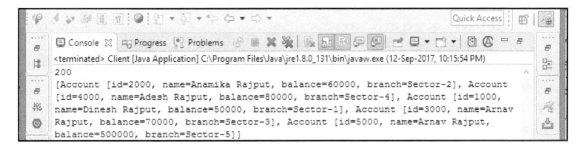

It creates a new record and fetch all five record in the form of JSON list.

 The `AsyncRestTemplate` also supports non-blocking interactions. The main difference is that it can't support non-blocking streaming, for example, Twitter one, because, fundamentally, it's still based and relies on `InputStream` and `OutputStream`.

In the next section, we'll talk about the request and response body parameters in a reactive web application.

Request and response body conversion

Conversion is required in the case of a Reactive web application . The spring core module provides reactive Encoder and Decoder to enable the serialization of a Flux of bytes to and from the typed objects.

Let's see the following example for request body type conversions. Developers do not need to forcefully do type conversion--the Spring Framework automatically converts it for you in both types of approaches: Annotation-based programming, and functional-based programming.

- **Account account**: This means that the account object is deserialized before the controller is called without blocking.
- **Mono<Account> account**: This means that `AccountController` can use the Mono to declare logic. The account object is first deserialized, and then this logic is executed.
- **Flux<Account> accounts**: This means that `AccountController` can use Flux in case of the input streaming scenario.
- **Single<Account> account**: This is very similar to the Mono, but here the Controller uses RxJava.
- **Observable<Account> accounts**: This is also very similar to Flux, but in this case, the Controller uses input streaming with RxJava.

In the preceding list, you saw the Spring Framework for type conversion in the reactive programing model. Let's see the following return types in the example for the response body:

- **Account**: This serializes without blocking the given Account; implies a synchronous, non-blocking controller method.
- **void**: This is specific to the annotation-based programming model. Request handling completes when the method returns; this implies a synchronous, non-blocking controller method.
- **Mono<Account>**: This serializes without blocking the given Account when the Mono completes.
- **Mono<Void>**: This implies that request handling completes when the Mono completes.

- **Flux<Account>**: This is used in the streaming scenario, possibly, the SSE depends on the requested content type.
- **Flux<ServerSentEvent>**: This enables SSE streaming.
- **Single<Account>**: The same, but uses RxJava.
- **Observable<Account>**: The same, but uses the RxJava Observable type.
- **Flowable<Account>**: The same, but uses the RxJava 2 Flowable type.

In the preceding list, you have seen the return types of the handler methods. The Spring Framework does type conversions in the reactive programing model.

Summary

In this chapter, you learned about the Reactive pattern and its principles. It is not a new innovation in programming--it is a very old concept, but it very fits in very well with the demands of modern applications.

Reactive programming has four principles: responsiveness, resilience, elasticity, and message-driven architecture. Responsiveness means a system must be responsive in all conditions: odd conditions and even conditions.

The Spring 5 Framework provides support for the reactive programming model by using the Reactor framework and reactive stream. Spring has introduced new a reactive web module, that is, spring-web-reactive. It provides the reactive programming approach to a web application by either using Spring MVC's annotations, such as `@Controller`, `@RestController`, and `@RequestMapping`, or by using the functional programming approach using the Java 8 Lambda expression.

In this chapter, we created a web application by using the spring web reactive modules. The code for this application is available on GitHub. In the next chapter, you will learn about implementation of concurrency patterns.

8
Implementing Concurrency Patterns

In Chapter 7, *Implementing Reactive Design Patterns*, we discussed the Reactive Design Pattern and how it fulfills the requirements of today's applications. Spring 5 Framework has introduced the Reactive Web Application Modules for the web application. In this chapter, we will explore some of the Concurrency Design Patterns and how these patterns solve the common problems of the multithreaded application. Spring 5 Framework's reactive modules also provide the solution for the multithreaded application.

If you are a software engineer or are in the process of becoming one, you must be aware of the term *concurrency*. In geometric properties, concurrent circles or shapes are those shapes that have a common center point. These shapes can differ in dimensions but have a common center or midpoint.

The concept is similar in terms of software programming as well. The term *concurrent programming* in the technical or programming means the ability of a program to carry out multiple computations in parallel and also the capability of a program to handle multiple external activities taking place in a single time interval.

As we are talking in terms of software engineering and programming, concurrency patterns are those design patterns that help in dealing with multi-threaded programming models. Some of the concurrency patterns are as follows:

- Handling concurrency with concurrency patterns
- Active object pattern
- Monitor object pattern
- Half-Sync/Half-Async patterns
- Leader/followers pattern
- Thread-specific storage
- Reactor pattern

- Best practices for concurrency module

Let's now explore each of these five concurrency design patterns in depth.

Active object pattern

The active object type of concurrency design pattern differentiates/distinguishes the method execution from the method invocation. The job of this pattern is the enhancement of concurrency along with simplification in the synchronized access to objects that reside in separate and distinguishable threads of control. It is used for dealing with the multiple client requests that arrive all at once, and also for improving the quality of the service. Let's see the following diagrams, which illustrates the active object design pattern in the concurrency and multithread-based application:

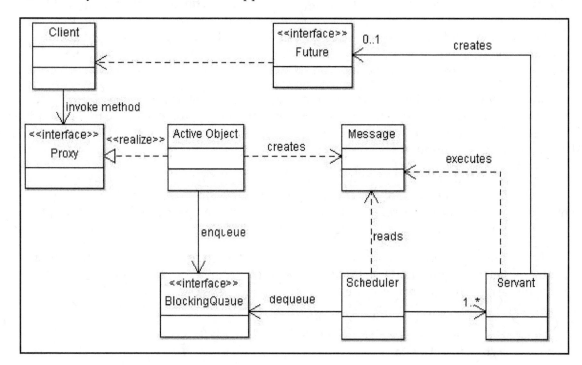

As you can see in the preceding diagram, the following components of this concurrency design pattern:

- **Proxy**: This is the active object that is visible to the client. The proxy advertises its interface.
- **Servant**: There is a method that is defined in the interface of the proxy. The servant is the provider of its implementation.
- **Activation list**: This is a serialized list that contains method request objects that the proxy inserts. This list allows the servant to run concurrently.

So, how does this design pattern work? Well, the answer to this is that every concurrent object belongs to or resides in a separate thread of control. This is also independent of the thread of control of the client. This invokes one of its methods, which means that both the method execution and method invocation take place in separate threads of control. However, the client sees this process as an ordinary method. In order for the proxy to pass the requests of the client to the servant at runtime, both must be run in separate threads.

In this design pattern, what the proxy does after receiving a request is that it sets up a method request object and inserts it in an activation list. This method carries out two jobs; holds the method request objects and keeps track of on which method request it can execute. Request parameters and any other information are contained in the method request object for executing the desired method later. This activation list in return helps the proxy and the servant to run concurrently.

Let's see another concurrency design pattern in the upcoming section, which is the monitor object pattern.

Monitor object pattern

The monitor object pattern is another concurrency design pattern that helps in the execution of multi-threaded programs. It is a design pattern implemented to make sure that at a single time interval, only one method runs in a single object, and for this purpose, it synchronizes concurrent method execution.

Unlike the active object design pattern, the monitor object pattern does not have a separate thread of control. Every request received is executed in the thread of control of the client itself, and until the time the method returns, the access is blocked. At a single time interval, a single synchronized method can be executed in one monitor.

The following solutions are offered by the monitor object pattern:

- The synchronization boundaries are defined by the interface of the object, and it also makes sure that a single method is active in a single object.
- It must be ensured that all the objects keep a check on every method that needs synchronization and serialize them transparently without letting the client know. Operations, on the other hand, are mutually exclusive, but they are invoked like ordinary method calls. Wait and signal primitives are used for the realization of condition synchronization.
- To prevent the deadlock and use the concurrency mechanisms available, other clients must be allowed to access the object when the method of the object blocks during execution.
- The invariants must always hold when the thread of control is interrupted voluntarily by the method.

Let's see the following diagram, which illustrates more about the monitor object design pattern in the concurrency application:

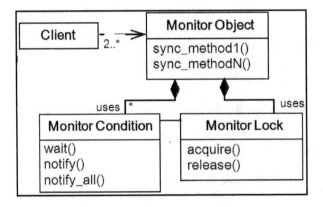

In this preceding diagram, the client object calls the monitor object that has several synchronized methods and the monitor object associated with the monitor conditions and monitor locks. Let's explore each component of this concurrency design pattern as follows:

- **Monitor object**: This component exposes the methods that are synchronized to the clients
- **Synchronized methods**: The thread-safe functions that are exported by the interface of the object are implemented by these methods
- **Monitor conditions**: This component along with the monitor lock decides whether the synchronized method should resume its processing or suspend it

The active object and the monitor object patterns are the branches of design patterns of concurrency.

Now, the other type of concurrency patterns that we will discuss are the branches of architectural patterns for concurrency.

Half-Sync/Half-Async patterns

The job of Half-Sync and Half-Async is to distinguish between the two types of processing called asynchronous and synchronous, for the simplification of the program without hindering its performance.

The two layers intercommunicating are introduced for both asynchronous and synchronous services for the purpose of processing with a queuing layer in between.

Every concurrent system contains both asynchronous and synchronous services. To enable these services to communicate with each other, the Half-Sync/Half-Async pattern decomposes the services in the system into layers. Using the queuing layer, both these services pass messages to each other for intercommunication.

Let's see the following diagram that illustrates these design patterns:

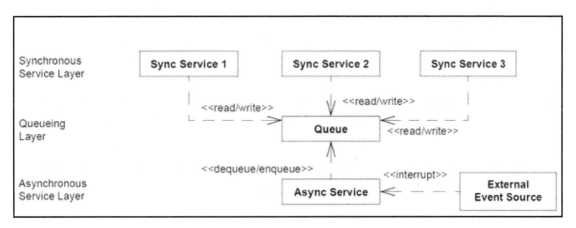

As you can see in the preceding diagram, there are three layers--**Synchronous Service Layer**, **Queuing Layer**, and **Asynchronous Service Layer**. Synchronous layer contains the services that are working synchronously to the queue at the **Queuing Layer**, and this query performs asynchronously using Asynchronous services at the **Asynchronous Service Layer**. These Asynchronous Services at this layer are using the external event-based resources.

As you can see in the preceding diagram, there are three layers included here. Let's look at these layers:

- **Synchronous Task Layer**: The tasks in this layer are active objects. High-level input and output operations are carried by these tasks, which transfer the data synchronously towards the queuing layer.
- **Queuing Layer**: This layer provides the synchronization and buffering required between the synchronous and asynchronous task layers.
- **Asynchronous Task Layer**: The events from the external sources are handled by the tasks present in this layer. These tasks do not contain a separate thread of control.

We have discussed the Half-Sync and Half-Async design patterns of the concurrency pattern. Let's move to another concurrency pattern, that is, the leader/follower Pattern.

Leader/follower pattern

Detection, demultiplexing, dispatching, and processing of service requests in the event sources is carried out in an efficient way in a concurrency model, in which many multiple threads process one by one to use the set on event sources. Another replacement for the Half-Sync/Half-Async is the leader/follower pattern. This pattern can be used instead of the Half-Sync/Half-Async and active object patterns for improvement in the performance. The condition of using this is that there must be neither ordering nor synchronization constraints while processing multiple threads of requests:

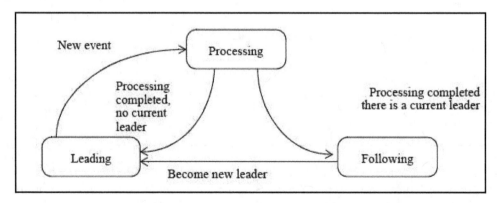

The focused job of this pattern is to process multiple events concurrently or simultaneously. Due to concurrency-related overheads, it might not be possible to connect a separate thread with each single socket handle. The highlighted feature of this design is that by using this pattern, demultiplexing the associations between threads and event source becomes possible. When the events arrive on the event sources, this pattern builds up a pool of threads. This is done to share a set of event sources efficiently. These event sources demultiplex the arriving events turn by turn. Also, the events are synchronously dispatched to application services for processing. Out of the pool of threads structured by the leader/follower pattern, only a single thread waits for the occurrence of the event; other threads queue up waiting. A follower is promoted as the leader when a thread detects an event. It then processes the thread and dispatches the event to the application handler.

In this type of pattern, processing threads can be run concurrently, but only one thread is allowed to wait for the upcoming new events.

Let's see another concurrency-based design pattern in the upcoming section.

Reactor pattern

The reactor pattern is used to handle service requests that are received concurrently by a service handler from a single or multiple input sources. The received service requests are then demultiplexed by the service handler and dispatched to the associated request handlers. All the reactor systems are commonly found in single threads, but they are also said to exist in a multi-threaded environment.

The key benefit of using this pattern is that the application components can be divided into multiple parts such as modular or reusable. Furthermore, this allows simple coarse-grain concurrency without the additional complexity of multiple threads to the system.

Let's see the following diagram about the reactor design pattern:

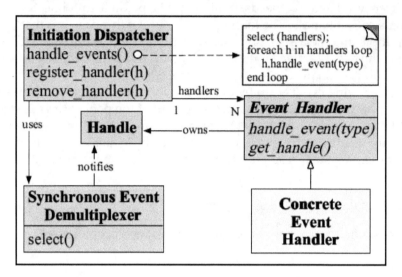

As you can see in the preceding diagram, the dispatcher uses the demultiplexer to notify handler and the handler performs the actual work to be done with an I/O event. A reactor responds to I/O events by dispatching the appropriate handler. Handlers perform non-blocking actions. The preceding diagram has the following components of this design pattern:

- **Resources:** These are the resources through which input is provided or output is consumed.
- **Synchronous event demultiplexer:** This blocks all resources via an event loop. When there is a possibility that a synchronous operation will start, the resource is sent to the dispatcher through the demultiplexer without blocking.
- **Dispatcher:** The registering or unregistering of request handler is handled by this component. Resources are dispatched to the respective request handler through the dispatcher.
- **Request Handler:** This handles the request dispatched by the dispatcher.

Now, we are moving on to our next and the last concurrency pattern that is the thread-specific storage pattern.

Thread-specific storage pattern

A single logical global access point can be used to retrieve an object local to the thread. This concurrency design pattern allows multiple threads to carry this function out. This is done without incurring locking overhead on each access to the object. Sometimes, this particular pattern can be viewed as an antithesis among all the concurrency design patterns. This is due to the fact that several complexities are addressed by the thread-specific storage by prevention of sharing of the available resources among the threads.

The method appears to be invoked on an ordinary object by the application thread. Actually, it is invoked on a thread-specific object. A single thread-specific object proxy can be used by multiple application threads for accessing the unique thread-specific objects associated to each of them. The proxy to distinguish between the thread-specific object it encapsulates uses the application thread identifier.

Best practices for concurrency module

Here is a list of considerations that a programmer must look into when carrying out concurrency. Let's look at the following best practices to consider when you to get a chance to work with the concurrent application module.

- **Obtaining an executor**: The Executor Framework for obtaining an executor supplies the executors utility class. Various types of executors offer specific thread executions policies. Here are three examples:
    - **ExecutorService newCachedThreadPool()**: This creates a thread pool using the previously constructed threads if available. The performance of the programs that make use of the short-lived asynchronous tasks is enhanced using this type of thread pool.
    - **ExecutorService newSingleThreadExecutor()**: A worker thread that is operating in an unbounded queue is used here to create an executor. In this type, the tasks are added to the queue that is then executed one by one. In case, this thread fails during the execution, a new thread will be created and replace the failed thread so that the tasks can be executed without interruption.

- **ExecutorService newFixedThreadPool(int nThreads)**: A fixed number of threads that are operating in a shared unbounded queue are reused in this case for the creation of a thread pool. At threads, the tasks are being actively processed. While all the threads in the pool are active and new tasks are submitted, the tasks will be added in the queue until a thread becomes available for the processing of the new task. If before the shutdown of the executor, the thread fails, a new thread will be created for carrying out the execution of the task. Note that these thread pools exist only when the executor is active or on.

- **Use of cooperative synchronized constructs**: It is recommended to use cooperative synchronized constructs when possible.

- **No unnecessary lengthy tasks and oversubscription**: Lengthy tasks are known to cause deadlock, starvation, and even prevent other tasks from functioning properly. Larger tasks can be broken down into smaller tasks for proper performance. Oversubscription is also a way to avoid the deadlock, starvation, and so on. Using this, more threads than the available number of threads can be created. This is highly efficient when a lengthy task contains a lot of latency.

- **Use of concurrent memory-management functions**: If in a situation, ensuing concurrent memory management functions can be used, it is highly recommended to use it. These can be used when objects with a short lifetime are used. The functions such as `Allot` and `Free` are used to free memory and allocate, without memory barriers or using locks.

- **Use of RAII to manage the lifetime of concurrency objects**: RAII is the abbreviation for **Resource Acquisition Is Initialization**. This is an efficient way to manage the lifetime of a concurrency object.

This was all about the concurrency and it's design patterns that can be used to handle and implement concurrency. These are the most common five design patterns for concurrency programs. Also, some of the best practices for carrying out concurrency modules were discussed. Hope this was an informative a piece and helped you understand how concurrency patterns work!

Summary

In this chapter, you learned several concurrency design patterns and also saw the use cases of these patterns. In this book, I have covered only the basic of the concurrency design patterns. We have included the active object, monitor object, Half-Sync/Half-Async, leader/followers, thread-specific storage, and reactor patterns. These all are the part of the concurrency design patterns in the multithreaded environment of the application. We also discussed some best practices consideration to use the concurrency design pattern in the application.

Demystifying Microservices

9

Microservices is an architecture style and an approach for software development to satisfy modern business demands. Microservices are not invented, it is more of an evolution from the previous architecture styles.

We will start the chapter by taking a closer look at the evolution of microservices architecture from the traditional monolithic architectures. We will also examine the definition, concepts, and characteristics of microservices.

By the end of this chapter, you will have learned about the following:

- Evolution of microservices
- Definition of microservices architecture with examples
- Concepts and characteristics of microservices architecture

Evolution of microservices

Microservices is one of the increasingly popular architecture patterns next to **Service Oriented Architecture (SOA)**, complemented by DevOps and Cloud. Its evolution has been greatly influenced by the disruptive digital innovation trends in modern business and the evolution of technology in the last few years. We will examine these two catalysts--business demands and technology--in this section.

Business demand as a catalyst for microservices evolution

In this era of digital transformation, enterprises are increasingly adopting technologies as one of the key enablers for radically increasing their revenue and customer base. Enterprises are primarily using social media, mobile, cloud, big data, and **Internet of Things (IoT)** as vehicles for achieving the disruptive innovations. Using these technologies, enterprises are finding new ways to quickly penetrate the market, which severely pose challenges to the traditional IT delivery mechanisms.

The following graph shows the state of traditional development and microservices against the new enterprise challenges, such as agility, speed of delivery, and scale:

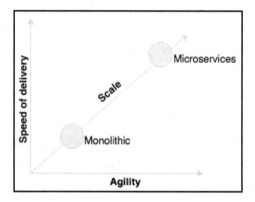

Microservices promises more agility, speed of delivery, and scale compared to traditional monolithic applications.

Gone are the days where businesses invested in large application developments with turnaround times of a few years. Enterprises are no longer interested in developing consolidated applications for managing their end-to-end business functions as they did a few years ago.

The following graph shows the state of traditional monolithic application and microservices in comparison with the turnaround time and cost:

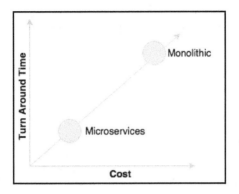

Microservices provides an approach for developing quick and agile applications, resulting in a lesser overall cost.

Today, for instance, airlines are not investing in rebuilding their core mainframe reservation systems as another monolithic monster. Financial institutions are not rebuilding their core banking systems. Retailers and other industries are not rebuilding heavyweight supply chain management applications, such as their traditional ERP's. Focus has been shifted from building large applications to building quick win, point solutions that cater to the specific needs of the business in the most agile way possible.

Let's take an example of an online retailer running with a legacy monolithic application. If the retailer wants to innovate their sales by offering their products personalized to a customer based on the customer's past shopping preferences and much more, or they want to enlighten customers by offering products to customer based on propensity to buy a product.

In such cases, enterprises want to quickly develop a personalization engine or an offer engine based on their immediate needs, and plug them into their legacy application, as shown here:

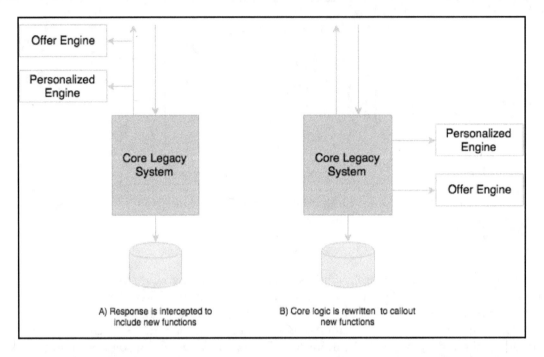

A) Response is intercepted to include new functions

B) Core logic is rewritten to callout new functions

As shown in the preceding diagram, rather than investing on rebuilding the **Core Legacy System**, this will either be done by passing the responses through the new functions, as shown in the diagram marked **A**, or modifying the **Core Legacy System** to call out these functions as part of the processing, as shown in the diagram marked **B**. These functions are typically written as microservices.

This approach gives organizations a plethora of opportunities to quickly try out new functions with lesser cost in an experimental mode. Business can later validate key performance indicators change or replace these implementations if required.

Modern architectures are expected to maximize the ability to replace its parts and minimize the cost of replacing them. Microservices' approach is a means to achieve this.

Technology as a catalyst for microservices evolution

Emerging technologies have made us rethink the way we build software systems. For example, a few decades ago, we couldn't even imagine a distributed application without a two-phase commit. Later, **NoSQL** databases made us think differently.

Similarly, these kinds of paradigm shifts in technology have reshaped all layers of software architecture.

The emergence of HTML 5, CSS3, and the advancement of mobile applications repositioned user interfaces. Client-side JavaScript frameworks, such as Angular, Ember, React, Backbone, and more, are immensely popular due to their capabilities around responsive and adaptive designs.

With cloud adoptions steamed into the mainstream, **Platform as a Services (PaaS)** providers, such as Pivotal CF, AWS, Sales Force, IBM Bluemix, Redhat OpenShift, and more, made us rethink the way we build middleware components. The container revolution created by **Docker** radically influenced the infrastructure space. Container orchestration tools, such as **Mesosphere DCOS**, made infrastructure management much easier. Serverless added further easiness in application managements.

Integration landscape has also changed with the emerging **Integration Platform as a Services (iPaaS)**, such as Dell Boomi, Informatica, MuleSoft, and more. These tools helped organizations stretch integration boundaries beyond the traditional enterprise.

NoSQL and **NewSQL** have revolutionized the space of the database. A few years ago, we had only a few popular databases, all based on relational data modeling principles. Today, we have a long list of databases: **Hadoop**, **Cassandra**, **CouchDB**, **Neo 4j**, and **NuoDB**, to name a few. Each of these databases addresses certain specific architectural problems.

Imperative architecture evolution

Application architecture has always been evolving alongside with demanding business requirements and evolution of technologies.

Different architecture approaches and styles, such as mainframes, client server, *n*-tier, and service oriented were popular at different times. Irrespective of the choice of architecture styles, we always used to build one or the other forms of monolithic architectures. Microservices architecture evolved as a result of modern business demands, such as agility, speed of delivery, emerging technologies, and learning from previous generations of architectures:

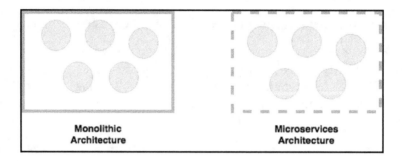

Microservices help us break the boundaries of the monolithic application and build a logically independent smaller system of systems, as shown in the preceding diagram.

 If we consider the monolithic application as a set of logical subsystems encompassed with a physical boundary, microservices are a set of independent subsystems with no enclosing physical boundary.

What are Microservices?

Microservices are an architectural style used by many organizations today as a game changer to achieve high degrees of agility, speed of delivery, and scale. Microservices gives us a way to develop physically separated modular applications.

Microservices are not invented. Many organizations, such as Netflix, Amazon, and eBay had successfully used the divide and conquer technique for functionally partitioning their monolithic applications into smaller atomic units, each performing a single function. These organizations solved a number of prevailing issues they were experiencing with their monolithic application. Following the success of these organizations, many other organizations started adopting this as a common pattern for refactoring their monolithic applications. Later, evangelists termed this pattern microservices architecture.

Microservices originated from the idea of **Hexagonal Architecture**, which was coined by Alister Cockburn back in 2005. Hexagonal Architecture, or Hexagonal pattern, is also known as the **Ports and Adapters** pattern.

 Read more about Hexagonal Architecture here:
`http://alistair.cockburn.us/Hexagonal+architecture`

In simple terms, Hexagonal architecture advocates to encapsulate business functions from the rest of the world. These encapsulated business functions are unaware of their surroundings. For example, these business functions are not even aware of input devices or channels and message formats used by those devices. Ports and adapters at the edge of these business functions convert messages coming from different input devices and channels to a format that is known to the business function. When new devices are introduced, developers can keep adding more and more ports and adapters to support those channels without touching business functions. One may have as many ports and adapters to support their needs. Similarly, external entities are not aware of business functions behind these ports and adapters. They will always interface with these ports and adapters. By doing so, developers enjoy the flexibility to change channels and business functions without worrying too much about future proofing interface designs.

The following diagram shows the conceptual view of Hexagonal Architecture:

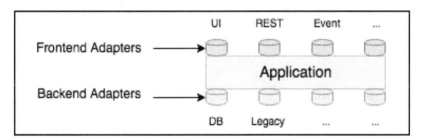

In the preceding diagram, the application is completely isolated and exposed through a set of frontend adapters, as well as a set of backend adapters. Frontend adaptors are generally used for integrating UI and other APIs, whereas backend adapters are used for connecting to various data sources. Ports and adapters on both sides are responsible for converting messages coming in and going out to appropriate formats expected by external entities. Hexagonal architecture was the inspiration for microservices.

When we look for a definition for microservices, there is no single standard way of describing them. Martin Fowler defines microservices as follows:

> *"The microservice architectural style is an approach to developing a single application as a suite of small services, each running in its own process and communicating with lightweight mechanisms, often an HTTP resource API. These services are built around business capabilities and independently deployable by fully automated deployment machinery. There is a bare minimum of centralized management of these services, which may be written in different programming languages and use different data storage technologies."*--(http://www.martinfowler.com/articles/microservices.html)

The definition used in this book is as follows:

Microservices is an architectural style or an approach for building IT systems as a set of business capabilities that are autonomous, self contained, and loosely coupled.

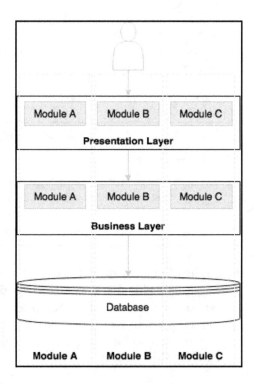

The preceding diagram depicts a traditional *n*-tier application architecture, having a **Presentation Layer**, **Business Layer**, and **Database Layer**. Modules **A**, **B**, and **C** represent three different business capabilities. The layers in the diagram represent separation of architecture concerns. Each layer holds all three business capabilities pertaining to that layer. The presentation layer has web components of all three modules, the business layer has business components of all three modules, and the database host tables of all three modules. In most cases, layers are physically spreadable, whereas modules within a layer are hardwired.

Let's now examine a microservices-based architecture:

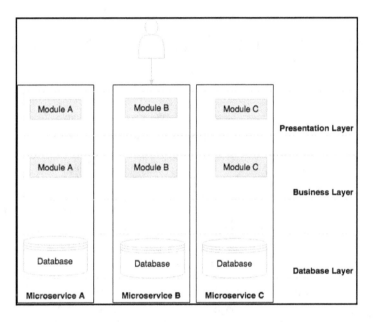

As we can see in the preceding diagram, the boundaries are inversed in the microservices architecture. Each vertical slice represents a microservice. Each microservice will have its own presentation layer, business layer, and database layer. Microservices are aligned towards business capabilities. By doing so, changes to one microservice does not impact others.

There is no standard for communication or transport mechanisms for microservices. In general, microservices communicate with each other using widely adopted lightweight protocols, such as HTTP and REST, or messaging protocols, such as **JMS** or **AMQP**. In specific cases, one might choose more optimized communication protocols, such as **Thrift**, **ZeroMQ**, **Protocol Buffers**, or **Avro**.

Since microservices are more aligned to business capabilities and have independently manageable life cycles, they are the ideal choice for enterprises embarking on DevOps and cloud. DevOps and cloud are two facets of microservices.

 DevOps is an IT realignment to narrow the gap between traditional IT development and operations for better efficiency.

Read more about DevOps at `http://dev2ops.org/2010/02/what-is-devops/`.

Microservices - The honeycomb analogy

A honeycomb is an ideal analogy for representing the evolutionary microservices architecture:

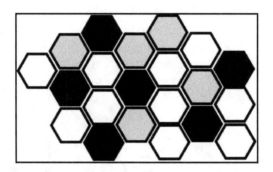

In the real world, bees build a honeycomb by aligning hexagonal wax cells. They start small, using different materials to build the cells. Construction is based on what is available at the time of building. Repetitive cells form a pattern, and result in a strong fabric structure. Each cell in the honeycomb is independent, but also integrated with other cells. By adding new cells, the honeycomb grows organically to a big, solid structure. The content inside the cell is abstracted and is not visible outside. Damage to one cell does not damage other cells, and bees can reconstruct those cells without impacting the overall honeycomb.

Principles of microservices

In this section, we will examine some of the principles of the microservices architecture. These principles are a must have when designing and developing microservices. The two key principles are single responsibility and autonomous.

Single responsibility per service

The single responsibility principle is one of the principles defined as part of the **SOLID** design pattern. It states that a unit should only have one responsibility.

 Read more about the SOLID design pattern at `http://c2.com/cgi/wiki?PrinciplesOfObjectOrientedDesign`.

It implies that a unit, either a class, a function, or a service, should have only one responsibility. At no point do two units share one responsibility, or one unit perform more than one responsibility. A unit with more than one responsibility indicates tight coupling:

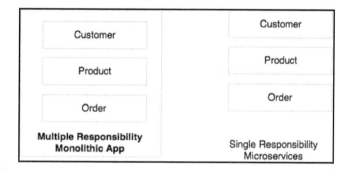

As shown in the preceding diagram, **Customer**, **Product**, and **Order** are different functions of an e-commerce application. Rather than building all of them into one application, it is better to have three different services, each responsible for exactly one business function, so that changes to one responsibility will not impair the others. In the preceding scenario, **Customer**, **Product**, and **Order** were treated as three independent microservices.

Microservices are autonomous

Microservices are self-contained, independently deployable, and autonomous services that take full responsibility of a business capability and its execution. They bundle all dependencies including the library dependencies; execution environments, such as web servers and containers; or virtual machines that abstract the physical resources.

One of the major differences between microservices and SOA is in its level of autonomy. While most of the SOA implementations provide the service-level abstraction, microservices go further and abstract the realization and the execution environment.

In traditional application developments, we build a war or a ear, then deploy it into a JEE application server, such as **JBoss**, **Weblogic**, **WebSphere**, and more. We may deploy multiple applications into the same JEE container. In the microservices approach, each microservice will be built as a fat jar embedding all dependencies and run as a standalone Java process:

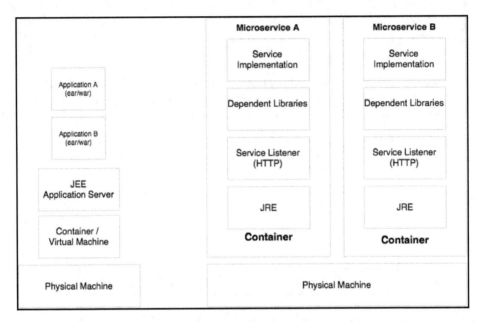

Microservices may also get their own containers for execution, as shown in the preceding diagram. Containers are portable, independently manageable, and lightweight runtime environments. **Container** technologies, such as Docker, are an ideal choice for microservices deployments.

Characteristics of microservices

The microservices definition discussed earlier in this chapter is arbitrary. Evangelists and practitioners have strong, but sometimes, different opinions on microservices. There is no single, concrete, and universally accepted definition for microservices. However, all successful microservices implementations exhibit a number of common characteristics. Therefore, it is important to understand these characteristics rather than sticking to theoretical definitions. Some of the common characteristics are detailed in this section.

Services are first class citizens

In the microservices world, services are first class citizens. Microservices expose service endpoints as APIs and abstract all their realization details. The internal implementation logic, architecture, and technologies, including programming language, database, quality of services mechanisms, and more, are completely hidden behind the service API.

Moreover, in the microservices architecture, there is no more application development, instead organizations will focus on service development. In most enterprises, this requires a major cultural shift in the way applications are built.

In a customer profile microservice, the internals, such as data structure, technologies, business logic, and so on, will be hidden. It wont be exposed or visible to any external entities. Access will be restricted through the service endpoints or APIs. For instance, customer profile microservices may expose register customer and get customers as two APIs for others to interact.

Characteristics of service in a microservice

Since microservices are more or less like a flavor of SOA, many of the service characteristics defined in the SOA are applicable to microservices as well.

The following are some of the characteristics of services that are applicable to microservices as well:

- **Service contract**: Similar to SOA, microservices are described through well-defined service contracts. In the microservices world, JSON and REST are universally accepted for service communication. In case of JSON/REST, there are many techniques used to define service contracts. JSON Schema, WADL, Swagger, and RAML are a few examples.
- **Loose coupling**: Microservices are independent and loosely coupled. In most cases, microservices accept an event as input and respond with another event. Messaging, HTTP, and REST are commonly used for interaction between microservices. Message-based endpoints provide higher levels of decoupling.
- **Service abstraction**: In microservices, service abstraction is not just abstraction of service realization, but also provides complete abstraction of all libraries and environment details, as discussed earlier.
- **Service reuse**: Microservices are course grained reusable business services. These are accessed by mobile devices and desktop channels, other microservices, or even other systems.

- **Statelessness**: Well-designed microservices are a stateless, shared nothing with no shared state, or conversational state maintained by the services. In case there is a requirement to maintain state, they will be maintained in a database, perhaps in-memory.
- **Services are discoverable**: Microservices are discoverable. In a typical microservices environment, microservices self-advertise their existence and make themselves available for discovery. When services die, they automatically take themselves out from the microservices ecosystem.
- **Service interoperability**: Services are interoperable as they use standard protocols and message exchange standards. Messaging, HTTP, and more are used as the transport mechanism. REST/JSON is the most popular method to develop interoperable services in the microservices world. In cases where further optimization is required on communications, then other protocols such as Protocol Buffers, Thrift, Avro, or Zero MQ could be used. However, use of these protocols may limit the overall interoperability of the services.
- **Service Composeability**: Microservices are composeable. Service composeability is achieved either through service orchestration or service choreography.

 More details on SOA principles can be found at `http://serviceorientation.com/serviceorientation/index`.

Microservices are lightweight

Well-designed microservices are aligned to a single business capability; therefore, they perform only one function. As a result, one of the common characteristics we see in most of the implementations are microservices with smaller footprints.

When selecting supporting technologies, such as web containers, we will have to ensure that they are also lightweight so that the overall footprint remains manageable. For example, Jetty or Tomcat are better choices as application containers for microservices as compared to more complex traditional application servers, such as Weblogic or WebSphere.

Container technologies such as Docker also helps us keep the infrastructure footprint as minimal as possible compared to hypervisors such as VMware or **Hyper-V**.

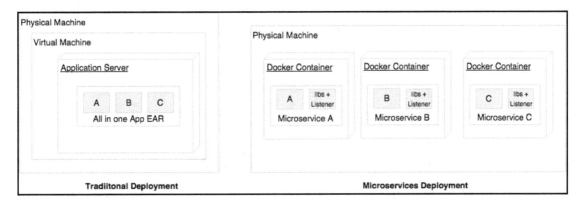

As shown in the preceding diagram, microservices are typically deployed in Docker containers, which encapsulate the business logic and needed libraries. This helps us quickly replicate the entire setup on a new machine, a completely different hosting environment, or even move across different cloud providers. Since there is no physical infrastructure dependency, containerized microservices are easily portable.

Microservices with polyglot architecture

Since microservices are autonomous and abstract everything behind the service APIs, it is possible to have different architectures for different microservices. A few common characteristics that we see in microservices implementations are as follows:

- Different services use different versions of the same technologies. One microservice may be written on Java 1.7 and another one could be on Java 1.8.
- Different languages for developing different microservices, such as one microservice in Java and another one in **Scala**.
- Different architectures such as one microservice using **Redis** cache to serve data while another microservice could use MySQL as a persistent data store.

A polyglot language scenario is depicted in the following diagram:

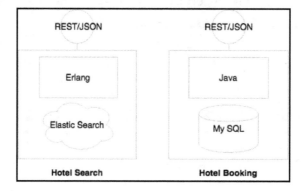

In the preceding example, since **Hotel Search** is expected to have high transaction volumes with stringent performance requirements, it is implemented using **Erlang**. In order to support predictive search, **Elastic Search** is used as the data store. At the same time, Hotel Booking needs more **ACID** transactional characteristics. Therefore, it is implemented using MySQL and Java. The internal implementations are hidden behind service endpoints defined as REST/JSON over HTTP.

Automation in microservices environment

Most of the microservices implementations are automated to a maximum, ranging from development to production.

Since microservices break monolithic applications into a number of smaller services, large enterprises may see a proliferation of microservices. Large numbers of microservices are hard to manage until and unless automation is in place. The smaller footprint of microservices also helps us automate the microservices development to deployment life cycle. In general, microservices are automated end to end, for example, automated builds, automated testing, automated deployment, and elastic scaling:

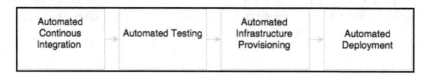

As indicated in the diagram, automations are typically applied during the development, test, release, and deployment phases.

Different blocks in the preceding diagram are explained as follows:

- The development phase will be automated using version control tools, such as Git, together with **continuous integration** (**CI**) tools, such as Jenkins, Travis CI, and more. This may also include code quality checks and automation of unit testing. Automation of a full build on every code check-in is also achievable with microservices.
- The testing phase will be automated using testing tools such as **Selenium, Cucumber**, and other **AB testing strategies**. Since microservices are aligned to business capabilities, the number of test cases to automate will be fewer compared to the monolithic applications; hence, regression testing on every build also becomes possible.
- Infrastructure provisioning will be done through container technologies, such as Docker, together with release management tools, such as Chef or Puppet, and configuration management tools, such as Ansible. Automated deployments are handled using tools such as Spring Cloud, **Kubernetes**, **Mesos**, and Marathon.

Microservices with a supporting ecosystem

Most of the large scale microservices implementations have a supporting ecosystem in place. The ecosystem capabilities include DevOps processes, centralized log management, service registry, API gateways, extensive monitoring, service routing, and flow control mechanisms:

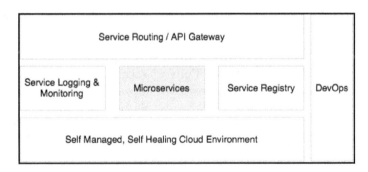

Microservices work well when supporting capabilities are in place, as represented in the preceding diagram.

Microservices are distributed and dynamic

Successful microservices implementations encapsulate logic and data within the service. This results in two unconventional situations:

- Distributed data and logic
- Decentralized governance

Compared to traditional applications, which consolidate all logic and data into one application boundary, microservices decentralize data and logic. Each service, aligned to a specific business capability, owns its own data and logic:

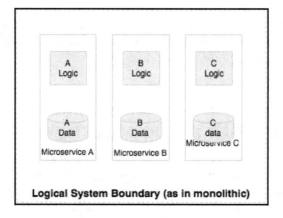

Logical System Boundary (as in monolithic)

The dotted line in the preceding diagram implies the logical monolithic application boundary. When we migrate this to microservices, each microservice, **A**, **B**, and **C**, creates its own physical boundaries.

Microservices don't typically use centralized governance mechanisms the way they are used in SOA. One of the common characteristics of microservices implementations are that they are not relaying on heavyweight enterprise-level products, such as an **Enterprise Service Bus** (**ESB**). Instead, the business logic and intelligence are embedded as a part of the services themselves.

A retail example with ESB is shown as follows:

![Shopping Logic diagram with ESB connecting to Customer, Product, and Order]

A typical SOA implementation is shown in the preceding diagram. **Shopping Logic** is fully implemented in the ESB by orchestrating different services exposed by **Customer**, **Order**, and **Product**. In the microservices approach, on the other hand, shopping itself will run as a separate microservice, which interacts with **Customer**, **Product**, and **Order** in a fairly decoupled way.

SOA implementations are heavily relaying on static registry and repository configurations to manage services and other artifacts. Microservices bring a more dynamic nature into this. Hence, a static governance approach is seen as an overhead in maintaining up-to-date information. This is why most of the microservices implementations use automated mechanisms to build registry information dynamically from the runtime topologies.

Antifragility, fail fast, and self healing

Antifragility is a technique successfully experimented with at Netflix. It is one of the most powerful approaches to build fail-safe systems in modern software development.

 The antifragility concept is introduced by Nassim Nicholas Taleb in his book, *Antifragile: Things That Gain from Disorder*.

In the antifragility practice, software systems are consistently challenged. Software systems evolve through these challenges, and, over a period of time, get better and better to withstand these challenges. Amazon's Game Day exercise and Netflix's **Simian Army** are good examples of such antifragility experiments.

Fail Fast is another concept used to build fault-tolerant, resilient systems. This philosophy advocates systems that expect failures versus building systems that never fail. Importance has to be given to how quickly the system can fail, and, if it fails, how quickly it can recover from that failure. With this approach, the focus is shifted from **Mean Time Between Failures** (**MTBF**) to **Mean Time To Recover** (**MTTR**). A key advantage of this approach is that if something goes wrong, it kills itself, and the downstream functions won't be stressed.

Self-Healing is commonly used in microservices deployments, where the system automatically learns from failures and adjusts itself. These systems also prevent future failures.

Microservices examples

There is no *one size fits all* approach when implementing microservices. In this section, different examples are analyzed to crystalize the microservices concept.

An example of a holiday portal

In the first example, we will review a holiday portal--**Fly By Points**. **Fly By Points** collects points that are accumulated when a customer books a hotel, flight, or car through their online website. When a customer logs in to the **Fly By Points** website, they will be able to see the points accumulated, personalized offers that can be availed by redeeming the points, and upcoming trips, if any:

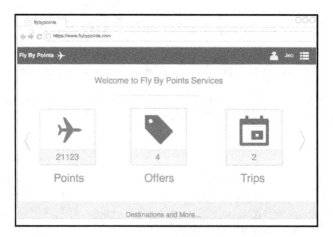

Let's assume that the preceding page is the home page after login. There are **2** upcoming trips for **Jeo**, **4** personalized offers, and **21123** points. When the user clicks on each of the boxes, details will be queried and displayed.

Holiday portal has a Java, Spring-based traditional monolithic application architecture, as follows:

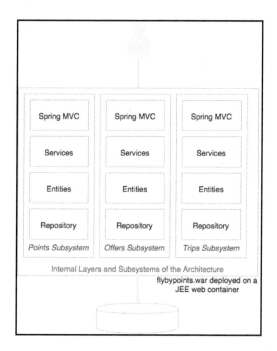

As shown in the preceding diagram, Holiday portal's architecture is web-based and modular with clear separation between layers. Following the usual practice, Holiday portal is also deployed as a single war file deployed on a web server such as **Tomcat**. Data is stored in an all encompassing backing relational database. This is a good fit for the purposes of architecture when the complexities are less. As the business grows, the user base expands and the complexity also increases.

This results in a proportional increase in the transaction volumes. At this point, enterprises should look for rearchitecting the monolithic application to microservices for better speed of delivery, agility, and manageability:

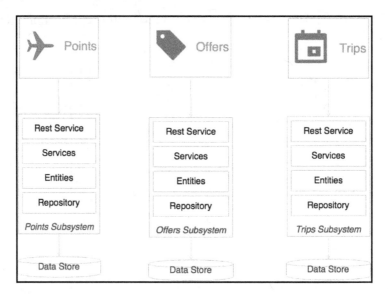

Upon examining the simple microservices version of this application, we will immediately see a few things in this architecture:

- Each subsystem has now become an independent system by itself--a microservice. There are three microservices representing three business functions--**Trips**, **Offers**, and **Points**. Each one has its internal data store and middle layer. The internal structure of each service remains the same.
- Each service encapsulates its own database as well as its own HTTP listener. As opposed to the previous model, there is no web server and there is no war. Instead, each service has its own embedded HTTP listener, such as Jetty, Tomcat, and more.
- Each microservice exposes a rest service to manipulate the resources/entities that belong to that service.

It is assumed that the presentation layer is developed using a client-side JavaScript MVC framework, such as Angular JS. These client-side frameworks are capable of invoking REST calls directly.

When the web page is loaded, all three boxes, **Trips, Offers,** and **Points**, will be displayed with details such as points, number of offers, and number of trips. This will be done by each box independently making asynchronous calls to the respective backend microservices using REST. There is no dependency between the services at the service layer. When the user clicks on any of the boxes, the screen will be transitioned and will load the details of the clicked item. This will be done by making another call to the respective microservice.

An example of a travel agent portal

This third example is a simple travel agent portal application. In this example, we will see both synchronous REST calls as well as asynchronous events.

In this case, portal is just a container application with multiple menu items or links in the portal. When specific pages are requested, for example, when the menu is clicked or a link is clicked, they will be loaded from the specific microservices:

The architecture of the **Travel Agent Portal** backed with multiple microservices is shown as follows:

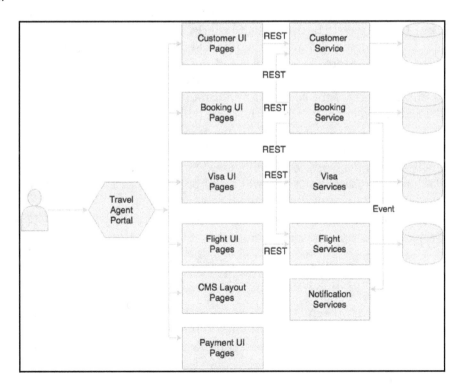

When a customer requests a booking, the following events will take place internally:

- The travel agent opens the flight UI, searches for a flight, and identifies the right flight for the customer. Behind the scenes, the flight UI will be loaded from the Flight microservice. The flight UI only interacts with its own backend APIs within the Flight microservice. In this case, it makes a REST call to the Flight microservice to load the flights to be displayed.
- The travel agent then queries the customer details by accessing the customer UI. Similar to the flight UI, the customer UI will be loaded from the Customer microservices. Actions in the customer UI will invoke REST calls on the Customer microservice. In this case, the customer details will be loaded by invoking appropriate APIs on the Customer microservice.
- Then the travel agent checks the visa details to see the eligibility to travel to the selected country. This will also follow the same pattern as mentioned in the previous two points.
- Then the travel agent makes a booking using the booking UI from the Booking microservices, which again follows the same pattern.
- The payment pages will be loaded from the Payment microservice. In general, the payment service will have additional constraints, including the **Payment Card Industry Data Security Standard** (**PCIDSS**) compliance, such as protecting and encrypting data in motion and data at rest. The advantage of the microservices approach is that none of the other microservices need to be considered under the purview of PCIDSS as opposed to the monolithic application, where the complete application comes under the governing rules of PCIDSS. Payment also follows the same pattern described earlier.
- Once the booking is submitted, the **Booking Service** calls the flight service to validate and update the flight booking. This orchestration is defined as a part of the Booking microservices. Intelligence to make a booking is also held within the Booking microservices. As a part of the booking process, it also validates, retrieves, and updates the Customer microservice.
- Finally, the Booking microservice sends a booking event, which the **Notification Services** picks up, and sends a notification to the customer.

The interesting factor here is that we can change the user interface, logic, and data of a microservice without impacting any other microservices.

This is a clean and neat approach. A number of portal applications could be built by composing different screens from different microservices, especially for different user communities. The over all behavior and navigation will be controlled by the portal application.

The approach has a number of challenges unless the pages are designed with this approach in mind. Note that the site layouts and static contents will be loaded from the **Content Management System** (**CMS**) as layout templates. Alternately, this could be stored in a web server. The site layout may have fragments of User Interfaces, which will be loaded from the microservices at runtime.

Microservices benefits

Microservice offers a number of benefits over the traditional multi-tier monolithic architectures. This section explains some of the key benefits of the microservices architecture approach.

Supports polyglot architecture

With microservices, architects and developers get flexibility in choosing the most suitable technology and architecture for a given scenario. This gives the flexibility to design better fit solutions in a more cost-effective way.

Since microservices are autonomous and independent, each service can run with its own architecture or technology, or different versions of technologies.

The following image shows a simple, practical example of polyglot architecture with microservices:

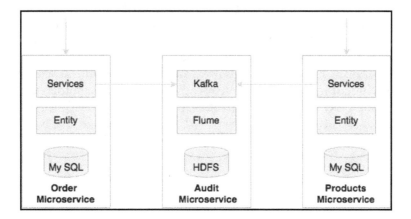

There is a requirement to audit all system transactions and record transaction details such as request and response data, users who initiated the transaction, the service invoked, and so on.

As shown in the preceding diagram, while core services like Order microservice and Product microservice use a relational data store, the Audit microservice persists data in a **Hadoop File System** (**HDFS**). A relational data store is neither ideal nor cost effective to store large data volumes, like in the case of audit data. In the monolithic approach, the application generally uses a shared, single database that stores the **Order**, **Product**, and **Audit** data.

In this example, audit service is a technical microservice using a different architecture. Similarly, different functional services could also use different architectures.

In another example, there could be a Reservation microservice running on Java 7, while a Search microservice could be running on Java 8. Similarly, an Order microservice could be written on Erlang, whereas a Delivery microservice could be on the Go language. None of these are possible with a monolithic architecture.

Enables experimentation and innovation

Modern enterprises are thriving toward quick wins. Microservices is one of the key enablers for enterprises to do disruptive innovation by offering the ability to experiment and Fail Fast.

Since services are fairly simple and smaller in size, enterprises can afford to experiment with new processes, algorithms, business logic, and more. With large monolithic applications, experimentation was not easy, straightforward, or cost effective. Businesses had to spend a large sum of money to build or change an application to try out something new. With microservices, it is possible to write a small microservice to achieve the targeted functionality, and plug it into the system in a reactive style. One can then experiment with the new function for a few months. Moreover, if the new microservice is not working as expected, change or replace it with another one. The cost of change will be considerably less compared to the monolithic approach:

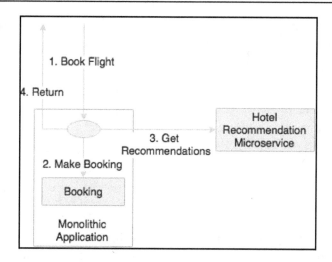

In another example of an airline booking website, the airline wants to show personalized hotel recommendations in their booking page. The recommendations have to be displayed on the booking confirmation page.

As shown in the preceding diagram, it is convenient to write a microservice that can be plugged into the monolithic applications booking flow rather than incorporating this requirement in the monolithic application itself. The airline may choose to start with a simple recommendation service, and keep replacing it with newer versions until it meets the required accuracy.

Elastically and selectively scalable

Since microservices are smaller units of work, it enables us to implement selective scalability and other **Quality of Services (QoS)**.

Scalability requirements may be different for different functions in an application. Monolithic applications are generally packaged as a single war or an ear. As a result, applications can only be scaled as a whole. There is no option to scale a module or a subsystem level. An I/O intensive function, when streamed with high velocity data, could easily bring down the service levels of the entire application.

In the case of microservices, each service could be independently scaled up or down. Since scalability can be selectively applied for each service, the cost of scaling is comparatively less with the microservices approach.

In practice, there are many different ways available to scale an application, and this is largely constraint to the architecture and behavior of the application. The **Scale Cube** defines primarily three approaches to scale an application:

- X-axis scaling, by horizontally cloning the application
- Y-axis scaling, by splitting different functionality
- Z-axis scaling, by partitioning or sharding the data.

 Read more about Scale Cube at http://theartofscalability.com/.

When Y-axis scaling is applied to monolithic applications, it breaks the monolithic into smaller units aligned with business functions. Many organizations successfully applied this technique to move away from monolithic application. In principle, the resulting units of functions are inline with the microservices characteristics.

For instance, on a typical airline website, statistics indicates that the ratio of flight search versus flight booking could be as high as 500:1. This means one booking transaction for every 500 search transactions. In this scenario, search needs 500 times more scalability than the booking function. This is an ideal use case for selective scaling:

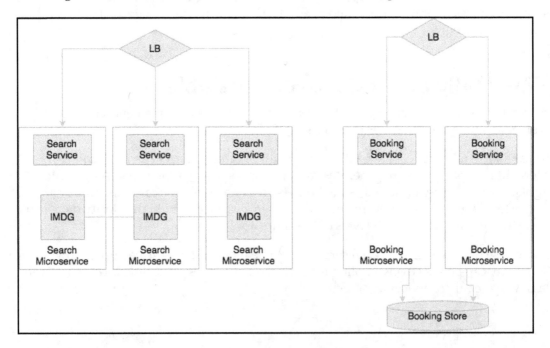

The solution is to treat search requests and booking requests differently. With a monolithic architecture, this is only possible with *Z* scaling in the scale cube. However, this approach is expensive, as, in *Z* scale, the entire codebase will be replicated.

In the preceding diagram, Search and **b** are designed as different microservices so that Search can be scaled differently from Booking. In the diagram, Search has three instances and Booking has two instances. Selective scalability is not limited to the number of instances, as shown in the preceding diagram, but also in the way in which the microservices are architected. In the case of Search, an **In-Memory Data Grid** (**IMDG**) such as Hazelcast can be used as the data store. This will further increase the performance and scalability of Search. When a new Search microservice instance is instantiated, an additional IMDG node will be added to the IMDG cluster. Booking does not require the same level of scalability. In the case of Booking, both instances of the Booking microservices are connected to the same instance of the database.

Allows substitution

Microservices are self-contained independent deployment modules, enabling us to substitute one microservice with another similar microservice.

Many large enterprises follow buy-versus-build policies for implementing software systems. A common scenario is to build most of the functions in-house and buy certain niche capabilities from specialists outside. This poses challenges in the traditional monolithic applications since these application components are highly cohesive. Attempting to plug in third-party solutions to the monolithic applications results in complex integrations. With microservices, this is not an afterthought. Architecturally, a microservice can be easily replaced by another microservice developed, either in-house or even extended by a microservice from a third party:

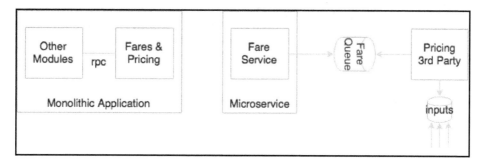

A pricing engine in the airline business is complex. Fares for different routes are calculated using complex mathematical formulas known as pricing logic. Airlines may choose to buy a pricing engine from the market instead of building the product in-house. In the monolithic architecture, **Pricing** is a function of **Fares** and **Booking**. In most cases, Pricing, Fares, and Bookings are hardwired, making it almost impossible to detach.

In a well-designed microservices system, Booking, Fares, and Pricing will be independent microservices. Replacing the Pricing microservice will have only a minimal impact on any other services, as they are all loosely coupled and independent. Today, it could be a third-party service, tomorrow, it could be easily substituted by another third-party service or another home grown service.

Enables to build organic systems

Microservices help us build systems that are organic in nature. This is significantly important when migrating monolithic systems gradually to microservices.

Organic systems are systems that grow laterally over a period of time by adding more and more functions to it. In practice, applications grow unimaginably large in its lifespan, and, in most cases, the manageability of the application reduces dramatically over that same period of time.

Microservices are all about independently manageable services. This enables us to keep adding more and more services as the need arises, with minimal impact on the existing services. Building such systems do not need huge capital investment. Hence, businesses can keep building as part of their operational expenditure.

A loyalty system in an airline was built years ago, targeting individual passengers. Everything was fine until the airline started offering loyalty benefits to their corporate customers. Corporate customers are individuals grouped under corporations. Since the current system's core data model is flat, targeting individuals, the corporate requirement needs a fundamental change in the core data model, and hence, a huge rework to incorporate this requirement.

As shown in the following diagram, in a microservices-based architecture, customer information would be managed by the Customer microservices, and loyalty by the Loyalty microservice:

In this situation, it is easy to add a new Corporate Customer microservice to manage corporate customers. When a corporation is registered, individual members will be pushed to the Customer microservices to manage them as usual. The Corporate Customer microservice provides a corporate view by aggregating data from the Customer microservice. It will also provide services to support corporate-specific business rules. With this approach, adding new services will have only a minimal impact on existing services.

Helps managing technology debt

Since microservices are smaller in size and have minimal dependencies, they allow the migration of services that are using end-of-life technologies with minimal cost.

Technology changes are one of the barriers in software development. In many traditional monolithic applications, due to the fast changes in technology, today's next generation applications could easily become legacy, even before releasing to production. Architects and developers tend to add a lot of protection against technology changes by adding layers of abstractions. However, in reality, this approach doesn't solve the issue, but, instead, it results in over-engineered systems. Since technology upgrades are often risky and expensive, with no direct returns for the business, the business may not be happy to invest in reducing the technology debt of the applications.

With microservices, it is possible to change or upgrade technology for each service individually, rather than upgrading an entire application.

Upgrading an application with, for instance, five million lines written on **EJB 1.1** and Hibernate to Spring, **JPA**, and REST services is almost like rewriting the entire application. In the microservices world, this could be done incrementally.

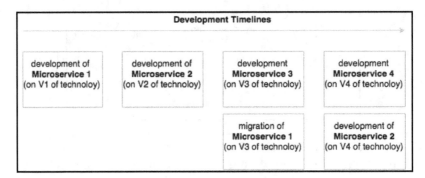

As shown in the preceding diagram, while older versions of the services are running on old versions of technologies, new service developments can leverage the latest technologies. The cost of migrating microservices with end-of-life technologies will be considerably less compared to enhancing monolithic applications.

Allowing co-existence of different versions

Since microservices package the service runtime environment along with the service itself, it enables multiple versions of the service to coexist in the same environment.

There will be situations where we will have to run multiple versions of the same service at the same time. Zero downtime promote, where one has to gracefully switch over from one version to another, is one example of such a scenario, as there will be a time window where both services will have to be up and running simultaneously. With monolithic applications, this is a complex procedure, since upgrading new services in one node of the cluster is cumbersome as, for instance, this could lead to class loading issues. A Canary release, where a new version is only released to a few users to validate the new service, is another example where multiple versions of the services have to coexist.

With microservices, both these scenarios are easily manageable. Since each microservice uses independent environments, including the service listeners such as embedded Tomcat or Jetty, multiple versions can be released and gracefully transitioned without many issues. Consumers, when looking up services, look for specific versions of services. For example, in a canary release, a new user interface is released to user A. When user A sends a request to the microservice, it looks up the canary release version, whereas all other users will continue to look up the last production version.

Care needs to be taken at database level to ensure that the database design is always backward compatible to avoid breaking changes.

As shown in the following diagram, version V01 and V02 of the Customer service can coexist as they are not interfering with each other, given their respective deployment environment:

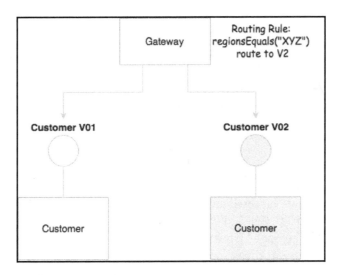

Routing rules can be set at the gateway to divert traffic to specific instances, as shown in the diagram. Alternatively, clients can request specific versions as a part of the request itself. In the diagram, the gateway selects the version based on the region from which the request originated.

Supporting building self-organizing systems

Microservices help us build self-organizing systems. A self-organizing system supporting automated deployment will be resilient and exhibits self-healing and self-learning capabilities.

In a well-architected microservice system, services are unaware of other services. It accepts a message from a selected queue and processes the message. At the end of the process, it may send out another message that triggers other services. This allows us to drop any service into the ecosystem without analyzing the impact on the overall system. Based on the input and output, the service will self-organize into the ecosystem. No additional code changes or service orchestration is required. There is no central brain to control and coordinate the processes.

Imagine an existing notification service that listens to an INPUT queue and sends notifications to a **Simple Mail Transfer Protocol (SMTP)** server as follows:

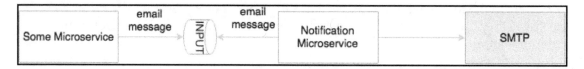

If later, a personalization engine needs to be introduced to personalize messages before sending it to the customer, the personalization engine is responsible for changing the language of the message to the customer's native language.

The updated service linkage is shown as follows:

With microservices, a new personalization service will be created to do this job. The input queue will be configured as INPUT in an external configuration server. The personalization service will pick up the messages from the INPUT queue (earlier, this was used by the notification service), and send the messages to the OUTPUT queue after completing the process. The notification service's input queue will then send to OUTPUT. From the very next moment onward, the system automatically adopts this new message flow.

Supporting event-driven architecture

Microservices enable us to develop transparent software systems. Traditional systems communicate with each other through native protocols and hence behave like a black-box application. Business events and system events, unless published explicitly, are hard to understand and analyze. Modern applications require data for business analysis, to understand dynamic system behaviors, and analyze market trends, and they also need to respond to real-time events. Events are useful mechanisms for data extraction.

A well-architected microservice always works with events for both input and output. These events can be tapped by any services. Once extracted, events can be used for a variety of use cases.

For example, businesses want to see the velocity of orders categorized by the product type in real-time. In a monolithic system, we will need to think about how to extract these events, which may impose changes in the system.

The following diagram shows the addition of **New Event Aggregation Service** without impacting existing services:

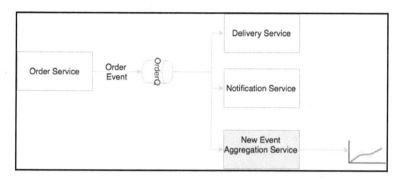

In the microservices world, **Order Event** is already published whenever an order is created. This means that it is just a matter of adding a new service to subscribe to the same topic, extract the event, perform the requested aggregations, and push another event for the dashboard to consume.

Enables DevOps

Microservices are one of the key enablers of DevOps. DevOps is widely adopted as a practice in many enterprises, primarily to increase the speed of delivery and agility. Successful adoption of DevOps requires cultural changes and process changes, as well as architectural changes. It advocates to have agile development, high velocity release cycles, automatic testing, automatic infrastructure provisioning, and automated deployment. Automating all these processes is extremely hard to achieve with traditional monolithic applications. Microservices are not the ultimate answer, but microservices are at the center stage in many DevOps implementations. Many DevOps tools and techniques are also evolving around the use of microservices.

Considering a monolithic application takes hours to complete a full build and twenty to thirty minutes to start the application, one can see that this kind of application is not ideal for DevOps automation. It is hard to automate continuous integration on every commit. Since large monolithic applications are not automation friendly, continuous testing and deployments are also hard to achieve.

On the other hand, small footprint microservices are more automation-friendly, and, therefore, they can more easily support these requirements.

Microservices also enables smaller, focused agile teams for development. Teams will be organized based on the boundaries of microservices.

Summary

In this chapter, we learned about the fundamentals of microservices with the help of a few examples.

We explored the evolution of microservices from traditional monolithic applications. We examined some of the principles and mind shift required for modern application architectures. We also looked at some of the common characteristics repeatedly seen in most of the successful microservices implementations. Finally, we also learned the benefits of microservices.

10
Related Architecture Styles and Use Cases

Microservices are on top of the hype at this point. At the same time, there are noises around certain other architecture styles, for instance, serverless architecture. Which is good? Are they competing against each other? What are the appropriate scenarios and the best ways to leverage microservices? These are the obvious questions raised by many developers.

In this chapter, we will analyze various other architecture styles and establish the and relationships between microservices and other buzz words such as **Service Oriented Architecture (SOA), Twelve-Factor Apps, serverless computing, Lambda architectures, DevOps, Cloud, Containers, and Reactive Microservices**. Twelve-Factor Apps defines a set of software engineering principles to develop applications targeting cloud. We will also analyze typical use cases of microservices and review some of the popular frameworks available for the rapid development of microservices.

By the end of this chapter, you will have learned about the following:

- Relationship of microservices with SOA and Twelve-Factor Apps
- Link to serverless computing and Lambda architecture style used in the context of Big Data, **cognitive computing**, and the **Internet of Things (IoT)**
- Supporting architecture elements such as Cloud, Containers, and DevOps
- Reactive Microservices
- Typical use cases of microservices architecture
- A few popular microservices frameworks

Service-Oriented Architecture (SOA)

SOA and microservices follow similar concepts. In the Chapter 9, *Demystifying Microservices*, we saw that microservices are evolved from SOA and many service characteristics are common in both approaches.

However, are they the same or are they different?

Since microservices are evolved from SOA, many characteristics of microservices are similar to SOA. Let's first examine the definition of SOA.

The Open Group definition of SOA (http://www.opengroup.org/soa/ source-book/soa/p1.htm) is as follows:

SOA is an architectural style that supports service-orientation. Service-orientation is a way of thinking in terms of services and service-based development and the outcomes of services.

A service:

- *Is a logical representation of a repeatable business activity that has a specified outcome (e.g., check customer credit, provide weather data, consolidate drilling reports)*
- *Is self-contained*
- *May be composed of other services*
- *Is a "black box" to consumers of the service*

We have learned similar aspects in microservices as well. *So, in what way are microservices different?* The answer is--it depends.

The answer to the previous question could be yes or no, depending on the organization and its adoption of SOA. SOA is a broader term, and different organizations approached SOA differently to solve different organizational problems. The difference between microservices and SOA is based on the way an organization approaches SOA.

In order to get clarity, a few scenarios will be examined in the following section.

Service-oriented integration

Service-oriented integration refers to a service-based integration approach used by many organizations:

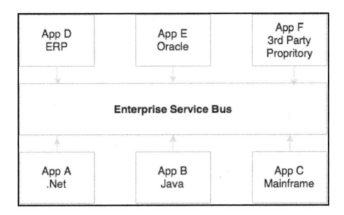

Many organizations would have used SOA primarily to solve their integration complexities, also known as integration spaghetti. Generally, this is termed as **Service-Oriented Integration (SOI)**. In such cases, applications communicate with each other through a common integration layer using standard protocols and message formats, such as SOAP/XML based web services over HTTP or **Java Message Service (JMS)**. These types of organizations focus on **Enterprise Integration Patterns (EIP)** to model their integration requirements. This approach strongly relies on heavyweight **Enterprise Service Bus (ESB)**, such as TIBCO BusinessWorks, WebSphere ESB, Oracle ESB, and the likes. Most of the ESB vendors also packed a set of related products, such as Rules Engines, Business Process Management Engines, and so on, as an SOA suite. Such organization's integrations are deeply rooted into these products. They either write heavy orchestration logic in the ESB layer or business logic itself in the service bus. In both cases, all enterprise services are deployed and accessed via the ESB. These services are managed through an enterprise governance model. For such organizations, microservices is altogether different from SOA.

Legacy modernization

SOA is also used to build service layers on top of legacy applications:

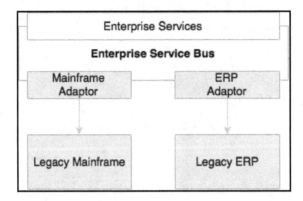

Another category of organizations would have used SOA in transformation projects or legacy modernization projects. In such cases, the services are built and deployed in the ESB connecting to backend systems using ESB adapters. For these organizations, microservices are different from SOA.

Service-oriented application

Some organizations would have adopted SOA at an application level:

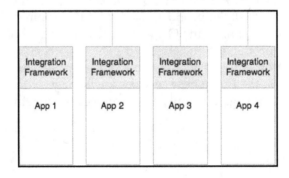

In this approach, lightweight integration frameworks, such as **Apache Camel** or **Spring Integration**, are embedded within applications to handle service-related cross-cutting capabilities, such as protocol mediation, parallel execution, orchestration, and service integration. Since some of the lightweight integration frameworks had native Java object support, such applications would have even used native **Plain Old Java Objects** (**POJO**) services for integration and data exchange between services. As a result, all services have to be packaged as one monolithic web archive. Such organizations could see microservices as the next logical step of their SOA.

Monolithic migration using SOA

The following diagram shows a monolithic application, broken down into three micro applications:

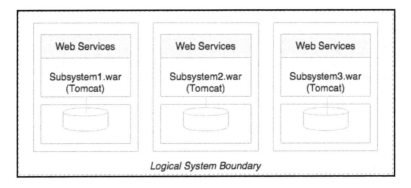

The last possibility is transforming a monolithic application into smaller units after hitting the breaking point with the monolithic system. They would have broken the application into smaller, physically deployable subsystems, similar to the **Y-axis scaling** approach explained earlier, and deployed them as web archives on web servers, or as jars deployed on some homegrown containers. These subsystems as service would have used web services or other lightweight protocols to exchange data between services. They would have also used SOA and service-design principles to achieve this. For such organizations, they may tend to think that microservices are the same old wine in a new bottle.

Twelve-Factor Apps

Cloud computing is one of the most rapidly evolving technologies. It promises many benefits, such as cost advantage, speed, agility, flexibility, and elasticity. There are many cloud providers offering different services. They are lowering the cost models to make it more attractive to the enterprises. Different cloud providers, such as AWS, Microsoft, Rackspace, IBM, Google, and so on, use different tools, technologies, and services. On the other hand, enterprises are aware of this evolving battlefield and, therefore, they are looking for options for de-risking from lockdown to a single vendor.

Many organizations do a lift and shift of their applications to cloud. In such cases, the applications may not realize all benefits promised by the cloud platforms. Some applications need to undergo an overhaul, whereas some may need minor tweaking before moving to the cloud. This is, by and large, depends upon how the application is architectured and developed.

For example, if the application has its production database server URLs hardcoded as a part of the applications war, this needs to be modified before moving the application to cloud. In the cloud, the infrastructure is transparent to the application and, especially, the physical IP addresses cannot be assumed.

How do we ensure that an application, or even microservices, can run seamlessly across multiple cloud providers and take advantages of cloud services such as elasticity?

It is important to follow certain principles while developing cloud-native applications.

Cloud native is a term used to develop applications that can work efficiently in a cloud environment, and understand and utilize cloud behaviors, such as elasticity, utilization-based charging, fail aware, and so on.

Twelve-Factor App, forwarded by Heroku, is a methodology describing characteristics expected from a modern cloud-ready application. These twelve factors are equally applicable for microservices as well. Hence, it is important to understand the Twelve-Factors.

Single code base

The code base principle advices that each application should have a single code base. There can be multiple instances of deployment of the same code base, such as development, testing, or production. The code is typically managed in a source-control system such as Git, Subversion, and so on:

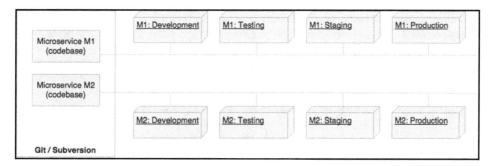

Extending the same philosophy for microservices, each microservice should have its own code base, and this code base is not shared with any other microservice. It also means that one microservice will have exactly one code base.

Bundle dependencies

As per this principle, all applications should bundle their dependencies along with the application bundle. With build tools such as **Maven** and **Gradle**, we explicitly manage dependencies in a **Project Object Model** (**POM**) or gradle file, and link them using a central build artifact repository such as **Nexus** or **Archiva**. This will ensure that the versions are managed correctly. The final executables will be packaged as a war file or an executable jar file embedding all dependencies:

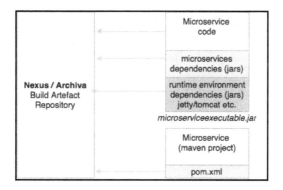

In the context of microservices, this is one of the fundamental principles to be followed. Each microservices should bundle all required dependencies and execution libraries, such as HTTP listener and more, in the final executable bundle.

Externalizing configurations

The Externalize configurations principle gives you an advice to externalize all configuration parameters from the code. An application's configuration parameters vary between environments such as support email IDs or URL of an external system, username, passwords, queue name, and more. These will be different for development, testing, and production. All service configurations should be externalized:

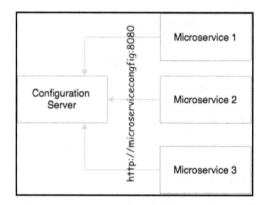

The same principle is obvious for microservices as well. Microservices configuration parameters should be loaded from an external source. This will also help you automate the release and deployment process as the only change between these environments are the configuration parameters.

Backing services are addressable

All backing services should be accessible through an addressable URL. All services need to talk to some external resources during the life cycle of their execution. For example, they could be listening to or sending messages to a messaging system, sending an email, or persisting data to a database. All these services should be reachable through a URL without complex communication requirements:

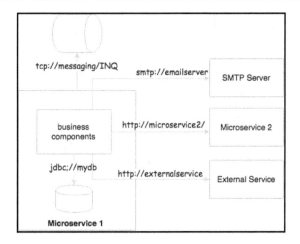

In the microservices world, microservices can either talk to a messaging system to send or receive messages, or they can accept or send messages to another service API. In a regular case, these are either HTTP endpoints using REST and JSON or TCP or HTTP-based messaging endpoints.

Isolation between build, release, and run

This principle advocates strong isolation between the build stage, the release stage, and the run stage. The build stage refers to compiling and producing binaries by including all assets required. The release stage refers to combining binaries with environment-specific configuration parameters. The run stage refers to running applications on a specific execution environment. The pipeline is unidirectional. Hence, it is not possible to propagate changes from run stages back to the build stage. Essentially, it also means that it is not recommended to do specific builds for production; rather, it has to go through the pipeline:

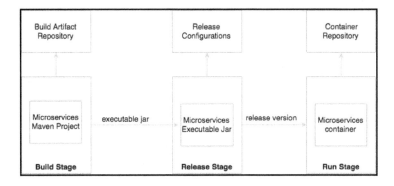

In microservices, the build will create executable jar files, including the service runtime, such as the HTTP listener. During the release phase, these executables will be combined with release configurations, such as production URLs, and so on, and create a release version, most probably as a container like **Docker**. In the run stage, these containers will be deployed on production via a container scheduler.

Stateless, shared nothing processes

This principle suggests that processes should be stateless and share nothing. If the application is stateless, then it is fault tolerant, and can be scaled out easily.

All microservices should be designed as stateless functions. If there is any requirement to store a state, it should be done with a backing database or in an in-memory cache.

Expose services through port bindings

A Twelve-Factor App is expected to be self-contained or standalone. Traditionally, applications are deployed into a server--a web server or an application server, such as Apache Tomcat or JBoss, respectively. A Twelve-Factor App ideally does not relay on an external web server. A HTTP listener, such as Tomcat, **Jetty**, and more, has to be embedded in the service or application itself.

Port binding is one of the fundamental requirements for microservices to be autonomous and self-contained. Microservice embeds the service listeners as a part of the service itself.

Concurrency for scale out

The concurrency for scale out principle states that processes should be designed to scale out by replicating the processes. This is in addition to the use of threads within the process.

In the microservices world, services are designed for a scale out rather than scale up. The *X*-axis scaling technique is primarily used for scaling a service by spinning up another identical service instance. The services can be elastically scaled or shrunk, based on the traffic flow. Furthermore, microservices may make use of parallel processing and concurrency frameworks to further speed up or scale up the transaction processing.

Disposability, with minimal overhead

The disposability with minimal overhead principle advocates to build applications with minimal startup and shutdown times, and with a graceful shutdown support. In an automated deployment environment, we should be able to bring up or bring down instances as quickly as possible. If the application's startup or shutdown takes considerable time, it will have an adverse effect on automation. The startup time is proportionally related to the size of the application. In a cloud environment targeting auto scaling, we should be able to spin up a new instance quickly. This is also applicable when promoting new versions of services.

In the microservices context, in order to achieve full automation, it is extremely important to keep the size of the application as thin as possible, with minimal startup and shutdown times. Microservices should also consider lazy loading of objects and data.

Development, production parity

The development, production parity principle states the importance of keeping the development and production environments as identical as possible. For example, let's consider an application with multiple services or processes, such as a job scheduler service, cache services, or one or more application services. In a development environment, we tend to run all of them on a single machine. Whereas, in production, we will facilitate independent machines to run each of these processes. This is primarily to manage cost of the infrastructure. The downside is that, if production fails, there is no identical environment to reproduce and fix the issues.

This principle is not only valid for microservices, but it is also applicable to any application development.

Externalizing logs

A Twelve-Factor App never attempts to store or ship log files. In a cloud, it is better to avoid local I/Os or file systems. If the I/Os are not fast enough in a given infrastructure, they could create a bottleneck. The solution to this is to use a centralized logging framework. **Splunk, greylog, Logstash, Logplex, Loggly** are some examples of log shipping and analysis tools. The recommended approach is to ship logs to a central repository by tapping the logback appenders and write to one of the shipper's endpoints.

In a microservices ecosystem, this is very important, as we are breaking a system into a number of smaller services, which could result in decentralized logging. If they store logs in a local storage, it would be extremely difficult to correlate logs between services:

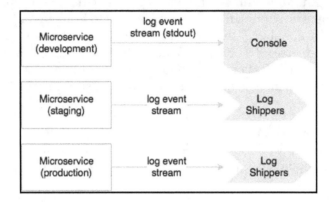

In development, microservice may direct the log stream to **stdout**, whereas, in production, these streams will be captured by the log shippers and sent to a central log service for storage and analysis.

Package admin processes

Apart from application requests, most of the applications provision for admin tasks. This principle advices you to target the same release and an identical environment as the long running processes runs to perform these activities. Admin code should also be packaged along with the application code.

This principle is not only valid for microservices, but it is also applicable to any application development.

Serverless computing

Serverless computing architecture or **Functions as a Service (FaaS)** has gained quite a bit of popularity these days. In serverless computing, developers need not worry about application servers, virtual machines, Containers, infrastructure, scalability, and other quality of services. Instead, developers write functions and drop those functions into an already running computing infrastructure. Serverless computing improves faster software deliveries as it eliminates the provisioning and management part of the infrastructure required by microservices. Sometimes, this is even referred to as **NoOps**.

FaaS platforms support multiple language runtimes, such as Java, Python, Go, and so on. There are many serverless computing platforms and frameworks available. Moreover, this space is still evolving. **AWS Lambda**, **IBM OpenWhisk**, **Azure Functions**, **Google Cloud Functions** are some of the popular managed infrastructures for serverless computing. **Red Hat Funktion** is another serverless computing platform on top of **Kubernetes**, which can be deployed on any cloud or on premise. **IronFunctions** is one of the recent entrants--a cloud-agnostic, serverless computing platform. There are other serverless computing platforms, such as Webtask for web-related functions. **BrightWork** is another serverless computing platform for JavaScript applications that offers minimal vendor locking.

There are many other frameworks intended to simplify AWS Lambda development and deployment supporting different languages. **Apex**, **Serverless**, **Lambda Framework for Java**, **Chalice for Python**, **Claudia for Node JS**, **Sparta for Go**, and **Gordon** are some of the popular frameworks in this category.

Serverless computing is closely related to microservices. In other words, microservices are the basis for serverless computing. There are a number of characteristics shared by both, serverless computing as well as microservices. Similar to microservices, functions generally perform one task at a time, are isolated in nature, and communicate through designated APIs that are either event-based or HTTP. Also, functions have smaller footprints like microservices. It is safe to say that functions follow microservices-based architecture.

The following diagram shows a serverless computing scenario based on AWS Lambda:

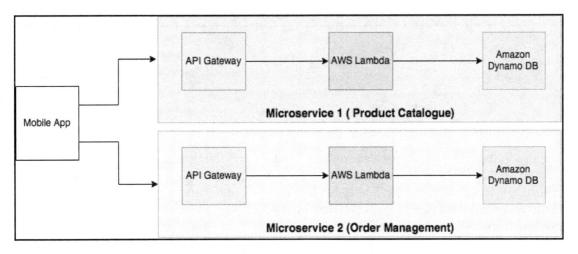

In this scenario, each microservice will be developed as a separate AWS Lambda function and independently wired through an API gateway for HTTP-based communication. In this case, each microservice holds its own data in an Amazon DynamoDB.

Generally, the FaaS billing model is truly based on the **pay as you use** model, as opposed to pay for what is reserved model followed in case of virtual machines or EC2 instances. Moreover, developers need not worry about passivating images when they are no longer used. When there are only a few transactions, just enough computing power will be charged. As the load increases, more resources will be automatically allocated. This makes serverless computing an attractive model for many enterprises.

The new style of microservices use cases such as big data, cognitive computing, IoT, and bots, which are perfect candidates for serverless computing. More about these use cases is explained in the next section.

It is also important to note that the disadvantage of serverless computing is its strong vendor locking. This space is still getting matured, and, perhaps, we will see more tooling in this space to reduce these gaps. In the future, we will also see a large number of services available in the market place that can be utilized by microservice developers when developing on serverless computing platforms. Serverless computing, together with microservices architecture, is definitely a promising choice for developers.

Lambda architecture

There are new styles of microservices use cases in the context of big data, cognitive computing, bots, and IoT:

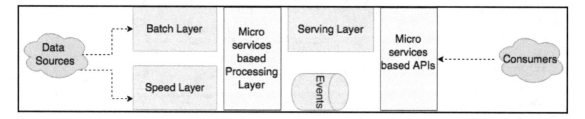

The preceding diagram shows a simplified **Lambda architecture** commonly used in the context of big data, cognitive, and IoTs. As you can see in the diagram, microservices play a critical role in the architecture. The batch layer process data, and store typically in a **Hadoop Distributed File System** (HDFS) file system. Microservices are written on top of this batch layer process data and build serving layer. Since microservices are independent, when they encounter new demands, it is easy to add those implementations as microservices.

Speed-layer microservices are primarily reactive microservices for stream processing. These microservices accept a stream of data, apply logic, and then respond with another set of events. Similarly, microservices are also used for exposing data services on top of the serving layer.

The following are different variations of the preceding architecture:

- **Cognitive computing** scenarios, such as integrating an optimization service, forecasting service, intelligent price calculation service, prediction service, offer service, recommendation service, and more, are good candidates for microservices. These are independent stateless computing units that accepts certain data, applies algorithms, and returns the results. These are cognitive computing microservices run on top of either speed layer or batch layer. Platforms such as Algorithmia uses microservices-based architecture.
- **Big Data** processing services that run on top of big data platforms to provide answer sets is another popular use case. These services connect to the big data platform's read-relevant data, process those records, and provide necessary answers. These services typically run on top of the batch layer. Platforms such as **MapR** embrace microservices.
- **Bots** that are conversational in nature use the microservices architecture. Each service is independent and executes one function. This can be treated as either API service on top of the serving layer or stream processing services on top of the speed layer. Bots platforms, such as the Azure bot service, leverages the microservices architecture.
- **IoT** scenarios such as machine or sensor data stream processing utilize microservices to process data. These kinds of services run on top of the speed layer. Industrial internet platforms such as Predix are based on the microservices philosophy.

DevOps, Cloud, and Containers

The trios Cloud (more specifically, Containers), Microservices and **DevOps**, are targeting a set of common objectives--speed of delivery, business value, and cost benefits. All three can stay evolved independently, but they complement each other to achieve the desired common goals. Organizations embarking on any of these naturally tend to consider the others as they are closely linked together:

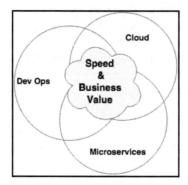

Many organizations start their journey with DevOps as an organizational practice to achieve high velocity release cycles, but eventually move to microservices architecture and cloud. However, it is not mandatory to have microservices and Cloud to support DevOps. However, automating release cycles of large monolithic applications does not make much sense, and, in many cases, it would be impossible to achieve. In such scenarios, microservices architecture and Cloud will be handy when implementing DevOps.

If we flip the coin, Cloud does not need a microservices architecture to achieve its benefits. However, to effectively implement microservices, both Cloud and DevOps are essential.

In summary, if the objective of an organization is to achieve speed of delivery and quality in a cost-effective way, the trio together can bring tremendous success.

DevOps as the practice and process for microservices

Microservice is an architecture style that enables quick delivery. However, microservices cannot provide the desired benefits by itself. A microservices-based project with a delivery cycle of six months does not give the targeted speed of delivery or business agility. Microservices need a set of supporting delivery practices and processes to effectively achieve their goal.

DevOps is the ideal candidate as the underpinning process and practices for microservice delivery. It processes and practices gel well with the microservices architecture philosophies.

Cloud and Containers as the self-service infrastructure for microservices

The main driver for cloud is to improve agility and reduce cost. By reducing the time to provision the infrastructure, the speed of delivery can be increased. By optimally utilizing the infrastructure, one can bring down the cost. Therefore, cloud directly helps you achieve both speed of delivery and cost.

Without having a cloud infrastructure with the cluster management software, it would be hard to control the infrastructure cost when deploying microservices. Hence, the cloud with self-service capabilities is essential for microservices to achieve their full potential benefits. In a microservices context, the cloud not only helps you abstract the physical infrastructure, but also provides software APIs for dynamic provisioning and automatic deployments. This is referred to as **infrastructure as code** or **software defined infrastructure**.

Containers further provide benefits when dealing with DevOps and microservices. They provide better manageability and a cost-effective way of handling large volumes of deployments. Furthermore, container services and container orchestration tools helped you manage infrastructures.

Reactive microservices

The reactive programming paradigm is an effective way to build scalable, fault-tolerant applications. The reactive manifesto defines basic philosophy of reactive programming.

Read more about the reactive manifesto here:
http://www.reactivemanifesto.org

By combining the reactive programming principles together with the microservices architecture, developers can build low latency high throughput scalable applications.

Microservices are typically designed around business capabilities. Ideally, well-designed microservices will exhibit minimal dependencies between microservices. However, in reality, when microservices are expected to deliver same capabilities delivered by monolithic applications, many microservices have to work in collaboration. Dividing services based on business capabilities will not solve all issues. Isolation and communication between services are also equally important. Even though microservices are often designed around business capabilities, wiring them with synchronous calls can form hard dependencies between them. As a result, organizations may not realize the full benefits of microservices. Distributed systems with strong dependencies between them have its own overheads and are hard to manage. For example, if an upgrade is required for one of the microservices, it can seriously impact other dependent services. Hence, adopting reactive style is important for successful microservices implementations.

Let's examine reactive microservices a bit more. There are four pillars when dealing with reactive programming. These attributes are **resilient**, **responsive**, **message based**, and **elastic**. Resilient and responsive are closely linked to isolation. Isolation is the foundation for both reactive programming as well as microservices. Each microservice is autonomous and is the building block of a larger system. By and large, these microservices are isolated from the rest of its functional components by drawing boundaries around business functions. By doing so, failures of one service can be well isolated from the others. In case of failures, it should not cause issues to its downstream services. Either a fallback service or a replica of the same service will takeover its responsibility temporarily. By introducing isolation, each isolated components can be scaled, managed, and monitored independently.

Even though isolation is in place, if the communication or dependencies between services are modeled as synchronous blocking RPC calls, then failures cannot be fully isolated. Hence, it is extremely important to design communications between services in a reactive style by using asynchronous non-blocking calls:

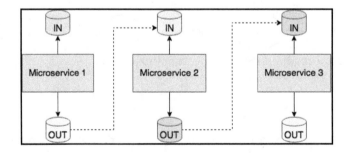

As shown in the preceding diagram, in a reactive system, each microservice will listen to an event. The service reacts upon receiving an input event. The service then starts processing the event and sends out another response event. The microservice itself is not aware of any other services running in the ecosystem. In this example, **Microservice 1** does not have any knowledge of **Microservice 2** and **Microservice 3**. Choreography can be achieved by connecting an output queue of one service to the input queue of another service, as shown in the diagram.

Based on the velocity of events, services can automatically scale up by spinning out replicas of instances. For example, in a reactive style order management system, as soon as an order is placed, the system will send out an **Order Event**. There could be many microservices listening to an **Order Event.** Upon consuming this event, they perform various things. This design also allows developers to keep adding more and more reactive routines as need arises.

The flow control or choreography in case of reactive microservices will be taken care of automatically, as shown earlier in the diagram. There is no central command and control. Instead, messages and input and output contracts of microservices itself will establish flow. Changing the message flow is easy to achieve by rewiring input and output queues.

 The **Promise theory** proposed by Mark Burgess in 2004 has so much relevance in this situation. The Promise theory defines an autonomous collaboration model for systems or entities to interact in a distributed environment using voluntary cooperation. The theory claims that promise-based agents can reproduce the same behavior exhibited by traditional command and control systems that follows the obligation model. Reactive microservices are inline with the Promise theory, in which, each service is independent and can collaborate in a completely autonomous manner. **Swarm Intelligence** is one of these formal architecture mechanisms, increasingly applied in the modern artificial intelligent systems for building highly scalable intelligence routines.

A highly scalable and reliable message system is the single most important component in a reactive microservices ecosystem. **QBit**, **Spring Reactive**, **RxJava**, and **RxJS** are some of the frameworks and libraries that help you build reactive microservices. Spring 5 has inbuilt support to develop reactive web applications. **Spring Cloud Streams** are good choice to build truly reactive microservices using Spring Framework.

A reactive microservice-based order management system

Let's examine another microservices example: an online retail web site. In this case, we will focus more on the backend services, such as the order event generated when the customer places an order through the website:

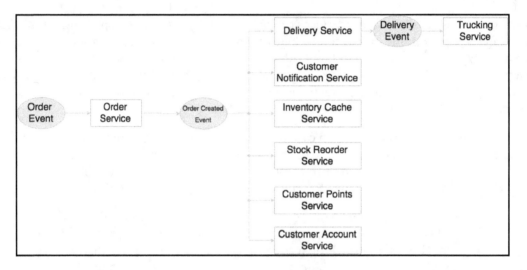

This microservices system is completely designed based on reactive programming practices.

When an event is published, a number of microservices are ready to kick start upon receiving the event. Each one of them is independent and is not relying on other microservices. The advantage of this model is that we can keep adding or replacing microservices to achieve specific needs.

In the preceding diagram, there are eight microservices shown. The following activities take place on arrival of an **OrderEvent**:

- **OrderService** kicks off when an **OrderEvent** is received. **OrderService** creates an order and saves details to its own database.
- If the order is successfully saved, an **OrderSuccessfulEvent** is created by **OrderService** and published.

- A series of actions will take place when **OrderSuccessfulEvent** arrives.
- **DeliveryService** accepts the event and places a **DeliveryRecord** to deliver the order to the customer. This in turn generates **DeliveryEvent** and publishes the event.
- The **TruckingService** picks up the **DeliveryEvent** and processes it. For instance, **TruckingService** creates a trucking plan.
- **CustomerNotificationService** sends a notification to the customer informing the customer that an order is placed.
- **InventoryCacheService** updates the inventory cache with the available product count.
- **StockReorderService** checks whether the stock limits are adequate and generates **ReplenishEvent** if required.
- **CustomerPointsService** recalculates the customer's loyalty points based on this purchase.
- **CustomerAccountService** updates the order history in the customer account.

In this approach, each service is responsible for only one function. Services accept and generate events. Each service is independent and is not aware of its neighborhoods. Hence, the neighborhood can organically grow as mentioned in the **honeycomb analogy**. New services could be added as and when necessary. Adding a new service does not impact any of the existing service.

Microservice use cases

Microservice is not a silver bullet, and it will not solve all the architectural challenges of today's world. There is no hard and fast rule, or a rigid guideline on when to use microservices.

Microservices may not fit in each and every use case. The success of microservices largely depends on the selection of use cases. The first and the foremost activity is to do a litmus test of the use case against the microservices benefits. The litmus test must cover all microservices benefits we had discussed earlier in this chapter. For a given use case, if there are no quantifiable benefits, or if the cost is outweighing the benefits, then the use case may not be the right choice for microservices.

Let's discuss some commonly used scenarios that are suitable candidates for a microservice architecture:

- Migrating a monolithic application due to improvements required in scalability, manageability, agility, or speed of delivery. Another similar scenario is rewriting an end-of-life heavily-used legacy application. In both cases, microservices presents an opportunity. Using a microservices architecture, it is possible to replatform the legacy application by slowly transforming functions to microservices. There are benefits in this approach. There is no humongous upfront investment required, no major disruption to business, and there are no severe business risks. Since the service dependencies are known, the microservices dependencies can be well managed.

- In many cases, we build headless business applications or business services that are autonomous in nature. For instance, payment service, login service, flight search service, customer profile service, notification service, and more. These are normally reused across multiple channels, and, hence, are good candidates for building them as microservices.

- There could be micro or macro applications that serves a single purpose and performs a single responsibility. A simple time-tracking application is an example of this category. All it does is capture time, duration, and the task performed. Common use enterprise applications are also candidates for microservices.

- Backend services of a well architected, responsive, client side MVC web application (**Backend as a Service (BaaS)**). In most of these scenarios, data could be coming from multiple logically different data sources, as described in the *Fly By Points* example mentioned in Chapter 9, *Demystifying Microservices*.

- Highly agile applications, applications demanding speed of delivery or time to market, innovation pilots, applications selected for DevOps, System of Innovation type of applications, and so on, could also be considered as potential candidates for microservices architecture.

- Applications that we could anticipate getting benefits from microservices, such as polyglot requirements; applications that require **Command Query Responsibility Segregation (CQRS)**; and so on, are also potential candidates of microservices architecture.

- Independent technical services and utility services, such as communication service, encryption service, authentication services and so on, are also good candidates for microservices.

If the use case falls into any of these categories, they are potential candidates for microservices architecture. There are a few scenarios that we should consider avoiding in microservices:

- If the organization policies are forced to use centrally-managed heavyweight components, such as ESBs, to host the business logic, or if the organization has any other policies that are hindering the fundamental principles of microservices, then microservices are not the right solution, unless the organizational process is relaxed.

- If the organizations culture, processes, and more are based on traditional waterfall delivery model, lengthy release cycles, matrix teams, manual deployments and cumbersome release processes, no infrastructure provisioning, and more, then microservices may not be the right fit. This is underpinned by the **Conway's law**. The Conway's law states that there is a strong link between organizational structure and the software they create.

Read more about the conveys law here:
`http://www.melconway.com/Home/Conways_Law.html`

Microservices early adopters - Is there a common theme?

Many organizations had already successfully embarked on their journey to the microservices world. In this section, we will examine some of the front runners on the microservices space to analyze why they did what they did, and how they did it? The following is a curated list of organizations adopted microservices, based on the information available on the internet:

- **Netflix** (`www.netflix.com`): Netflix, an international, on-demand, media streaming company, is a pioneer in the microservices space. Netflix transformed their large pool of developers developing traditional monolithic code to smaller development teams producing microservices. These microservices work together to stream digital media to millions of Netflix customers. At Netflix, engineers started with monolithic architecture, went through the pain, and then broke the application into smaller units that are loosely coupled and aligned to business capability.

- **Uber** (www.uber.com): Uber, an international transportation network company, was started in 2008 with a monolithic architecture with single codebase. All services were embedded into the monolithic application. When Uber expanded their business from one city to multiple cities, challenges started. Uber then moved to SOA-based architecture by breaking the system into smaller independent units. Each module was given to different teams, empowered to choose their language, framework, and database. Uber has many microservices deployed in their ecosystem using RPC and REST.

- **Airbnb** (www.airbnb.com): Airbnb, a world leader providing trusted marketplace for accommodations, started with a monolithic application that performed all required functions of the business. It faced scalability issues with increased traffic. A single codebase became too complicated to manage, resulting in poor separation of concerns, and running into performance issues. Airbnb broke their monolithic application into smaller pieces, with separate codebases, running on separate machines, with separate deployment cycles. Airbnb has developed their own microservices or SOA ecosystem around these services.

- **Orbitz** (www.orbitz.com): Orbitz, an online travel portal, started with a monolithic architecture in the 2000s with a web layer, a business layer, and a database layer. As Orbitz expanded their business, they faced manageability and scalability issues with the monolithic-tiered architecture. Orbitz had then gone through continuous architecture changes. Later, Orbitz broke down their monolithic application in to many smaller applications.

- **eBay** (www.ebay.com): eBay, one of the largest online retailers, started in the late 90s with a monolithic Perl application with **FreeBSD** as its database. eBay went through scaling issues as the business grew. It was consistently invested on improving architecture. In the mid 2000s, eBay moved to smaller decomposed systems based on Java and web services. They employed database partitions and functional segregation to meet the required scalability.

- **Amazon** (www.amazon.com): Amazon, one of the largest online retailer's website in 2001 was running on a big monolith application written on C++. The well-architected monolithic application was based on tiered architecture with many modular components. However, all these components were tightly coupled. As a result, Amazon was not able to speed up their development cycle by splitting teams into smaller groups. Amazon then separated out code as independent functional services wrapped with web services, and eventually advanced to microservices.

- **Gilt** (www.gilt.com): Gilt, an online shopping website, started in 2007 with a tiered monolithic Rails application with Postgres database at the back. Just like many other applications, as traffic volumes increased, this web application was not able to provide the required resiliency. Gilt went through an architecture overhaul by introducing Java and polyglot persistence. Later, Gilts moved to many smaller applications using microservices concept.
- **Twitter** (www.twitter.com): Twitter, one of the largest social websites, started with a three-tiered monolithic rails application in the mid 2000s. Later, when Twitter experienced growth in the user base, it went through an architecture refactoring cycle. With that refactoring, Twitter moved away from a typical web application to an API-based event-driven core. Twitter is using Scala and Java to develop microservices with polyglot persistence.
- **Nike** (www.nike.com): Nike, the world leader in apparels and footwear, transformed their monolithic applications to microservices. Like many other organizations, Nike was running with age old legacy applications that are hardly stable. In their journey, Nike moved to heavyweight commercial products with an objective to stabilize legacy applications, but ended up in monolithic applications that are expensive to scale, have long release cycles, and require too much manual work to deploy and manage applications. Later, Nike moved to microservices-based architecture, which brought down the development cycle considerably.

Monolithic migration as the common use case

When we analyze the preceding enterprises, there is one common theme. All these enterprises started with monolithic applications and transitioned to microservices architecture by applying learning and pain points from their previous editions.

Even today, many start-ups are starting with monolith as it is easy to start, conceptualize, and then slowly move them to microservices when the demand arises. Monolithic to microservices migration scenarios have an added advantage that we have all information upfront, readily available for refactoring.

Although it is a monolithic transformation for all of those enterprises, the catalysts were different for different organizations. Some of the common motivations are lack of scalability, long development cycles, process automation, manageability, and changes in business models.

While monolithic migrations are no brainers, there are opportunities to build ground-up microservices. More than building ground-up systems, look for an opportunity to build smaller services that are quick wins for the business. For example, adding a trucking service to an airline's end-to-end cargo management system, or adding a customer scoring service to a retailer's loyalty system. These could be implemented as independent microservices exchanging messages with their respective monolithic applications.

Another point is that many of the organizations are using microservices only for their business' critical and customer engagement applications, leaving the rest of their legacy monolithic applications to take its own trajectory.

Another important observation is that most of the organizations examined previously are at different levels of maturity in their microservices journey. When eBay transitioned from the monolithic application in the early 2000s, they functionally split the application into smaller, independent, deployable units. These logically divided units are wrapped with web services. While single responsibility and autonomy are their underpinning principles, the architectures are limited to the technologies and tools available at that point in time. Organizations such as Netflix and Airbnb built capabilities of their own to solve specific challenges they faced. To summarize, all of them are not truly microservices, but are small, business-aligned services following the same characteristics.

There is no state called definite or ultimate microservices. It is a journey, and it is evolving and maturing day by day. The mantra for architects and developers is the replaceability principle--build an architecture that maximizes the ability to replace its parts and minimizes the cost of replacing its parts. The bottom line is that enterprises shouldn't attempt to develop microservices by just following the hype.

Microservice frameworks

Microservices are already in the main stream. When developing microservices, there are some cross-cutting concerns that need to be implemented, such as externalized logging, tracing, embedded HTTP listener, health checks, and so on. As a result, significant efforts will go into developing these cross-cutting concerns. Microservices frameworks are emerged in this space to fill these gaps.

There are many microservices frameworks available apart from those that are mentioned specifically under the serverless computing. The capabilities vary between these microservice frameworks. Hence, it is important to choose the right framework for development.

Spring Boot, **Dropwizard**, and **Wildfly Swarm** are popular enterprise-grade HTTP/REST implementations for the development of microservices. However, these frameworks only provide minimalistic support for large-scale microservices development. Spring Boot, together with **Spring Cloud**, offers sophisticated support for microservices. **Spring Framework 5** introduced the reactive web framework. Combining Spring Boot and Spring Framework 5 reactive is a good choice for reactive style microservices. Alternatively, **Spring Streams** can also be used for the microservices development.

The following is a curated list of other microservices frameworks:

- Lightbend's **Lagom** (`www.lightbend.com/lagom`) is a full-fledged, sophisticated, and popular microservices framework for Java and Scala.
- WSO2 **Microservices For Java - MSF4J** (`github.com/wso2/msf4j`) is a lightweight, high performance microservices framework.
- **Spark** (`sparkjava.com`) is a micro framework to develop REST services.
- **Seneca** (`senecajs.org`) is a microservices toolkit for Node JS in a fast and easy way similar to Spark.
- **Vert.x** (`vertx.io`) is a polyglot microservices toolkit to build reactive microservices quickly.
- **Restlet** (`restlet.com`) is a framework used to develop REST-based APIs in a quick and efficient way.
- **Payra-micro** (`payara.fish`) is used to develop web applications (war files) and run them on a standalone mode. Payra is based on Glass Fish.
- **Jooby** (`jooby.org`) is another micro-web framework that can be used to develop REST-based APIs.
- **Go-fasthttp** (`github.com/valyala/fasthttp`) is a high performance HTTP package for Go, useful to build REST services.
- **JavaLite** (`javalite.io`) is a framework to develop applications with HTTP endpoints.
- **Mantl** (`mantl.io`) is open source microservices framework come from Cisco for the microservice development and deployments.
- **Fabric8** (`fabric8.io`) is an integrated microservices development platform on top of Kubernetes, backed by Red Hat.
- **Hook.io** (`hook.io`) is another microservices deployment platform.
- **Vamp** (`vamp.io`) is an open source self-hosted platform to manage microservices that relies on container technologies.

- **Go Kit** (`github.com/go-kit/kit`) is a standard library for microservices using the Go language.
- **Micro** (`github.com/micro/micro`) is a microservice toolkit for Go language.
- **Lumen** (`lumen.laravel.com`) is a lightweight, fast micro-framework.
- **Restx** (`restx.io`) is a lightweight, REST development framework.
- **Gizmo** (`github.com/NYTimes/gizmo`) is a reactive microservices framework for Go.
- **Azure service fabric** (`azure.microsoft.com/en-us/services/service-fabric/`) has also emerged as a microservice development platform.

This list does not end here. There are many more in this category, such as Kontena, Gilliam, Magnetic, Eventuate, LSQ, and Stellient, which are some of the platforms supporting microservices.

The rest of this book will focus on building microservices using Spring Framework projects.

Summary

In this chapter, we learned about the relationship of the microservices architecture with a few other popular architecture styles.

We started with microservices relationships with SOA and Twelve-Factor Apps. We also examined the link between the microservices architecture and other architectures, such as serverless computing architecture and Lambda Architecture. We also learned the advantages of using microservices together with cloud and DevOps. We then analyzed examples of a few enterprises from different industries that successfully adopted microservices and their use cases. Finally, we reviewed some of the microservices frameworks evolved over a period of time.

In the next chapter, we will develop a few sample microservices to bring more clarity to our learnings in this chapter.

11
Building Microservices with Spring Boot

Developing microservices is not so tedious anymore--thanks to the powerful Spring Boot framework. Spring Boot is a framework for developing production-ready microservices in Java.

This chapter will move from the microservices theory explained in the previous chapters to hands-on practice by reviewing code samples. Here, we will introduce the Spring Boot framework, and explain how Spring Boot can help building RESTful microservices inline with the principles and characteristics discussed in the previous chapter. Finally, some of the features offered by Spring Boot for making the microservices production ready will be reviewed.

At the end of this chapter, you will have learned about the following:

- Setting up the latest Spring development environment
- Developing RESTful services using Spring Framework 5 and Spring Boot
- Building reactive microservices using Spring WebFlux and Spring Messaging
- Securing microservices using Spring Security and OAuth2
- Implementing cross-origin microservices
- Documenting Spring Boot microservices using Swagger
- Spring Boot Actuator for building production-ready microservices

Setting up a development environment

To crystalize microservices' concepts, a couple of microservices will be built. For that, it is assumed that the following components are installed:

- **JDK 1.8** (http://www.oracle.com/technetwork/java/javase/downloads/jdk8-downloads-2133151.html)
- **Spring Tool Suite 3.8.2 (STS)** (https://spring.io/tools/sts/all)
- **Maven 3.3.1** (https://maven.apache.org/download.cgi)

Alternately, other IDEs like **IntelliJ IDEA/NetBeans/Eclipse** could be used. Similarly, alternate build tools like **Gradle** can be used. It is assumed that Maven repository, class path, and other path variables are set properly for running STS and Maven projects.

This chapter is based on the following versions of Spring libraries:

- Spring Framework 5.0.0.RC1
- Spring Boot 2.0.0. M1

The focus of this chapter is not to explore the full features of Spring Boot, but to understand some of the essential and important features of Spring Boot, required when building microservices.

Spring Boot for building RESTful microservices

Spring Boot is a utility framework from the Spring team for bootstrapping Spring-based applications and microservices quickly and easily. The framework uses an opinionated approach over configurations for decision making, thereby reducing the effort required on writing a lot of boilerplate code and configurations. Using the 80-20 principle, developers should be able to kick start a variety of Spring applications with many default values. Spring Boot further presents opportunities to the developers for customizing applications by overriding auto-configured values.

Spring Boot not only increases the speed of development, but also provides a set of production-ready ops features such as health checks and metrics collections. Since Spring Boot masks many configuration parameters and abstracts many lower level implementations, it minimizes the chances of errors to a certain extent. Spring Boot recognizes the nature of the application based on the libraries available in the classpath, and runs the auto-configuration classes packaged in those libraries.

Often, many developers mistakenly see Spring Boot as a code generator, but, in reality, it is not. Spring Boot only auto-configures build files, for example, pom files in the case of Maven. It also sets properties, such as data source properties, based on certain opinionated defaults.

Consider the following dependencies in the file `pom.xml`:

```
<dependency>
  <groupId>org.springframework.boot</groupId>
  <artifactId>spring-boot-starter-data-jpa</artifactId>
</dependency>

<dependency>
  <groupId>org.hsqldb</groupId>
  <artifactId>hsqldb</artifactId>
  <scope>runtime</scope>
</dependency>
```

For instance, in the preceding case, Spring Boot understands that the project is set to use the Spring Data JPA and HSQL database. It automatically configures the driver class and other connection parameters.

One of the great outcomes of Spring Boot is that it almost eliminates the need to have traditional XML configurations. Spring Boot also enables microservices development by packaging all the required runtime dependencies into a fat executable jar.

Getting started with Spring Boot

These are the different ways in which Spring Boot-based application development can be started:

- By using **Spring Boot CLI** as a command-line tool
- By using IDEs like **Spring Tool Suite** (**STS**), which provide Spring Boot, supported out of the box

- By using the **Spring Initializr** project at `http://start.spring.io`
- By using **SDKMAN! (The Software Development Kit Manager)** from `http://sdkman.io`

The first three options will be explored in this chapter, developing a variety of example services.

Developing a Spring Boot microservice

The easiest way to develop and demonstrate Spring Boot's capabilities is by using the Spring Boot CLI, a command-line tool.

The following are the steps to set up and run Spring Boot CLI:

1. Install the Spring Boot command-line tool by downloading the `spring-boot-cli-2.0.0.BUILD-M1-bin.zip` file from the following location URL: `https://repo.spring.io/milestone/org/springframework/boot/spring-boot-cli/2.0.0.M1/`

2. Unzip the file into a directory of choice. Open a terminal window, and change the terminal prompt to the `bin` folder.

 Ensure that the `/bin` folder is added to the system path so that Spring Boot can be run from any location. Otherwise, execute from the `bin` folder by using the command `./spring`.

3. Verify the installation with the following command. If successful, the Spring CLI version will be printed on the console as shown:

   ```
   $spring --version
   Spring CLI v2.0.0.M1
   ```

4. As the next step, a quick REST service will be developed in groovy, which is supported out of the box in Spring Boot. To do so, copy and paste the following code using any editor of choice, and save it as `myfirstapp.groovy` into any folder:

   ```
   @RestController
   class HelloworldController {
     @RequestMapping("/")
     String sayHello(){
       return "Hello World!"
   ```

```
        }
    }
```

5. In order to run this groovy application, go to the folder where `myfirstapp.groovy` is saved, and execute the following command. The last few lines of the server startup log will be as shown in the following command snippet:

```
$spring run myfirstapp.groovy
2016-12-16 13:04:33.208  INFO 29126 --- [ runner-0]
s.b.c.e.t.TomcatEmbeddedServletContainer : Tomcat started on
port(s):
8080 (http)
2016-12-16 13:04:33.214  INFO 29126 --- [ runner-0]
o.s.boot.SpringApplication : Started application in 4.03
seconds (JVM running for 104.276)
```

6. Open a browser window, and point the URL to `http://localhost:8080`; the browser will display the following message:

   Hello World!

There is no war file created and no Tomcat server was running. Spring Boot automatically picked up Tomcat as the web server, and embedded it into the application. This is a very basic, minimal microservice. The `@RestController`, used in the previous code, will be examined in detail in the next example.

Developing our first Spring Boot microservice

In this section, we will demonstrate how to develop a Java-based REST/JSON Spring Boot service using STS.

 The full source code of this example is available as the `chapter3.Bootrest` project in the code files of this book under the following Git repository: `https://github.com/rajeshrv/Spring5Microservice`

1. Open STS, right-click in **Project Explorer** window, select **New Project**, then select `Spring Starter Project` as shown in the following screenshot. Then click on **Next**:

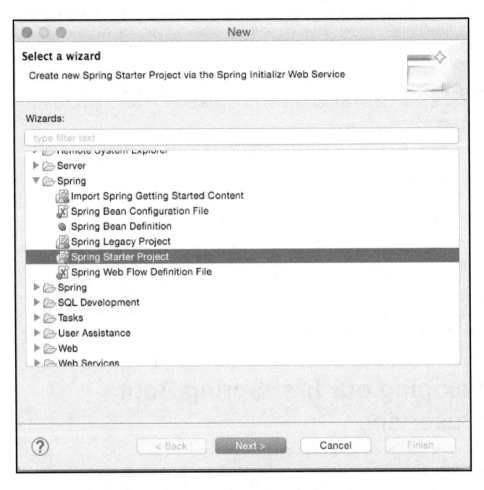

2. The `Spring Starter Project` is a basic template wizard, which provides a selection of a number of other starter libraries.
3. Type the project name as `chapter3.bootrest`, or any other name of your choice. It is important to choose the packaging as Jar. In traditional web applications, a war file is created, and then deployed into a servlet container, whereas, Spring Boot packages all the dependencies into a self-contained, autonomous jar with an embedded HTTP listener.

4. Select **Java Version** as **1.8**. Java 1.8 is recommended for Spring 5 applications. Change other Maven properties such as **Group, Artifact**, and **Package** as shown in the following screenshot:

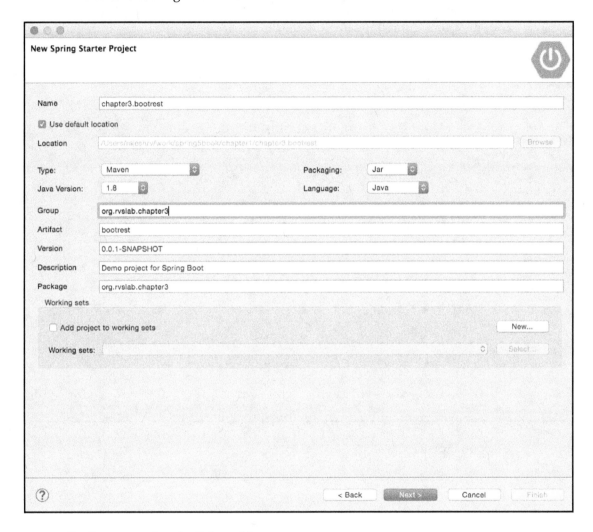

5. Once completed, click on **Next**.

6. The wizard will show the library options. In this case, since we are developing REST services, select **Web** under **Web**. This is an interesting step, which tells Spring Boot that a Spring MVC web application is being developed so that spring boot can include the necessary libraries, including Tomcat, as the HTTP listener and other configurations as required:

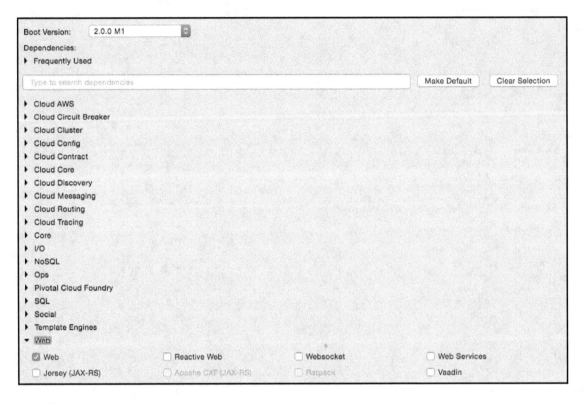

7. Click on **Finish**.

8. This will generate a project named `chapter3.bootrest` in **STS Project Explorer**:

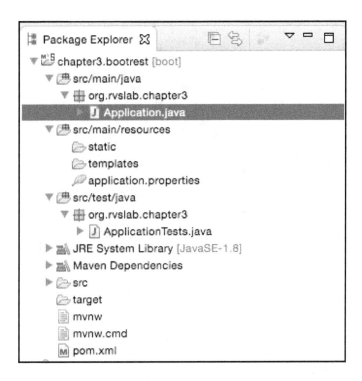

9. Let us examine the `pom` file. The parent element is one of the interesting aspects in `pom.xml`:

```
<parent>
  <groupId>org.springframework.boot</groupId>
  <artifactId>spring-boot-starter-parent</artifactId>
  <version>2.0.0.M1</version>
</parent>
```

`Spring-boot-starter-parent` is a **bill-of-materials** (**BOM**), a pattern used by Maven's dependency management. The BOM is a special kind of pom used for managing different library versions required for a project. The advantage of using the `spring-boot-starter-parent` pom is that developers need not worry about finding the right, compatible versions of different libraries such as Spring, Jersey, Junit, Logback, Hibernate, Jackson, and more.

The starter pom has a list of Boot dependencies, sensible resource filtering, and sensible plug-in configurations required for the Maven builds.

Refer to the following link to see the different dependencies provided in the starter parent (version 2.0.0). All these dependencies can be overridden if required: `https://github.com/spring-projects/spring-boot/blob/a9503abb94b203a717527b81a94dc9d3cb4b1afa/spring-boot-dependencies/pom.xml`

The starter pom itself does not add jar dependencies to the project. Instead, it only adds library versions. Subsequently, when dependencies are added to `pom.xml`, they refer to the library versions from this `pom.xml`. Some of the properties are as shown next:

```xml
<activemq.version>5.14.5</activemq.version>
<commons-collections.version>3.2.2
</commons-collections.version>
<hibernate.version>5.2.10.Final</hibernate.version>
<jackson.version>2.9.0.pr3</jackson.version>
<mssql-jdbc.version>6.1.0.jre8</mssql-jdbc.version>
<spring.version>5.0.0.RC1</spring.version>
<spring-amqp.version>2.0.0.M4</spring-amqp.version>
<spring-security.version>5.0.0.M1</spring-security.version>
<thymeleaf.version>3.0.6.RELEASE</thymeleaf.version>
<tomcat.version>8.5.15</tomcat.version>
```

Reviewing the dependency section of our `pom.xml`, one can see that this is a clean and neat `pom` file with only two dependencies:

```xml
<dependencies>
  <dependency>
    <groupId>org.springframework.boot</groupId>
    <artifactId>spring-boot-starter-web</artifactId>
  </dependency>
  <dependency>
    <groupId>org.springframework.boot</groupId>
    <artifactId>spring-boot-starter-test</artifactId>
    <scope>test</scope>
  </dependency>
</dependencies>
```

Since **Web** is selected, `spring-boot-starter-web` adds all dependencies required for a Spring MVC project. It also includes dependencies to Tomcat as an embedded HTTP listener. This provides an effective way to get all the dependencies required as a single bundle. Individual dependencies could be replaced with other libraries, such as replacing Tomcat with Jetty.

Similar to web, Spring Boot also comes up with a number of `spring-boot-starter-*` libraries, such as amqp, aop, batch, data-jpa, thymeleaf, and so on.

The last thing to be reviewed in the file `pom.xml` is the Java 8 property as shown here:

```
<java.version>1.8</java.version>
```

By default, the parent pom adds Java 6. It is recommended to override the Java version to 8 for Spring 5.

10. Let us now examine `Application.java`. Spring Boot, by default, generated a class `org.rvslab.chapter3.Application.java` under `src/main/java` for bootstrapping:

```
@SpringBootApplication
public class Application {
    public static void main(String[] args) {
        SpringApplication.run(Application.class, args);
    }
}
```

There is only a main method in the application, which will be invoked at startup, as per the Java convention. The main method bootstraps the Spring Boot application by calling the run method on `SpringApplication`. `Application.class` is passed as a parameter to tell Spring Boot that this is the primary component.

More importantly, the magic is done by the `@SpringBootApplication` annotation. `@SpringBootApplication` is a top-level annotation, which encapsulates three other annotations, as shown in the following code snippet:

```
@Configuration
@EnableAutoConfiguration
@ComponentScan
public class Application {
```

The `@Configuration` annotation hints that the contained class declares one or more `@Bean` definitions. `@Configuration` is meta-annotated with `@Component`, therefore, they are candidates for component scanning.

`@EnableAutoConfiguration` tells Spring Boot to automatically configure the Spring application based on the dependencies available in the class path.

11. Let us examine `application.properties`--a default `application.properties` file is placed under `src/main/resources`. It is an important file for configuring any required properties for the Spring Boot application. At the moment, this file is kept empty, and will be revisited with some test cases later in this chapter.

12. Let us examine `ApplicationTests.java` under `src/test/java`. This is a placeholder for writing test cases against the Spring Boot application.

13. As the next step, add a REST endpoint. Let us edit `Application.java` under `src/main/java`, and add a RESTful service implementation. The RESTful service is exactly the same as what was done in the previous project. Append the following code at the end of the `Application.java` file:

```
@RestController
class GreetingController{
  @GetMapping("/")
  Greet greet(){
    return new Greet("Hello World!");
  }
}
class Greet{
  private String message;
  public Greet() {}
  public Greet(String message){
    this.message = message;
  }
  //add getter and setter
}
```

14. To run, go to **Run As | Spring Boot App**. Tomcat will be started on the 8080 port:

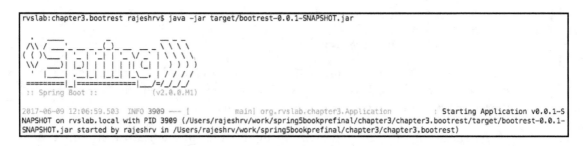

15. We can notice the following things from the log:
    - Spring Boot gets its own process ID (in this case, `3909`)
    - Spring Boot automatically starts the Tomcat server at the local host, port `8080`
    - Next, open a browser and point to `http://localhost:8080`. This will show the JSON response as follows:

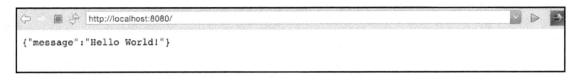

The key difference between the legacy service and this one is that the Spring Boot service is self-contained. To make this clearer, run the Spring Boot application outside STS.

Open a terminal window, go to the project folder, and run Maven as follows:

```
$ maven install
```

This preceding command will generate a fat jar under the target folder of the project. Running the application from the command line shows the following:

```
$java -jar target/bootrest-0.0.1-SNAPSHOT.jar
```

As one can see, `bootrest-0.0.1-SNAPSHOT.jar` is self-contained, and could be run as a standalone application. At this point, the jar is as thin as 14 MB. Even though the application is not more than just a *hello world*, the spring boot service just developed practically follows the principles of microservices.

Testing Spring Boot microservice

There are multiple ways to test REST/JSON Spring Boot microservices. The easiest way is to use a web browser or a curl command pointing to the URL, like this:

```
curl localhost:8080
```

There are number of tools available for testing RESTful services such as Postman, Advanced Rest Client, SOAP UI, Paw, and more.

In this example, for testing the service, the default test class generated by Spring Boot will be used. Adding a new test case to `ApplicatonTests.java` results in this:

```
@RunWith(SpringRunner.class)
@SpringBootTest(webEnvironment = WebEnvironment.RANDOM_PORT)
public class ApplicationTests {
  @Autowired
  private TestRestTemplate restTemplate;
  @Test
  public void testSpringBootApp() throws JsonProcessingException,
  IOException {
    String body = restTemplate.getForObject("/", String.class);
    assertThat(new ObjectMapper().readTree(body)
      .get("message")
      .textValue())
      .isEqualTo("Hello World!");
  }
}
```

Note that `@SpringBootTest` is a simple annotation for testing Spring Boot applications, which enables Spring Boot features during test execution. `webEnvironment=WebEnvironment.RANDOM_PORT` property directs the Spring Boot application to bind to a random port. This will be handy when running many Spring Boot services as part of a regression test. Also note that `TestRestTemplate` is being used for calling the RESTful service. `TestRestTemplate` is a utility class, which abstracts the lower-level details of the HTTP client, and also automatically discovers the actual port used by Spring Boot.

To test this, open a terminal window, go to the project folder, and run `mvn install`.

HATEOAS-enabled Spring Boot microservice

In the next example, **Spring Initializr** will be used to create a Spring Boot project. Spring Initializr is a drop-in replacement for the STS project wizard, and provides a web UI for configuring and generating a Spring Boot project. One of the advantages of the Spring Initializr is that it can generate a project through the website, which can then be imported into any IDE.

In this example, the concept of **HyperMedia As The Engine Of Application State (HATEOAS)** for REST-based services and the **Hypertext Application Language (HAL)** browser will be examined.

HATEOAS is useful for building conversational style microservices which exhibit strong affinity between UI and its backend services.

HATEOAS is a REST service pattern in which navigation links are provided as part of the payload metadata. The client application determines the state, and follows the transition URLs provided as part of the state. This methodology is particularly useful in responsive mobile and web applications where the client downloads additional data based on user navigation patterns.

The HAL browser is a handy API browser for hal+json data. HAL is a format based on JSON, which establishes conventions for representing hyperlinks between resources. HAL helps APIs to be more explorable and discoverable.

> The full source code of this example is available as the
> `chapter3.boothateoas` project in the code files of this book under the
> following Git repository: `https://github.com/rajeshrv/`
> `Spring5Microservice`

Here are the concrete steps for developing a HATEOAS sample using Spring Initilizr:

1. In order to use Spring Initilizr, go to `https://start.spring.io`:

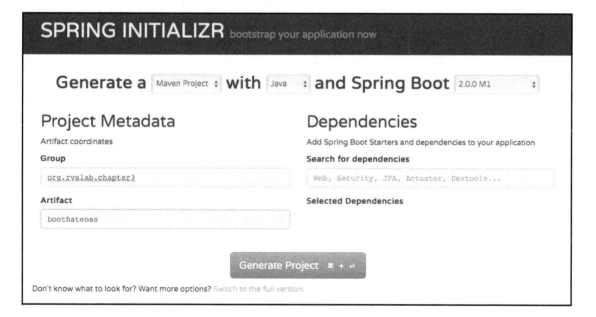

2. Fill the details such as **Maven Project**, Spring Boot version, **Group**, and **Artifact**, as shown in the preceding screenshot, and click on **Switch to the full** version below the **Generate Projects** button. Select **Web, HATEOAS**, and **Rest Repositories HAL Browser**. Make sure the Java version is 8, and the package type is selected as Jar, as shown in the following screenshot:

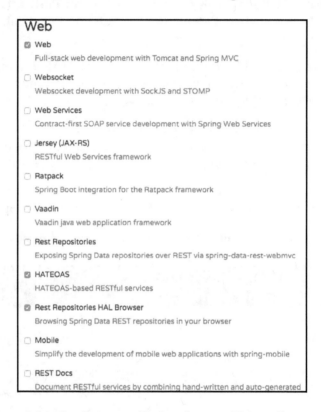

3. Once selected, hit the **Generate Project** button. This will generate a Maven project, and download the project as a zip file into the download directory of the browser.

4. Unzip the file, and save it to a directory of your choice.

5. Open STS, go to the **File** menu, and click on **Import**:

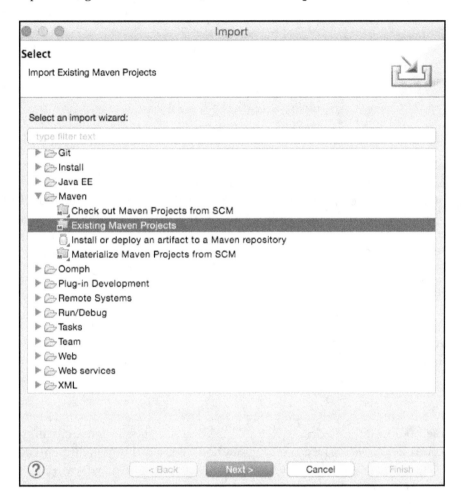

6. Navigate to `Maven | Existing Maven Projects`, then click on **Next**.
7. Click on browse next to the root directory, and select the unzipped folder. Click on **Finish**. This will load the generated Maven project in **STS Project Explorer**.

8. Edit `BoothateoasApplication.java` to add a new REST endpoint as follows:

```
@RequestMapping("/greeting")
@ResponseBody
public HttpEntity<Greet> greeting(@RequestParam(value = "name",
   required = false, defaultValue = "HATEOAS") String name) {
  Greet greet = new Greet("Hello " + name);
  greet.add(linkTo(methodOn(GreetingController.class)
    .greeting(name)).withSelfRel());
  return new ResponseEntity<Greet>(greet, HttpStatus.OK);
}
```

9. Note that this is the same `GreetingController` class as in the previous example. But a method named greeting was added this time. In this new method, an additional optional request parameter is defined and defaulted to HATEOAS. The following code adds a link to the resulting JSON--in this case, it adds the link to the same API.

10. The following code adds a self-reference web link to the Greet object: `"href"`: `"http://localhost:8080/greeting?name=HATEOAS"`:

```
greet.add(linkTo(methodOn(
   GreetingController.class).greeting(name)).withSelfRel());
```

In order to do this, we need to extend the `Greet` class from `ResourceSupport` as shown in following code. The rest of the code remains the same:

```
class Greet extends ResourceSupport{
```

11. `Add` is a method on `ResourceSupport`. The `linkTo` and `methodOn` are static methods of `ControllerLinkBuilder`, a utility class for creating links on controller classes. The `methodOn` method does a dummy method invocation, and `linkTo` creates a link to the controller class. In this case, we use `withSelfRel` to point it to self.

12. This will essentially produce a link, `/greeting?name=HATEOAS`, by default. A client can read the link, and initiate another call.

13. Run as Spring Boot App. Once the server startup is completed, point the browser to `http://localhost:8080`.

14. This will open the HAL browser window. In the **Explorer** field, type `/greeting?name=World!`, and click on the **Go** button. If everything is fine, the response details will be seen in the HAL browser as shown in the following screenshot:

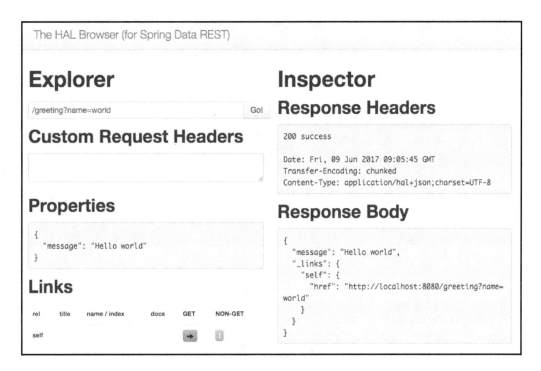

As shown in the preceding screenshot, the **Response Body** has the result with a link, `href`, which points back to the same service. This is because we pointed the reference to itself. Also, review the **Links** section. The little green box against self is the navigable link.

It does not make much sense in this simple example, but this could be handy in larger applications with many related entities. Using the links provided, the client can easily navigate back and forth between these entities with ease.

Reactive Spring Boot microservices

Reactive microservices highlight the need of asynchronously integrating microservices in an ecosystem. Even though external service calls primarily get benefits from reactive style programming, reactive principles are useful in any software development, as it improves resource efficiency and scalability characteristics. Therefore, it is important build microservices using reactive programming principles.

There are two ways we can implement reactive microservices. The first approach is to use the Spring **WebFlux** in the Spring Framework 5. This approach uses reactive style web server for microservices. The second approach is to use a messaging server such as RabbitMQ for asynchronous interaction between microservices. In this chapter, we will explore both the options mentioned here.

Reactive microservices using Spring WebFlux

Reactive programming in Java is based on the **Reactive Streams** specification. Reactive stream specification defines the semantics for asynchronous stream processing or flow of events between disparate components in a non-blocking style.

Unlike the standard observer pattern, Reactive Streams allow to maintain sequence, notification on completion, and notification when there is an error with full backpressure support. With backpressure support, a receiver can set terms such as how much data it wants from the publisher. Also, the receiver can start receiving data only when data is ready to be processed. Reactive Streams are particularly useful for handling different thread pools for different components, or in the case of integrating slow and fast components.

 Reactive streams specification is now adopted as part of Java 9 `java.util.concurrent.Flow`. Its semantics are similar to `CompletableFuture` in Java 8 with lambda expressions for collecting results.

Spring Framework 5 integrates reactive programming principles at its core as WebFlux. Spring 5 WebFlux is based on Reactive Streams specification. Under the hood, Spring's Web Reactive Framework uses the Reactor project (`https://projectreactor.io`) for implementing reactive programming. Reactor is an implementation of Reactive Streams specification. With Spring Framework, developers can also choose to use RxJava instead of Reactor.

In this section, we will see how to build Reactive Spring Boot microservices using Spring 5 WebFlux libraries. These libraries help developers to create asynchronous, non-blocking HTTP servers with full backpressure support, without coding callback methods. Note that it is not a one-size-fits solution in all cases and, if not used property, this can backfire on the quality of services. Also, developers need to be sure that the downstream components support full reactive programming.

In order to get full power of reactive programming, reactive constructs should be used end-to-end from client, endpoint, and to the repository. That means, if a slow client accesses a reactive server, then the data read operations in the repository can slow down to match the slowness of the client.

At the time of writing this book, Spring Data Kay M1 supports reactive drivers for Mongo DB, Apache Cassandra, and Redis. The reactive CRUD repository, `ReactiveCrudRepository`, is a handy interface for implementing reactive repositories.

Spring WebFlux supports two options for implementing Spring Boot applications. The first approach is annotation based with `@Controller` and the other annotations generally used with Spring Boot. The second approach is functional programming Java 8 lambda style coding.

Let us build a sample using the annotation style reactive programming using WebFlux.

The full source code of this example is available as the `chapter3.webflux` project in the code files of this book under the following Git repository: `https://github.com/rajeshrv/Spring5Microservice`

Follow these steps to build a reactive Spring Boot application:

1. Go to `https://start.spring.io`, and generate a new Spring Boot project.

2. Select **Reactive Web** under the **Web** section:

3. Generate project, and import the newly generated project into STS.
4. Examine `pom.xml`; there is only one difference. Instead of `spring-boot-starter-web`, this project uses `spring-boot-starter-webflux` in the dependency section. Following is the dependency to Spring Webflux:

```
<dependency>
    <groupId>org.springframework.boot</groupId>
    <artifactId>spring-boot-starter-webflux</artifactId>
</dependency>
```

5. Add the `GreetingController` and `Greet` classes from `chapter3.bootrest` to the `Application.java` class.
6. Run this project, and test with a browser by pointing to `http://localhost:8080`. You will see the same response.
7. Let us add some Reactive APIs to enable reactive programming to the Boot application. Let us modify `RestController`. Let us add a construct, `Mono`, as follows:

```
@RequestMapping("/")
Mono<Greet> greet(){
    return Mono.just(new Greet("Hello World!"));
}
```

In this case, the response body uses `Mono`, which means that the Greet object will be serialized only when `Mono` is completed in an asynchronous non-blocking mode. Since we have used Mono, this method just creates a single definitive item.

In this case, Mono is used to declare a logic which will get executed as soon as the object is deserialized. You may consider Mono as a placeholder (deferred) for zero or one object with a set of callback methods.

In case of Mono as a parameter to a controller method, the method may be executed even before the serialization gets over. The code in the controller will decide what we want to do with the Mono object. Alternately, we can use **Flux**. Both these constructs will be explained in detail in the next section.

Let us now change the client. Spring 5 reactive introduced WebClient and WebTestClient as an alternate to RestTemplate. WebClient is fully support reactive under the hood.

The client-side code is as follows:

```
@RunWith(SpringRunner.class)
@SpringBootTest(webEnvironment = WebEnvironment.DEFINED_PORT)
public class ApplicationTests {
  WebTestClient webClient;
  @Before
  public void setup() {
    webClient = WebTestClient.bindToServer()
      .baseUrl("http://localhost:8080").build();
  }

  @Test
  public void testWebFluxEndpoint() throws Exception {
    webClient.get().uri("/")
      .accept(MediaType.APPLICATION_JSON)
      .exchange()
      .expectStatus().isOk()
      .expectBody(Greet.class).returnResult()
      .getResponseBody().getMessage().equals("Hello World!");
  }
}
```

WebTestClient is a purpose build class for testing WebFlux server. WebClient, another client class similar to RestTemplate is more handy when invoking WebFlux from a non-testing client. The preceding test code first creates a WebTestClient with the server URL. Then it executes a get method on the / URL, and verifies it against the existing result.

8. Run the test from the command prompt using mvn install. You will not notice any difference in functionality, but the execution model has changed under the hood.

Understanding Reactive Streams

Let us understand the Reactive Streams specification. Reactive Streams has just four interfaces, which are explained as follows:

Publisher

A `Publisher` holds the source of data, and then publishes data elements as per the request from a subscriber. A `Subscriber` can then attach a subscription on the `Publisher`. Note that the `subscribe` method is just a registration method, and will not return any result:

```
public interface Publisher<T> {
  public void subscribe(Subscriber<? super T> s);
}
```

Subscriber

`Subscriber` subscribes to a `Publisher` for consuming streams of data. It defines a set of callback methods, which will be called upon those events. Complete is when everything is done and success. Note, that all these are callback registrations, and the methods themselves do not respond with any data:

```
public interface Subscriber<T> {
  public void onSubscribe(Subscription s);
  public void onNext(T t);
  public void onError(Throwable t);
  public void onComplete();
}
```

Subscription

A `Subscription` is shared by exactly one `Publisher` and one `Subscriber` for the purpose of mediating data exchange between this pair. Data exchange happens when the subscriber calls `request`. `cancel` is used basically to stop the subscription as seen in this example:

```
public interface Subscription {
  public void request(long n);
  public void cancel();
}
```

Processor

A `Processor` represents a processing stage--which is both a `Subscriber` and a `Publisher`, and **MUST** obey the contracts of both. A of can be chained by connecting a `Publisher` and `Subscriber`:

```
public interface Processor<T, R> extends Subscriber<T>,
  Publisher<R> {
}
```

Reactor has two implementations for `Publisher`--**Flux** and **Mono**. Flux can emit 0...N events, whereas, Mono is for a single event (0...1). Flux is required when many data elements or a list of values is transmitted as Streams.

Reactive microservices using Spring Boot and RabbitMQ

In an ideal case, all microservice interactions are expected to happen asynchronously using publish subscribe semantics. Spring Boot provides a hassle-free mechanism to configure messaging solutions:

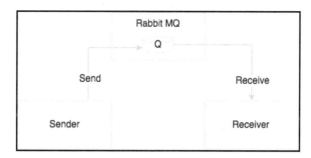

In this next example, we will create a Spring Boot application with a sender and receiver, both connected through an external queue.

The full source code of this example is available as the `chapter3.bootmessaging` project in the code files of this book under the following Git repository: `https://github.com/rajeshrv/Spring5Microservice`

Let us follow these steps to create a string boot reactive microservice using RabbitMQ:

1. Create a new project using STS to demonstrate this capability. In this example, instead of selecting **Web**, select **AMQP** under **I/O**:

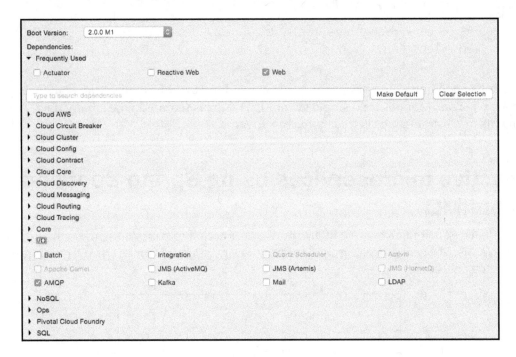

2. RabbitMQ will also be needed for this example. Download and install the latest version of RabbitMQ from `https://www.rabbitmq.com/download.html`. RabbitMQ 3.5.6 is used in this book.

3. Follow the installation steps documented on the site. Once ready, start the RabbitMQ server like this:

```
$./rabbitmq-server
```

4. Make the configuration changes to the `application.properties` file to reflect the RabbitMQ configuration. The following configuration uses the default port, username, and password of RabbitMQ:

```
spring.rabbitmq.host=localhost
spring.rabbitmq.port=5672
spring.rabbitmq.username=guest
spring.rabbitmq.password=guest
```

5. Add a message sender component and a queue named `TestQ` of the type `org.springframework.amqp.core.Queue` to `Application.java` under `src/main/java`. The `RabbitMessagingTemplate` template is a convenient way to send messages, and abstracts all the messaging semantics. Spring Boot provides all boilerplate configurations for sending messages:

```
@Component
class Sender {
  @Autowired
  RabbitMessagingTemplate template;

  @Bean
  Queue queue() {
    return new Queue("TestQ", false);
  }
  public void send(String message){
    template.convertAndSend("TestQ", message);
  }
}
```

6. For receiving a message, all that is needed is a `@RabbitListener` annotation. Spring Boot auto-configures all required boilerplate configurations:

```
@Component
class Receiver {
  @RabbitListener(queues = "TestQ")
  public void processMessage(String content) {
    System.out.println(content);
  }
}
```

7. The last piece of this exercise is to wire the sender to our main application, and implement the `CommandLineRunner` interface's run method to initiate the message sending. When the application is initialized, it invokes the run method of the `CommandLineRunner`:

```
@SpringBootApplication
public class Application implements CommandLineRunner{
  @Autowired
  Sender sender;
  public static void main(String[] args) {
    SpringApplication.run(Application.class, args);
  }
  @Override
  public void run(String... args) throws Exception {
    sender.send("Hello Messaging..!!!");
```

```
    }
  }
```

8. Run the application as a Spring Boot application, and verify the output. The following message will be printed on the console:

```
Hello Messaging..!!!
```

Implementing security

It is important to secure the microservices. This will be more significant when there are many microservices communicating with each other. Each service needs to be secured, but at the same time, security shouldn't surface as an overhead. In this section, we will learn some basic measures to secure microservices.

 The full source code of this example is available as the `chapter3.security` project in the code files of this book under the following Git repository: `https://github.com/rajeshrv/Spring5Microservice`

Perform the following steps for building this example:

- Create a new Spring Starter project, and select **Web** and **Security** (under core)
- Name the project as `chapter3.security`
- Copy rest endpoint from `chapter3.bootrest`

Securing a microservice with basic security

Adding basic authentication to Spring Boot is pretty simple. The `pom.xml` file will have the following dependency. This will include the necessary Spring security library files:

```
<dependency>
    <groupId>org.springframework.boot</groupId>
    <artifactId>spring-boot-starter-security</artifactId>
</dependency>
```

This will, by default, assume that basic security is required for this project. Run the application, and test it with a browser. The browser will ask for the login username and password.

The default basic authentication assumes the . The default password will be printed on the console at startup:

```
Using default security password: a7d08e07-ef5f-4623-b86c-
63054d25baed
```

Alternately, the username and password can be added in `application.properties` as shown next:

```
security.user.name=guest
security.user.password=guest123
```

Securing microservice with OAuth2

In this section, we will see the basic Spring Boot configuration for OAuth2. When a client application requires access to a protected resource, the client sends a request to an authorization server. The authorization server validates the request, and provides an access token. This access token will be validated for every client-to-server request. The request and response sent back and forth depends on the grant type.

 Read more about OAuth and grant types at this link: `http://oauth.net`

The resource owner password credentials grant approach will be used in the following example:

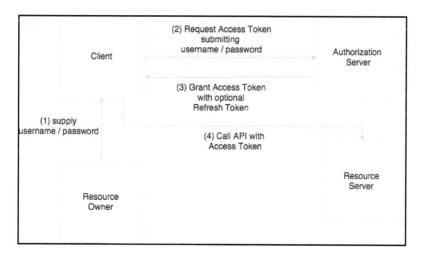

In this case, as shown in the preceding diagram, the resource owner provides the client with a username and password. The client then sends a token request to the authorization server by providing the credentials. The authorization server authorizes the client, and returns an access token. On every subsequent request, the server validates the client token.

To implement OAuth2 in our example, follow these steps:

1. As the first step, update `pom.xml` with oauth2 dependency as follows:

    ```
    <dependency>
      <groupId>org.springframework.security.oauth</groupId>
      <artifactId>spring-security-oauth2</artifactId>
    </dependency>

    <!-- below dependency is explicitly required when
     testing OAuth2 with Spring Boot 2.0.0.M1 -->
    <dependency>
      <groupId>org.springframework.security</groupId>
      <artifactId>spring-security-crypto</artifactId>
      <version>4.2.2.RELEASE</version>
    </dependency>
    ```

2. Next, add two new annotations-- `@EnableAuthorizationServer` --and `@EnableResourceServer` to `Application.java`. The `@EnableAuthorizationServer` annotation creates an authorization server with an in-memory repository to store client tokens and to provide clients with a username, password, client ID, and secret. `@EnableResourceServer` is used to access the tokens. This enables a spring security filter that authenticates via an incoming OAuth2 token.

 In our example, both, authorization server and resource server, are the same. But in practice, these two will be running.

    ```
    @EnableResourceServer
    @EnableAuthorizationServer
    @SpringBootApplication
    public class Application {
    ```

3. Add the following properties to the `application.properties` file:

```
security.user.name=guest
security.user.password=guest123
security.oauth2.client.client-id: trustedclient
security.oauth2.client.client-secret: trustedclient123
security.oauth2.client.authorized-grant-types:
authorization_code, refresh_token, password
```

4. Add another test case to test OAuth2 as follows:

```
@Test
public void testOAuthService() {
  ResourceOwnerPasswordResourceDetails resource =
    new ResourceOwnerPasswordResourceDetails();
  resource.setUsername("guest");
  resource.setPassword("guest123");
  resource.setAccessTokenUri("http://localhost:8080/oauth
    /token");
  resource.setClientId("trustedclient");
  resource.setClientSecret("trustedclient123");
  resource.setGrantType("password");
  resource.setScope(Arrays.asList(new String[]
    {"read","write","trust"}));
  DefaultOAuth2ClientContext clientContext =
    new DefaultOAuth2ClientContext();
  OAuth2RestTemplate restTemplate =
    new OAuth2RestTemplate(resource, clientContext);

  Greet greet = restTemplate
    .getForObject("http://localhost:8080", Greet.class);
  Assert.assertEquals("Hello World!", greet.getMessage());
}
```

As shown in the preceding code, a special rest template, `OAuth2RestTemplate`, is created by passing the resource details encapsulated in a resource details object. This rest template handles the OAuth2 processes underneath. The access token URI is the endpoint for the token access.

5. Rerun the application using maven install. The first two test cases will fail, and the new one will succeed. This is because the server accepts only OAuth2-enabled requests.

These are quick configurations provided by Spring Boot out of the box, but are not good enough to be production grade. We may need to customize `ResourceServerConfigurer` and `AuthorizationServerConfigurer` to make them production ready. Regardless, the approach remains the same.

Enabling cross origin for microservices interactions

Browsers are generally restricted when client-side web applications running from one origin request data from another origin. Enabling cross origin access is generally termed as **CORS (Cross Origin Resource Sharing)**.

This is particularly important when dealing with microservices, such as when the microservices run on separate domains, and the browser tries to access these microservices from one browser after another:

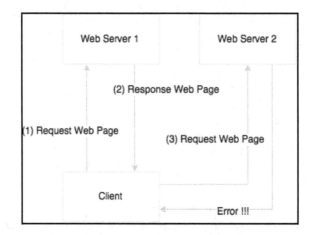

The preceding example showcases how to enable cross origin requests. With microservices, since each service runs with its own origin, it will easily get into the issue of a client-side web application, which consumes data from multiple origins. For instance, a scenario where a browser client accesses customers from the customer microservice, and order history from the order microservices is very common in microservices world.

Spring Boot provides a simple declarative approach for enabling cross origin requests.

The following code example shows how to use a microservice to enable cross origin:

```
@RestController
class GreetingController{
  @CrossOrigin
  @RequestMapping("/")
  Greet greet(){
    return new Greet("Hello World!");
  }
}
```

By default, all origins and headers are accepted. We can further customize the cross origin annotations by giving access to a specific origin as follows. The `@CrossOrigin` annotation enables a method or a class to accept cross origin requests:

```
@CrossOrigin("http://mytrustedorigin.com")
```

Global CORS could be enabled by using the `WebMvcConfigurer` bean, and customizing the `addCorsMappings` (`CorsRegistry registry`) method.

Spring Boot actuators for microservices instrumentation

The previous sections explored most of the Spring Boot features required for developing a microservices. In this section, we will explore some of the production-ready operational aspects of Spring Boot.

Spring Boot actuators provide an excellent out-of-the-box mechanism for monitoring and managing Spring Boot microservices in production.

> The full source code of this example is available as the `chapter3.bootactuator` project in the code files of this book under the following Git repository: `https://github.com/rajeshrv/Spring5Microservice`

Create another Spring starter project, and name it as `chapter3.bootactuator.application`; this time, select the **Web**, **HAL browser, hateoas,** and **Actuator** dependencies. Similar to `chapter3.bootrest`, add a `GreeterController` endpoint with the greet method. Add `management.security.enabled=false` to the `application.properties` file to grant access to all endpoints.

Do the following to execute the application:

1. Start the application as Spring Boot App.
2. Point the browser to `localhost:8080/application`. This will open the HAL browser. Review the **Links** section.

   A number of links are available under the **Links** section. These are automatically exposed by the Spring Boot actuator:

Some of the important links are listed as follows:

- **dump**: Performs a thread dump and displays the result
- **mappings**: Displays a list of all the http request mappings
- **info**: Displays information about the application

- **health**: Displays the health condition of the application
- **autoconfig**: Displays the auto configuration report
- **metrics**: Shows different metrics collected from the application

From the browser, individual endpoints are accessible using
`/application/<endpoint_name>`. For example, to access the `/health` endpoint, point
the browser to `localhost:8080/application/health`.

Monitoring using JConsole

Alternately, we can use the JMX console to see Spring Boot information. Connect to the
remote Spring Boot instance from a jconsole. The Boot information will be shown as
follows:

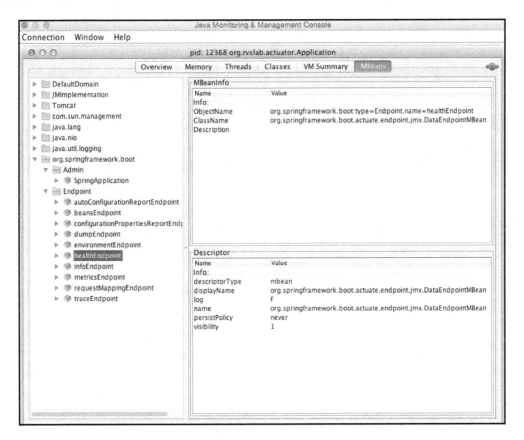

Monitoring using ssh

Spring Boot provides remote access to the Boot application using ssh. The following command connects to the Spring Boot application from a terminal window. The password can be customized by adding the `shell.auth.simple.user.password` property in the `application.properties` file. The updated `application.properties` will look as follows:

```
shell.auth.simple.user.password=admin
```

Use a terminal window to connect to the remote boot application using the following code:

```
$ ssh -p 2000 user@localhost
```

When connected with the preceding command, similar actuator information can be accessed. The following is an example of the metrics information accessed through the CLI:

- **help**: lists all the options available
- **dashboard**: dashboard is one interesting feature, which shows a lot of system-level information

Adding a custom health module

Adding a new custom module to the Spring Boot application is not so complex. For demonstrating this feature, assume that if a service gets more than two transactions in a minute, then the server status will be set as `Out of Service`.

In order to customize this, we have to implement the `HealthIndicator` interface, and override the `health` method. The following code is a quick and dirty implementation to do the job:

```
class TPSCounter {
  LongAdder count;
  int threshold = 2;
  Calendar expiry = null;

  TPSCounter(){
    this.count = new LongAdder();
    this.expiry = Calendar.getInstance();
    this.expiry.add(Calendar.MINUTE, 1);
  }
  boolean isExpired(){
    return Calendar.getInstance().after(expiry);
  }
```

```
  boolean isWeak(){
    return (count.intValue() > threshold);
  }

  void increment(){
    count.increment();
  }
}
```

The preceding code is a simple **Plain Old Java Object (POJO)** class, which maintains the transaction counts window. The isWeak method checks whether the transaction in a particular window has reached its threshold. isExpired checks whether the current window is expired or not. The increment method simply increases the counter value.

As the next step, implement our custom health indicator class, TPSHealth. This is done by extending HealthIndicatoras follows:

```
@Component
class TPSHealth implements HealthIndicator {
  TPSCounter counter;
  @Override
  public Health health() {
    boolean health = counter.isWeak();
    if (health) {
      return Health.outOfService()
        .withDetail("Too many requests", "OutofService")
        .build();
    }
    return Health.up().build();
  }

  void updateTx(){
    if(counter == null || counter.isExpired()){
      counter = new TPSCounter();
    }
  counter.increment();
  }
}
```

The health method checks whether the counter isWeak or not. If it is weak, it marks the instance as out of service.

Finally, we autowire `TPSHealth` into the `GreetingController` class, and then call `health.updateTx()` in the greet method, like this:

```
Greet greet(){
    logger.info("Serving Request....!!!");
    health.updateTx();
    return new Greet("Hello World!");
}
```

Go to the `/application/health` endpoint in the HAL browser, and see the status of the server.

Now open another browser, point to `http://localhost:8080`, and fire the service twice or thrice. Go back to the `/application/health` endpoint, and refresh to see the status. It would have been changed to out of service.

In this example, since there is no action taken other than collecting the health status, new service calls will still go through even though the status is out of service. But in the real world, a program should read the `/application/health` endpoint, and block further requests going to that instance.

Building custom metrics

Just like health, customization of the metrics is also possible. The following example shows how to add a counter service and gauge service, just for demonstration purpose:

```
@Autowired
CounterService counterService;

@Autowired
GaugeService gaugeService;
```

And add the following methods to the `greet` method:

```
this.counterService.increment("greet.txnCount");
this.gaugeService.submit("greet.customgauge", 1.0);
```

Restart the server, and go to `/application/metrics` to see the new gauge and counter added already reflected there.

Documenting microservices

The traditional approach of API documentation is either to write service specification documents or to use static service registries. With a large number of microservices, it would be hard to keep the documentation of APIs in sync.

Microservices can be documented in many ways. This section will explore how microservices can be documented using the popular Swagger framework. In the following examples, we will use `Springfox` libraries for generating REST API documentation. `Springfox` is a set of Java Spring-friendly library.

Create a new `Spring Starter` project, and choose **Web** in the library selection window. Name the project as `chapter3.swagger`.

> The full source code of this example is available as the `chapter3.swagger` project in the code files of this book under the following Git repository:
> https://github.com/rajeshrv/Spring5Microservice

Since `Springfox` libraries are not part of the Spring suite, edit the `pom.xml` file, and add the `springfox-swagger` library dependencies. Add the following dependencies to the project:

```
<dependency>
  <groupId>io.springfox</groupId>
  <artifactId>springfox-swagger2</artifactId>
  <version>2.6.1</version>
</dependency>

<dependency>
  <groupId>io.springfox</groupId>
  <artifactId>springfox-swagger-ui</artifactId>
  <version>2.6.1</version>
</dependency>
```

Create a REST service similar to the services created earlier, but also add the `@EnableSwagger2` annotation as shown next:

```
@SpringBootApplication
@EnableSwagger2
public class Application {
```

This is all that is required for a basic swagger documentation. Start the application, and point the browser to `http://localhost:8080/swagger-ui.html`. This will open the **swagger** API documentation page, as seen in this screenshot:

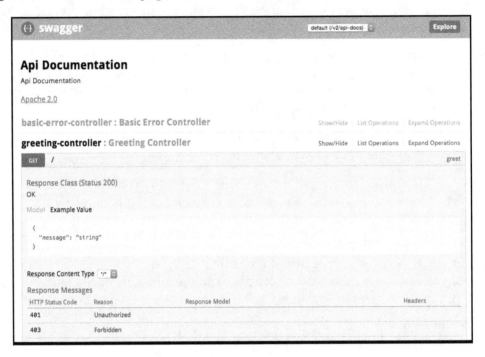

As shown in the preceding screenshot, the Swagger lists out the possible operations on the `GreetingController` class. Click on the **GET** operation. This expands the **GET** row, which provides an option to try out the operation.

Putting it all together - Developing a customer registration microservice example

So far, the examples we have seen are not more than just a simple *hello world*. Putting our learnings together, this section demonstrates an end-to-end customer profile microservice implementation. The customer profile microservices will demonstrate the interaction between different microservices. It will also demonstrate microservices with business logic and primitive data stores.

In this example, two microservices--**Customer Profile Service** and **Customer Notification Service**-- will be developed:

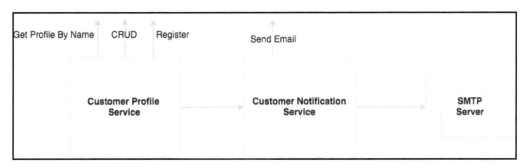

As shown in the preceding diagram, the customer profile microservice exposes methods to create, read, update, and delete a customer, and a registration service for registering a customer. The registration process applies certain business logic, saves the customer profile, and sends a message to the customer notification microservice. The customer notification microservice accepts the message sent by the registration service, and sends an e-mail message to the customer using an SMTP server. Asynchronous messaging is used for integrating customer profile with the customer notification service.

The customer microservices class domain model is shown in the following diagram:

<<RestController>> CustomerController	<<Component>> CustomerComponent	<<JPA Entity>> Customer	<<JpaRepository>> CustomerRepository
register : Customer	register : Customer	+ id: Long	findByName: Customer
		+ name: String	
		+ email: String	

The `CustomerController` in the diagram is the REST endpoint, which invokes a component class, `CustomerComponent`. The component class/bean handles all the business logic. `CustomerRepository` is a Spring data JPA repository defined for handling persistence of the Customer entity.

 The full source code of this example is available as the `chapter3.bootcustomer` and `chapter3.bootcustomernotification` projects in the code files of this book.

Follow the steps listed next to build this example:

1. Create a new Spring Boot project, and call it `chapter3.bootcustomer` the same way as earlier. Select the checkbox of the following options in the starter module selection screen:

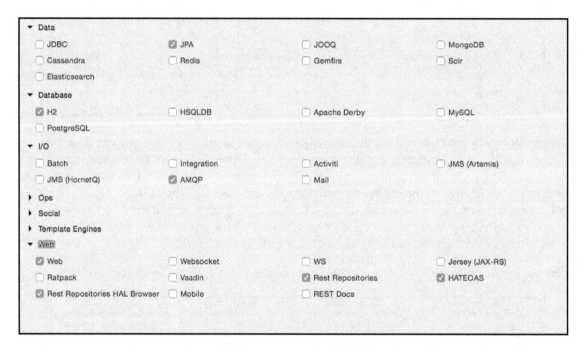

This will create a web project with **JPA**, **Rest Repository**, and **H2** as database. **H2** is a tiny in-memory embedded database with easy-to-demonstrate database features. In the real world, it is recommended to use an appropriate enterprise-grade database. This example uses **JPA** for defining persistence entities and the REST repository for exposing REST-based repository services.

The project structure will look like the following screenshot:

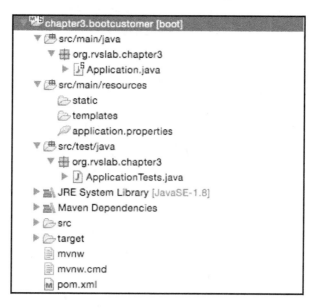

2. Start building the application by adding an entity class named `Customer`. For simplicity, there are only three fields added to the customer entity which are auto-generated--`Id` field, `name`, and `email`:

```
@Entity
class Customer  {
  @Id
  @GeneratedValue(strategy = GenerationType.AUTO)

  private Long id;
  private String name;
  private String email;
```

3. Add a `Repository` class for handling persistence handling of customer. The `CustomerRepository` extends the standard `JpaRepository`. That means, all the CRUD methods and default finder methods are automatically implemented by the Spring Data JPA:

```
@RepositoryRestResource
interface CustomerRespository extends JpaRepository
<Customer,Long>{
  Optional<Customer> findByName(@Param("name")  String name);
}
```

In the preceding example, we added a new method, `findByName`, to the `Repository` class, which essentially searches for a customer based on customer name, and returns a `Customer` object if there is a matching name.

`@RepositoryRestResource` enables repository access through RESTful services. This also enables **HATEOAS** and **HAL** by default. Since for CRUD methods there is no additional business logic required, we will leave it as it is, without controller or component classes. Using **HATEOAS** helps us to navigate through the `CustomerRepository` methods effortlessly.

 Note that there is no configuration added anywhere to point to any database. Since **H2** libraries are in the class path, all configurations are done by default by Spring Boot, based on **H2** auto-configuration.

4. Update `Application.java` by adding `CommandLineRunner` to initialize the repository with some customer records, as follows:

```
@SpringBootApplication
public class Application {
  public static void main(String[] args) {
    SpringApplication.run(Application.class, args);
  }
  @Bean
  CommandLineRunner init(CustomerRespository repo) {
    return (evt) ->    {
      repo.save(new Customer("Adam","adam@boot.com"));
      repo.save(new Customer("John","john@boot.com"));
      repo.save(new Customer("Smith","smith@boot.com"));
      repo.save(new Customer("Edgar","edgar@boot.com"));
      repo.save(new Customer("Martin","martin@boot.com"));
      repo.save(new Customer("Tom","tom@boot.com"));
      repo.save(new Customer("Sean","sean@boot.com"))
    };
  }
}
```

`CommandLineRunner`, defined as a bean, indicates that it should run when it is contained in a `SpringApplication`. This will insert six sample customer records to the database at startup.

5. At this point, run the application as Spring Boot App. Open the HAL browser by pointing the browser URL to `http://localhost:8080`.

6. In the **Explorer**, point to `http://localhost:8080/customers` and click on **Go**. This will list all customers in the **Response Body** section of the HAL browser.

7. In the **Explorer** section, enter the following URL, and click on **Go**. This will automatically execute paging and sorting on the repository, and return the result--`http://localhost:8080/customers?size=2&page=1&sort=name`

   Since the page size is set as two, and first page is requested, it will come back with two records in a sorted order.

8. Review the **Links** section. As shown in the following diagram, it will facilitate navigating first, next, previous, and last. These are done using the HATEOAS links automatically generated by the repository browser:

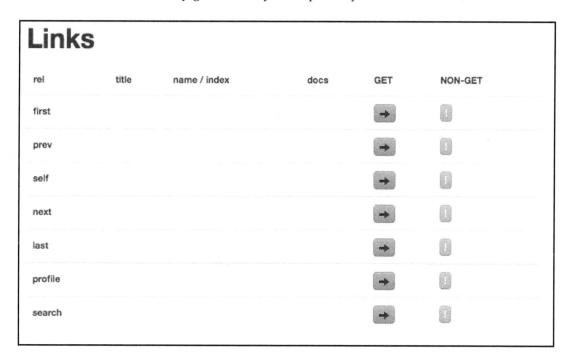

9. Also, one can explore the details of a customer by selecting the appropriate link, `http://localhost:8080/customers/2`.

10. As the next step, add a controller class, `CustomerController`, for handling the service endpoints. There is only one endpoint in this class, `/register`, which is used for registering a customer. If successful, it returns the customer object as the response:

```
@RestController
class CustomerController{
  @Autowired
  CustomerRegistrar customerRegistrar;

  @RequestMapping( path="/register", method =
  RequestMethod.POST)
  Customer register(@RequestBody Customer customer){
    return customerRegistrar.register(customer);
  }
}
```

The `CustomerRegistrar` component is added for handling business logic. In this case, there is only minimal business logic added to the component. In this component class, while registering a customer, we will just check whether the customer name already exists in the database or not. If it does not exist, then a new record should be inserted, otherwise, an error message should be returned:

```
@Component
class CustomerRegistrar {
  CustomerRespository customerRespository;
  @Autowired
  CustomerRegistrar(CustomerRespository customerRespository){
    this.customerRespository = customerRespository;
  }
  // ideally repository will return a Mono object
  public Mono<Customer> register(Customer customer){
    if(customerRespository
      .findByName(customer.getName())
      .isPresent())
      System.out.println("Duplicate Customer.
        No Action required");
    else {
      customerRespository.save(customer);
    }
    return Mono.just(customer);
  }
}
```

11. Restart the Boot application, and test using the HAL browser using the following URL: `http://localhost:8080`.

12. Point the Explorer field to `http://localhost:8080/customers`. Review the results in the **Links** section:

13. Click on **NON-GET** against self. This will open a form for creating a new customer.
14. Fill the form and change the action as shown in the preceding screenshot. Click on the **Make Request** button. This will call the register service and register the customer. Try giving a duplicate name to test the negative case as follows:

Let us complete the last part in the example by integrating the customer notification service for notifying the customer. When registration is successful, an e-mail should be sent to the customer by asynchronously calling the customer notification microservice.

Perform the following steps to build the customer notification microservice:

1. First update `CustomerRegistrar` for calling the second service. This is done through messaging. In this case, we inject a `Sender` component for sending a notification to the customer by passing the customer's e-mail address to the sender:

```
@Component
@Lazy
class CustomerRegistrar {
  CustomerRespository customerRespository;
  Sender sender;
  @Autowired
  CustomerRegistrar(CustomerRespository customerRespository,
  Sender sender){
    this.customerRespository = customerRespository;
    this.sender = sender;
  }
  // ideally repository will return a Mono object
  public Mono<Customer> register(Customer customer){
    if(customerRespository.findByName(
      customer.getName()).isPresent())
      System.out.println("Duplicate Customer.
      No Action required");
    else {
      customerRespository.save(customer);
      sender.send(customer.getEmail());
    }
    return Mono.just(customer); //HARD CODED BECOSE THERE
      IS NO REACTIVE REPOSITORY.
  }
}
```

The sender component will be based on RabbitMQ and AMQP. In this example, `RabbitMessagingTemplate` is used as explored in the last messaging example:

```
@Component
@Lazy
class Sender {
  @Autowired
  RabbitMessagingTemplate template;
  @Bean
  Queue queue() {
```

```
      return new Queue("CustomerQ", false);
  }
  public void send(String message){
   template.convertAndSend("CustomerQ", message);
  }
}
```

@Lazy is a useful annotation, which helps to increase the boot startup time. Those beans will be initialized only when the need arises.

2. We will also update the Application.property file to include RabbitMQ-related properties:

```
spring.rabbitmq.host=localhost
spring.rabbitmq.port=5672
spring.rabbitmq.username=guest
spring.rabbitmq.password=guest
```

3. We are ready to send the message. For consuming the message and sending emails, we will create a notification service. For this, let us create another Spring Boot service, chapter3.bootcustomernotification. Make sure that the AMQP and Mail starter libraries are selected when creating the Spring Boot service. Both AMQP and Mail are under I/O.

The package structure of the chapter3.bootcustomernotifcation project is as shown in following screenshot:

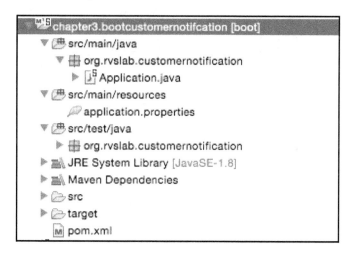

4. Add a `Receiver` class. The `Receiver` class waits for a message on the customer. This will receive a message sent by the Customer Profile service. On the arrival of a message, it sends an email:

```
@Component
class Receiver {
  @Autowired
  Mailer mailer;

  @Bean
  Queue queue() {
    return new Queue("CustomerQ", false);
  }

  @RabbitListener(queues = "CustomerQ")
  public void processMessage(String email)  {
    System.out.println(email);
    mailer.sendMail(email);
  }
}
```

5. Add another component for sending an email to the customer. We use `JavaMailSender` to send the email:

```
@Component
class Mailer  {
  @Autowired
  private  JavaMailSender  javaMailService;

  public void sendMail(String email) {
    SimpleMailMessage mailMessage=new SimpleMailMessage();
    mailMessage.setTo(email);
    mailMessage.setSubject("Registration");
    mailMessage.setText("Successfully Registered");
    javaMailService.send(mailMessage);
  }
}
```

Behind the scene, Spring Boot automatically configures all the parameters required for `JavaMailSender`.

Perform the following steps to test the application:

1. To test SMTP, a test setup for SMTP is required to ensure that the mails are going out. In this example, Fake SMTP will be used.
2. Download the Fake SMTP server from `http://nilhcem.github.io/FakeSMTP`.
3. Once you have downloaded `fakeSMTP-2.0.jar`, run the SMTP server by executing the following command:

```
$ java -jar fakeSMTP-2.0.jar
```

4. This will open a GUI for monitoring email messages. Click on the **Start Server** button next to the listening port text box.
5. Update `Application.properties` with the following configuration parameters to connect to RabbitMQ as well as to the mail server:

```
spring.rabbitmq.host=localhost
spring.rabbitmq.port=5672
spring.rabbitmq.username=guest
spring.rabbitmq.password=guest
spring.mail.host=localhost
spring.mail.port=2525
```

6. We are ready to test our microservices end to end. Start both Spring Boot Apps. Open the browser, and repeat the customer creation steps through the HAL browser. In this case, immediately after submitting the request, we will be able to see the e-mail in the SMTP GUI.

7. Internally, the Customer Profile service asynchronously calls the Customer Notification service, which, in turn, sends the email message to the SMTP server:

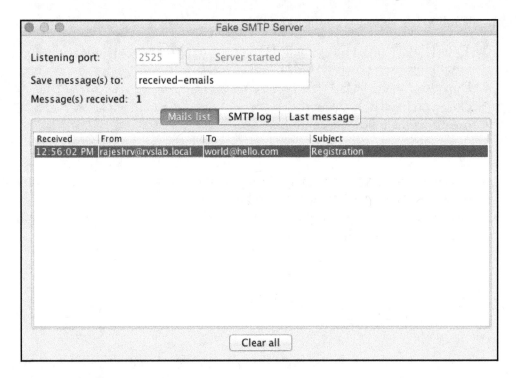

Summary

In this chapter, we learned about Spring Boot, and its key features for building production-ready applications.

We explored the previous generation web applications, and then compared how Spring Boot makes developers' lives easier in developing fully qualified microservices. We also saw HTTP-based and message-based asynchronous reactive microservices. Further, we explored how to achieve some of the key capabilities required for microservices such as security, HATEOAS, cross-origin, and so on, with practical examples. We also saw how the Spring Boot actuators help the operations teams, and also how to customize our needs. Then, documenting microservices APIs was also discussed. We closed the chapter with a complete example that puts together all our learnings.

Scale Microservices with Spring Cloud Components

12

In order to manage Internet-scale microservices, one requires more capabilities than what is offered by the Spring Boot framework. The Spring Cloud project has a suite of purpose-built components to achieve these additional capabilities effortlessly.

This chapter will provide a deep insight into the various components of the Spring Cloud project, such as Eureka, Zuul, Ribbon, and Spring Config, by positioning them against the microservices capability model. This chapter will demonstrate how the Spring Cloud components help to scale the BrownField Airline's PSS microservices system.

At the end of this chapter, we will have learned about the following:

- The Spring **Config Server** for externalizing configuration
- The Eureka Server for service registration and discovery
- Understanding the relevance of Zuul as a service proxy and gateway
- The implementation of automatic microservice registration and service discovery
- Spring Cloud messaging for asynchronous reactive microservice composition

What is Spring Cloud?

Add a link to Netflix OSS. The Spring Cloud project is an umbrella project from the Spring team, which implements a set of common patterns required by distributed systems as a set of easy-to-use Java Spring libraries. Despite its name, Spring Cloud by itself is not a cloud solution. Rather, it provides a number of capabilities, which are essential when developing applications targeting cloud deployments that adhere to the Twelve-Factor Application principles. By using Spring Cloud, developers just need to focus on building business capabilities using Spring Boot, and leverage the distributed, fault-tolerant, and self-healing capabilities available out-of-the-box from Spring Cloud.

The Spring Cloud solutions are agnostic to the deployment environment and can be developed and deployed on a desktop PC or in an elastic cloud. The cloud-ready solutions, which are developed using Spring Cloud, are also agnostic, and portable across many cloud providers, such as Cloud Foundry, AWS, Heroku, and others. When not using Spring Cloud, developers will end up using services natively provided by the cloud vendors, resulting in deep coupling with the PaaS providers. An alternate option for developers is to write quite a lot of boilerplate code to build these services. Spring Cloud also provides simple, easy-to-use Spring-friendly APIs, which abstract the cloud provider's service APIs, such as those APIs coming with the AWS Notification service.

Built on Spring's *convention over configuration* approach, Spring Cloud defaults all configurations, and helps developers to a quick start. Spring Cloud also hides complexities, and provides simple declarative configurations to build systems. The smaller footprints of the Spring Cloud components make it developer-friendly, and also make it easy to develop cloud-native applications.

Spring Cloud offers many choices of solutions for developers based on their requirements. For example, the service registry can be implemented using popular options such as Eureka, Zookeeper, or Consul. The components of Spring Cloud are fairly decoupled, hence, developers get the flexibility to pick and choose what is required.

 What is the difference between Spring Cloud and Cloud Foundry? Spring Cloud is a developer kit for developing Internet-scale Spring Boot applications, whereas, Cloud Foundry is an open source Platform as a Service for building, deploying, and scaling applications.

Spring Cloud releases

The Spring Cloud project is an overarching Spring project, which includes a combination of different components. The versions of these components are defined in the *spring-cloud-starter-parent* BOM.

 In this book, we are relying on the **Dalston SR1** version of the Spring Cloud. Dalston does not support Spring Boot 2.0.0 and Spring Framework 5. Spring Cloud Finchley, planned for the end of this year, is expected to support Spring Boot 2.0.0. Hence, examples in the previous chapters need to downgrade to the Spring Boot 1.5.2.RELEASE version.

Add the following dependency in `pom.xml` to use Spring Cloud Dalston dependency:

```
<dependency>
  <groupId>org.springframework.cloud</groupId>
  <artifactId>spring-cloud-dependencies</artifactId>
  <version>Dalston.SR1</version>
  <type>pom</type>
  <scope>import</scope>
</dependency>
```

Setting up the environment for the BrownField PSS

We will examine how to make these services enterprise grade using the Spring Cloud components.

In order to prepare the environment for this chapter, import and rename (`chapter6.*` to `chapter7.*`) projects into a new STS workspace.

 The full source code of this chapter is available under the `chapter7` project in the code files under `https://github.com/rajeshrv/Spring5Microservice`.

Spring Cloud Config

Simplify this section. The Spring Cloud Config Server is an externalized configuration server in which applications and services can deposit, access, and manage all runtime configuration properties. The Spring Config Server also supports version control of the configuration properties.

In earlier examples with Spring Boot, all configuration parameters were read from a property file packaged inside the project, either `application.properties` or `application.yaml`. This approach is good, since all properties are moved out of code to a property file. However, when microservices are moved from one environment to another, these properties need to undergo changes, which require application rebuild. This is in violation of one of the Twelve-Factor Application principles, which advocates one time build and moving the binaries across environments.

A better approach is to use the concept of profiles. Profiles, as discussed in `Chapter 11`, *Building Microservices with Spring Boot*, is used to partition different properties for different environments. The profile specific configuration will be named as `application-{profile}.properties`. For example, `application-development.properties` represents a property file targeted for the development environment.

However, the disadvantage of this approach is that the configurations are statically packaged along with the application. Any changes in the configuration properties require the application to be rebuilt.

There are alternate ways to externalize configuration properties from the application deployment package. Configurable properties can also be read from an external source in a number of ways, which are as follows:

- From an external JNDI server using the JNDI namespace (`java:comp/env`)
- Using the Java system properties (`System.getProperties()`), or by using the `-D` command-line option
- Using the `PropertySource` configuration

```
@PropertySource("file:${CONF_DIR}/application.properties")
public class ApplicationConfig {
}
```

- Using a command-line parameter pointing a file to an external location

```
java -jar myproject.jar --spring.config.location=<file location>
```

JNDI operations are expensive, lack flexibility, have difficulties in replication, and are not version controlled. `System.properties` is not flexible enough for large-scale deployments. The last two options rely on a local or a shared filesystem mounted on the server.

For large-scale deployments, a simple, yet powerful, centralized configuration management solution is required.

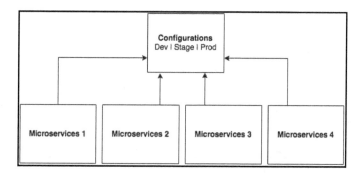

As shown in the preceding diagram, all microservices point to a central server to get the required configuration parameters. The microservices then locally cache these parameters to improve performance. The Config Server propagates the configuration state changes to all subscribed microservices so that the local cache's state can be updated with the latest changes. The Config Server also uses profiles to resolve values specific to an environment.

As shown in the next diagram, there are multiple options available under the Spring Cloud project for building the configuration server. Config Server, Zookeeper Configuration, and Consul Configuration are available as options. However, this chapter will only focus on the Spring Config Server implementation:

The Spring Config Server stores properties in a version-controlled repository such as Git or SVN. The Git repository can be local or remote. A highly available remote Git server is preferred for large-scale distributed microservices deployments.

The Spring Cloud Config Server architecture is shown in the following diagram:

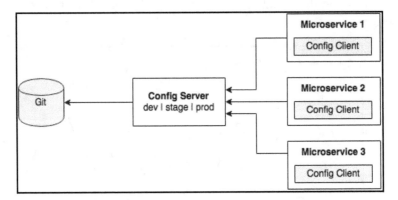

As shown in the diagram, the **Config Client** embedded in the Spring Boot microservices does a configuration lookup from a central configuration server using simple declarative mechanisms and stores properties into the Spring environment. The configuration properties can be application-level configurations such as trade limit per day, or infrastructure-related configurations such as server URLs, credential and so on.

Unlike Spring Boot, Spring Cloud uses a bootstrap context, which is a parent context of the main application. Bootstrap context is responsible for loading configuration properties from the **Config Server**. The bootstrap context looks for bootstrap.yaml or bootstrap.properties for loading the initial configuration properties. To make this work in a Spring Boot application, rename the application.* file as bootstrap.*.

Building microservices with Config Server

The next few sections demonstrate how to use the Config Server in a real-world scenario. In order to do this, we will modify our search microservice (chapter7.search) to use the Config Server. The following diagram depicts the scenario:

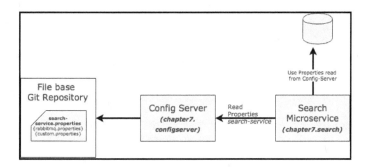

In this example, the search service will read the **Config Server** at startup by passing the service name. In this case, the service name of the search service will be **search-service**. The properties configured for the **search-service** include the RabbitMQ properties as well as a custom property.

Setting up the Config Server

The following steps need to be followed to create a new Config Server using STS:

1. Create a new Spring Starter project and select **Config Server** and **Actuator**, as shown in this screenshot:

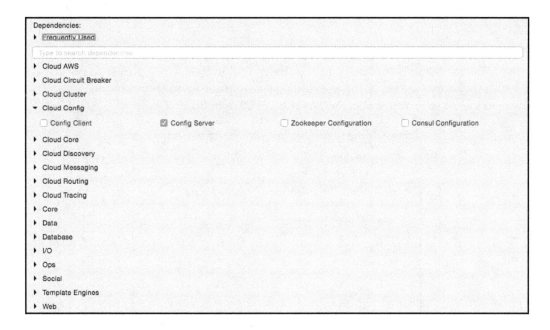

2. Set up a Git repository. This could be done by pointing to a remote Git configuration repository, such as `https://github.com/spring-cloud-samples/config-repo`. This URL is an indicative one, a Git repository used by the Spring Cloud examples. We will have to use our own Git repository instead.

3. Alternatively, a local-file-system-based Git repository can be used. In a real production scenario, an external Git is recommended. The Config Server in this chapter will use a local-file-system-based Git repository for demonstration purposes.

4. Use the following set of commands to set up a local Git repository:

```
$ cd $HOME
$ mkdir config-repo
$ cd config-repo
$ git init .
$ echo message : helloworld > application.properties
$ git add -A .
$ git commit -m "Added sample application.properties"
```

This will create a new Git repository on the local filesystem. A property file, named `application.properties`, with a property message and value `helloworld` is also created.

 `application.properties` is created for demonstration purposes. We will change this in subsequent sections.

5. The next step is to change the configuration in the Config Server to use the Git repository created in the previous step. In order to do this, rename `application.properties` as `bootstrap.properties`:

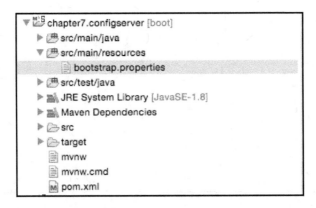

6. Edit the contents of the new `bootstrap.properties` to match the following:

```
server.port=8888
spring.cloud.config.server.git.uri:
    file://${user.home}/config-repo
```

 Port `8888` is the default port for the Config Server. Even without configuring the `server.port`, the Config Server should bind to `8888`. In a Windows environment, an extra / is required in the file URL.

7. Also add `management.security.enabled=false` to disable security validation.
8. Optionally, rename the default package of the autogenerated `Application.java` from `com.example` to `com.brownfield.configserver`. Add `@EnableConfigServer` in `Application.java`.

```
@EnableConfigServer
@SpringBootApplication
public class ConfigserverApplication {
```

9. Run the Config Server by right-clicking the project, and run as Spring Boot App.
10. Check `curl http://localhost:8888/env` to see whether the server is running. If everything is fine, this will list all environment configurations. Note that `/env` is an Actuator endpoint.
11. Check `http://localhost:8888/application/default/master` to see the properties specific to `application.properties`, which was added in the earlier step. The browser will display properties configured in the `application.properties`. The browser should display content similar to this:

```
{"name":"application","profiles":["default"],"label":"master",
  "version":"6046fd2ff4fa09d3843767660d963866ffcc7d28",
  "propertySources":[{"name":"file:///Users/rvlabs
  /config-repo /application.properties","source":
  {"message":"helloworld"}}]}
```

Understanding the Config Server URL

In the previous section, we used `http://localhost:8888/application/default/master` to explore the properties. How do we interpret the given URL?

The first element in the URL is the application name. In the last example, the application name should be `application`. The application name is a logical name given to the application, using the `spring.application.name` property in the `bootstrap.properties` of the Spring Boot application. Each application must have a unique name. The Config Server will use the name to resolve and pick up appropriate properties from the Config Server repository. The application name is also sometimes referred to as service ID. If there is an application with the name `myapp`, then there should a `myapp.properties` in the configuration repository to store all properties related to that application.

The second part of the URL represents the profile. There can be more than one profile configured within the repository for an application. The profiles can be used in various scenarios. The two common scenarios are to segregate different environments such as Dev, Test, Stage, Prod, and so on, or to segregate server configurations such as primary, secondary, and others. The first one represents different environments of an application, whereas the second one represents different servers where an application is deployed.

The profile names are logical names, which will be used for matching the filename in the repository. The default profile is named as `default`. To configure properties for different environments, we have to configure different files, as shown next. In this example, the first file is for the development environment, whereas the second is for the production environment:

```
application-development.properties
application-production.properties
```

These are accessible using the following URLs:

`http://localhost:8888/application/development`

`http://localhost:8888/application/production`

The last part of the URL is the `label`, and is named as `master` by default. The `label` is an optional Git label, which can be used if required.

In short, the URL is based on this pattern:

`http://localhost:8888/{name}/{profile}/{label}`

The configuration can also be accessed by ignoring the profile. In the given example, all the following three URLs point to the same configuration:

```
http://localhost:8888/application/default
```

```
http://localhost:8888/application/master
```

```
http://localhost:8888/application/default/master
```

There is an option to have different Git repositories for different profiles. This makes sense for production systems, since the access to different repositories could be different.

Accessing the Config Server from clients

In the previous section, a Config Server is set up and accessed using a web browser. In this section, the Search microservice will be modified to use the Config Server. The Search microservice will act as a Config Client.

Follow the steps listed next to use the Config Server instead of reading properties from the application.properties file:

1. Add the Spring Cloud Config dependency and the Actuator (if Actuator is not already in place) to pom.xml. The Actuator is mandatory for refreshing the configuration properties:

```
<dependency>
  <groupId>org.springframework.cloud</groupId>
  <artifactId>spring-cloud-starter-config</artifactId>
</dependency>
```

2. Add the following to include the Spring Cloud dependencies. This is not required if the project is created from scratch:

```
<dependencyManagement>
  <dependencies>
  <dependency>
<groupId>org.springframework.cloud</groupId>
<artifactId>spring-cloud-dependencies</artifactId>
<version>Dalston.BUILD-SNAPSHOT</version>
<type>pom</type>
<scope>import</scope>
</dependency>
</dependencies>
</dependencyManagement>
```

3. The following screenshot shows the Cloud starter library selection screen. If the application is built from the ground up, select the libraries as shown here:

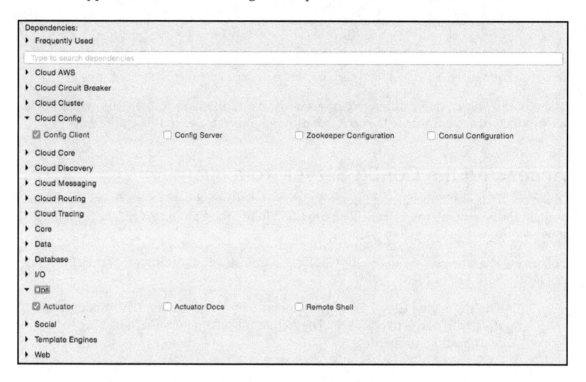

4. Rename the `application.properties` to `bootstrap.properties`, and add an application name and a configuration server URL. The configuration server URL is not mandatory if the Config Server is running on the default port (`8888`) on the local host.

The new `bootstrap.properties` file will look like this:

```
spring.application.name=search-service
spring.cloud.config.uri=http://localhost:8888
server.port=8090
spring.rabbitmq.host=localhost
spring.rabbitmq.port=5672
spring.rabbitmq.username=guest
spring.rabbitmq.password=guest
```

search-service is a logical name given to the Search microservices. This will be treated as the service ID. The Config Server will look for search-service.properties in the repository to resolve the properties.

5. Create a new configuration file for search-service. Create a new search-service.properties under the config-repo folder where the Git repository is created. Note that search-service is the service ID given to the Search microservice in the bootstrap.properties file. Move service-specific properties from bootstrap.properties to the new search-service.properties. The following properties will be removed from bootstrap.properties and added to search-service.properties:

```
spring.rabbitmq.host=localhost
spring.rabbitmq.port=5672
spring.rabbitmq.username=guest
spring.rabbitmq.password=guest
```

6. In order to demonstrate the centralized configuration of properties and propagation of changes, add a new application-specific property to the property file. We will add originairports.shutdown to temporarily take out an airport from the search. Users will not get any flights when searching with an airport mentioned in the shutdown list:

```
originairports.shutdown=SEA
```

In this preceding example, we will not return any flights when searching with SEA as origin.

7. Commit this new file into the Git repository by executing the following commands:

```
git add -A .
git commit -m "adding new configuration"
```

The final search-service.properties file should look like this:

```
spring.rabbitmq.host=localhost
spring.rabbitmq.port=5672
spring.rabbitmq.username=guest
spring.rabbitmq.password=guest
originairports.shutdown:SEA
```

The `chapter7.search` project's `bootstrap.properties` should look like the following:

```
spring.application.name=search-service
server.port=8090
spring.cloud.config.uri=http://localhost:8888
```

8. Modify the Search microservice code to use the configured parameter, `originairports.shutdown`. A `RefreshScope` annotation has to be added at the class level to allow properties to be refreshed when there is a change. In this case, we are adding a refresh scope to the `SearchRestController` class.

```
@RefreshScope
```

9. Add the following instance variable as a placeholder for the new property that is just added in the Config Server. The property names in the `search-service.properties` must match:

```
@Value("${originairports.shutdown}")
private String originAirportShutdownList;
```

10. Change the application code to use this property. This is done by modifying the search method as follows:

```
@RequestMapping(value="/get", method = RequestMethod.POST)
List<Flight> search(@RequestBody SearchQuery query){
    logger.info("Input : "+ query);
    if(Arrays.asList(originAirportShutdownList.split(","))
    .contains(query.getOrigin())){
        logger.info("The origin airport is in shutdown state");
        return new ArrayList<Flight>();
    }
    return searchComponent.search(query);
}
```

The search method is modified to read the parameter `originAirportShutdownList` and see whether the requested origin is in the shutdown list. If there is a match, instead of proceeding with the actual search, the search method will return an empty flight list.

11. Start the Config Server. Then start the Search microservice. Make sure that the Rabbit MQ server is running.

12. Modify the `chapter7.website` project to match the `bootstrap.properties` content, as follows, to utilize the Config Server:

```
spring.application.name=test-client
server.port=8001
spring.cloud.config.uri=http://localhost:8888
```

13. Change the `CommandLineRunner`'s run method in Application.java to query SEA as origin airport.

```
SearchQuery searchQuery = new SearchQuery(
  "SEA","SFO","22-JAN-18");
```

14. Run the `chapter7.website` project. `CommandLineRunner` will now return an empty flight list. The following message will be printed in the server:

```
The origin airport is in shutdown state
```

Handling configuration changes

The `/refresh` endpoint will refresh the locally cached configuration properties and reload fresh values from the Config Server.

In order to force reloading the configuration properties, call the `/refresh` endpoint of the microservice. This is actually the Actuator's refresh endpoint. The following command will send an empty POST to the `/refresh` endpoint:

```
curl -d {} localhost:8090/refresh
```

Spring Cloud Bus for propagating configuration changes

With the preceding approach, configuration parameters can be changed without restarting the microservices. This is good when there are only one or two instances of the services running. What happens if there are many instances?

For example, if there are five instances, then we have to hit `/refresh` against each service instance. This is definitely a cumbersome activity.

The following diagram shows the solution using Spring Cloud Bus:

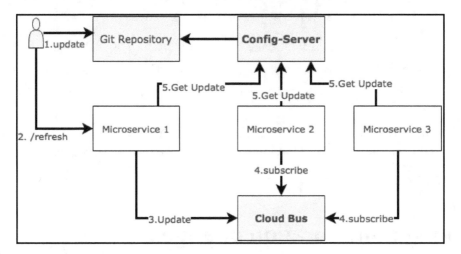

The Spring Cloud Bus provides a mechanism to refresh configurations across multiple instances without knowing how many instances there are, nor their locations. This is particularly handy when there are many service instances of a microservice running, or when there are many microservices of different types running. This is done by connecting all service instances through a single message broker. Each instance subscribes for change events and refreshes its local configuration when required. This refresh is triggered by making a call to any one instance by hitting the `/bus/refresh` endpoint, which then propagates the changes through the cloud bus and the common message broker.

Setting up high availability for the Config Server

The previous sections explored how to setup the Config Server, allowing real-time refresh of configuration properties. However, the Config Server is a single point of failure in this architecture.

There are three single points of failure in the default architecture established in the previous section. One of them is the availability of the Config Server itself, the second one is the Git repository, and the third one is the RabbitMQ server.

The following diagram shows a high-availability architecture for the Config Server:

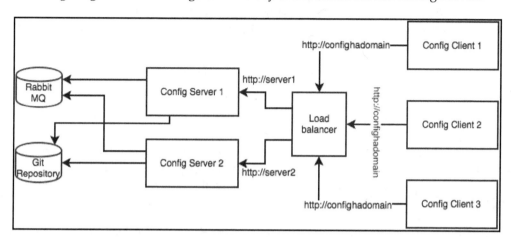

The architecture mechanisms and rationale are explained as follows:

The Config Server requires high availability, since the services won't be able to bootstrap if the Config Server is not available. Hence, redundant Config servers are required for high availability. However, the applications can continue to run if the Config Server is unavailable after the services are bootstrapped. In this case, services will run with the last-known configuration state. Hence, the Config Server availability is not at the same critical level as the microservices availability.

In order to make the Config Server highly available, we need multiple instances of the Config servers. Since the Config Server is a stateless HTTP service, multiple instances of configuration servers can be run in parallel. Based on the load on the configuration server, a number of instances have to be adjusted. The bootstrap.properties is not capable of handling more than one server address. Hence, multiple configuration servers should be configured to run behind a load balancer or behind a local DNS with failover and fallback capabilities. The load balancer or DNS server URL will be configured in the microservices bootstrap.properties. This is with the assumption that the DNS or the load balancer is highly available and capable of handling failovers.

In a production scenario, it is not recommended to use a local-file-based Git repository. The configuration server should be typically backed with a highly available Git service. This is possible by either using an external high available Git service or a highly available internal Git service. SVN can also be considered.

Having said that, an already bootstrapped Config Server is always capable of working with a local copy of the configuration. Hence, we need a highly available Git only when the Config Server needs to be scaled. Therefore, this too is not as critical as the microservices availability or the Config Server availability.

 The GitLab example for setting up high availability is available at the following link: https://about.gitlab.com/high-availability/

RabbitMQ also has to be configured for high availability. The high availability for RabbitMQ is needed only to push configuration changes dynamically to all instances. Since this is more of an offline, controlled activity, it does not really require the same high availability as required by the components.

Rabbit MQ high availability can be achieved by either using a cloud service or a locally configured highly available Rabbit MQ service.

 Setting up high availability for Rabbit MQ is documented at the link https://www.rabbitmq.com/ha.html.

Monitoring Config Server health

The Config Server is nothing but a Spring Boot application, and is, by default, configured with an Actuator. Hence, all Actuator endpoints are applicable for the Cloud Server. The health of the server can be monitored using the following Actuator URL:

```
http://localhost:8888/health
```

Config Server for configuration files

We may run into scenarios where we need a complete configuration file to be externalized, such as `logback.xml`. The Config Server provides a mechanism to configure and store such files. This is achievable by using the URL format as follows:

```
/{name}/{profile}/{label}/{path}
```

The `name`, `profile`, and `label` has the same meaning as explained earlier. The path indicates the filename, such as `logback.xml`.

Completing changes to use Config Server

In order to build this capability to the complete BrownField Airline's PSS, we have to make use of the configuration server for all services.

 All microservices in our `chapter7.*` examples need to make similar changes to look to the Config Server for getting the configuration parameters.

We are not externalizing the queue names used in the Search, Booking, and Check-in services at the moment. Later in this chapter, these will be changed to use Spring Cloud Streams.

Eureka for registration and discovery

So far, we have achieved externalizing configuration parameters, as well as load balancing across many service instances.

Ribbon-based load balancing is sufficient for most of the microservices requirements. However, this approach falls short in these scenarios:

- If there is a large number of microservices, and if we want to optimize infrastructure utilization, we will have to dynamically change the number of service instances and associated servers. It is not easy to predict and preconfigure the server URLs in a configuration file.
- When targeting cloud deployments for highly scalable microservices, static registration and discovery is not a good solution considering the elastic nature of the cloud environment.
- In cloud deployment scenarios, IP addresses are not predictable and will be difficult to statically configure in a file. We will have to update the configuration file every time there is a change in address.

The Ribbon approach partially addresses this issue. With Ribbon, we can dynamically change the service instances, but whenever we add new service instances or shut down instances, we will have to manually go and update the Config Server. Though the configuration changes will be automatically propagated to all required instances, manual configuration changes will not work with large-scale deployments. When managing large deployments, automation, wherever possible, is paramount.

To fix this gap, the microservices should self-manage their life cycle by dynamically registering service availability and provision-automated discovery for consumers.

Understanding dynamic service registration and discovery

Dynamic registration is primarily from the service provider's point of view. With dynamic registration, when a new service is started, it automatically enlists its availability in a central service registry. Similarly, when a service goes out of service, it is automatically delisted from the service registry. The registry always keeps up-to-date information of the services available, as well as their metadata.

Dynamic discovery is applicable from the service consumer's point of view. Dynamic discovery is where clients look for the service registry to get the current state of the services topology and then invoke the services accordingly. In this approach, instead of statically configuring the service URLs, the URLs are picked up from the service registry.

The clients may keep a local cache of the registry data for faster access. Some registry implementations allow clients to keep a watch on the items they are interested in. In this approach, the state changes in the registry server will be propagated to the interested parties to avoid using stale data.

There are a number of options available for dynamic service registration and discovery. Netflix Eureka, Zookeeper, and Consul are available as part of Spring Cloud, as shown in the start.spring.io screenshot that follows. Etcd is another service registry available outside of Spring Cloud to achieve dynamic service registration and discovery. In this chapter, we will focus on the Eureka implementation:

Cloud Discovery

Eureka Discovery
Service discovery using spring-cloud-netflix and Eureka

Eureka Server
spring-cloud-netflix Eureka Server

Zookeeper Discovery
Service discovery with Zookeeper and spring-cloud-zookeeper-discovery

Cloud Foundry Discovery
Service discovery with Cloud Foundry

Consul Discovery
Service discovery with Hashicorp Consul

Understanding Eureka

Spring Cloud Eureka also comes from the Netflix OSS. The Spring Cloud project provides a Spring-friendly declarative approach for integrating Eureka with Spring-based applications. Eureka is primarily used for self-registration, dynamic discovery, and load balancing. The Eureka internally uses Ribbon for load balancing.

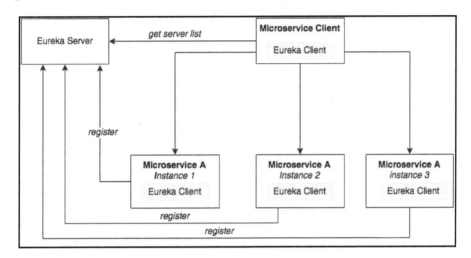

As shown in the preceding diagram, Eureka consists of a server component and a client-side component. The server component is the registry in which all microservices register their availability. The registration typically includes service identity and its URLs. The microservices use the **Eureka Client** for registering their availability. The consuming components will also use the **Eureka Client** for discovering the service instances.

When a microservice is bootstrapped, it reaches out to the **Eureka Server** and advertises its existence with the binding information. Once registered, the service endpoint sends ping requests to the registry every 30 seconds to renew its lease. If a service endpoint cannot renew its lease for a few times, that service endpoint is taken out of the service registry. The registry information is replicated to all Eureka clients so that the clients need to go to the remote **Eureka Server** for each and every request. Eureka clients fetch the registry information from the server and cache it locally. After that, the clients use that information to find other services. This information is updated periodically (every 30 seconds) by getting the delta updates between the last fetch cycle and the current one.

When a client wants to contact a microservice endpoint, the **Eureka Client** provides a list of currently available services based on the requested service ID. The **Eureka Server** is zone-aware. Zone information can also be supplied when registering a service.

When a client requests for a services instance, the Eureka service tries to find the service running in the same zone. The Ribbon client then load balances across these available service instances supplied by the **Eureka Client**. The communication between the **Eureka Client** and **Eureka Server** uses REST and JSON.

Setting up the Eureka Server

In this section, we will run through the steps required for setting up the Eureka Server.

The full source code of this section is available under the `chapter7.eurekaserver` project in the code files under `https://github.com/rajeshrv/Spring5Microservice`. Note that the Eureka Server registration and refresh cycles takes up to 30 seconds. Hence, when running services and clients, wait for 40-50 seconds.

Start a new Spring Starter project and select **Config Client**, **Eureka Server**, and **Actuator**, as shown in the following screenshot:

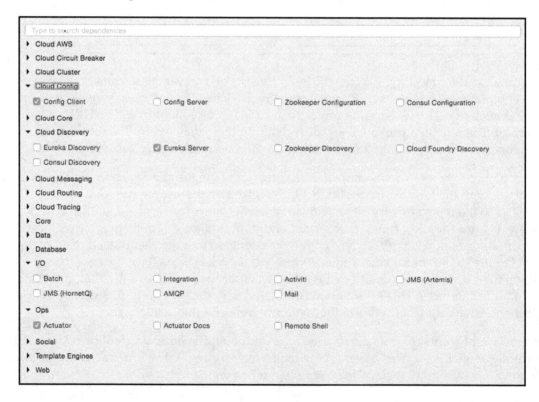

The project structure of the Eureka server is shown in the following screenshot:

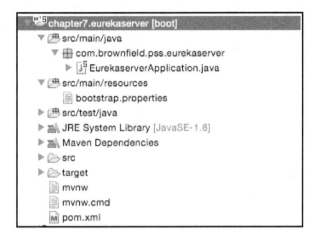

Note that the main application is named EurekaserverApplication.java.

Rename application.properties to bootstrap.properties, as this is using the Config Server. As we have done earlier, configure the details of the Config Server in the bootsratp.properties so that it can locate the Config Server instance. The bootstrap.properties will look like this:

```
spring.application.name=eureka-server1
server.port:8761
spring.cloud.config.uri=http://localhost:8888
```

The Eureka Server can be set up in a standalone mode or in a clustered mode. We will start with the standalone mode. By default, the Eureka Server itself is another Eureka Client. This is particularly useful when there are multiple Eureka servers running for high availability. The client component is responsible for synchronizing the state from other Eureka servers. The Eureka Client is taken to its peers by configuring the eureka.client.serviceUrl.defaultZone property.

In the standalone mode, we will point the `eureka.client.serviceUrl.defaultZone` back to the same standalone instance. Later, we will see how we can run Eureka servers in a clustered mode.

Perform the following steps to set up Eureka server:

1. Create a `eureka-server1.properties` file and update it in the Git repository. `eureka-server1` is the name of the application given in the applications `bootstrap.properties` in the previous step. As shown next, the `serviceUrl` points back to the same server. Once the following properties are added, commit the file to the Git repository:

   ```
   spring.application.name=eureka-server1
   eureka.client.serviceUrl.defaultZone:http:
     //localhost:8761/eureka/
   eureka.client.registerWithEureka:false
   eureka.client.fetchRegistry:false
   ```

2. Change the default `Application.java`. In this example, the package is renamed as `com.brownfield.pss.eurekaserver` and the class name is also changed to `EurekaserverApplication`. In `EurekaserverApplication`, add `@EnableEurekaServer`:

   ```
   @EnableEurekaServer
   @SpringBootApplication
   public class EurekaserverApplication {
   ```

3. We are now ready to start the Eureka Server. Ensure the Config Server is also started. Right-click on the application and `Run As`, `Spring Boot App`. Once the application starts, open the following link in a browser to see the Eureka console:

   ```
   http://localhost:8761
   ```

4. In the console, note that there is no instance registered under the instances currently registered with Eureka. Since there are no services started with the Eureka Client enabled, the list is empty at this point.

5. Making a few changes to our microservices will enable dynamic registration and discovery using the Eureka service. To do this, first we have to add Eureka dependencies in `pom.xml`. If the services are being built up fresh using the Spring Starter project, then select **Config Client**, **Actuator**, **Web**, as well as the **Eureka Discovery** client, as shown in the following screenshot:

▸ Cloud AWS			
▸ Cloud Circuit Breaker			
▸ Cloud Cluster			
▾ Cloud Config			
☑ Config Client	☐ Config Server	☐ Zookeeper Configuration	☐ Consul Configuration
▸ Cloud Core			
▾ Cloud Discovery			
☑ Eureka Discovery	☐ Eureka Server	☐ Zookeeper Discovery	☐ Cloud Foundry Discovery
☐ Consul Discovery			
▸ Cloud Messaging			
▸ Cloud Routing			
▸ Cloud Tracing			
▸ Core			
▸ Data			
▸ Database			
▸ I/O			
▾ Ops			
☑ Actuator	☐ Actuator Docs	☐ Remote Shell	
▸ Social			
▸ Template Engines			
▾ Web			
☑ Web	☐ Websocket	☐ WS	☐ Jersey (JAX-RS)
☐ Ratpack	☐ Vaadin	☐ Rest Repositories	☐ HATEOAS
☐ Rest Repositories HAL Browser	☐ Mobile	☐ REST Docs	

6. Since we are modifying all our microservices, add the following additional dependency to all the microservices in their `pom.xml` files:

```
<dependency>
  <groupId>org.springframework.cloud</groupId>
  <artifactId>spring-cloud-starter-eureka</artifactId>
</dependency>
```

The following property has to be added to all the microservices in their respective configuration files under `config-repo`. This will help the microservices to connect to the Eureka Server. Commit to Git once the updates are completed:

```
eureka.client.serviceUrl.defaultZone:
  http://localhost:8761/eureka/
```

7. Add `@EnableDiscoveryClient` to all the microservices in their respective Spring Boot main classes. This will ask Spring Boot to register these services at startup to advertise its availability.

8. Instead of `RestTemplate`, we will use `@FeignClient` in this example by introducing a `FareServciesProxy`, as shown next:

```
@FeignClient(name="fares-service")
public interface FareServiceProxy {
  @RequestMapping(value = "fares/get",
  method=RequestMethod.GET)
  Fare getFare(@RequestParam(value="flightNumber")
  String flightNumber, @RequestParam(value="flightDate")
  String flightDate);
}
```

9. In order to do this, we have to add a Feign dependency:

```
<dependency>
  <groupId>org.springframework.cloud</groupId>
  <artifactId>spring-cloud-starter-feign</artifactId>
</dependency>
```

10. Start all services except website service.

11. If you go to the Eureka URL, you can see that all three instances are up and running:

```
http://localhost:8761
```

Instances currently registered with Eureka			
Application	AMIs	Availability Zones	Status
BOOK-SERVICE	n/a (1)	(1)	UP (1) - 192.168.0.102:book-service:8060
CHECKIN-SERVICE	n/a (1)	(1)	UP (1) - 192.168.0.102:checkin-service:8070
FARES-SERVICE	n/a (1)	(1)	UP (1) - 192.168.0.102:fares-service:8080
SEARCH-SERVICE	n/a (1)	(1)	UP (1) - 192.168.0.102:search-service:8090

12. Change the website project `bootstrap.properties` to make use of Eureka rather than connecting directly to the service instances. We will use the load-balanced `RestTemplate`. Commit these changes to the Git repository:

```
spring.application.name=test-client
eureka.client.serviceUrl.defaultZone:
  http://localhost:8761/eureka/
```

13. Add `@EnableDiscoveryClient` to the Application class to make the client Eureka aware.

14. Edit both `Application.java` as well as `BrownFieldSiteController.java`. Add `RestTemplate` instances. This time, we annotate them with `@Loadbalanced` to ensure that we are using the load balancing features using Eureka and Ribbon. `RestTemplate` cannot be automatically injected. Hence, we have to provide a configuration entry, as follows:

```
@Configuration
class AppConfiguration {
  @LoadBalanced
  @Bean
  RestTemplate restTemplate() {
    return new RestTemplate();
  }
}
@Autowired
RestTemplate restClient;
```

15. We will use these `RestTemplate` instances to call the microservices. We will replace the hard-coded URLs with service IDs, which are registered in the Eureka Server. In the following code, we use the service names `search-service`, `book-service` and `checkin-service` instead of explicit host names and ports:

```
Flight[] flights = searchClient.postForObject(
  "http://search-service/search/get",
   searchQuery, Flight[].class);=

long bookingId = bookingClient.postForObject(
    "http://book-service/booking/create", booking, long.class);

long checkinId = checkInClient.postForObject(
  "http://checkin- service/checkin/create", checkIn,
   long.class);
```

16. We are now ready to test. Run the website project. If everything is fine, the website project's `CommandLineRunner` will successfully perform search, book, and check-in.

17. The same can also be tested using the browser by pointing the browser to `http://localhost:8001`.

High availability for Eureka

In the previous example, there was only one Eureka Server in the standalone mode. This is not good enough for a real production system.

The Eureka Client connects to the server, fetches registry information, and stores it locally in a cache. The client always works with this local cache. The Eureka Client checks the server periodically for any state changes. In case of a state change, it downloads the changes from the server and updates the cache. If the Eureka Server is not reachable, then the Eureka Client can still work with the last known state of the servers based on the data available in the client cache. However, this could lead to stale state issues quickly.

This section will explore high availability of the Eureka Server. The high availability architecture is shown in this diagram:

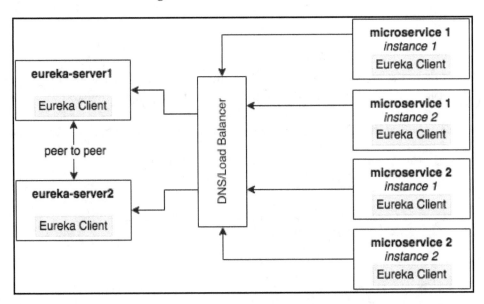

The Eureka Server is built with a peer-to-peer data synchronization mechanism. The run-time state information is not stored in a database, but managed using an in-memory cache. The high availability implementation favors availability and partition tolerance in the CAP theorem, leaving out consistency. Since the Eureka Server instances are synchronized with each other using asynchronous mechanism, the states may not always match between server instances. Peer-to-peer synchronization is done by pointing service URLs to each other. If there is more than one Eureka Server, each one has to be connected to at least one of the peer servers. Since the state is replicated across all peers, Eureka clients can connect to any one of the available Eureka servers.

The best way to achieve high availability for Eureka is to cluster multiple Eureka servers and run them behind a load balancer or a local DNS. The clients always connect to the server using the DNS or load balancer. At runtime, the load balancer will take care of selecting the appropriate servers. This load balancer address will be provided to the Eureka clients.

This section will showcase how to run two Eureka servers in a cluster for high availability. For this, define two property files--eureka-server1 and eureka-server2. These are peer servers--if one fails, the other one will take over. Each of these servers will also act as a client for the other so that they can sync their states. The two property files defined are defined next. Upload and commit these properties to the Git repository. In the following configurations, the client URLs are pointing to each other, forming a peer network:

```
#eureka-server1.properties
eureka.client.serviceUrl.defaultZone:http://localhost:8762/eureka/
eureka.client.registerWithEureka:false
eureka.client.fetchRegistry:false

#eureka-server2.properties
eureka.client.serviceUrl.defaultZone:http://localhost:8761/eureka/
eureka.client.registerWithEureka:false
eureka.client.fetchRegistry:false
```

Update bootstrap.properties of Eureka and change the application name to eureka. Since we are using two profiles, the Config Server will look for either eureka-server1 or eureka-server2 based on the active profile supplied at startup:

```
spring.application.name=eureka
spring.cloud.config.uri=http://localhost:8888
```

Start two instances of the Eureka servers--server1 on 8761 and server2 on 8762:

```
java -jar -Dserver.port=8761 -Dspring.profiles.active=server1
    demo-0.0.1-SNAPSHOT.jar

java -jar -Dserver.port=8762 -Dspring.profiles.active=server2
    demo-0.0.1-SNAPSHOT.jar
```

All our services are still pointing to the first server, server1. Open both the browser windows.

```
http://localhost:8761
http://localhost:8762
```

Start all microservices. The one which opened 8761 will immediately reflect the changes, whereas the other one will take 30 seconds to reflect the states. Since both the servers are in a cluster, the state is synchronized between these two servers. If we keep these servers behind a load balancer or DNS, then the client will always connect to one of the available servers.

After completing this exercise, switch back to the standalone mode for the remaining exercises.

Zuul proxy as the API Gateway

In most microservices implementations, internal microservices endpoints are not exposed outside. They are kept as private services. A set of public services will be exposed to the clients using an API Gateway. There are many reasons to do this, some of which are listed as follows:

- Only a selected set of microservices are required by the clients.
- If there are client-specific policies to be applied, it is easy to apply them in a single place rather than in multiple places. An example of such a scenario is the cross-origin access policy.
- It is hard to implement client-specific transformations at the service endpoint.
- If there is data aggregation required, especially to avoid multiple client calls in a bandwidth restricted environment, then a gateway is required in the middle.

Zuul is a simple gateway service or edge service, which well suits such situations. Zuul also came from the Netflix family of microservices products. Unlike many enterprise API gateway products, Zuul provides complete control to developers to configure or program based on specific requirements.

The following diagram shows Zuul acting as a proxy and load balancer for **Microservice A**:

```
                                    ┌──────────────────┐
                                    │       Zuul       │
              ┌──discover───────────│  Eureka Client   │
              │                     └──────────────────┘
              │                          │        │
              ▼                          │        │
    ┌──────────────────┐                 │        │
    │                  │                 │        │
    │  Eureka Server   │                 ▼        ▼
    │                  │      ┌──────────────┐ ┌──────────────┐
    └──────────────────┘      │ Microservice A│ │ Microservice A│
       ▲        ▲             │   instance 1  │ │   instance 2  │
       │        └──register───└──────────────┘ └──────────────┘
       │                              
       └────────register─────────────────────────────
```

The Zuul proxy internally uses the **Eureka Server** for service discovery, and Ribbon for load balancing between service instances.

The Zuul proxy is also capable of routing, monitoring, managing resiliency, security, and so on. In simple terms, we can consider Zuul as a reverse proxy service. With Zuul, we can even change the behaviors of the underlying services by overriding them at the API layer.

Setting up Zuul

Unlike the Eureka Server and the Config Server, in typical deployments, Zuul is specific to a microservice. However, there are deployments in which one API Gateway covers many microservices. In this case, we are going to add Zuul for each of our microservices--Search, Booking, Fare, and Check-In.

The full source code of this section is available under the `chapter7.*-apigateway` project in the code files.

Perform the following steps for setting up Zuul:

1. Convert the microservices one by one. Start with the Search API Gateway. Create a new Spring Starter project and select **Zuul**, **Config Client**, **Actuator**, and **Eureka Discovery**:

▶ Cloud Circuit Breaker
▶ Cloud Cluster
▼ Cloud Config

☑ Config Client	☐ Config Server	☐ Zookeeper Configuration	☐ Consul Configuration

▶ Cloud Core
▼ Cloud Discovery

☑ Eureka Discovery	☐ Eureka Server	☐ Zookeeper Discovery	☐ Cloud Foundry Discovery
☐ Consul Discovery			

▶ Cloud Messaging
▼ Cloud Routing

☑ Zuul	☐ Ribbon	☐ Feign

▶ Cloud Tracing
▶ Core
▶ Data
▶ Database
▶ I/O
▼ Ops

☑ Actuator	☐ Actuator Docs	☐ Remote Shell

▶ Social   API documentation for the Actuator endpoints
▶ Template Engines
▼ Web

☐ Web	☐ Websocket	☐ WS	☐ Jersey (JAX-RS)
☐ Ratpack	☐ Vaadin	☐ Rest Repositories	☑ HATEOAS
☑ Rest Repositories HAL Browser	☐ Mobile	☐ REST Docs	

The project structure for the `search-apigateway` is shown in this screenshot:

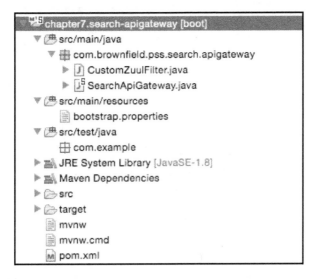

2. The next step is to integrate the API Gateway with Eureka and the Config Server. Create a `search-apigateway.property` file with the contents as given next, and commit to the Git repository.

   This configuration also sets a rule on how to forward traffic. In this case, any request coming on the `/api` endpoint of the API Gateway should be sent to the search-service:

   ```
   spring.application.name=search-apigateway
   zuul.routes.search-apigateway.serviceId=search-service
   zuul.routes.search-apigateway.path=/api/**
   eureka.client.serviceUrl.defaultZone:
   http://localhost:8761/eureka/
   ```

   The `search-service` is the service ID of Search service, and it will be resolved using the Eureka Server.

3. Update `bootstrap.properties` of `search-apigateway` as follows. There is nothing new in this configuration--a name to the service, port, and the Config Server URL:

   ```
   spring.application.name=search-apigateway
   server.port=8095
   spring.cloud.config.uri=http://localhost:8888
   ```

4. Edit `Application.java`. In this case, the package name and the class name also change to `com.brownfield.pss.search.apigateway` and `SearchApiGateway` respectively. Also add `@EnableZuulProxy` to tell Spring Boot that this is a Zuul proxy:

```
@EnableZuulProxy
@EnableDiscoveryClient
@SpringBootApplication
public class SearchApiGateway {
```

5. Run this as Spring Boot app. Before that, ensure that the Config Server, the Eureka Server, and the Search microservice are running.
6. Change the website project's CommandLineRunner, as well as `BrownFieldSiteController`, to make use of the API Gateway:

```
Flight[] flights = searchClient.postForObject(
    "http://search-apigateway/api/search/get",
    searchQuery, Flight[].class);
```

In this case, the Zuul proxy acts as a reverse proxy, which proxies all microservice endpoints to consumers. In the preceding example, the Zuul proxy does not add much value, as we just pass through the incoming requests to the corresponding backend service.

Zuul is particularly useful when we have one or more requirements like these:

- Enforcing authentication and other security policies at the gateway instead of doing that on every microservice endpoint. The gateway can handle security policies, token handling, and so on before passing the request to the relevant services behind. It can also do basic rejections based on some business policies, such as blocking requests coming from certain black-listed users.
- Business insights and monitoring can be implemented at the gateway level. Collect real-time statistical data and push it to an external system for analysis. This will be handy, as we can do this at one place rather than applying it across many microservices.
- API gateways are useful in scenarios where dynamic routing is required based on fine-grained controls. For example, send requests based on certain specific business values such as gold customer to a different service instances. For example, all requests coming from a region to be sent to one group of service instances. Another example--all requests requesting for a particular product have to be routed to a group of service instances.

- Handling the load shredding and throttling requirements is another scenario where API gateways are useful. This is when we have to control load based on set thresholds such as number of requests in a day. For example, control requests coming from a low-value third-party online channel.
- The Zuul gateway is useful for fine-grained load balancing scenarios. Zuul, Eureka Client, and Ribbon together provide fine-grained controls over load balancing requirements. Since the Zuul implementation is nothing but another Spring Boot application, the developer has full control of the load balancing.
- The Zuul gateway is also useful in scenarios where data aggregation requirements are in place. If the consumer wants higher-level coarse-grained services, then the gateway can internally aggregate data by calling more than one service on behalf of the client. This is particularly applicable when the clients are working in low-bandwidth environments.

Zuul also provides a number of filters. These filters are classified under pre-filters, routing filters, post filters, and error filters. As the names indicate, these are applied at different life cycle stages of a service call. Zuul also provides an option for developers to write custom filters. In order to write a custom filter, extend from the abstract `ZuulFilter`, and implement methods shown as follows:

```
public class CustomZuulFilter extends ZuulFilter{
public Object run(){}
public boolean shouldFilter(){}
public int filterOrder(){}
public String filterType(){}
```

Once a custom filter is implemented, add that class to the main context. In our example case, add this to the `SearchApiGateway` class as follows:

```
@Bean
public CustomZuulFilter customFilter() {
  return new CustomZuulFilter();
}
```

As mentioned earlier, the Zuul proxy is a Spring Boot service. We can customize the gateway programmatically in the way we want. As shown in the following code, we can add custom endpoints to the gateway, which in turn can call the backend services:

```
@RestController
class SearchAPIGatewayController {
  @RequestMapping("/")
  String greet(HttpServletRequest req){
```

```
    return "<H1>Search Gateway Powered By Zuul</H1>";
    }
  }
```

In the preceding case, it just adds a new endpoint, and returns a value from the gateway. We can further use the @Loadbalanced RestTemplate to call a backend service. Since we have full control, we can do transformations, data aggregation, and so on. We can also use the Eureka APIs to get the server list and implement completely independent load balancing or traffic shaping mechanisms instead of the out-of-the-box load balancing features provided by Ribbon.

High availability of Zuul

Zuul is just a stateless service with an HTTP endpoint, hence, we can have as many Zuul instances as we need. There is no affinity or stickiness required. However, the availability of Zuul is extremely critical, as all the traffic from the consumer to the provider flows through the Zuul proxy. However, the elastic scaling requirements are not as critical as the backend microservices, where all the heavy lifting is happening.

The high availability architecture of Zuul is determined by the scenario in which we are using Zuul. The typical usage scenarios are as follows:

- When a client-side java script MVC such as Angular JS accesses Zuul services from a remote browser
- Another microservice or non-microservice accesses services via Zuul

In some cases, the client may not have capabilities to use the Eureka Client libraries, such as a legacy application written on PL/SQL. In some cases, organization policies do not allow Internet clients to handle client-side load balancing. In the case of browser-based clients, there are third-party Eureka JavaScript libraries available.

It all boils down to whether the client is using Eureka Client libraries or not. Based on this, there are two ways we can set up Zuul for high availability.

High availability of Zuul when the client is also a Eureka Client

In this case, since the client is also another Eureka Client, Zuul can be configured just like other microservices. Zuul itself registers to Eureka with a service ID. The clients then use Eureka and the service ID to resolve Zuul instances.

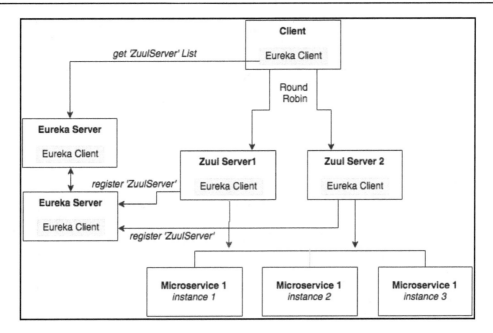

As shown in the preceding diagram, Zuul services register themselves with Eureka with a service ID, `search-apigateway` in our case. The **Eureka Client** will ask for the server list with the ID `search-apigateway`. The **Eureka Server** returns the list of servers based on the current Zuul topology. The **Eureka Client**, based on this list, picks up one of the servers, and initiates the call.

As we saw earlier, the client will use the service ID to resolve the Zuul instance. In the following case, `search-apigateway` is the Zuul instance ID registered with Eureka:

```
Flight[] flights = searchClient.postForObject(
    "http://search-apigateway/api/search/get",
    searchQuery, Flight[].class);
```

High availability when client is not a Eureka Client

In this case, the client is not capable of handling the load balancing by using the Eureka Server. As shown in the following diagram, the client sends the request to a load balancer, which, in turn, identifies the right Zuul service instance.

The Zuul instances, in this case, will be running behind a load balancer such as HAProxy, or a hardware load balancer like NetScaler:

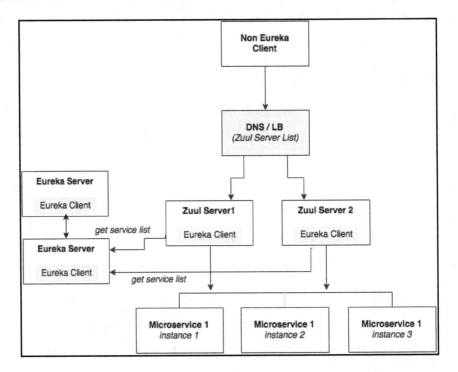

The microservices will still be load balanced by Zuul using the Eureka Server.

Completing Zuul for all other services

In order to complete this exercise, add an API Gateway for all our microservices. The following steps are required to achieve this task:

1. Create new property files per service and check in to Git repositories.
2. Change `application.properties` to `bootstrap.properties` and add the required configurations.
3. Add `@EnableZuulProxy` in the application.
4. `@EnableDiscoveryClient` in all applications.
5. Optionally, change the default generated package names and the filenames.

In the end, we will have the following API Gateway projects:

- `chapter7.fares-apigateway`
- `chapter7.search-apigateway`
- `chapter7.checkin-apigateway`
- `chapter7.book-apigateway`

Streams for reactive microservices

Spring Cloud Streams provides an abstraction over the messaging infrastructure. The underlying messaging implementation can be RabbitMQ, Redis, or Kafka. Spring Cloud Streams provides a declarative approach for sending and receiving messages.

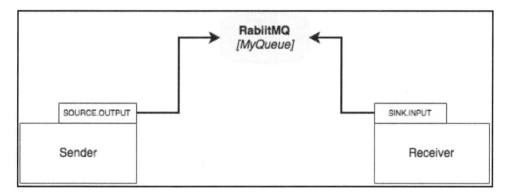

As shown in the preceding diagram, the Cloud Streams work with the concept of a Source and a Sink. The Source represents the sender perspective of the messaging, and Sink represents the receiver perspective of the messaging.

In the given example, the **Sender** defines a logical queue called `Source.OUTPUT` to which the **Sender** sends messages. The **Receiver** defines a logical queue called `Sink.INPUT` from which the **Receiver** retrieves messages. The physical binding of `OUTPUT` to `INPUT` is managed through the configuration. In this case, both link to the same physical queue, `MyQueue` on RabbitMQ. So, at one end, `Source.OUTPUT` will be pointed to `MyQueue`, and on the other end, `Sink.INPUT` will be pointed to the same `MyQueue`.

Spring Cloud offers the flexibility to use multiple messaging providers in one application, such as connecting an input stream from the Kafka to a Redis output stream without managing the complexities. Spring Cloud Streams is the basis for message-based integration. The Cloud Stream Modules sub-project is another Spring Cloud library that provides many endpoint implementations.

As the next step, rebuild the inter-microservice messaging communication with the Cloud Streams. As shown in the diagram, we will define a `SearchSink` connected to `InventoryQ` under the Search microservice. Booking will define a `BookingSource` for sending inventory change messages connected to `InventoryQ`. Similarly, Checkin defines a `CheckinSource` for sending check-in messages. Booking defines a sink `BookingSink` for receiving messages, both bound to the `CheckinQ` queue on Rabbit MQ.

The following diagram shows the example setup using stream based architecture:

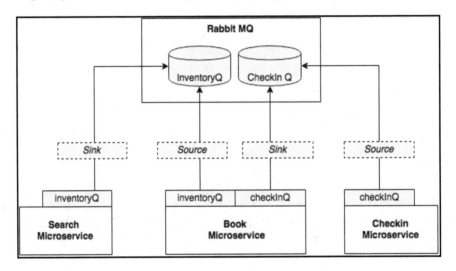

In this example, we will use RabbitMQ as the message broker. Perform the following steps:

1. Add the following Maven dependency to Booking, Search, and Check-in, as these are the three modules using messaging:

```
<dependency>
    <groupId>org.springframework.cloud</groupId>
    <artifactId>spring-cloud-starter-stream-rabbit</artifactId>
</dependency>
```

2. Add the following two properties to `booking-service.properties`. These properties bind the logical queues, `inventoryQ` to the physical `inventoryQ`, and the logical `checkinQ` to physical `checkinQ`.

```
spring.cloud.stream.bindings.inventoryQ.destination=inventoryQ
spring.cloud.stream.bindings.checkInQ.destination=checkInQ
```

3. Add the following property to `search-service.properties`. This property binds the logical queue `inventoryQ` to the physical `inventoryQ`:

```
spring.cloud.stream.bindings.inventoryQ.destination=inventoryQ
```

4. Add this next property to the `checkin-service.properties`. This property binds the logical queue `checkinQ` to the physical `checkinQ`:

```
spring.cloud.stream.bindings.checkInQ.destination=checkInQ
```

5. Commit all files to the Git repository.
6. The next step is to edit the code. The Search microservice consumes messages from the Booking microservice. In this case, Booking is the source and Search is the sink.
7. Add `@EnableBinding` to the `Sender` class of the Booking service. This enables the Cloud Stream to work on auto-configurations based on the message broker library available in the class path. In our case, it is RabbitMQ. The parameter, `BookingSource` defines the logical channels to be used for this configuration:

```
@EnableBinding(BookingSource.class)
public class Sender {
```

In this case, `BookingSource` defines a message channel called `inventoryQ`, which is physically bound to the Rabbit MQ `inventoryQ`, as configured in the configuration. `BookingSource` uses an annotation, `@Output`, to indicate that this is of the type output--a message that is outgoing from a module. This information will be used for the auto-configuration of the message channel:

```
interface BookingSource {
  public static String InventoryQ="inventoryQ";
  @Output("inventoryQ")
  public MessageChannel inventoryQ();
}
```

8. Instead of defining a custom class, we can also use the default `Source` class that comes with Spring Could Streams, if the service has only one source and sink:

```
public interface Source {
  @Output("output")
  MessageChannel output();
}
```

9. Define a message channel in the sender based on `BookingSource`. The following code will inject an output message channel with the name inventory, which is already configured in `BookingSource`:

```
@Output (BookingSource.InventoryQ)
@Autowired
private MessageChannel messageChannel;
```

10. Reimplement the send message method in the Booking sender:

```
public void send(Object message){
  messageChannel.send(
  MessageBuilder.withPayload(message).build());
}
```

11. Now add the following to the Search `Receiver` class the same way we did it for the Booking service:

```
@EnableBinding(SearchSink.class)
public class Receiver {
```

12. In this case, the `SearchSink` interface will look like the following. This will define the logical sink queue it is connected with. The message channel in this case is defined as `@Input` to indicate that this message channel is to accept messages:

```
interface SearchSink {
  public static String INVENTORYQ="inventoryQ";

  @Input("inventoryQ")
  public MessageChannel inventoryQ()
}
```

13. Amend the Search service to accept this message:

```
public void accept(Map<String,Object> fare){
  searchComponent.updateInventory(
  (String)fare.get("FLIGHT_NUMBER"),
  (String)fare.get("FLIGHT_DATE"),
  (int)fare.get("NEW_INVENTORY"));}
```

14. We will still need the RabbitMQ configurations that we have in our configuration files to connect to the message broker:

```
spring.rabbitmq.host=localhost
spring.rabbitmq.port=5672
spring.rabbitmq.username=guest
spring.rabbitmq.password=guest
server.port=8090
```

15. Run all the services, and run the website project. If everything is fine, the website project successfully executes the search, book, and check-in functions. The same can also be tested using the browser by pointing to `http://localhost:8001`.

Protecting microservices with Spring Cloud Security

In a monolithic web application, once the user is logged in, user-related information will be stored in an HTTP session. All subsequent requests will be validated against the HTTP session. This is simple to manage, since all requests will be routed through the same session, either through the session affinity or offloaded, shared session store.

In the case of microservices, it is harder to protect from unauthorised access, especially, when many services are deployed and accessed remotely. A typical or rather simple pattern for microservices is to implement perimeter security by using gateways as security watchdogs. Any request coming to the gateway will be challenged and validated. In this case, it is then important to ensure that all requests to downstream microservices are funneled through the API Gateway. Generally, the load balancer sitting in the front will be the only client that sends requests to the gateway. In this approach, downstream microservices processes all requests, assuming they are trusted, without authenticating. It means all microservice endpoints will be open for all.

However, this solution may not be acceptable for enterprise cyber security. One of the ways to eliminate this concern is to create network segregation and zones so that the services are exposed only for the gateways to access. In order to simplify this landscape, a common pattern is to set up consumer-driven gateways, which combine multiple microservices access instead of the one-to-one gateways we have used in our example.

Another way of accomplishing this is through token relay, as shown in this diagram:

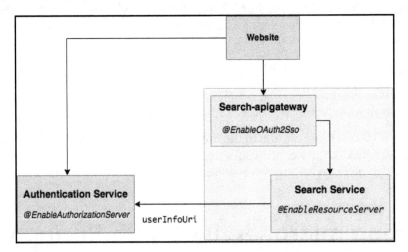

In this case, each microservice will also act as a resource server with a central server for authentication. The API Gateway will forward the request with the token to the downstream microservices for authentication.

Summarising the BrownField PSS architecture

The next diagram shows the overall architecture that we have created with the Config Server, Eureka, Feign, Zuul, and Cloud Streams.

The architecture also includes high availability of all the components. In this case, we are assuming that the client is using the Eureka Client libraries:

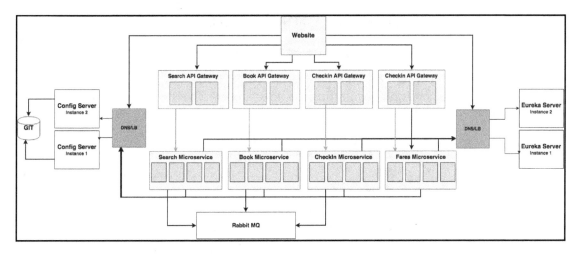

The summary of the projects and the port they are listening to is given in the following table:

Microservice	Projects	Port
Book Microservice	chapter7.book	8060-8064
Check In Microservice	chapter7.checkin	8070-8074
Fare Microservice	chapter7.fares	8080-8084
Search Microservice	chapter7.search	8090-8094
Website Client	chapter7.website	8001
Spring Cloud Config Server	chapter7.configserver	8888 / 8889
Spring Cloud Eureka Server	chapter7.eurekaserver	8761 / 8762
Book API Gateway	chapter7.book-apigateway	8095-8099
Check In API Gateway	chapter7.checkin-apigateway	8075-8079
Fares API Gateway	chapter7.fares-apigateway	8085-8089
Search API Gateway	chapter7.search-apigateway	8065-8069

Follow these steps to do a final run:

1. Run RabbitMQ.
2. Build all projects using `pom.xml` at the root level:

    ```
    mvn -Dmaven.test.skip=true clean install
    ```

3. Run the following projects from the respective folders. Note that you should wait for 40-50 seconds before starting the next service. This will ensure that the dependent services are registered and are available before we start a new service.

    ```
    java -jar target/config-server-1.0.jar
    java -jar target/eureka-server-1.0.jar
    java -jar target/fares-1.0.jar
    java -jar target/fares-1.0.jar
    java -jar target/search-1.0.jar
    java -jar target/checkin-1.0.jar
    java -jar target/book-1.0.jar
    java -jar target/fares-apigateway-1.0.jar
    java -jar target/search-apigateway-1.0.jar
    java -jar target/checkin-apigateway-1.0.jar
    java -jar target/book-apigateway-1.0.jar
    java -jar target/website-1.0.jar
    ```

4. Open the browser window, and point to `http://localhost:8001`.

Summary

In this chapter, we learned how to scale Twelve-Factor Spring Boot microservices using the Spring Cloud project. Our learnings were applied on the BrownField Airline's PSS microservice, which we developed in the previous chapter.

We explored the Spring Config Server for externalizing microservices configurations, and how to deploy the Config Server for high availability. We also learned Eureka for load balancing, dynamic service registration, and discovery. Implementation of an API Gateway was examined by implementing Zuul. Finally, we concluded with the reactive style integration of microservices using Spring Cloud Streams.

The BrownField Airline's PSS microservices are now deployable for Internet scale. Other Spring Cloud components such as Hyterix, Sleuth, and others will be covered in the next chapter.

13
Logging and Monitoring Microservices

One of the biggest challenges due to the very distributed nature of internet-scale microservices deployment is the logging and monitoring of individual microservices. It is difficult to trace end-to-end transactions by correlating logs emitted by different microservices. Like monolithic applications, there is no single pane of glass for monitoring microservices. This is important, especially when we deal with enterprise-scale microservices with a number of technologies, as discussed in the previous chapter.

This chapter will cover the necessity and importance of logging and monitoring in microservice deployments. This chapter will further examine the challenges and solutions to address logging and monitoring with a number of potential architectures and technologies.

By the end of this chapter, you will have learned about the following:

- The different options, tools, and technologies for log management
- The use of **Spring Cloud Sleuth** for microservices
- The different tools for end-to-end monitoring of microservices
- The use of **Spring Cloud Hystrix** and **Turbine** for circuit monitoring
- The use of **Data Lake** for enabling business data analysis

Understanding log management challenges

Logs are nothing but streams of events coming from a running process. For traditional JEE applications, a number of frameworks and libraries are available for logging. **Java Logging (JUL)** is an option off-the-shelf from Java itself. Log4j, Logback, and SLF4J are some of the other popular logging frameworks available. These frameworks support both UDP as well as TCP protocols for logging. The applications send log entries to the console or the filesystem. File recycling techniques are generally employed to avoid logs filling up all disk space.

One of the best practices for log handling is to switch off most of the log entries in production due to the high cost of disk IOs. The disk IOs not only slow down the application, but can also severely impact the scalability. Writing logs into the disk also requires a high disk capacity. Running out of the disk space scenario can bring down the application. Logging frameworks provide options to control logging at runtime to restrict what has to be printed and what not. Most of these frameworks provide fine-grained controls over the logging controls. It also provides options for changing these configurations at runtime.

On the other hand, logs may contain important information and have a high value if properly analyzed. Therefore, restricting log entries essentially limits our ability to understand the application behavior.

When moved from traditional deployment to cloud deployment, applications are no longer locked to a particular, predefined machine. Virtual machines and containers are not hardwired with an application. The machines used for deployment can change from time to time. Moreover, containers such as Docker are ephemeral. This essentially means one cannot rely on the persistent state of the disk. Logs written to the disk will be lost once the container is stopped and restarted. Therefore, we cannot rely on the local machine's disk to write log files.

As we discussed in Chapter 10, *Related Architecture Styles and Use Cases*, one of the principles of the Twelve-Factor application is to avoid routing or storing log files by the application itself. In the context of microservices, they will be running on isolated physical or virtual machines, resulting in fragmented log files. In this case, it would be almost impossible to trace end-to-end transactions that span across multiple microservices.

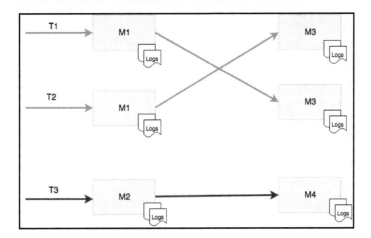

As shown in the preceding diagram, each microservice emits logs to a local file system. In this case, transaction **T1** calls **M1** followed by **M3**. Since **M1** and **M3** runs on different physical machines, both of them writes respective logs to different log files. This makes it harder to correlate and understand the end-to-end transactions flow. Also, since two instances of **M1** and **M3** are running on two different machines, log aggregation at service level is hard to achieve.

Centralized logging solution

In order to address the earlier stated challenges, traditional logging solutions require serious rethinking. The new logging solution, in addition to addressing the preceding challenges, is also expected to support the capabilities summarized here:

- Ability to collect all log messages and run analytics on top of the log messages
- Ability to correlate and track transactions end-to-end
- Ability to keep log information for longer time periods for trending and forecasting
- Ability to eliminate dependency on the local disk system
- Ability to aggregate log information coming from multiple sources, such as network devices, operating system, microservices, and so on

The solution to these problems is to centrally store and analyze all log messages, irrespective of the source of the log. The fundamental principle employed in the new logging solution is to detach log storage and processes from the service execution environments. Big data solutions are better suited for storing and processing a large amount of log messages more effectively than storing and processing them in the microservice execution environments.

In the centralized logging solution, log messages will be shipped from the execution environment to a central big data store. Log analysis and processing will be handled using big data solutions.

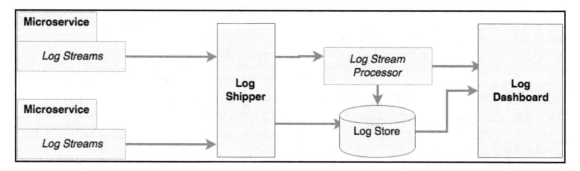

As shown in the preceding logical diagram, there are a number of components in the centralized logging solution. These are explained as follows:

- **Log streams**: These are streams of log messages coming out of the source systems. The source system can be microservices, other applications, or even network devices. In typical Java-based systems, these are equivalent to streaming the Log4j log messages.
- **Log shippers**: These are responsible for collecting the log messages coming from different sources or endpoints. The log shippers then send these messages to another set of endpoints, such as writing to a database, pushing to a dashboard, or sending it to a stream processing endpoint for further real-time processing.
- **Log store**: This is the place where all log messages will be stored for real-time analysis, trending, and so on. Typically, the log store will be a NoSQL database, such as HDFS, capable of handling large data volumes.
- **Log stream processor**: This is capable of analyzing real-time log events for quick decision making. Stream processors take actions such as sending information to a dashboard, sending alerts, and so on. In the case of self-healing systems, stream processors can even take action to correct the problems.

- **Log dashboard**: This dashboard is a single pane of glass for displaying log analysis results, such as graphs and charts. These dashboards are meant for operational and management staff.

The benefits of this centralized approach is that there are no local IOs or blocking disk writes. It is also not using the local machine's disk space. This architecture is fundamentally similar to Lambda architecture for big data processing.

 Follow this link to read more on Lambda architecture:
`http://lambda-architecture.net`

It is important to have each log message, a context, message and a correlation ID. The context typically will have the timestamp, IP address, user information, process details (such as service, class, functions), log type, classification, and so on. The message will be plain and simple free text information. The correlation ID will be used to establish the link between service calls so that calls spanning across microservices can be traced.

Selection of logging solutions

There are a number of options available for implementing a centralized logging solution. These solutions use different approaches, architectures, and technologies. It is important to understand the capabilities required and select the right solution that meets the needs.

Cloud services

There are a number of cloud logging services available as SaaS solution. **Loggly** is one of the most popular cloud-based logging service. The Spring Boot microservices can use the Loggly's Log4j and Logback appenders to directly stream log messages into the Loggly service.

If the application or service is deployed in AWS, the AWS **CloudTrail** can be integrated with Loggly for log analysis.

Papertrial, **Logsene**, **Sumo Logic**, **Google Cloud Logging**, and **Logentries** are examples of other cloud-based logging solutions. Some of the tools in the **Security Operations Center** (**SOC**) are also qualified for centralized log management.

The cloud logging services take away the overhead of managing complex infrastructures and large storage solutions by providing them as simple to integrate services. However, latency is one of the key factors to be considered when selecting cloud logging as a service.

Off-the-shelf solutions

There are many purpose-built tools to provide end-to-end log management capabilities that are installable locally on an on-premise data center or in the cloud.

Graylog is one of the popular open source log management solutions. It uses Elasticsearch for log storage and MongoDB as a metadata store. It also uses GELF libraries for Log4j log streaming.

Splunk is one of the popular commercial tools available for log management and analysis. It uses the log file shipping approach compared to log streaming used by other solutions for collecting logs.

Best of the breed integration

The last approach is to pick and choose the best of the breed components and build a custom logging solution.

Log shippers

There are log shippers that can be combined with other tools to build an end-to-end log management solution. The capabilities differ between different log shipping tools.

Logstash is a powerful data pipeline tool that can be used for collecting and shipping log files. It acts as a broker that provides a mechanism to accept streaming data from different sources and sinks them to different destinations. Log4j and Logback appenders can also be used to send log messages directly from Spring Boot microservices to Logstash. The other end of the Logstash will be connected to Elasticsearch, HDFS, or any other databases.

Fluentd is another tool that is very similar to Logstash. Logspout is another similar tool to Logstash, but it is more appropriate in a Docker container-based environment.

Log stream processors

Stream processing technologies are optionally used for processing log streams on the fly. For example, if a 404 error is continuously received as a response to a particular service call, it means there is something wrong with the service. Such situations have to be handled as soon as possible. Stream processors are pretty handy in such cases, as they are capable of reacting to certain streams of events compared to traditional reactive analysis.

A typical architecture used for stream processing is a combination of **Flume** and **Kafka** together, with either **Storm** or **Spark Streaming**. Log4j has Flume appenders that are useful for collecting log messages. These messages will be pushed into distributed Kafka message queues. The stream processors collect data from Kafka and process it on the fly before sending it to Elasticsearch and other log stores.

Spring Cloud Stream, **Spring Cloud Stream modules**, and **Spring Cloud Data Flow** can also be used to build the log stream processing.

Log storage

Real-time log messages are typically stored in Elasticsearch, which allows clients to query based on the text-based indexes. Apart from Elasticsearch, HDFS is also commonly used to store archived log messages. MongoDB or Cassandra are used to store summary data, such as monthly aggregated transaction counts. Offline log processing can be done using Hadoop map reduce programs.

Dashboards

The last piece required in the central logging solution is a dashboard. The most commonly used dashboard for log analysis is **Kibana** on top of an Elasticsearch data store. **Graphite** and **Grafana** are also used to display log analysis reports.

Custom logging implementation

The tools mentioned in the preceding section can be leveraged to build a custom end-to-end logging solution. The most commonly used architecture for custom log management is a combination of **Logstash**, **Elasticsearch**, and **Kibana**, also known as the **ELK** stack.

The full source code of this chapter is available under the `chapter8` projects in the code files under `https://github.com/rajeshrv/Spring5Microservice`. Copy `chapter7.configserver`, `chapter7.eurekaserver`, `chapter7.search`, `chapter7.search-apigateway`, and `chapter7.website` into a new STS workspace and rename `chapter8.*`.

Note: Even though Spring Cloud Dalston SR1 officially supports Spring Boot 1.5.2.RELEASE, there are a few issues around Hystrix. In order to run the Hystrix examples, it is advised to upgrade the Spring Boot version to 1.5.4.RELEASE.

The following diagram shows the log monitoring flow:

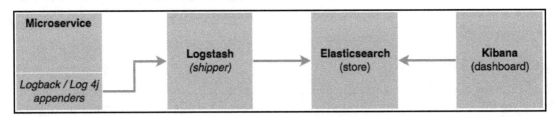

In this section, a simple implementation of a custom logging solution using the ELK stack will be examined.

Follow these steps to implement the ELK stack for logging:

1. Download and install Elasticsearch, Kibana, and Logstash from `https://www.elastic.co`.
2. Update the Search microservice (`chapter8.search`). Review and ensure that there are some log statements in `Application.java` of the Search microservice. The log statements are nothing special but simple log statements using slf4j as shown in the following code snippet:

```
import org.slf4j.Logger;
import org.slf4j.LoggerFactory;
//other code goes here
private static final Logger logger = LoggerFactory
    .getLogger(SearchRestController.class);

//other code goes here

logger.info("Looking to load flights...");
```

```
for (Flight flight : flightRepository
  .findByOriginAndDestinationAndFlightDate
  ("NYC", "SFO", "22-JAN-18")) {
    logger.info(flight.toString());
}
```

3. Add the Logstash dependency to integrate `logback` to `logstash` in the Search service's `pom.xml`:

```xml
<dependency>
  <groupId>net.logstash.logback</groupId>
  <artifactId>logstash-logback-encoder</artifactId>
  <version>4.6</version>
</dependency>
```

4. Override the default `logback` configuration. This can be done by adding a new `logback.xml` under `src/main/resources`. A sample log configuration is shown as follows:

```xml
<?xml version="1.0" encoding="UTF-8"?>
<configuration>
  <include resource="org/springframework/boot/logging
    /logback/defaults.xml"/>
  <include resource="org/springframework/boot/logging
    /logback/console-appender.xml" />
  <appender name="stash"
    class="net.logstash.logback.appender
    .LogstashTcpSocketAppender">
    <destination>localhost:4560</destination>
    <!-- encoder is required -->
    <encoder class="net.logstash.logback.encoder
    .LogstashEncoder" />
  </appender>
  <root level="INFO">
   <appender-ref ref="CONSOLE" />
   <appender-ref ref="stash" />
  </root>
</configuration>
```

The preceding configuration overrides the default `logback` configuration by adding a new TCP socket appender, which streams all log messages to a Logstash service that is listening on port `4560`. It is important to add an encoder, as mentioned in the preceding configuration.

5. Create a configuration, as shown next, and store it in a `logstash.conf` file. The location of this file is irrelevant, since it will be passed as an argument when starting Logstash. This configuration will take input from the socket, listening on port `4560` and send the output to Elasticsearch running on port `9200`. The `stdout` is optional and set for debugging:

```
input {
  tcp {
    port => 4560
    host => localhost
  }
}
output {
  elasticsearch { hosts => ["localhost:9200"] }
  stdout { codec => rubydebug }
}
```

6. Run Logstash, Elasticsearch, and Kibana from their respective installation folders:

```
./bin/elasticsearch
./bin/kibana
./bin/logstash -f logstash.conf
```

7. Run the Search microservice. This will invoke the unit test cases and result in printing the log statements mentioned earlier. Ensure that RabbitMQ, Config Server, and Eureka servers are running.
8. Go to a browser and access Kibana:

```
http://localhost:5601
```

Go to settings and configure an index pattern, as shown in the following screenshot:

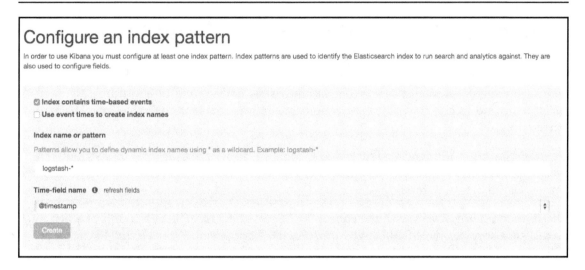

9. Go to discover menu to see the logs. If everything is successful, we will see the following Kibana screenshot. Note that the log messages are displayed in the Kibana screen.

   Kibana provides out-of-the-box features to build summary charts and graphs using log messages.

   The Kibana UI will look like the following screenshot:

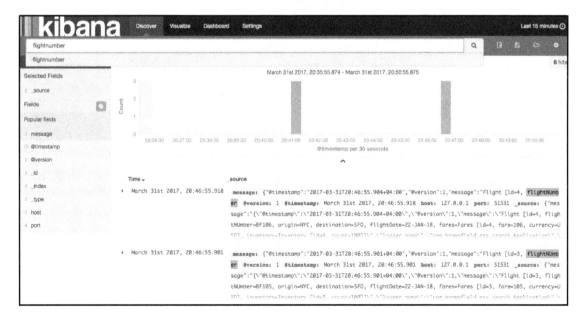

Distributed tracing with Spring Cloud Sleuth

The previous section addressed the microservices distributed and fragmented the logging issue by centralizing the log data. With the central logging solution, we have all the logs in central storage. However, still, it is almost impossible to trace end-to-end transactions. In order to do end-to-end tracking, transactions spanning across microservices need to have a correlation ID.

Twitter's **Zipkin**, Cloudera's **HTrace**, and Google's **Dapper** are examples of distributed tracing systems. The Spring Cloud provides a wrapper component on top of these using the Spring Cloud Sleuth library.

Distributed tracing works with the concepts of **Span** and **Trace**. Span is a unit of work, such as **calling a service**, identified by a 64-bit span ID. A set of spans form a tree-like structure called trace. Using the trace ID, a call can be tracked end-to-end as shown in the following diagram:

As shown in the preceding diagram, **Microservice 1** calls **2**, and **2** calls **3**. In this case, as shown in the diagram, the same **Trace-id** will be passed across all microservices, which can be used to track transactions end-to-end.

In order to demonstrate this, we will use the Search API Gateway and Search microservices. A new endpoint has to be added in the Search API Gateway (`chapter8.search-apigateway`), which internally calls the Search service to return data. Without the trace ID, it is almost impossible to trace or link calls coming from a website to `search-apigateway` to the Search microservice. In this case, it only involves two to three services; whereas, in a complex environment, there can be many interdependent services.

Follow these steps to create an example using Sleuth:

1. Update Search and Search API Gateway. Before that, the Sleuth dependency has to be added to the respective pom files:

    ```
    <dependency>
      <groupId>org.springframework.cloud</groupId>
      <artifactId>spring-cloud-starter-sleuth</artifactId>
    </dependency>
    ```

2. Add the Logstash dependency to the Search service as well as the `logback` configuration, as shown in the previous example.

3. The next step is to add the service name `property` in the `logback` configuration of the respective microservices:

```
<property name="spring.application.name"
  value="search-service"/>
<property name="spring.application.name"
  value="search-apigateway"/>
```

4. Add a new endpoint to the Search API Gateway, which will call the Search service, as follows. This is to demonstrate the propagation of the trace ID across multiple microservices. This new method in the gateway returns the operating hub of the airport by calling the search service. Note--the Rest Template (with `@Loadbalanced`) and Logger details also need to be added to the `SearchAPIGateway.java` class:

```
@RequestMapping("/hubongw")
String getHub(HttpServletRequest req){
  logger.info("Search Request in API gateway
   for getting Hub, forwarding to search-service ");
  String hub = restTemplate.getForObject("http://search-
   service/search/hub", String.class);
  logger.info("Response for hub received,  Hub "+ hub);
  return hub;
}
```

5. Add another endpoint in the Search service, as follows:

```
@RequestMapping("/hub")
String getHub(){
  logger.info("Searching for Hub, received from
   search-apigateway ");
  return "SFO";
}
```

6. Once added, run both services. Hit the gateway's new hub on the gateway (`/hubongw`) endpoint using a browser. Copy and paste the following link:

```
http://localhost:8095/hubongw
```

As mentioned earlier, the Search API Gateway service is running on `8095` and the Search service is running on `8090`.

7. Notice the console logs to see the trace ID and span IDs printed. The following print is from the Search API Gateway:

```
2017-03-31 22:30:17.780  INFO [search-
apigateway,9f698f7ebabe6b83,9f698f7ebabe6b83,false]
47158 --- [nio-8095-exec-1]
c.b.p.s.a.SearchAPIGatewayController: Response for hub
received,  Hub SFO
```

The following log is coming from the Search service:

```
2017-03-31 22:30:17.741 INFO [search-
service,9f698f7ebabe6b83,3a63748ac46b5a9d,false]
47106---[nio-8090-exec-
1]c.b.p.s.controller.SearchRestController  : Searching
for Hub, received from search-apigateway
```

Note that the trace IDs are the same in both cases.

8. Open the Kibana console and search for the trace ID using the trace ID printed in the console. In this case, it is `9f698f7ebabe6b83`. As shown in the following screenshot, with a trace ID, one can trace service calls that span across multiple services:

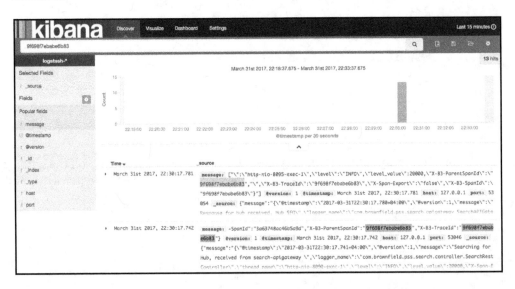

Monitoring microservices

Microservices are truly distributed systems with fluid deployment topology. Without a sophisticated monitoring in place, the operations team may run into trouble managing large-scale microservices. Traditional monolithic application deployments are limited to a number of known services, instances, machines, and so on. This is easier to manage as compared to a large number of microservices instances potentially running across different machines. To add more complications, these services dynamically change its topologies. The centralized logging capability only addresses part of the issue. It is important for the operations team to understand the runtime deployment topology, and also the behavior of the systems. This demands more than centralized logging can offer.

In general, application monitoring is more of a collection of metrics and aggregation and validating them against certain baseline values. If there is a service-level breach, then monitoring tools generate alerts and send to administrators. With hundreds and thousands of interconnected microservices, traditional monitoring does not really offer true value. A one-size-fits-all approach to monitoring, or monitoring everything with a single pane of glass is not easy to achieve in large-scale microservices.

One of the main objectives of microservice monitoring is to understand the behaviors of the system from the user experience point of view. This will ensure that the end-to-end behavior is consistent and in line with what is expected by users.

Monitoring challenges

Similar to the fragmented logging issue, the key challenge in monitoring microservices is that there are many moving parts in a microservice ecosystem.

Typical issues are summarized as follows:

- The statistics and metrics are fragmented across many services, instances, and machines.
- Heterogeneous technologies may be used to implement microservices, making things even more complex. A single monitoring tool may not give all required monitoring options.
- Microservices deployment topologies are dynamic, making it impossible to preconfigure servers, instances, and monitoring parameters.

Many of the traditional monitoring tools are good for monitoring monolithic applications, but fall short in monitoring large-scale distributed and interlinked microservice systems. Many of the traditional monitoring systems are agent-based, preinstall agents on the target machines or application instances. This poses the following two challenges:

- If the agents require deep integration with the services or operating systems, then this will be hard to manage in a dynamic environment
- If these tools impose overheads when monitoring or instrumenting the application, they can hinder performance issues

Many traditional tools need baseline metrics. Such systems work with preset rules, such as if the CPU utilization goes above 60% and remains at that level for two minutes, then send an alert to the administrator. It is extremely hard to preconfigure these values in large internet-scale deployments.

New generation monitoring applications self learn the application behavior and set automatic threshold values. This frees up the administrators from performing this mundane task. Automated baselines are sometimes more accurate than human forecasts.

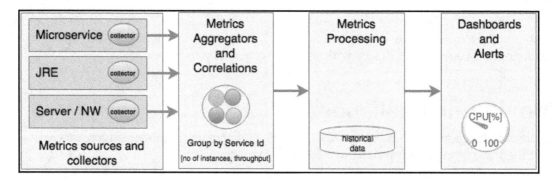

As shown in the preceding diagram, key areas of microservices monitoring are as follows:

- **Metrics sources and data collectors**: The metrics collection at the source will be done by either the server pushing metrics information to a central collector or by embedding lightweight agents to collect information. The data collectors collect monitoring metrics from different sources, such as network, physical machines, containers, software components, application, and so on. The challenge is to collect this data using auto-discovery mechanisms instead of static configurations.

  This will be done by either running agents on the source machines, streaming data from the sources, or polling at regular intervals.

- **Aggregation and correlation of metrics**: The aggregation capability is required to aggregate metrics collected from different sources, such as user transaction, service, infrastructure, network, and so on. Aggregation can be challenging, as it requires some level of understanding of the applications behaviors, such as service dependencies, service grouping, and so on. In many cases, these are automatically formulated based on the metadata provided by the sources.

  Generally, this will be done by an intermediary that accepts the metrics.

- **Processing metrics and actionable insights**: Once the data is aggregated, then the next step is to take measurements. Measurements are typically done by using set thresholds. In the new generation monitoring systems, these thresholds are automatically discovered. The monitoring tools then analyze the data and provide actionable insights.

  These tools may use big data and stream analytics solutions.

- **Alerting, actions and dashboards**: As soon as issues are detected, they have to be notified to the relevant people or systems. Unlike traditional systems, the microservices monitoring systems should be capable of taking actions on a real-time basis. Proactive monitoring is essential to achieving self-healing. Dashboards are used to display SLAs, KPIs, and so on.

  Dashboards and alerting tools are capable of handling these requirements.

Microservice monitoring is typically done with three approaches. A combination of them is really required for effective monitoring:

- **Application Performance Monitoring (APM)** (sometimes referred to as **Digital Performance Monitoring** or **DPM**) is is more of a traditional approach of system metrics collection, processing, alerting, and rendering dashboards. These are more from the system's point of view. Application topology discovery and visualization are new capabilities implemented by many of the APM tools. The capabilities vary between different APM providers.
- **Synthetic monitoring** is is a technique that is used to monitor system behavior using end-to-end transactions with a number of test scenarios in a production or production-like environment. Data will be collected to validate the system behavior and potential hotspots. Synthetic monitoring helps us understand system dependencies as well.

- **Real user monitoring** (**RUM**) or user experience monitoring is typically a browser-based software that records real user statistics, such as response times, availability, and service levels. With microservices, with a more frequent release cycle and dynamic topology, users experience that monitoring is more important.

Monitoring tools

There are many tools available for monitoring microservices. There are also overlaps between many of these tools. Selection of monitoring tools really depends upon the ecosystem that needs to be monitored. In most cases, more than one tool is required to monitor the overall microservice ecosystem.

The objective of this section is to familiarize a number of common microservices-friendly monitoring tools:

- **AppDynamics**, **Dynatrace** and **New Relic** are top commercial vendors in the APM space, as per Gartner magic quadrant 2015. These tools are microservice-friendly and support microservice monitoring effectively in a single console. **Ruxit**, **Datadog**, and **Dataloop** are other commercial offerings that are purpose-built for distributed systems that are essentially microservices-friendly. Multiple monitoring tools can feed data to Datadog using plugins.
- Cloud vendors come with their own monitoring tools, but, in many cases, these monitoring tools alone may not be sufficient for large-scale microservices monitoring. For instance, AWS uses **CloudWatch** and Google Cloud Platform uses **Cloud Monitoring** to collect information from various sources.
- Some of the data collecting libraries, such as **Zabbix**, **statd**, **collectd**, **jmxtrans**, and so on, operate at a lower level in collecting runtime statistics, metrics, gauges, and counters. Typically, this information will be fed into data collectors and processors, such as **Riemann**, **Datadog**, and **Librato**, or dashboards, such as **Graphite**.
- Spring Boot **Actuator** is one of the good vehicles for collecting microservices metrics, gauges, and counters, as we saw in `Chapter 11`, *Building Microservices with Spring Boot*. Netflix's **Servo** is a metric collector similar to Actuator. **QBit** and **Dropwizard** metrics also fall in the same category of metric collectors. All these metrics collectors need an aggregator and dashboard to facilitate full-sized monitoring.

- Monitoring through logging is popular, but a less effective approach in microservices monitoring. In this approach, as discussed in the previous section, log messages will be shipped from various sources, such as microservices, containers, networks, and so on, to a central location. Then, use the log files to trace transactions, identify hotspots, and so on. **Loggly**, **ELK**, **Splunk**, and **Trace** are candidates in this space.
- **Sensu** is a popular choice for microservice monitoring from the open source community. **Weave scope** is another tool, primarily targeting containerized deployments. SimianViz (formerly **Spigo**) is one of the purpose-built microservices, monitoring the system closely aligned with the Netflix stack. Cronitor is also another useful tool.
- **Pingdom**, **New Relic synthetic**, **Runscope**, **Catchpoint**, and so on, provide options for synthetic transaction monitoring and user experience monitoring on live systems.
- **Circonus** is classified more towards DevOps monitoring tools, but can also do microservices monitoring. **Nagios** is a popular open source monitoring tool, but it falls more into the traditional monitoring systems.
- **Prometheus** provides a time series database and visualization GUI useful for building custom monitoring tools.

Monitoring microservice dependency

When there are a large number of microservices with dependencies, it is important to have a monitoring tool that can show the dependencies between microservices. It is not a scalable approach to statically configure and manage these dependencies. There are many tools that are useful for monitoring microservice dependencies.

Mentoring tools, such as **AppDynamics**, **Dynatrace**, and **New Relic**, can draw dependencies between microservices. End-to-end transaction monitoring can also trace transaction dependencies. Other monitoring tools such as Spigo are also useful for microservices dependency management.
CMDB tools, such as **Device42**, or purpose-built tools, such as **Accordance**, are useful for managing dependency of microservices. **Vertias Risk Advisor (VRA)** is also useful for infrastructure discovery.

A custom implementation with a Graph database such as Neo4j can also be used. In this case, microservices has to be preconfigured with its direct and indirect dependencies. At the startup of the service, it publishes and cross-checks its dependencies with this Neo4j database.

Spring Cloud Hystrix for fault-tolerant microservices

This section will explore the Spring Cloud Hystrix as a library for fault-tolerant and latency-tolerant microservice implementation. The Hystrix is based on fail-fast and rapid recovery principles. If there is an issue with a service, Hystrix helps isolate the issue. It helps to fail-fast quickly by falling back to another preconfigured fallback service. It is another battle-tested library from Netflix and is based on the **Circuit Breaker** pattern.

 Read more about the Circuit Breaker pattern at `https://msdn.microsoft.com/en-us/library/dn589784.aspx`.

In this section, we will build a circuit breaker with the Spring Cloud Hystrix. Follow these steps to change the Search API Gateway service to integrate with the Hystrix. Update the Search API Gateway service.

Add the Hystrix dependency to the service, as follows:

```
<dependency>
    <groupId>org.springframework.cloud</groupId>
    <artifactId>spring-cloud-starter-hystrix</artifactId>
</dependency>
```

If developing from scratch, select the following libraries:

```
▶  Cloud AWS
▼  Cloud Circuit Breaker
    ☑ Hystrix              ☑ Hystrix Dashboard        ☐ Turbine                 ☐ Turbine AMQP
    ☐ Turbine Stream
▶  Cloud Cluster
▶  Cloud Config
▶  Cloud Core
▶  Cloud Data Flow
▶  Cloud Discovery
▶  Cloud Messaging
▶  Cloud Routing
▶  Cloud Tracing
▶  Core
▶  Data
▶  Database
▶  I/O
▼  Ops
    ☑ Actuator            ☐ Actuator Docs            ☐ Remote Shell
▶  Social
▶  Template Engines
▼  Web
    ☑ Web                 ☐ Websocket                ☐ WS                      ☐ Jersey (JAX-RS)
    ☐ Ratpack             ☐ Vaadin                   ☐ Rest Repositories       ☐ HATEOAS
    ☐ Rest Repositories HAL Browser  ☐ Mobile        ☐ REST Docs
```

In the Spring Boot Application class (`SearchAPIGateway`), add
`@EnableCircuitBreaker`. This command will tell Spring Cloud Hystrix to enable circuit
breaker for this application. It also exposes the `/hystrix.stream` endpoint for metrics
collection.

Add a component class to the Search API Gateway service with a method; in this case;
`getHub` annotated with `@HystrixCommand`. This tells Spring that this method is prone to
failure. The Spring Cloud libraries wrap these methods to handle fault-tolerance and
latency-tolerance by enabling circuit breaker. The `HystrixCommand` typically follows with
a `fallbackMethod`. In case of failure, Hystrix automatically enables the `fallbackMethod`
mentioned and diverts the traffic to the `fallbackMethod`.

As shown in the following code, in this case, `getHub` will fall back to `getDefaultHub`:

```
@Component
class SearchAPIGatewayComponent {
  @LoadBalanced
  @Autowired
  RestTemplate restTemplate;
  @HystrixCommand(fallbackMethod = "getDefaultHub")
  public String getHub(){
    String hub = restTemplate
      .getForObject("http://search-service/search/hub",
      String.class);
    return hub;
  }

  public String getDefaultHub(){
    return "Possibily SFO";
  }
}
```

The `getHub` method of `SearchAPIGatewayController` calls the `getHub` method of `SearchAPIGatewayComponent`:

```
@RequestMapping("/hubongw")
String getHub(){
  logger.info("Search Request in API gateway for getting Hub,
    forwarding to search-service ");
  return component.getHub();
}
```

The last part of this exercise is to build a Hystrix dashboard. For this, build another Spring Boot application. Include **Hystrix**, **Hystrix Dashboard**, and **Actuator** when building this application.

In the Spring Boot Application class, add the `@EnableHystrixDashboard` annotation.

Start the Search service, Search API Gateway, and Hystrix Dashboard applications. Point the browser to the Hystrix dashboard application's URL. In this example, the Hystrix dashboard is started on port 9999.

Open the following URL:
`http://localhost:9999/hystrix`

A screen as shown in the following screenshot will be displayed. In the **Hystrix Dashboard**, enter the URL of the service to be monitored.

In this case, the Search API Gateway is running on the `8095` port. Hence the `hystrix.stream` URL will be `http://localhost:8095/hytrix.stream`:

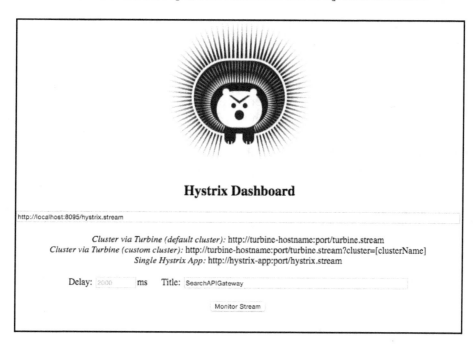

The Hystrix dashboard will be displayed as follows:

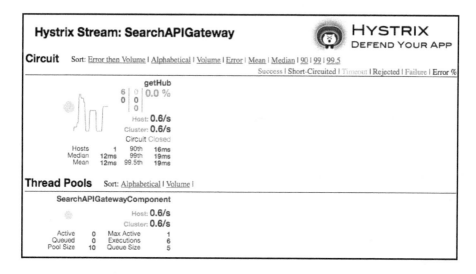

Note that at least one transaction has to be executed to see the display. This can be done by hitting `http://localhost:8095/hubongw`.

Create a failure scenario by shutting down the Search service. Note that the fallback method will be called when hitting the following URL:
`http://localhost:8095/hubongw`

If there are continuous failures, then the circuit status will be changed to open. This can be done by hitting the preceding link a number of times. In the open state, the original service will no longer be checked. The Hystrix dashboard will show the status of the circuit as **Open**, as shown in the following screenshot. Once the circuit is opened, periodically, the system will check for the original service status for recovery. When the original service is back, the circuit breaker falls back to the original service and the status will be set to **Closed**:

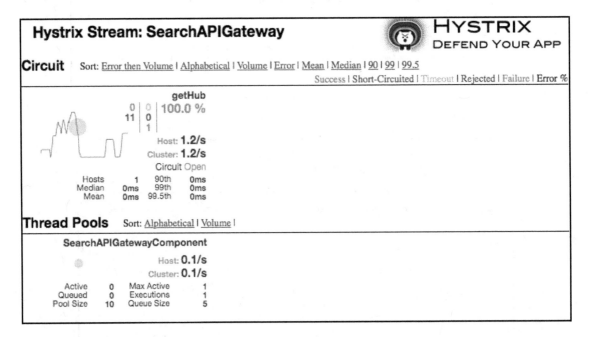

The following Hystrix Wiki URL shows the meaning of each of these parameters:
`https://github.com/Netflix/Hystrix/wiki/Dashboard`

Aggregate Hystrix streams with Turbine

In the previous example, the /hystrix.stream endpoint of our microservice was given in the Hystrix dashboard. Hystrix dashboard can only monitor one microservice at a time. If there are many microservices, then the Hystrix dashboard pointing to the service has to be changed every time when switching the microservices to the monitor. Looking into one instance at a time is tedious, especially when there are many instances of a microservice or multiple microservices.

We have to have a mechanism to aggregate data coming from multiple /hystrix.stream instances, and consolidate them into a single dashboard view. Turbine does exactly the same. It is another server that collects the Hystrix streams from multiple instances and consolidates them into one /turbine.stream. Now the Hystrix dashboard can point to /turbine.stream to get the consolidated information. Take a look at the following diagram:

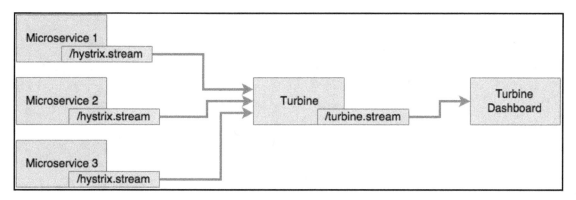

Turbine works only with different host names. Each instance has to run on separate hosts. If testing multiple services locally on the same host, update the host file (/etc/hosts) to simulate multiple hosts. Once done, the bootstrap.properties have to be configured as follows:
eureka.instance.hostname: localdomain2.

The following example showcases how to use Turbine to monitor circuit breakers across multiple instances and services. We will use the Search service and Search API Gateway in this example. Turbine internally uses Eureka to resolve service IDs that are configured for monitoring.

Follow these steps to build and execute this example.

1. The Turbine server can be created as just another Spring Boot application using Spring Boot Starter. Select **Turbine** to include the Turbine libraries.

2. Once the application is created, add `@EnableTurbine` to the main Spring Boot Application class. In this example, both the Turbine and the Hystrix dashboard are configured to run on the same Spring Boot Application. This is possible by adding the following annotations to the newly created Turbine application:

```
@EnableTurbine
@EnableHystrixDashboard
@SpringBootApplication
public class TurbineServerApplication {
```

3. Add the following configuration to the `yaml` or property file to point to instances that we are interested in `monitor.spring`:

```
application:
  name : turbineserver
turbine:
  clusterNameExpression: new String('default')
  appConfig : search-service,search-apigateway
  server:
    port: 9090
  eureka:
  client:
    serviceUrl:
      defaultZone: http://localhost:8761/eureka/
```

4. The preceding configuration instructs the Turbine server to look up the Eureka server to resolve the `search-service` and `search-apigateway` services. The `search-service` and `search-apigateways` services are the service IDs used to register services with Eureka. Turbine will use these names to resolve the actual service host and port by checking with the Eureka server. It then uses this information to read `/hystrix.stream` from each of these instances. Turbine then reads all individual Hystrix streams, aggregates all of them together, and exposes them under the Turbine server's `/turbine.stream` URL.
The cluster name expression points to the default cluster, since there is no explicit cluster configurations done in this example. If clusters are manually configured, then the following configuration has to be used:

```
turbine:
  aggregator:
    clusterConfig: [comma separated clusternames]
```

5. Change the Search service and `SearchComponent` to add another circuit breaker:

```
@HystrixCommand(fallbackMethod = "searchFallback")
public List<Flight> search(SearchQuery query){
```

6. Also add `@EnableCircuitBreaker` to the main class in the Search service. In this example, we will run two instances of `search-apigateway`--One on `localdomain1:8095` and another one on `localdomain2:8096`. We will also run one instance of `search-service` on `localdomain1:8090`.

7. Run the microservices with command-line overrides to manage different host addresses, as follows:

```
java -jar -Dserver.port=
  8096 -Deureka.instance.hostname=localdomain2 -
  Dserver.address=localdomain2
  target/search-apigateway-1.0.jar

java -jar -Dserver.port=
  8095 -Deureka.instance.hostname=localdomain1 -
  Dserver.address=localdomain1
  target/search-apigateway-1.0.jar

java -jar -Dserver.port=
  8090 -Deureka.instance.hostname=localdomain1 -
  Dserver.address=localdomain1
  target/search-1.0.jar
```

8. Open the Hystrix dashboard by pointing the browser to the following URL: `http://localhost:9090/hystrix`

9. Instead of giving `/hystrix.stream`, this time, we will point to `/turbine.stream`. In this example, the Turbine stream is running on `9090`. Hence, the URL to be given in the Hystrix dashboard is as follows: `http://localhost:9090/turbine.stream`

10. Fire a few transactions by opening the browser window and hitting `http://localhost:8095/hubongw` and `http://localhost:8096/hubongw`.

11. Once this is done, the dashboard page will show the `getHub` service.

12. Run `chapter8.website`. Execute the search transaction using the following website: `http://localhost:8001`

13. After executing the preceding search, the dashboard page will show `search-service` as well. This is shown in the following screenshot:

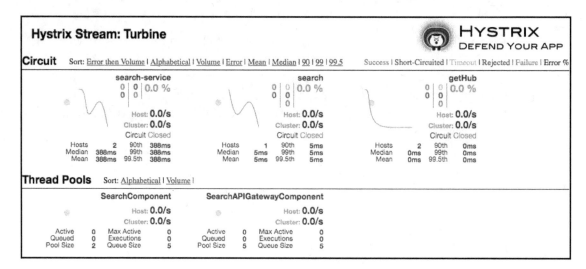

As we can see in the dashboard, `search-service` and `getHub` is coming from the Search API Gateway. Since we have two instances of the Search API Gateway, `getHub` is coming from two hosts, indicted by **Hosts 2**. The search is coming from the Search microservice. Data has been provided by the two components we created--`SearchComponent` in Search microservice and the `SearchAPIGateway` component in the Search API Gateway microservices.

Data analysis using Data Lake

Just like the scenario of fragmented logs and monitoring, fragmented data is another challenge in microservice architecture. Fragmented data poses challenges in data analytics. This data may be used for simple business event monitoring, data auditing, or even for deriving business intelligence out of the data.

Data Lake or a data hub is an ideal solution to handle such scenarios. The event-sourced architecture pattern is generally used to share state and state changes as events with an external data store. When there is a state change, microservices publish the state change as events. Interested parties may subscribe to these events and process them based on their requirements. A central event store can also subscribe to these events and store them in a big data store for further analysis.

One of the commonly followed architectures for such data handling is shown in the following diagram:

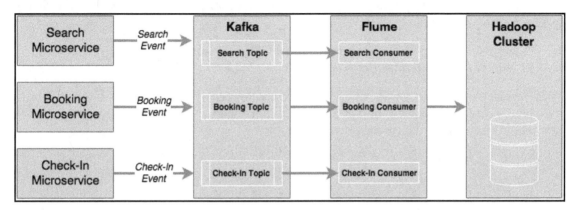

The state change events generated from the microservices, in our case, **Search**, **Booking**, and **Check-In** events, are pushed to a distributed high performance messaging system such as **Kafka**. A data ingestion, such as **Flume**, can subscribe these events and update them to an **HDFS** cluster. In some cases, these messages will be processed in real time by **Spark Streaming**. To handle heterogeneous sources of events, **Flume** can also be used between event sources and **Kafka**.

Spring Cloud Streams, **Spring Cloud Streams modules**, and **Spring Cloud Data Flow** are also useful as an alternative for high velocity data ingestion.

Summary

In this chapter, we learned about the challenges around logging and monitoring when dealing with internet-scale microservices.

We explored the various solutions for centralized logging and also learned how to implement a custom centralized logging using **Elasticsearch**, **Logstash**, and **Kibana** (**ELK**). In order to understand distributed tracing, we upgraded the BrownField microservices using the Spring Cloud Sleuth.

In the second half of this chapter, we went deeper into the capabilities required for microservices monitoring solutions and different approaches for monitoring. Subsequently, we examined a number of tools available for microservices monitoring.

The BrownField microservices were further enhanced with the Spring Cloud Hystrix and Turbine for monitoring latencies and failures in inter-service communications. The examples also demonstrated how to use the Circuit Breaker pattern to fall back to another service in case of failures.

Finally, we also touched upon the importance of Data Lake and how to integrate a Data Lake architecture in a microservice context.

Microservice management is another important challenge we have to tackle when dealing with large-scale microservices deployments. The next chapter will explore how containers can help in simplifying microservice management.

14
Containerizing Microservices with Docker

In the context of microservices, containerized deployment is like the icing on the cake. It helps microservices to be further autonomous by self-containing the underlying infrastructure, thereby making microservices cloud-neutral.

This chapter will introduce the concepts and relevance of virtual machine images and containerized deployments of microservices. Then, this chapter will further familiarize you with how to build Docker images for BrownField PSS microservices developed with Spring Boot and Spring Cloud. Finally, this chapter will also touch base on how to manage, maintain, and deploy Docker images in a production-like environment.

By the end of this chapter, you will have learned about the following:

- The concept of containerization and its relevance in the context of microservices
- How to build and deploy microservices as Docker images and containers
- Using AWS as an example of cloud-based Docker deployments

Understanding gaps in the BrownField PSS microservices

In Chapter 12, *Scale Microservices with Spring Cloud Components*, the BrownField PSS microservices were developed using Spring Boot and Spring Cloud. Those microservices are deployed as versioned fat jar files on bare metals, specifically on a local development machine. In Chapter 13, *Logging and Monitoring Microservices*, challenges around logging and monitoring were addressed using centralized logging and monitoring solutions.

This is good enough for most implementations. However, there are still a few gaps in our BrownField PSS implementation. So far, the implementation has not used any cloud infrastructure. Dedicated machines, as in the traditional monolithic application deployments, are not the best solution for deploying microservices. Automation such as automatic provisioning, the ability to scale on demand, self service, and payment based on usage are essential capabilities required to manage large-scale microservice deployments efficiently. In general, a cloud infrastructure provides all these essential capabilities. Therefore, a private or public cloud with the capabilities mentioned earlier is better suited for deploying internet-scale microservices.

Additionally, running one microservice instance per bare metal is not cost-effective. Therefore, in most cases, enterprises end up deploying multiple microservices on a single bare metal server. Running multiple microservices on a single bare metal could create a noisy neighbor problem. There will not be any isolation between microservice instances running on the same machine. As a result, the services deployed on a single machine can eat other's space, and, thus, impact the performance of other microservices.

An alternative approach is to run microservices on VMs. However, VMs are heavyweight in nature. Therefore, running many smaller VMs on a physical machine is not resource-efficient. This generally results in resource wastage. In cases of sharing a VM for deploying multiple services, developers will end up facing the same issues of sharing the bare metal, as explained earlier.

In the case of Java-based microservices, sharing a VM or bare metal for deploying multiple microservices also results in sharing the JRE between microservices. This is because the fat jars created in our BrownField PSS abstract only the application code and its dependencies, but not JREs. Any update on the JRE installed on the machine will have implications for all microservices deployed on that machine. Similarly, if there are OS-level parameters, libraries, or tunings that are required for specific microservices, then it will be hard to manage them on a shared environment.

One of the microservice principles insists on being self-contained and autonomous by fully encapsulating its end-to-end runtime environment. In order to align with this principle, all components, such as the OS, JRE, and microservices binaries, have to be self-contained and isolated. The only option to achieve this is to follow the approach of deploying one microservice per VM. However, this will result in under-utilized virtual machines, and, in many cases, extra costs due to this can nullify the benefits of microservices.

What are containers?

Containers are not revolutionary groundbreaking concepts. It has been in action for quite a while. However, the world is witnessing the reentry of containers, mainly due to the wide adoption of cloud computing. The shortcomings of traditional virtual machines in the cloud computing space has also accelerated the use of containers. Container providers, such as Docker, simplified container technologies to a great extent, which also helped the large adoption of container technologies in today's world. The recent popularity of DevOps and microservices also acted as catalysts for the rebirth of container technologies.

So, what are containers? Containers provide private spaces on top of the operating system. This technique is also called operating system virtualization. In this approach, the kernel of the operating system provides isolated virtual spaces. Each of these virtual spaces are called **containers** or **virtual engines** (**VEs**). Containers allow processes to run on an isolated environment, on top of the host operating system. A representation of multiple containers running on the same host is shown in the following figure:

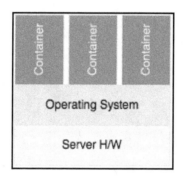

Containers are easy mechanisms to build, ship, and run compartmentalized software components. Generally, containers package all binaries and libraries that are essential for running an application. Containers reserve their own filesystem, IP address, network interfaces, internal processes, name spaces, OS libraries, application binaries, dependencies, and other application configurations.

There are billions of containers used by organizations. Moreover, there are many large organizations heavily investing in container technologies. Docker is, by far, ahead of the competition, supported by many large operating system vendors and cloud providers. **Lmctfy, Systemd Nspawn, Rocket, Drawbridge, LXD, Kurma**, and **Calico** are some of the other containerization solutions. Open-container specification is also under development.

Difference between VM and containers

Virtual machines such as **Hyper-V**, **VMWare**, and **Zen** were popular choices for data center virtualization a few years back. Enterprises experienced cost savings by implementing virtualization over traditional bare metal usage. It has also helped many enterprises to utilize their existing infrastructure in a much more optimized manner. Since VMs support automation, many enterprises have experienced less management efforts with virtual machines. Virtual machines have also helped organizations to get isolated environments for applications to run.

On prima facie, both virtualization and containerization exhibit exactly the same characteristics. However, in a nutshell, containers, and virtual machines are not the same. Therefore, it is unfair to make an apple-to-apple comparison between VMs and containers. Virtual machines and containers are two different techniques that address different problems of virtualization. This difference is evident in the following diagram:

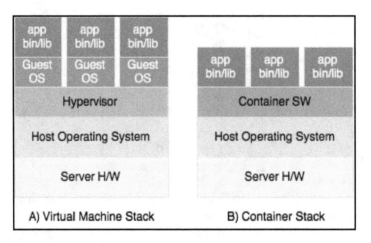

The **Virtual Machine** (**VM**) operates at a much lower level compared to containers. VMs provide hardware virtualization, such as virtualization of CPUs, motherboards, memory, and so on. A VM is an isolated unit with an embedded operating system, generally called a **Guest OS**. VMs replicate the whole operating system and run it within the VM with no dependency on the host operating system environment. Since VMs embed the full operating system environment, these are heavyweight in nature. This is an advantage as well as a disadvantage. The advantage is that VMs offer full isolation to the processes running on the VMs. The disadvantage is that it limits the number of VMs one can spin up in a bare metal due to the resource requirements of VMs. The size of the VMs have a direct impact on the time to start and stop them.

Since starting a VM intern will boot the OS, the start time for it is generally high. VMs are more friendly for the infrastructure teams, since they require low-level infrastructure competency to manage VMs. Processes running inside the VMs are completely isolated from the processes on a different VM running on the same host.

In the container world, containers do not emulate the entire hardware or operating system. Unlike VMs, containers share certain parts of host kernels and the operating system. There is no concept of Guest OS in the case of containers. Containers provide an isolated execution environment directly on top of the host operating system. This is an advantage as well as a disadvantage. The advantage is that it is lighter as well as faster. Since containers on the same machine share the host operating system, the overall resource utilization of containers is fairly small. As a result, many smaller containers can be run on the same machine compared to heavyweight VMs. Since the containers on the same host share the host operating system, there are limitations as well. For example, it is not possible to set iptables firewall rules inside a container. Processes inside the container are completely independent from the processes on different containers running on the same host.

Unlike VMs, container images are publicly available on community portals. This makes the developer's life much easier, as they don't have to build images from scratch, instead, they can now take base images from certified sources and add additional layers of software components on top of the downloaded base image.

The lightweight nature of the containers is also opening up a plethora of opportunities, such as automated build, publishing, downloading, copying, and so on. The ability to download, build, ship, and run containers with few commands make containers more developer-friendly. Building a new container will not consume more than a few seconds. Containers are now a part and parcel of the continuous delivery pipelines as well.

In summary, there are many advantages for containers over VMs, but a VM has its own exclusive strengths. Many organizations use both containers together with VMs; for example, by running containers on top of VMs.

Benefits of containers

We have already seen many benefits of containers over VMs. This section will explain the overall benefits of containers beyond the benefits of VMs.

Some of the benefits of containers are summarized as follows:

- **Self contained**: Containers package essential application binaries and its dependencies together to make sure that there is no disparity between different environments, such as development, testing, or production. This promotes the concept of the Twelve-Factor applications and the concept of immutable containers. The Spring Boot microservices bundles all required application dependencies. Containers stretch this boundary further by embedding the JRE and other operating system-level libraries, configurations, and so on, if any.

- **Lightweight**: Containers, in general, are smaller in size with a lighter footprint. The smallest container, **Alpine**, has a size of only less than 5 MB. The simplest Spring Boot microservices packaged with an Alpine container with **Java 8** will only come at around 170 MB. Though the size is still on the higher side, it is much less than the VM image size, which will generally be in GBs. Smaller footprint of containers not only helps to spin new containers quickly, but also to make building, shipping, and storing easier.

- **Scalability**: Since container images are smaller in size, and there is no OS booting at the startup, containers are generally faster to spin up and shut down. This makes containers a popular choice for cloud-friendly elastic applications.

- **Portability**: Containers provide portability across machines and cloud providers. Once containers are built with all dependencies, they can be ported across multiple machines or multiple cloud providers without relying on the underlying machines. Containers are portable from desktops to different cloud environments.

- **License cost**: Many software license terms are based on the physical core. Since containers share the operating system and are not virtualized at the physical resources level, there is an advantage in terms of the license cost.

- **DevOps**: The lightweight footprint of containers makes them easy for automating builds and publishing and downloading containers from remote repositories. This makes them easy to use in agile and DevOps environments by integrating with automated delivery pipelines. Containers also support the concept of build once by creating immutable containers at build time and moving them across multiple environments. Since containers are not deep into the infrastructure, multi-disciplinary DevOps teams can manage containers as part of their day-to-day life.

- **Version controlled**: Containers support versions by default. This helps build versioned artifacts, just like versioned archive files.

- **Reusable**: Container images are reusable artifacts. If an image is built by assembling a number of libraries for a purpose, it can be reused in similar situations.

- **Immutable containers**: In this concept, the containers are created and disposed of after usage. They are never updated or patched. Immutable containers are used in many environments to avoid complexities in patching deployment units. Patching will result in a lack of traceability and an inability to recreate environments consistently.

Microservices and containers

There is no direct relationship between microservices and containers. Microservices can run without containers and containers can run monolithic applications. However, there is a sweet spot between microservices and containers.

Containers are good for monolithic applications; however, the complexities and the size of the monolith application may kill some of the benefits of containers. For example, spinning new containers quickly may not be easy with monolithic applications. In addition to that, monolithic applications generally have local environment dependencies, such as local disk, stove pipe dependencies with other systems, and more. Such applications are difficult to manage with container technologies. This is where microservices go hand in hand with containers.

The following diagram shows three polyglot microservices running on the same host machine and sharing the same operating system, but abstracts the runtime environment:

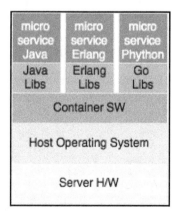

The real advantage of containers is when managing many polyglot microservices. For instance, one microservice in Java is another one in Erlang or some other language. Containers help developers to package microservices written in any language or technology in a uniform fashion. It also helps deployment team to distribute across multiple environments without spending too much attention to configuration of such environments. Containers eliminate the need to have different deployment management tools to handle polyglot microservices. Containers not only abstract the execution environment, but also abstract how to access the services. Irrespective of the technologies used, containerized microservices expose REST APIs. Once the container is up and running, it binds to certain ports and exposes its APIs. Since containers are self-contained and provide full-stack isolation between services, in a single VM or bare metal, one can run multiple heterogeneous microservices and handle them in a uniform way. Containers can really help avoid conflicting situations where dev, test, and prod teams blame each other for their configuration and operating environments.

Introduction to Docker

Previous sections talked about containers and their benefits. Containers have been present in the business for years, but the popularity of Docker has given containers a new outlook. As a result, many container definitions and perspectives have emerged from the Docker architecture. Docker is so popular, that even containerization is referred to as **Dockerization**.

Docker is a platform to build, ship, and run lightweight containers based on Linux kernels. Docker has a default support for Linux platforms. They also have support for Mac and Windows using **Boot2Docker**, which runs on top of Virtual Box.

Amazon **EC2 Container Service** (**ECS**) has out-of-the-box support for Docker on AWS EC2 instances. Docker can be installed on bare metals and also on traditional virtual machines such as VMWare or Hyper-V.

Key components of Docker

The Docker installation has two key components. A **Docker daemon** and a **Docker client**. Both, Docker daemon and Docker client are distributed as a single binary.

The following diagram shows the key components of a Docker installation:

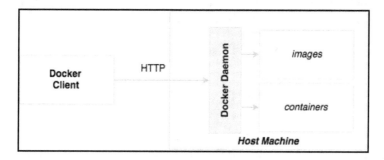

The Docker daemon

The Docker daemon is the server-side component that runs on the host machine responsible for building, running, and distributing the Docker containers. The Docker daemon exposes APIs for the Docker client to interact with the daemon. These APIs are primarily REST-based endpoints. One can imagine the Docker daemon as a controller service running on the host machine. Developers can programmatically use the APIs to build custom clients as well.

The Docker client

The Docker client is a remote command-line program that interacts with the Docker daemon either through a socket or through REST APIs. The CLI can run on the same host as the daemon is running on, or it can run on a completely different host and connect to the daemon remotely using the CLI. The Docker users will use the CLI to build, ship, and run Docker containers.

Docker concepts--The Docker architecture is built around a few concepts, such as images, containers, registry, and Dockerfile.

The Docker image

One of the key concepts of Docker is the image. The Docker image is the read-only copy of the operating system libraries and applications and their libraries. Once an image is created, it is guaranteed to run on any Docker platforms without alterations.

In Spring Boot microservices, a Docker image will package operating systems such as Ubuntu, Alpine, JRE, and the Spring Boot fat application jar file. It also includes instructions to run the application and how to expose services.

As shown in the preceding diagram, the Docker images are based on a layered architecture, where the base image will be one of the flavors of Linux. Each layer, as shown in the preceding diagram, gets added to the base image layer with the previous image as the parent layer. Docker uses the concept of the union filesystem to combine all these layers into a single image, forming a single filesystem.

In typical cases, developers will not build Docker images from scratch. Images, such as operating system, or other common libraries, such as Java 8 images are publicly available from trusted sources. Developers can start building on top of these base images. The base image in Spring microservices can be JRE 8 rather than starting from a Linux distribution image such as Ubuntu.

Every time we rebuild the application, only the changed layer gets rebuilt and the remaining layers are kept intact. All intermediate layers are cached and, hence, if there is no change, Docker will use the previously cached layer and build it on top. Multiple containers running on the same machine with the same type of base images will reuse the base image, thus reducing the size of the deployment. For instance, in a host, if there are multiple containers running with Ubuntu as the base image, they all reuse the same base image. This is applicable when publishing or downloading images as well.

As shown in the preceding figure, the first layer in the image is a boot filesystem called **bootfs**, which is similar to the **Linux kernel** and the boot loader. The boot filesystem acts as a virtual file system for all images.

On top of the boot filesystem, the operating system's filesystem will be placed, which is called **rootfs**. The root filesystem adds the typical operating system directory structure to the container. Unlike in the Linux systems, rootfs, in the case of Docker, will be in read-only mode.

On top of the **rootfs**, other required images will be placed, as per the requirements. In our case, these are **JRE** and the Spring Boot microservice jars. When a container is initiated, a writable filesystem will be placed on top of all other filesystems for the processes to run. Any changes made by the process to the underlying filesystem will not be reflected in the actual container. Instead, these will be written to the writable filesystem. This writable file system is volatile. Hence, the data will be lost once the container is stopped. Due to this reason, Docker containers are ephemeral in nature.

The base operating system packaged inside Docker is generally a minimal copy of just the OS filesystem. In reality, the process running on top may not use the entire OS service. In a Spring Boot microservice, in many cases, the container just initiates a CMD and JVM, and then invokes the Spring Boot fat jar.

The Docker container

Docker containers are the running instances of a Docker image. The containers use the kernel of the host operating system when running. Hence, they share the host kernel with other containers running on the same host. Docker runtime ensures that the container processes are allocated with their own isolated process space using kernel features, such as **cgroups**, and the kernel **namespace** of the operating system. In addition to resource fencing, the containers will get their own filesystem and network configurations as well.

The containers, when instantiated, can have a specific resource allocation, such as memory and CPU. Containers, when initiated from the same image, can have a different resource allocation. The Docker container, by default, gets an isolated **subnet** and **gateway** to the network.

The Docker registry

The Docker registry is a central place where Docker images are published and downloaded from. The central registry provided by Docker is `https://hub.docker.com`. The Docker registry has public images that one can download and use as a base registry. Docker also has private images that are specific to the accounts created in the Docker registry. The Docker registry screenshot is shown as follows:

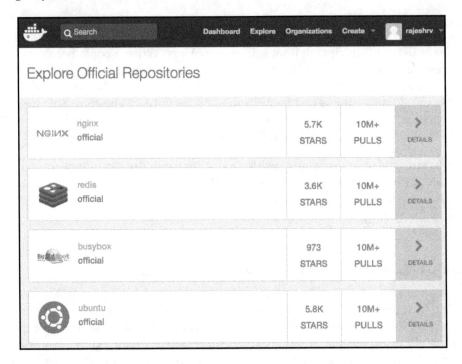

Docker also offers **Docker Trusted Registry (DTR)**, which can be used to set up registries locally on-premise.

Dockerfile

Dockerfile is a build file or a scripting file that contains instructions to build a Docker image. There can be multiple steps included in a Dockerfile, start with downloading a base image. Dockerfile is a text file generally named `Dockerfile`. The `docker build` command looks up the Dockerfile for instructions for building. One can compare `Dockerfile` as a `pom.xml` file used in the Maven build.

Deploying microservices into Docker

This section will operationalize our learning by showcasing how to build containers for our BrownField PSS microservices.

 The full source code of this chapter is available under the `chapter9` projects, in the code files under `https://github.com/rajeshrv/Spring5Microservice`. Copy `chapter6.*` into a new STS workspace and rename `chapter9.*`.

Follow these steps to build Docker containers for the BrownField microservices:

1. Install Docker from the official Docker site (`https://www.docker.com`).

2. Follow the *Get Started* link for the download and install instructions based on the operating system of choice.

3. Once installed, run `Docker.app` and then use the following command to verify the installation:

```
Client:
Version:      17.03.1-ce
API version:  1.27
Go version:   go1.7.5
Git commit:   c6d412e
Built:        Tue Mar 28 00:40:02 2017
OS/Arch:      darwin/amd64
Server:
Version:      17.03.1-ce
API version:  1.27 (minimum version 1.12)
Go version:   go1.7.5
Git commit:   c6d412e
Built:        Fri Mar 24 00:00:50 2017
OS/Arch:      linux/amd64
Experimental: true
```

4. Before we make any changes, we need to edit `application.properties` of all services to change from localhost to the IP address, since localhost is not resolvable from within the Docker containers. In the real world, this will point to a DNS or load balancer.

application.properties file looks like as follows:

```
server.port=8090
spring.rabbitmq.host=192.168.0.101
spring.rabbitmq.port=5672
spring.rabbitmq.username=guest
spring.rabbitmq.password=guest
```

 Note: Replace the IP address with the IP address of your machine.

5. Update Application.java and BrownFieldSiteController.java in the chapter9.website project to replace localhost with IP address.

6. Update BookingComponent.java under chapter9.book to reflect the IP address instead of localhost.

7. Create a Dockerfile under the root directory of all microservices. An example of the Dockerfile to search for a microservice will look like this:

```
FROM frolvlad/alpine-oraclejdk8
VOLUME /tmp
ADD  target/search-1.0.jar search.jar
EXPOSE 8090
ENTRYPOINT ["java","-jar","/search.jar"]
```

8. The following is a quick examination of the contents of the Dockerfile:

- FROM frolvlad/alpine-oraclejdk8 tells the Docker build to use a specific alpine-oraclejdk8 version as the basic image for this build. The frolvlad indicates the repository to locate the alpine-oraclejdk8 image. In this case, this is an image built with Alpine Linux and Oracle JDK 8. This will help layer our application on top of this base image without setting up Java libraries ourselves. In this case, since this image is not available on our local image store, the Docker build will go ahead and download this image from the remote Docker Hub registry.

- VOLUME /tmp enables access from the container to the directory specified in the host machine. In our case, this is pointing to the tmp directory where the Spring Boot application creates working directories for Tomcat. The tmp directory is a logical directory for the container that will indirectly point to one of the local directories of the host.

- ADD `target/search-1.0.jar search.jar` adds the application's binary file to the container with the destination file's name specified. In this case, the Docker build copies `target/search-1.0.jar` to the container as `search.jar`.

- `EXPOSE 8090` tells the container how to perform port mapping. This will associate `8090` as the external port binding for the internal Spring Boot service.

- `ENTRYPOINT ["java",”-jar", "/search.jar"]` tells the container which default application to run when it is started. In this case, we are pointing to the Java process and the Spring Boot fat jar file to initiate the service.

9. The next step is to run the `docker build` command from the folder where Dockerfile is stored. This will download the base image and run the entries in the Dockerfile one after the other.

   Docker build command for search is shown as follows:

   ```
   docker build -t search:1.0 .
   ```

   The preceding command will result in building a docker image for search. The log is shown as follows:

   ```
   rvslab:chapter9.search rajeshrv$ docker build -t search:1.0 .
   Sending build context to Docker daemon 57.01 MB
   Step 1/5 : FROM frolvlad/alpine-oraclejdk8
   latest: Pulling from frolvlad/alpine-oraclejdk8
   627beaf3eaaf: Pull complete
   95a531c0fa10: Pull complete
   b03e476748e7: Pull complete
   Digest: sha256:8ad40ff024bff6df43e3fa7e7d0974e31f6b3f346c666285e275afee72c74fcd
   Status: Downloaded newer image for frolvlad/alpine-oraclejdk8:latest
    ---> f656c77f5536
   Step 2/5 : VOLUME /tmp
    ---> Running in c816f2b47568
    ---> e6028f6a76bc
   Removing intermediate container c816f2b47568
   Step 3/5 : ADD target/search-1.0.jar search.jar
    ---> 39f28a242676
   Removing intermediate container b4463e6220fc
   Step 4/5 : EXPOSE 8090
    ---> Running in 2c25a35d20ea
    ---> d0738b1fb63a
   Removing intermediate container 2c25a35d20ea
   Step 5/5 : ENTRYPOINT java -jar /search.jar
    ---> Running in 095e60d75f13
    ---> a9f2ae1252c2
   Removing intermediate container 095e60d75f13
   Successfully built a9f2ae1252c2
   ```

10. Repeat the preceding step for all microservices.

11. Once the images are created, they can be verified by typing the following command. This command will list the images and their details, including the size of the image files:

```
docker images
```

The preceding command will show all images as follows:

```
rvslab:chapter9.website rajeshrv$ docker images
REPOSITORY              TAG              IMAGE ID          CREATED            SIZE
book                    1.0              8c0dbbe5ffc4      11 minutes ago     203 MB
checkin                 1.0              2ee2d759fecd      12 minutes ago     209 MB
fares                   1.0              13275668b4ea      12 minutes ago     202 MB
website                 1.0              b4b3c7d59ff8      13 minutes ago     187 MB
search                  1.0              8f42cd4d1f86      13 minutes ago     203 MB
```

12. Next, we will run the Docker container. This can be done using the following command. This command will load and run the container. Upon starting, container calls the Spring Boot executable jar to start the microservice:

```
docker run -p 8090:8090 -t search:1.0
docker run -p 8080:8080 -t fares:1.0
docker run -p 8060:8060 -t book:1.0
docker run -p 8070:8070 -t checkin:1.0
docker run -p 8001:8001 -t website:1.0
```

The preceding command starts the Search and Search API Gateway microservices and the website.

Once all the services are fully started, verify with the `docker ps` command:

```
rvslab:chapter9.website rajeshrv$ docker ps
CONTAINER ID   IMAGE         COMMAND               CREATED         STATUS          PORTS                     NAMES
9a11b3478e28   book:1.0      "java -jar /book.jar" 36 seconds ago  Up 34 seconds   0.0.0.0:8060->8060/tcp    hardcore_booth
2e629addd32b   website:1.0   "java -jar /websit..." 12 minutes ago Up 12 minutes   0.0.0.0:8001->8001/tcp    boring_mcclintock
bf0b4436a387   checkin:1.0   "java -jar /checki..." 12 minutes ago Up 12 minutes   0.0.0.0:8070->8070/tcp    angry_darwin
02d9c291b8b8   fares:1.0     "java -jar /fares.jar" 13 minutes ago Up 13 minutes   0.0.0.0:8080->8080/tcp    affectionate_sinoussi
8a40e771dbe2   search:1.0    "java -jar /search..." 14 minutes ago Up 14 minutes   0.0.0.0:8090->8090/tcp    loving_edison
```

The next step is to point the browser to the following URL. This will open the BrownField website:

```
http://localhost:8001
```

Running RabbitMQ on Docker

Since our example also uses RabbitMQ, let's explore how to set up RabbitMQ as a Docker container. The following command pulls the RabbitMQ image from the Docker Hub and starts RabbitMQ:

```
docker run rabbitmq
```

Using the Docker registry

The Docker Hub provides a central location to store all Docker images. The images can be stored as public as well as private. In many cases, organizations deploy their own private registries on-premise due to security related concerns.

Follow these steps to set up and run a local registry:

1. The following command will start a registry that will bind the registry on port 5000:

   ```
   docker run -d -p 5000:5000 --restart=always --name registry
       registry:latest
   ```

2. Tag search:1.0 to the registry:

   ```
   docker tag search:1.0 localhost:5000/search:1.0
   ```

3. Push the image to the registry:

   ```
   docker push localhost:5000/search:1.0
   ```

4. Pull the image back from the registry:

   ```
   docker pull localhost:5000/search:1.0
   ```

Setting up the Docker Hub

In the previous chapter, we played with a local Docker registry. This section will show us how to set up and use the Docker Hub to publish the Docker containers. This is a convenient mechanism to globally access the Docker images. Later in this chapter, the Docker images will be published to the Docker Hub from the local machine and downloaded from the EC2 instances.

Perform the steps mentioned in the following link for setting up a public Docker Hub account and a repository:

`https://docs.docker.com/engine/installation/`

The registry, in this case, act as the microservices repository where all the Dockerized microservices will be stored and accessed. This is one of the capabilities explained in the microservices capability model.

Publish microservices to the Docker Hub

In order to push the Dockerized services to the Docker Hub, follow these steps. The first step below tags the Docker image and the second command push the Docker image to the Docker hub repository:

```
docker tag search:1.0 brownfield/search:1.0
docker push brownfield/search:1.0
```

To verify whether the container images are published, go to the Docker Hub repository using the following URL:

`https://hub.docker.com/u/brownfield`

 Replace `brownfield` with the repository name used in the previous section.

Repeat this step for all the other microservices as well. At the end of this step, all the services will be published to the Docker Hub.

Microservices on Cloud

One of the capabilities mentioned in the microservices capability model is the use of the Cloud infrastructure for microservices. Earlier in this chapter, we also explored the necessity of using Cloud for microservices deployments. So far, we have not deployed anything to the Cloud. Once we have many microservices, it will be hard to run all of them on the local machine.

In the rest of this book, we will operate using AWS as the Cloud platform for deploying the BrownField PSS microservices.

Installing Docker on AWS EC2

In this section, we will install Docker on the EC2 instance. Follow these steps to install Docker.

This example assumes that you are familiar with AWS and an account has already been created on AWS:

Follow these steps to set up Docker on EC2:

1. Launch a new EC2 instance. In this case, if we have to run all instances together, we may need a large instance. The example uses t2.large.

> In this example, the following Ubuntu AMI is used.
> Ubuntu Server 16.04 LTS (HVM), SSD Volume Type - ami-a58d0dc5

2. Connect to the EC2 instance and run the following commands:

```
sudo apt-get update
sudo apt-get install docker.io
```

3. The preceding command will install Docker on the EC2 instance. Verify the installation with the following command:

```
sudo docker version
```

Running BrownField services on EC2

In this section, we will set up BrownField microservices on the EC2 instances created. In this case, the build is set up in the local desktop machine and the binaries will be deployed into AWS.
Follow these steps to set up services on the EC2 instance:

1. Change all IP addresses in *.properties to reflect the IP address of the EC2 instance.
2. Change the Java files mentioned earlier under chapter9.book and chapter9.website to reflect the IP addresses.
3. On the local machine, recompile all projects and create Docker images for all microservices. Push all of them to the Docker Hub registry.

4. Set up Java 8 on the EC2 instance.

5. Execute the following commands in sequence:

```
sudo docker run --net=host rabbitmq:3
sudo docker run -p 8090:8090 rajeshrv/search:1.0
sudo docker run -p 8001:8001 rajeshrv/website:1.0
```

6. Validate whether all services are working by opening the URL of the website and execute search. Note that we will be using the public IP of the EC2 instance in this case.

   The URL for the website application is as follows:

```
http://54.165.128.23:8001
```

Future of containerization

Containerization is still evolving, but the number of organizations adopting containerization techniques has gone up in recent times. In addition to Docker, Microsoft has already invested in Windows containers. While many organizations are aggressively adopting Docker and other container technologies, the downside of these techniques are still the size of the containers and security concerns. Container portability and standardization is another challenge.

Currently, the Docker images are, in general, heavy. In an elastic-automated environment, where containers are created and destroyed quite frequently, size is still an issue. A larger size indicates more code, and more code means they are more prone for security vulnerabilities.

The future is definitely in small-footprint containers. Docker is working on unikernels, a lightweight kernel or cloud operating system that can run Docker even on low-powered IoT devices. Unikernels are not full-fledged operating systems, but they provide the basic necessary libraries to support deployed applications. Unikernels offer better speed, scalability, a smaller size, and enhanced security.

Many organizations are moving toward hybrid cloud solutions to avoid vendor locking. This leads to work with a safe distance from the vendor, that helps organizations quickly build containers and deploy across various environments. There are efforts gone into standardizing container runtimes as well as container images such as **Open Container Initiative (OCI)**. Many container vendors have already been adopted as OCI standards.

Security concerns and security issues are much-discussed and debated on containers. Key security issues are around the user namespace segregation or user ID isolation. If a container is on root (by default), it can gain root privilege of the host. Using container images from untrusted sources is another security concern. The attacking surface is wider in the case of large-scale containers, as each container may expose endpoints.

Docker is closing these gaps as quickly as possible, but there are many organizations that use a combination of VMs and containers to circumvent some of the security concerns. Tools such as Docker Security Scanning could identify vulnerabilities associated with images automatically. There are other security control tools such as Docker Bench, Clair by CoreOS, and Twistlock.

Summary

In this chapter, we learned about the need to have a cloud environment when dealing with internet-scale microservices.

We explored the concept of containers and compared them with traditional virtual machines. We also learned the basics of Docker and were explained the concepts of Docker images, containers, and registry. The importance and benefits of containers were explained in the context of microservices.

This chapter then switched to a hands-on example by Dockerizing the BrownField microservices. We demonstrated how to deploy the Spring Boot microservices developed earlier on Docker. We learned the concept of registry by exploring a local registry, as well as the Docker Hub for pushing and pulling Dockerized microservices.

As a last step, we explored how to deploy Dockerized BrownField microservices in the AWS cloud environment.

15
Scaling Dockerized Microservices with Mesos and Marathon

In order to leverage full power of a cloud-like environment, the dockerized microservice instances should also be capable of scaling out and shrinking automatically, based on the traffic patterns. However, this could lead to another problem. Once there are many microservices, it is not easy to manually manage thousands of dockerized microservices. It is essential to have an infrastructure abstraction layer and a strong container orchestration platform to successfully manage internet-scale dockerized microservice deployments.

This chapter will explain the basic scaling approaches and the need and use of Mesos and Marathon as an infrastructure-orchestration layer to achieve optimized resource usage in a cloud-like environment when deploying microservices at scale. This chapter will also provide a step-by-step approach to setting up Mesos and Marathon in a cloud environment. Finally, this chapter will demonstrate how to manage dockerized microservices into the Mesos and Marathon environment.

By the end of this chapter, we will have learned about the following:

- Options to scale containerized Spring Boot microservices
- The need to have an abstraction layer and a container orchestration software
- An understanding Mesos and Marathon from the context of microservices
- How to manage dockerized BrownField Airline's PSS microservices with Mesos and Marathon

Scaling microservices

At the end of Chapter 12, *Scale Microservices with Spring Cloud Components*, we discussed two options for scaling either using Spring Cloud components or dockerized microservices using Mesos and Marathon. In Chapter 12, *Scale Microservices with Spring Cloud Components*, you learned how to scale the Spring Boot microservices using the Spring Cloud components.

The two key concepts of Spring Cloud that we have implemented are self-registration and self-discovery. These two capabilities enable automated microservices deployments. With self-registration, microservices can automatically advertise the service availability by registering service metadata to a central service registry as soon as the instances are ready to accept traffic. Once microservices are registered, consumers can consume newly registered services from the very next moment by discovering service instances using the registry service. In this model, registry is at the heart of this automation.

The following diagram shows the Spring Cloud method for scaling microservices:

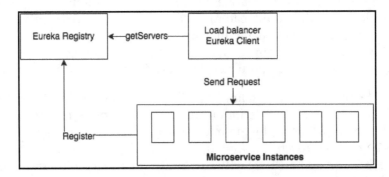

In this chapter, we will focus on the second approach, scaling dockerized microserices using Mesos and Marathon. It also provides us with one additional capability that you didn't learn about in Chapter 12, *Scale Microservices with Spring Cloud Components*. When there is a need for an additional microservice instance, a manual task is required to kick off a new instance. Similarly, when there is not enough traffic, there should be an option to turn off unused instances. In an ideal scenario, the start and stop of microservices instances also require automation. This is especially relevant when services are running on a pay as per usage cloud environment.

Understanding autoscaling

Autoscaling is an approach to automatically scale out instances based on the resource usage to meet agreed SLAs by replicating the services to be scaled.

The system automatically detects an increase in traffic, spins up additional instances, and makes them available for traffic handling. Similarly, when the traffic volumes go down, the system automatically detects and reduces the number of instances by taking active instances back from the service. It is also required to ensure that there is a set number of instances always up and running. In addition to this, the physical or virtual machines also need a mechanism to automatically provision machines. The latter part is much more easy to handle using APIs provided by different cloud providers.

Autoscaling can be done by considering different parameters and thresholds. Some of them are easy to handle whereas some of them are complex to handle. The following are the points that summarizes some of the commonly followed approaches:

- **Scale with resource constraints**: This approach is based on real-time service metrics collected through monitoring mechanisms. Generally, the resource scaling approach makes decisions based on the CPU, memory, or the disk of machines. It can also be done by looking at the statistics collected on the service instances itself, such as heap memory usage.
- **Scale during specific time periods**: Time-based scaling is an approach to scale services based on certain periods of the day, month, or year to handle seasonal or business peaks. For example, some services may experience higher number of transactions during office hours, and considerably less number of transactions outside office hours. In this case, during the day time, services autoscale to meet the demand and automatically downsizes during the off office hours.
- **Scale based on message queue length**: This is particularly useful when the microservices are based on asynchronous messaging. In this approach, new consumers will be automatically added when the messages in the queue goes beyond certain limits.
- **Scale based on business parameters**: In this case, adding instances will be based on certain business parameters. For example, spinning up a new instance just before handling sales, closing transactions. As soon as the monitoring service receives a preconfigured business event, such as sales closing minus 1 hour, a new instance will be brought up in anticipation of large volumes of transactions. This will provide fine grained controls on scaling based on business rules.

- **Predictive autoscaling**: This is a new paradigm of autoscaling, which is different from the traditional real-time metrics-based autoscaling. A prediction engine will take multiple inputs, such as historical information, current trends, and more, to predict possible traffic patterns. Autoscaling will be done based on these predictions. Predictive autoscaling helps in avoiding hardcoded rules and time windows. Instead, the system can automatically predict such time windows. In more sophisticated deployments, the predictive analysis may use cognitive computing mechanisms to predict autoscaling.

The missing pieces

In order to achieve autoscaling as mentioned previously, it requires a lot of scripting at the operating system level. Docker is a good step toward achieving this as it provides a uniform way of handling the containers, irrespective of the technologies used by the microservices. It also helped us in isolating microservices to avoid resource stealing by nosy neighbors.

However, Docker and scripting only address the issues partially. In the context of large-scale Docker deployments, some of the key questions to be answered are as follows:

- How do we manage thousands of containers?
- How do we monitor them?
- How do we apply rules and constraints when deploying artifacts?
- How do we ensure that we utilize containers properly to gain resource efficiency?
- How do we ensure that at least a certain number of minimal instances are running at any point in time?
- How do we ensure that dependent services are up and running?
- How do we do rolling upgrades and graceful migrations?
- How do we rollback faulty deployments?

All these preceding questions point to the need of having a solution to address the following two key capabilities:

- A container abstraction layer that provides a uniform abstraction over many physical or virtual machines
- A container orchestration and init system to manage deployments intelligently on top of the cluster abstraction

The rest of this chapter focuses on addressing these two points.

Container orchestration

Container orchestration tools provide a layer of abstraction for developers and infrastructure teams to deal with large-scale containerized deployments. The features offered by the container orchestration tools vary between providers. However, common denominators are provision, discovery, resource management, monitoring, and deployments.

Why is container orchestration is important

Since microservices break applications into different micro applications, many developers request more server nodes for deployment. In order to manage microservices properly, developers tend to deploy one microservice per VM, which further drives down the resource utilization. In many cases, this results in over-allocation of CPUs and memory.

In many deployments, the high availability requirements of microservices force engineers to add more and more service instances for redundancy. In reality, although it provides the required high availability, this will result in under-utilized server instances.

In general, microservices deployment requires more infrastructure compared to monolithic application deployments. Due to the increase in cost of the infrastructure, many organizations fail to see the value of microservices.

The following diagram shows dedicated VMs for each microservices:

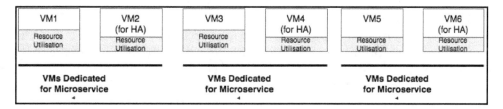

In order to address the issue stated in the preceding image, we need a tool that is capable of the following:

- Automating a number of activities such as allocation of containers to infrastructure efficiently, which are transparent to the developers and administrators
- Providing a layer of abstraction for the developers so that they can deploy their application against a data center without knowing which machine is to be used for hosting their applications

- Setting rules or constraints against deployment artifacts
- Offering higher levels of agility, with minimal management overheads for developers and administrators, perhaps with minimal human interactions
- Building, deploying, and managing applications cost effectively by driving maximum utilization of the available resources

Containers solve an important issue in this context. Any tools that we select with these capabilities can handle containers in a uniform way, irrespective of the undelaying microservice technologies.

What does container orchestration do?

Typical container orchestration tools help virtualize a set of machines and manage them as a single cluster. The container orchestration tools also help move the workload or containers across machines transparent to the consumer. Technology evangelists and practitioners use different terminologies, such as container orchestration, cluster management, data center virtualization, container schedulers, container life cycle management, data center operating system, and so on.

Many of these tools are currently supporting both Docker-based containers as well as non-containerized binary artifact deployments, such as the standalone Spring Boot application. The fundamental function for these container orchestration tools are to abstract the actual server instance from the application developers and administrators.

Container orchestration tools help self-service and provisioning of infrastructure rather than requesting the infrastructure teams to allocate the required machines with a predefined specification. In this automated container orchestration approach, machines are no longer provisioned upfront and preallocated to the applications. Some of the container orchestration tools also help virtualize the data centers across many heterogeneous machines, or even across data centers, and create an elastic private cloud-like infrastructure. There is no standard reference model for container orchestration tools. Therefore, the capabilities vary between vendors.

Some of the key capabilities of the container orchestration software are summarized as follows:

- **Cluster management**: This manages a cluster of VMs and physical machines as a single large machine. These machines could be heterogeneous in terms of resource capabilities, but, by and large, machines with Linux as the operating system. These virtual clusters can be formed on cloud, on premises, or a combination of both.

- **Deployments**: These handle automatic deployments of applications and containers with a large set of machines. It support multiple versions of the application containers, and also support rolling upgrades across a large number of cluster machines. These tools are also capable of handling a rollback of faulty promotes.
- **Scalability**: This handles automatic and manual scalability of application instances as and when required with optimized utilization as a primary goal.
- **Health**: This manages the health of the cluster, nodes, and applications. It removes faulty machines and application instances from the cluster.
- **Infrastructure abstraction**: This abstracts the developers from the actual machine where the applications are deployed. The developers need not worry about the machines, capacity, and so on. It is entirely the container orchestration software's decision to see how to schedule and run the applications. These tools also abstract the machine details, their capacity, utilization, and location from the developers. For application owners, these are equivalent to a single large machine with almost unlimited capacity.
- **Resource optimizations**: The inherent behavior of these tools is to allocate the container workloads across a set of available machines in an efficient way, thereby reducing the cost of ownership. Simple to extremely complicated algorithms can be used effectively to improve utilization.
- **Resource allocations**: These allocate servers based on resource availability and constraints set by the application developers. The resource allocation will be based on these constraints, affinity rules, port requirements, application dependencies, health, and so on.
- **Service availability**: This ensures that the services are up and running somewhere in the cluster. In case of a machine failure, container orchestration automatically handle failures by restarting those services on some other machine in the cluster.
- **Agility**: Agility tools are capable of quickly allocating workloads to available resources or move the workload across machines if there is change in resource requirements. Also, constraints can be set to realign resources based on business criticality, business priority, and more.

- **Isolation**: Some of these tools provide resource isolation out-of-the-box. Hence, even if the application is not containerized, resource isolation can be achieved.

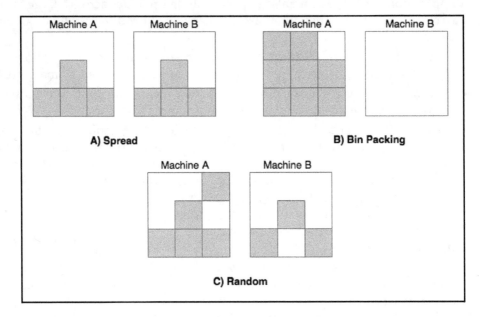

A variety of algorithms are used for resource allocation ranging from simple algorithms to complex algorithms with machine learning and artificial intelligence. The common algorithms used are **Random**, **Bin Packing**, and **Spread**. Constraints set against applications will override the default algorithms based on resource availability.

The preceding diagram shows how these algorithms fill the available machines with deployments. In this case, it is demonstrated with two machines.

Three common strategies of resource allocation are explained as follows:

- **Spread**: This equally distributes the allocation of workloads across available machines., which is shown in diagram **A**.
- **Bin packing**: This tries to fill machine by machine and ensure the maximum utilization of machines. Bin packing is especially good when using cloud services in a pay as you use style. This is shown in diagram **B**.
- **Random**: This algorithm randomly chooses machines and deploys containers on randomly selected machines, which is shown in diagram **C**.

There are possibilities of using cognitive computing algorithms such as machine learning and collaborative filtering to improve efficiency. Techniques such as **oversubscriptions** allow for better utilization of resources by utilizing under-utilized resources allocated for high priority tasks, including revenue generating services for best effort tasks such as analytics, video, image processing, and more.

Relationship with microservices

The infrastructure for microservices, if not properly provisioned, can easily result in over-sized infrastructures, and, essentially, higher cost of ownership. As discussed in the previous sections, a cloud-like environment with a container orchestration tool is essential to realize the cost benefits when dealing with large-scale microservices.

The Spring Boot microservices turbo, charged with the Spring Cloud project, is the ideal candidate workload to leverage container orchestration tools. Since the Spring Cloud based microservices are location unaware, these services can be deployed anywhere in the cluster. Whenever services come up, it automatically registers to the service registry and advertises its availability. On the other hand, consumers always look for the registry to discover available service instances. This way the application supports a full fluid structure without preassuming deployment topology. With Docker, we are able to abstract the runtime so that the services could run on any Linux-based environments.

Relationship with virtualization

The container orchestration solutions are different from server virtualization solutions in many aspects. Container orchestration solutions run on top of the VMs or physical machines as an application component.

Container orchestration solutions

There are many container orchestration software tools available. It is unfair to do an apple to apple comparison between them. Even though there are no one-to-one components, there are many areas of overlap in capabilities between them. In many situations, organizations use a combination of one or more of these tools to fulfill their requirements.

The following diagram shows the position of container orchestration tools from the microservices context:

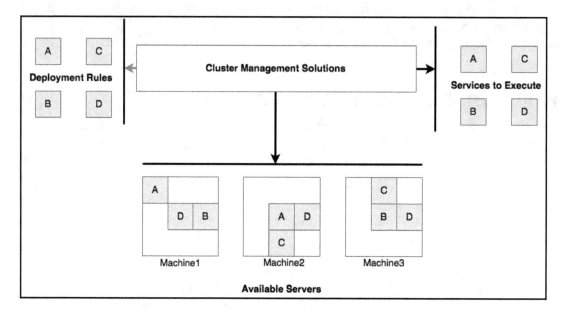

As shown in the preceding diagram, the container management or orchestration tools take a set of deployable artifacts in the form of containers (**Services to Execute**) and a set of constraints or rules as deployment descriptors then find the most optimal compute infrastructure for deployment which are available and fragmented across multiple machines.

In this section, we will explore some of the popular container orchestration solutions available in the market.

Docker Swarm

Docker Swarm is Docker's native container orchestration solution. Swarm provides native and deeper integration with Docker and exposes APIs that are compatible with Docker's remote APIs. It logically groups a pool of Docker hosts and manages them as a large single Docker virtual host. Instead of application administrators and developers deciding on which host the container is to be deployed, this decision making will be delegated to the Docker Swarm. It will decide which host to be used based on bin packing and spread algorithms.

Since the Docker Swarm is based on Docker's remote APIs, the learning curve for existing Docker users is much less compared to any other container orchestration tools. However, the Docker Swarm is a relatively new product in the market and it only supports the Docker containers.

Docker Swarm works with the concept of **manager** and **nodes**. The manager is the single point for administrations to interact and schedule the Docker containers for execution. The nodes are where the Docker containers are deployed and run.

Kubernetes

Kubernetes (**k8s**) is coming from Google's engineering, is written in Go language, and is battle tested for large-scale deployments at Google. Similar to Swarm, Kubernetes helps to manage containerized applications across a cluster of nodes. It helps to automate container deployments and scheduling and scalability of containers. It supports a number of useful out-of-the-box features, such as automatic progressive rollouts, versioned deployments, and container resiliency if containers fail for some reason.

Kubernetes architecture has the concept of **master**, **nodes**, and **pods**. The master and nodes together are called a Kubernetes cluster. The master node is responsible for allocating and managing the workload across a number of nodes. Nodes are nothing but a VM or a physical machine. Nodes are further subsegmented as pods. A node can host multiple pods. One or more containers are grouped and executed inside a pod. Pods are also helpful to manage and deploy co-located services for efficiency. Kubernetes also support the concept of labels as key-value pairs to query and find containers. Labels are user-defined parameters to tag certain types of nodes that perform common types of workloads, such as frontend web servers. The services deployed on the cluster will get a single IP/DNS to access the service.

Kubernetes has out-of-the-box support for Docker; however, Kubernetes' learning curve will be more compared to Docker Swarm. Red Hat offers commercial support for Kubernetes as part of its OpenShift platform.

Apache Mesos

Mesos is an open source framework originally developed by the University of California at Berkeley and is used by Twitter at scale. Twitter used Mesos primarily to manage a large Hadoop ecosystem.

Mesos is slightly different from the previous solutions. It is more of a resource manager that relies on other frameworks to manage workload execution. It sits between the operating system and the application, providing a logical cluster of machines.

Mesos is a distributed system kernel that logically groups and virtualizes many computers to a single large machine. It is capable of grouping a number of heterogeneous resources to a uniform resource cluster on which applications can be deployed. For these reasons, Mesos is also known as a tool for building a private cloud in a data center.

Mesos has the concept of the **master** and **slave** nodes. Similar to the earlier solutions, master nodes are responsible for managing the cluster, whereas slaves run the workloads. It internally uses **ZooKeeper** for cluster coordination and storage. It also supports the concept of frameworks. These frameworks are responsible for scheduling and running non-containerized applications and containers. **Marathon**, **Chronos**, and **Aurora** are popular frameworks for the scheduling and execution of applications. Netflix's **Fenzo** is another open source Mesos framework. Interestingly, Kubernetes also can be used as a Mesos framework.

Marathon supports the Docker container, as well as the non-containerized applications. The Spring Boot can be directly configured in Marathon. Marathon provides a number of out-of-the-box capabilities, such as support application dependencies, grouping of applications for scaling and upgrading services, start and shutdown of healthy and unhealthy instances, rolling promotes, rollback failed promoted, and so on.

Mesosphere offers commercial support for Mesos and Marathon as part of their DCOS platform.

HashiCorp Nomad

Nomad is from **HashiCorp**, another container orchestration software. Nomad is a container orchestration system that abstracts lower-level machine details and their locations. It has a simpler architecture compared to other solutions explored earlier. It is also lightweight. Similar to other container orchestration solutions, it will take care of resource allocations and the execution of applications. Nomad also accepts user-specific constraints and allocates resources based on that.

Nomad has the concept of servers where all jobs are managed. One server will act as the **leader** and others will act as **followers**. It has the concept of **tasks**, which are the smallest units of work. Tasks are grouped into **task groups**. A task group will have tasks that are to be executed in the same location. One or more task groups or tasks are managed as **jobs**.

Nomad supports many workloads, including Docker out of the box. Nomad also supports across data center deployments and is region data center aware.

CoreOS Fleet

Fleet is a container orchestration system from CoreOS. Feet runs on a lower level and works on top of the `systemd`. It can manage application dependencies and make sure that all required services are running somewhere in the cluster. If a service fails, it restarts the service on another host. Affinity and constraint rules are possible to supply when allocating resources.

Fleet has the concept of **engine** and **agents**. There will only be one engine at any point in the cluster with multiple agents. Tasks are submitted to the engine and the agents run these tasks on a cluster machine. Fleet also supports Docker out of the box.

In addition to this, **Amazon EC2 Container Services (ECS)**, **Azure Container Services (ACS)**, Cloud Foundry **Diego**, and **Google Container Engine** provide container orchestration functions as part of their respective cloud platform offerings.

Container orchestration with Mesos and Marathon

As we have seen in the previous section, there are many container orchestration solutions available. Different organizations choose different solutions to address problems based on their environments. Many organizations choose Kubernetes or Mesos with a framework such as Marathon. In most of the cases, Docker is used as a default containerization method to package and deploy workloads.

For the rest of this chapter, we will show how Mesos works with Marathon to provide the required container orchestration capability. Mesos is used by many organizations including Twitter, Airbnb, Apple, eBay, Netflix, Paypal, Uber, Yelp, and many others.

Mesos in details

Mesos can be treated as a data center kernel. Enterprise **DCOS** is the commercial version of Mesos supported by Mesosphere. In order to run multiples tasks on one node, Mesos uses resource isolation concepts. It relies on **cgroups** of the Linux kernel to achieve resource isolation similar to the container approach. It also supports containerized isolation using Docker. Mesos supports both, batch workloads as well as OLTP kind of workloads.

The following diagram shows Mesos logically abstracting multiple machines as a single resource cluster:

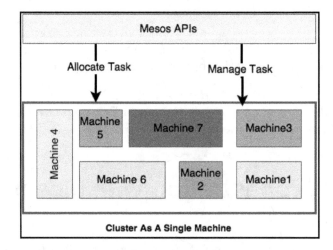

Mesos is an open source top-level Apache project under Apache License. It abstracts lower-level computing resources such as CPU, memory, and storage from the lower-level physical or virtual machines.

Before we examine why we need both Mesos and Marathon, let's understand the Mesos architecture.

Mesos architecture

The following diagram shows the simplest architecture representation of Mesos. The key components of Mesos include a **Mesos Master**, a set of slave nodes, a **ZooKeeper** service, and a Mesos framework. The Mesos framework is further subdivided into two components: a **Scheduler** and an **Executor**.

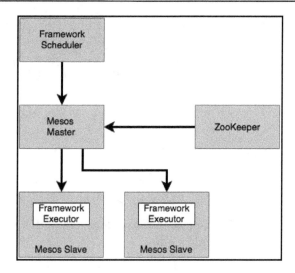

The boxes in the preceding diagram are explained as follows:

- **Master**: The **Mesos Master** is responsible for managing all Mesos slaves. It gets information on the resource availability from all slave nodes and takes responsibility of filling the resources appropriately, based on certain resource policies and constraints. The **Mesos Master** preempts available resources from all slave machines and pools them as a single large machine. Master offers resources to frameworks running on slave machines based on this resource pool.

  For high availability, the **Mesos Master** is supported by the Mesos master **standby** components. Even if the master is not available, existing tasks can be still executed. However, new tasks cannot be scheduled in the absence of a master node. The master standby nodes are nodes that wait for the failure of the active master and takeover the master role in case of a failure. They use **ZooKeeper** for the master leader election. Minimum quorum requirements must be met in this case for leader election.

- **Slave**: The Mesos slaves are responsible for hosting task execution frameworks. Tasks are executed on the slave nodes. Mesos slaves can be started with attributes as key value pairs, such as *datacenter* = *X*. This will be used for constraint evaluations when deploying workloads. Slave machines share resource availability to the **Mesos Master**.

- **ZooKeeper**: This is a centralized coordination server used in Mesos to coordinate activities across the Mesos cluster. Mesos uses **ZooKeeper** for leader election in case of a **Mesos Master** failure.

- **Framework**: The Mesos framework is responsible for understanding the application constraints, accepting resource offers from the master, and, finally, running the tasks on the slave resources offered by the master. The Mesos framework consists of two components: **Framework Scheduler** and **Framework Executor**.
- The **Scheduler** is responsible for registering to Mesos and handles resource offers.
- **Executor** runs the actual program on the Mesos slave nodes.

The framework is also responsible for enforcing certain policies and constraints. For example, a constraint can be, let's say, a minimum of 500 MB of RAM for execution.

The framework is a pluggable component and is replaceable with another framework. Its workflow is depicted in the following diagram:

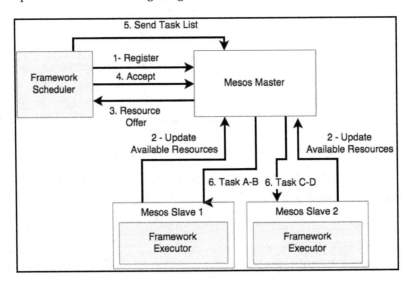

The steps denoted in the preceding workflow diagram are elaborated as follows:

1. The framework registers with the **Mesos Master** and waits for the resource offers. The scheduler may have many tasks in its queue to be executed with different resource constraints (task **A-D** in this example). A task, in this case, is a unit of work that is scheduled. For example, a Spring Boot microservice.
2. The Mesos slave offers available resources to the **Mesos Master**. For example, the slave advertizes the CPU and memory available with the slave machine.

3. **Mesos Master** creates a resource offer based on the allocation policies set and offers it to the scheduler component of the framework. The allocation policies determine to which framework the resources are to be offered and how many. The default policies can be customized by plugging additional allocation policies.

4. Scheduler framework components, based on the constraints, capabilities, and policies may accept or reject the resource offering. For example, the framework rejects the resource offer if the resources are insufficient as per the constraints and policies set.

5. If the scheduler component accepts the resource offer, it submits one or more task details to the **Mesos Master** with resource constraints per tasks. Let's say, in this example, it is ready to submit tasks **A-D**.

6. The **Mesos Master** sends this list of tasks to the slave where the resources are available. The framework executor components installed on the slave machines pick up and run these tasks.

Mesos supports a number of frameworks, such as the following:

- Marathon and Aurora for **long running** processes, such as web applications
- Hadoop, Spark, and Storm for **big data** processing
- Chronos and Jenkins for **batch scheduling**
- Cassandra and Elasticsearch for **data management**

In this chapter, we will use Marathon to run the dockerized microservices.

Marathon

Marathon is one of the Mesos framework implementations that can run both container as well as non-container execution. It is particularly designed for long running applications, such as a web server. It will ensure that the service started with Marathon will continue to be available even if the Mesos slave it is hosted on fails. This will be done by starting another instance.

Marathon is written in Scala and is highly scalable. It offers UI as well as REST APIs to interact with Marathon, such as starting, stopping, scaling, and monitoring applications.

Similar to Mesos, Marathon's high availability is achieved by running multiple Marathon instances pointing to a ZooKeeper instance. One of the Marathon instances will act as a leader and others will be in standby mode. In case the leading master fails, a leader election will take place and the next active master will be determined.

Some of the basic features of Marathon include the following:

- Setting resource constraints
- Scale up, scale down, and instance management of applications
- Application version management
    - Start and kill applications

Some of the advanced features of Marathon include the following:

- Rolling upgrades, rolling restarts, and rollbacks
- Blue-green deployments

Implementing Mesos and Marathon with DCOS

In Chapter 12, *Scale Microservices with Spring Cloud Components*, we discussed Eureka and Zuul for achieving load balancing. With container orchestration tools, load balancing and DNS services come out of the box and are much more simple to use. However, when developers need code-level control for load balancing and traffic routing, such as the business parameter based scaling scenarios mentioned earlier, Spring Cloud components may fit better.

In order to understand the technologies better, we will use Mesos and Marathon directly in this chapter. However, in all practical scenarios, it is better to go with Mesosphere DCOS rather than playing with plain vanilla Mesos and Marathon.

DCOS offers a number of supporting components on and above plain Mesos and Marathon to manage enterprise-scale deployments.

The DCOS architecture is well explained in the following link:
https://dcos.io/docs/1.9/overview/architecture

Let's do a side-by-side comparison of the components used for scaling microservices with Spring Cloud components and similar capabilities offered by DCOS.

The following points examines the major differences between Spring Cloud approach and DCOS:

- Configurations are managed using the Spring Cloud Config server when we approach with Spring Cloud for scaling microservices. When using DCOS, configurations can be managed by using one of Spring Cloud Config, Spring Profiles, or tools such as Puppet, Chef, and more.
- The Eureka server was used for managing service discovery and Zuul was used for load balancing with the Spring Cloud approach. DCOS has Mesos DNS, VIPs, and HAProxy based Marathon-lb components to achieve the same.
- Logging and monitoring, explained in `Chapter 13`, *Logging and Monitoring Microservices*, is accomplished using Spring Boot Actuator, Seluth, and Hystrix . DCOS offers various log aggregation and metrics collection features out of the box.

Implementing Mesos and Marathon for BrownField microservices

In this section, the dockerized Brownfield microservices developed in `Chapter 14`, *Containerizing Microservices with Docker*, will be deployed into the AWS cloud, and we will manage them with Mesos and Marathon.

For demonstration purposes, we will cover only two services (search and website deployment) in this chapter. Also, we will use one EC2 instance for the sake of simplicity.

Installing Mesos, Marathon, and related components

Launch a **t2.large** EC2 instance with the Ubuntu 16.04 version AMI, which will be used for this deployment. In this example, we are using another instance to run RabbitMQ; however, this can be done on the same instance as well.

Perform the following steps to install Mesos and Marathon:

- To install Mesos 1.2.0, follow the instructions documented in the following link. This will also install JDK 8:

  ```
  https://mesos.apache.org/gettingstarted/.
  ```

- To install Docker, perform the following steps:

  ```
  sudo apt-get update
  sudo apt-get install docker.io
  sudo docker version
  ```

- To install Marathon 1.4.3, follow the steps documented in the following link:

  ```
  curl -O http://downloads.mesosphere.com/marathon
    /v1.4.3/marathon-1.4.3.tgz
  tar xzf marathon-1.4.3.tgz
  ```

- To install ZooKeeper, perform the following steps:

  ```
  wget http://ftp.unicamp.br/pub/apache/zookeeper/zookeeper-
    3.4.9/zookeeper-3.4.9.tar.gz
  tar -xzvf zookeeper-3.4.9.tar.gz
  rm -rf zookeeper-3.4.9.tar.gz
  cd zookeeper-3.4.9/
  cp zoo_sample.cfg  zoo.cfg
  ```

Alternatively, you may use the DCOS package distribution on AWS using CloudFormation, which offers a high availability Mesos cluster out of the box.

Running Mesos and Marathon

Perform the following steps to run Mesos and Marathon:

1. Log in to the EC2 instance and run the following commands:

   ```
   ubuntu@ip-172-31-19-249:~/zookeeper-3.4.9
   $ sudo -E bin/zkServer.sh start

   ubuntu@ip-172-31-19-249:~/mesos-1.2.0/build/bin
   $ ./mesos-master.sh --work_dir=/home/ubuntu/mesos-
     1.2.0/build/mesos-server

   ubuntu@ip-172-31-19-249:~/marathon-1.4.3
   $ MESOS_NATIVE_JAVA_LIBRARY=/home/ubuntu/mesos-
   ```

```
1.2.0/build/src/.libs/libmesos.so ./bin/start --master
172.31.19.249:5050
```

ubuntu@ip-172-31-19-249:~/mesos-1.2.0/build

```
$ sudo ./bin/mesos-agent.sh --master=172.31.19.249:5050 --
containerizers=mesos,docker --work_dir=/home/ubuntu/mesos-
1.2.0/build/mesos-agent --resources='ports:[0-32000]'
```

Note that the relative path for a working directory may lead to execution problems. The `--resources` are required only if you want to force the host port to be in a certain range.

2. If you have more slave machines, you may repeat slave commands on those machines to add more nodes to the cluster.
3. Open the following URL to see the Mesos console. In this example, there are three slaves running, connecting to the master:

   `http://ec2-54-68-132-236.us-west-2.compute.amazonaws.com:5050`

You will see the Mesos console similar to the following screenshot:

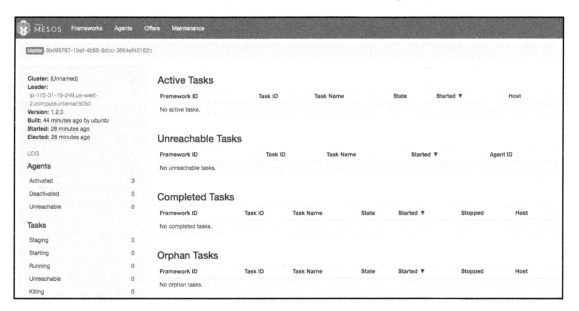

The **Agents** section of the console shows that there are three activated Mesos agents available for execution. It also indicates that there is no **Active Tasks**.

4. Open the following URL to inspect the Marathon UI. Replace the IP address with the public IP address of the EC2 instance:

```
http://ec2-54-68-132-236.us-west-2.compute.amazonaws.com:8080
```

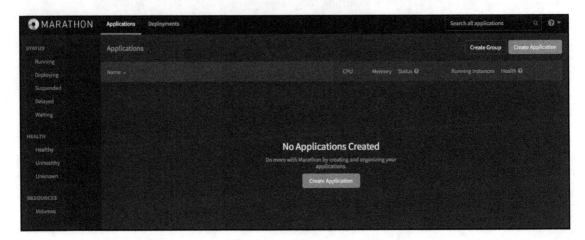

Since there are no applications deployed so far, the **Applications** section of the UI is empty.

Preparing BrownField PSS services

In the previous section, we successfully set up Mesos and Marathon. In this section, we will see how to deploy the BrownField PSS application previously developed using Mesos and Marathon.

The full source code of this chapter is available under the chapter10 projects in the code files under https://github.com/rajeshrv/ Spring5Microservice. Copy chapter9.* into a new STS workspace and rename it chapter10.*.

In this example, we will force the Mesos cluster to bind to fixed ports, but, in an ideal world, we will delegate the Mesos cluster to dynamically bind services to ports. Also, since we are not using a DNS or HA Proxy, we will hardcode the IP addresses. In the real world, a VIP for each service will be defined, and that VIP will be used by the services. This VIP will be resolved by the DNS and Proxy.

Perform the following steps to change the BrownField application to run on AWS:

1. Update search microservices (`application.properties`) to reflect the RabbitMQ IP and port. Also, update the website (`Application.java` and `BrownFieldSiteController.java`) to reflect the IP address of the EC2 machines.

2. Rebuild all microservices using Maven. Build and push the Docker images to the Docker Hub. The working directory has to be switched to the respective directories before executing these commands from the respective folders:

```
docker build -t search-service:1.0 .
docker tag search:1.0 rajeshrv/search:1.0
docker push rajeshrv/search:1.0

docker build -t website:1.0 .
docker tag website:1.0 rajeshrv/website:1.0
docker push rajeshrv/website:1.0
```

Deploying BrownField PSS services

The Docker images are now published to the Docker Hub registry. Perform the following steps to deploy and run the BrownFIeld PSS services:

1. Start the dockerized RabbitMQ:

```
sudo docker run --net=host rabbitmq:3
```

2. At this point, the Mesos Marathon cluster is up and running and is ready to accept deployments. The deployment can be done by creating one JSON file per service, as follows:

```
{
  "id": "search-3.0",
  "container": {
    "type": "DOCKER",
    "docker": {
      "image": "rajeshrv/search:1.0",
      "network": "BRIDGE",
      "portMappings": [
        { "containerPort": 8090, "hostPort": 8090 }
      ]

    }
  },
  "instances": 1,
```

```
    "cpus": 0.5,
    "mem": 512
}
```

3. The preceding JSON will be stored on the search.json file. Similarly, create a JSON file for other services as well.

The JSON structure is explained as follows:

- id: This is a unique id of the application and it can be a logical name.
- Cpus, mem: This sets the resource constraints for this application. If the resource offer does not satisfy this resource constraint, Marathon will reject that resource offer from the Mesos Master.
- instances: How many instances of this application to start with? In the preceding configuration, by default, it starts one instance as soon as it gets deployed. Marathon will maintain the number of instances mentioned at any point.
- container: This parameter tells the Marathon executor to use the Docker container for execution.
- image: This tells the Marathon scheduler which Docker image has to be used for deployment. In this case, this will download the search-service:1.0 image from the Docker Hub repository, rajeshrv.
- network: This value is used for Docker runtime to advice on the network mode to be used when starting the new Docker container. This can be BRIDGE or HOST. In this case, the BRIDGE mode will be used.
- portMappings: The port mapping provides information on how to map internal and external ports. In the preceding configuration, hostPort, set as 8090, tells the Marathon executor to use 8090 when starting the service. Since containerPort is set as 0, the same host port will be assigned to the container. Marathon picks up random ports if the hostPort value is 0.

4. Once this JSON is created and saved, deploy this to Marathon using the Marathon REST APIs as follows:

```
curl -X POST http://54.85.107.37:8080/v2/apps
    -d @search.json -H "Content-type: application/json"
```

5. Alternatively, use the Marathon console for deployment as follows:

```
New Application                                              JSON Mode ⬤

 1  {
 2    "id": "search-3.0",
 3    "container": {
 4      "type": "DOCKER",
 5      "docker": {
 6        "image": "rajeshrv/search:1.0",
 7        "network": "BRIDGE",
 8        "portMappings": [
 9          {  "containerPort": 8090, "hostPort": 8090 }
10        ]
11
12      }
13    },
14    "instances": 1,
15    "cpus": 0.5,
16    "mem": 512
17  }
18
                                              Cancel    Create Application
```

6. Repeat this step for the website as well.

7. Open the Marathon UI. As shown in the following diagram, the UI shows that both the applications are deployed and are in the **Running** state. It also indicates that a **1 of 1** instance is in the **Running** state.

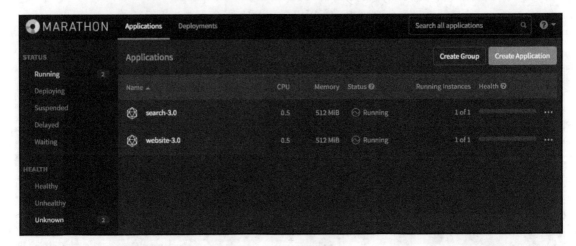

8. If you inspect the search service, it shows `ip` and the port it is bound to:

9. Open the following URL in a browser to verify the website application:

```
http://ec2-34-210-109-17.us-west-2.compute.amazonaws.com:8001
```

Summary

In this chapter, we learned the different aspects of autoscaling applications and the importance of a container orchestration to efficiently manage dockerized microservices at scale.

We explored the different container orchestration tools before deep diving into Mesos and Marathon. We also implemented Mesos and Marathon in the AWS cloud environment to demonstrate how to manage dockerized microservices developed for the BrownField PSS.

So far, we have seen all the core and supporting technology capabilities required for a successful microservices implementation. A successful microservice implementation also requires processes and practices beyond technology.

Other Books You May Enjoy

If you enjoyed this book, you may be interested in these other books by Packt:

Spring: Microservices with Spring Boot
Ranga Rao Karanam

ISBN: 9781789132588

- Use Spring Initializr to create a basic spring project
- Build a basic microservice with Spring Boot
- Implement caching and exception handling
- Secure your microservice with Spring security and OAuth2
- Deploy microservices using self-contained HTTP server
- Monitor your microservices with Spring Boot actuator
- Learn to develop more effectively with developer tools

Building Applications with Spring 5 and Kotlin
Miloš Vasić

ISBN: 9781788394802

- Explore Spring 5 concepts with Kotlin
- Learn both dependency injections and complex configurations
- Utilize Spring Data, Spring Cloud, and Spring Security in your applications
- Create efficient reactive systems with Project Reactor
- Write unit tests for your Spring/Kotlin applications
- Deploy applications on cloud platforms like AWS

Leave a review - let other readers know what you think

Please share your thoughts on this book with others by leaving a review on the site that you bought it from. If you purchased the book from Amazon, please leave us an honest review on this book's Amazon page. This is vital so that other potential readers can see and use your unbiased opinion to make purchasing decisions, we can understand what our customers think about our products, and our authors can see your feedback on the title that they have worked with Packt to create. It will only take a few minutes of your time, but is valuable to other potential customers, our authors, and Packt. Thank you!

Index